Everything You Need to Know to Teach First Grade

Pat Barrett Dragan

HEINEMANN
Portsmouth, NH

To all my family, especially my husband, George, my mom, and Sherry, Jim, Debi, Marsha, and Bev

Heinemann
A division of Reed Elsevier Inc.
361 Hanover Street
Portsmouth, NH 03801–3912
www.heinemann.com

Offices and agents throughout the world

Library of Congress Cataloging-in-Publication Data
Barrett Dragan, Patricia.
Everything you need to know to teach first grade / Pat Barrett Dragan.
p. cm.
ISBN 0-325-00391-2 (alk. paper)
1. First grade (Education)—Handbooks, manuals, etc. 2. Elementary school teaching—Handbooks, manuals, etc. I. Title.
LB15711st .B37 2003
372.1102—dc21 2003013817

Editor: Lois Bridges
Production: Sonja S. Chapman
Cover design: Joni Doherty
Compositor: House of Equations, Inc.
Manufacturing: Steve Bernier
Cover photo: Bob Doerr, Doerr Studios

Printed in the United States of America on acid-free paper
07 06 05 04 03 ML 1 2 3 4 5

CONTENTS

ACKNOWLEDGMENTS

There are several people I wish to acknowledge as I finish this book, and most of them are six or seven years old: my first graders at Martin Elementary School in South San Francisco. "My children" this year and last (as with previous classes) have shared with me their wonderfully honest reflections about learning, as well as their daily work, joys, and struggles. I appreciate so much my time in the classroom with them. No one sees the world like a first grader!

I thank my sweet mom for her patience and her understanding of our abbreviated time together in the two years I've been working on this book. She has smiled and been supportive throughout.

My sister Sherry has worked overtime to free me up so I could write. And my brother Jim and his wife, Debi, have given their valuable help long distance. They also gave me two of my favorite words in the book: *Gummilump Box*. The Gummilump Box is the treasure chest in which the Barrett family members keep their most prized photos and memories. When I was looking for a name for the place my first graders and I keep our written class compliments, the words *Gummilump Box* fit perfectly!

I thank my dear friend Marsha Oviatt, who has spent many hours listening to me and giving me invaluable input and support.

Phil Erskine tamed my troublesome computer so it would run faithfully throughout the writing, with only an occasional glitch.

My literature mentor, Kay Goines, has been my role model in so many ways throughout my teaching career. Most of what I have tried to be and become in my classroom I have learned from her.

I thank my visual arts mentor, Dick Sperisen. Dick is always generous in sharing ideas about helping children create. Whenever I talk with Dick, I come away with twenty ideas a minute.

Gloria Norton has facilitated three of the most important events of my life: meeting my husband, George, teaching in the credential program at San Francisco State University, and connecting with Heinemann. She is a wonderful friend.

I appreciate so much the wise advice of my dear friend Bev Hock who is always in my corner. I also want to acknowledge Carole Larson and Sue Fox for great ideas and Caroll Webster for chasing down pesky references.

Thanks to all at Heinemann for their gracious help and support, especially Editorial Director Leigh Peake, who said, "Yes!," and Associate Editorial Director Maura Sullivan for her great cover idea, and Sonja Chapman, my production editor. Thanks also to Karen Clausen, who has helped with so many technical details.

I want to say a special thank-you to my editor, Lois Bridges, who inspires me to write my best and always makes me feel both valued and energized. Whenever I am in a quandary in my classroom about how best to help a child, I think of Lois and all the ways she helps me. And then I know just what to do. . . .

Regie Routman, my favorite Heinemann author, has also been an inspiration to me.

Thanks to Bob and Ann Doerr, of Doerr Studios, for a wonderful photo shoot experience in my classroom, and a great cover photo.

Most of all I want to thank and acknowledge my husband, George, who has always given me incredible support, and even more so during the writing of this book. He makes me laugh, listens to ideas, and provides both cooked meals and wise perspective. And he helps me get up to write at 4:30 each morning before school. I now wake up laughing, thanks to George's present of a specially programmed alarm clock that gets me up daily with the words, "Author, author, time to wake up!"

George is most generous of heart and spirit and is full of fun. These gifts he shares with me help me to be the person I want to be in my first-grade classroom.

INTRODUCTION: THE MAGIC OF FIRST GRADE

Figure I–1
We share many miracles together during our first-grade year.

A hundred years from now
It will not matter
What my bank account was,
What sort of house I lived in,
Or what kind of car I drove.
But the world may be different
Because I was important
In the life of a child.

—*Anonymous*

First grade is a magical time. Children are open to everything, full of wonder and awe. They are enthusiastic and eager to learn. More than anything, they want to be able to do things and to be and become competent. They want very much to be up to the learning tasks at hand. At this age, five or six years old at the beginning of the first-grade school year, children are on the edge of becoming capable of many intellectual as well as physical and analytical tasks. They will accomplish more in this academic year than I ever would have dreamed possible. I have to remind myself each school year what first-grade children are like at the beginning. It is always a surprise. The end of the year is so full of achievements that it seems many years and worlds away.

This book covers first grade from before school starts to the last day and beyond. It encompasses everything from helpful tips and things I learned the hard way, to ways to accomplish curriculum goals and achieve joyful learning. I have taken a close look at the whole year and tried to bring it to life. I have especially tried to include things I would have loved to know when I began *my* teaching career.

You Can't Do It All . . .

My wise friend, first-grade teacher Laurel Sherry-Armstrong, always says, "You can do *anything*, but you cannot do *everything*." Since our time with our students is limited, and always being packed with yet more curricula to squeeze into our days, it is crucial that we make choices. We need to give our children the *best* of our knowledge and materials *first*, and get the biggest educational payoff we can for the time we have. We can't do it all, so we have to pick and choose with reflection and deliberation.

As elementary teachers we are generalists. We are responsible for teaching *all* curriculum areas in the most expert ways we can. Some of the best ways for us to become experts are to read and keep abreast of professional literature, take classes, attend conferences and in-services, and learn from colleagues whose work we respect. This kind of professional input helps me sharpen my skills and be at my best in my first-grade classroom.

With this in mind, I have included in this book some ideas and information I have learned from other educators whose work I value. Many are close friends. I work with some of them. I met others in workshops and classes and places like bookstores and educational conferences. I appreciate them giving me permission to include their wisdom and breakthrough ideas in my book.

Characteristics of First Graders

I feel fortunate to have spent so much of my life and teaching career among first graders. They want to like their teacher and hope their teacher will like them. A first grader can seem babyish one minute and at the cutting edge of independence the next. Children at this age like cheerful, upbeat people and adults with integrity and a sense of humor. So do I.

First graders are busy creating their own schemas—figuring out their ideas about the world. It is important to them that things are fair and just. They are sincere. And sometimes they are wise.

As Darnell, one of my first graders, told me earnestly on the first day of school last year, "Sometimes kids know things that big people don't know."

I had to agree with him.

No one is more candid than five- and six-year-olds. They will let you know exactly what they think, with complete and devastating honesty. One very articulate child, Maggie, said to me one day with perfect candor, "You are a wonderful teacher, and you teach us a lot, but you sure can't sing!" (My friend Laurel was right: We can't do it all! But we try.) Another child looked at my photograph in a children's book I had written and said critically, "You look different now, like way older." She was right. My unspoken response was to think, "Yes, I look *lots* older. I've had *you* in class all year!"

First grade is all about beginnings. Even for children who have learned to read at home or in kindergarten, this is still a time of starting many different things. I do try to stress with my new children right away, during our first morning together, that they know and can do so much already. I want them to feel competent, be in a can-do mode, and feel energized and ready to go, top of the heap, rather than feel like blank slates. I want this to be a year of learning together that is full of discovery, excitement, and *construction* of meaning, as opposed to one of *transmission*. I don't want to merely transfer to the children knowledge I think they need to learn. I want us to explore and discover together. I want to help children feel comfortable and capable as learners, to build on what they already know and to invite all of them to travel as far as they can go on their own learning journeys. I want their time at school with me to be the most joyful of experiences.

Acceleration of Knowledge

Whether you are a beginning teacher, are new to the grade level, or are a veteran, first grade has new challenges each year: changes in curriculum, shifts in materials available, even new knowledge about how children learn. Depending upon which source you consult, scientists estimate that knowledge now doubles every two to five years. The exact number is not important. The point is that knowledge is accelerating at an incredibly rapid rate. Even as I write, that pace is increasing. No wonder it can seem difficult to keep up with existing information and ideas.

Each new school year may bring reconfigurations of time schedules, often new staff and administration, and more importantly, new students. We are all locked in our own brains and even confined to our own classrooms. It is important to be as aware as possible of fresh developments in educational philosophy and to weigh and consider new learning strategies in light of our own beliefs. But the sheer amount of information out there can make it hard to get a grip on where to spend our energy, where to begin. I believe we need to pick one area at a time to focus on and get good at. When we are comfortable with that part of the curriculum, we can zero in on another subject area.

Exploration and Independence

Although I teach all areas of the curriculum, my own personal focus, passion, and emphasis for the first-grade year is reading/language arts. (And I *love* integrating the arts with this area of study.) Whenever possible, I connect learning across curriculum fields. Children particularly need reading and language arts skills to succeed in math, science, social studies—and all of the other things they will study.

I feel that one of my roles as a first-grade teacher is to convince children right away that they *can* read, and *are* learning to read, so they don't have to worry about it any more: they can just get on with it! As I expressed in my book *Literacy from Day One* (Portsmouth, NH: Heinemann, 2001), I want children to come to literacy easily, exuberantly. I feel they should learn the joys of literacy from someone who loves to read, loves books—reading, writing, and illustrations. I want to be that person for them.

Ideally, children have had wonderful years of being read to and talked with at home, before they ever start school. These experiences help make reading both a treasured pastime and an effortless learning endeavor. Children who have not been fortunate enough to have a literacy background will be helped so much by being read to at school and having the opportunity to experience wonderful literature in a nurturing environment.

According to scientists and archeologists, it took thousands of years for reading and writing to evolve. The concept of number, invention of numerals, and mathematic and scientific theories all took eons to develop as well. What is amazing to me, and I try to impress this upon my first graders, is that they will acquire some of these skills and more in a *single year*. It is a year for catching on to things and celebrating achievements—a time for "Ahas!" I expect to see lights go on, and hear lots of "Oooooohs," "*Now* I get it!" and "I can do it!"

There is nothing like the magic of seeing children take their first steps to literacy and watching them grow in knowledge and independence as they explore books and ideas, learn science and social studies concepts, and become mathematicians, artists, and musicians. That's what keeps me, ever fascinated, in the first-grade classroom.

First Graders Keep You on Your Toes

First grade definitely requires a light, whimsical, and imaginative touch. First-grade teachers walk a fine line between helping children learn to settle down and focus and introducing them to the excitement and pleasure of learning. A lot of what we do, especially at the beginning of the year, is to act as if children can do things. And before we know it, they really can!

I feel it is important to help children take subject matter seriously without intimidating them—to help them learn to work both independently and in large and small groups without overstructuring them. I believe most of all that we need to keep alive, and foster in children, the sense of play they need so much if they are to explore, achieve, and apply themselves with confidence to the learning tasks and adventures ahead of them.

Once upon a time, in my younger teaching days, I did a real slapstick routine in the classroom when I fell backward over a whole bank of desks. I think I possibly did a back flip—the only one of my life. At any rate, whatever I did, I landed on my feet. My children were absolutely beside themselves. They applauded and shouted with glee, convinced that I had executed this madcap move for their entertainment and edification. "Do it again, do it again, Teacher!" they all cried.

It was the only time I had the full attention of that class all year. With that group, accidental slapstick was my ticket to credibility.

Now I'm faced with the idea of credibility in a new way: The title of this book implies full expertise. I am a little intimidated by this, since there are certainly things I don't know about teaching first grade, especially with the knowledge base expanding and multiplying all the time. But first grade has been my life for more than thirty years; it still is, and I *do* know more than I used to. And, since I actively try hard to learn and grow, I always hope that tomorrow I will know more than I do today.

Since those beginning days of my career, I've given up back flips over desks and learned other ways to acquire integrity and credibility in my first-grade classroom—ways to inveigle, wangle, and keep children's attention to help them learn. These ideas are the ones I'd like to pass along in this book.

CHAPTER 1

Getting Ready to Teach

Now, let the wild rumpus start!

—From *Where the Wild Things Are*, Maurice Sendak

The Beginning—Or Is It?

It is the first day of school and the children are sitting with me on the rug in front of the room. I am explaining that they will use the bathrooms and then have recess. Before I finish my sentence, the children get up as a group and go to the classroom door, forming, incredibly for the first day of school, a single line. I'm trying to get their attention, saying things like "not yet" and "wait!" In unison they form a chorus line and do an intricate dance step. Clothed in white polo shirts and black shorts, my new first graders tip their black top hats to me and merrily zigzag out the door. I am helpless to stop this crazy exodus.

I wake up in a cold sweat. Later I will laugh, but not now. I'm thankful this is a first-day-of-school dream and not a true scenario! I realize I will have a few more of these before school actually starts.

The time before school begins can be stressful for both teachers and children. This is why I make contact with my new students *before* opening day.

The First Contact with Children: A Little Note

I write a little note to my new first graders about halfway through the summer. The school office sends it out with the school philosophy notes, emergency forms, and classroom placements. In my note I include one or two of my own drawings—the more primitive, the better—with brief information about things we will be learning. I also add brief personal information about things I enjoy. (See Figure 1–1.) I ask each child to make a drawing to bring to me on the first day of school. And I ask parents to write two or three special things they would like me to know about their son or daughter.

My little note is a link between us all—parents, teacher, and child. I always feel energized after this contact with my new first graders, and I believe that children and parents feel this way as well. Best of all, I am easing everyone's nervousness by taking action and making a tentative beginning.

Using These Notes and Drawings

On the first day of school, children hand me notes and drawings, some pristine, some smashed, smudged, and torn. These are little gifts from them to me. They enable me to whisper in a child's ear, "I know something special about you. You have a puppy, and you went backpacking in Yosemite!" The awed, smiling child usually doesn't connect my secret knowledge with the note from parents. My reputation as a magician is safe!

Children's drawings can be pinned up immediately to make a collage, a visual remembrance of all of us. I will put one of my little drawings and a few personal words on the bulletin board as well.

A variation of this idea, as I just learned from a colleague, Eveley Cha, who taught kindergarten at Martin School, is to call each new student before school starts. Usually she gets to speak to a parent, but often to her incoming kindergartner as well. Eveley says she spent about fifteen minutes on the telephone this year with a little girl who was really frightened. The child was thrilled to be able to talk with her new teacher, and made a good adjustment on the first day of school.

8/20

Dear Parents,

I am looking forward to having your child in first grade this year! He or she will learn a lot and have a good time too.

If possible, please send with your child on the first day of school a list of 2 or 3* wonderful things I should know about your child. On the first day I will be able to say, "I know something special about you!"

Thank you for your help and support!

(*or more)

Sincerely,
Mrs. Pat Barrett Dragan

A note for your child

8/20

Hi There!

Welcome to first grade! You will really like school, and you will learn a lot too! See you September 8th.

♡ Mrs. Pat Barrett Dragan

Figure 1–1
Sample summer note to students and parents

Visualizing the School Year

Visualizing is a powerful way of getting into the new school year. Being able to see the year ahead in my mind's eye is a dress rehearsal. It helps me arrange or rearrange my classroom, decide on some curriculum, and make some classroom discipline and management decisions. Sometimes I have solved problems through visualizations before those problems even arose. I save time because I have some things figured out before I reach the classroom door. And I enjoy "seeing" myself interacting successfully with joyful and engaged learners.

I visualize many lessons before I actually teach them. This is particularly helpful in the case of art lessons or lessons with many steps or activities. In thinking about how I will present content to my first graders, I am smoothing out, or averting, potential problems or snags. For example, if I were to decide that I will be making gingerbread men with my class on the first day of school (and I am *not* going to decide that!), I would mentally work through what the other children would be doing while I was cracking eggs and mixing dough with a few students at a time. I realize that this type of first-day lesson would not work for me. I have seen the pitfalls in my mind's eye—and as I visualized making gingerbread cookies on day one, it was not a pretty sight!

How to Use That Nervous Energy While You Wait for School to Start

My drama teacher always said, "*Use* that nervous energy! It will help you prepare for your role!" I feel this advice is as important for teachers as it is for actors and actresses. Here is a brief sampling of things you can accomplish while you wait for the curtain to go up on the first day of school. Add to the list and make it your own:

- Meet some colleagues, especially teachers at your grade level.
- Become familiar with the community.
- Learn what community resources are available: parks, parks and recreation classes, boys and girls clubs, after-school tutoring, sports, and music and art classes.
- Locate possible field trip locations such as the library, post office, fire station, police station, supermarket, pet store, shoe repair shop, museums, parks, and nurseries.
- Learn where your children live—types of neighborhoods and so on.
- Walk around—get a feel for what your first graders experience on the way to and from school.
- Make some room arrangement plans. Make drawings. Move some furniture around in the classroom if you have access to the room. Think about organizing the environment so that children can work independently. (See Chapter 2 for more on room arrangement.)

- Get an idea about what kind of discipline and classroom management techniques you will be using. It is important to have some plans in mind before school starts. (See Chapter 4 for more discipline and classroom management ideas.)
- Find out about ordering supplies and what supplies to expect. The school secretary can give you this information.
- Visit your district's or county's educational materials office and see about ordering some videos and books for units you know you will be teaching.
- Locate children's bookstores—choose some new books to read to your new class.
- Visit the local library. The children's section of the library is a good place to go to select some books for read-alouds. If you visit during summer library reading programs, you may even meet some of your new students.
- Start (or redo) a filing system.
- Make some personal notes of things you want to try out, achieve.
- If possible, spend some time working in your classroom.
- Get to know both the school secretary and the custodians.

It is certainly not crucial that you try to do the things on this list as you wait for school to start. The suggestions are just meant to give you ideas if you want to work on things ahead of time.

Custodial Work Schedules and Classroom Maintenance

Since I usually cannot get into my classroom until late in the summer because of custodial work schedules, visualizing the classroom and the year ahead helps me work on getting my room ready without even being there. However, I do try to get to school for several days before the school year begins. The optimum time, I think, is a week or even two before school starts. If you are a continuing teacher, you will

Figure 1–2
Instructions for eight-page booklet

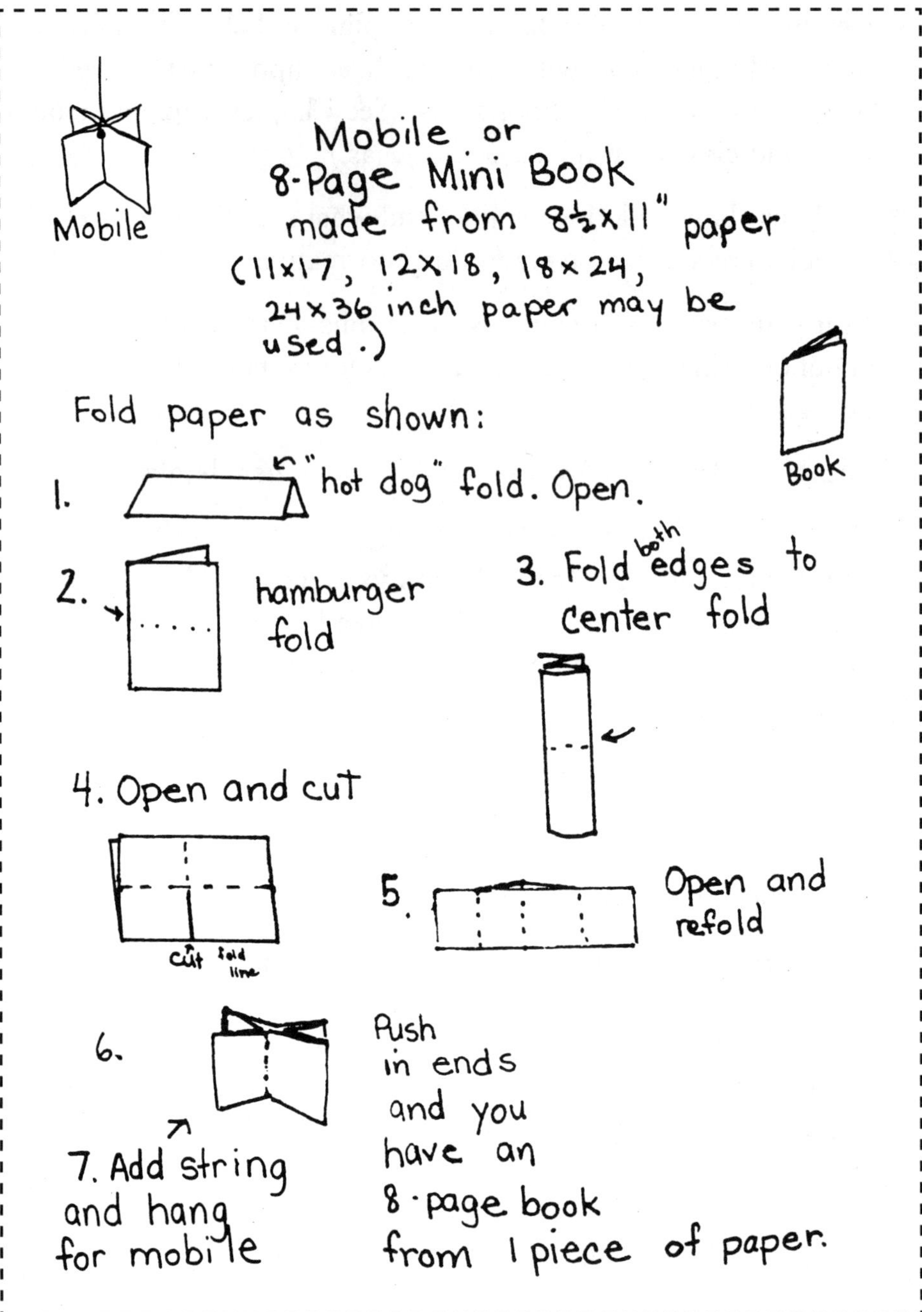

probably need less time because your room arrangement and some other things will probably be figured out to your satisfaction. Regardless of how much I like my room arrangement from the previous year, however, I usually find something I want to change so that things will run more smoothly.

We all have a lot of downtime as we wait in traffic, stand in line at the grocery store, and sit in the doctor's office. I try to use this time to puzzle out some of my own goals, objectives, and plans. I keep lists and notes on 3-by-5-inch cards or in a small eight-page folded book. (See Figure 1–2.) The trick is to make sure I am conscious enough of the real world around me that I can operate safely in it as I wool-gather!

In any event, I prefer to get to the classroom *before* the last days of vacation. This way I can rest and do some things I enjoy myself right before school begins.

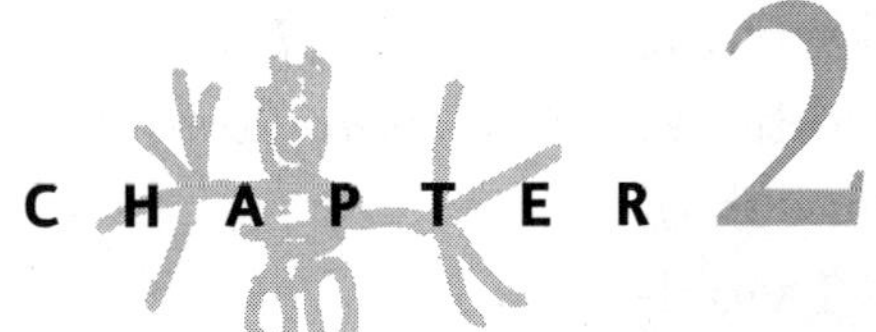

CHAPTER 2

Designing and Setting Up Your First-Grade Classroom

What we need is a plan.

—From *Winnie-the-Pooh and The House at Pooh Corner,* A. A. Milne

The more visualizing I do before school starts, and the more I have figured out in terms of classroom management strategies, the better my beginning days go. I can always change things as the school year evolves, but it is important to have a plan—and the *vision* that supports it. We also need to be flexible. As my friend and kindergarten teacher Peggy McNeil says, "If Plan A doesn't work, go to Plan B."

I like to bring the children into a beautiful and organized classroom. Although I prefer to do some of my classroom organization with the involvement of my new first graders, there are many things I can do before school starts to get the room ready for them.

The Power of Photographs—Record Your Efforts

When I first get into my classroom before the school year starts, I stand in the doorway and take a few photographs. I take more photos as I work in the room, and I have a colleague take some of me. I take other photos from the same spot when the room is ready. Then, when I compare the developed pictures, I can *see* the magic I have created. This before-and-after photo comparison is very empowering. I feel that if I can do this—make an attractive and organized classroom out of piles of boxes and bundled and packed materials—I can do *anything*.

Aside from being good confidence builders, these photographs are excellent public relations. Showcase the photos near your classroom doorway so that children and parents, as well as administrators, can see the difference you have made, even before school begins!

If you have purchased something special for your classroom, you may even wish to put a little sticker on it that says "Supplied by the teacher," or "Special present from Mr./Mrs. ________". (I haven't done this yet, but I've been thinking about it.)

Figure 2–1 *Moving to a new classroom*

Don't Even Try to Do It All!

Even though I work to create a classroom that will be exciting to enter on the first day of school, I do not attempt to finalize things. I want to leave a lot of opportunities for children to think, make decisions, and make things theirs—their school home for the year ahead.

When I work in my room before school begins, I put up fadeless background paper on bulletin boards. I have sometimes used fabric for bulletin board backgrounds. I stretch it as I staple it to the board so it will be smooth. It is best to use a fabric that does not fade, because I want this investment to last a while. Occasionally I have used leftover wallpaper on small bulletin boards.

Spaces and Places You Will Need in Your Room

Generally, I find I need these kinds of spaces on bulletin boards or somewhere else in the classroom:

- A place for ongoing student art or a mural
- A place for word wall words
- A math reference board, with calendar, clock, money chart, place value chart, number chart, birthday list, and other specific math topics we are working on. I make most of these myself. (See Chapter 12.)
- A phonics reference board—alphabet with key words across the classroom and some additional key word drawings, done by students
- Nursery rhyme, song, poetry, and book excerpt charts (I make some of these materials; children and parents make other charts.)
- Daily schedule—on chart paper or in a pocket chart, if available

Pat's Tip

Painter's tape is a handy item for putting up charts and chart paper. It looks like blue masking tape but is easily removed from walls and cabinets, and it doesn't damage paint. A roll is inexpensive and lasts a long time. Fun-tak, a blue gumlike substance, is also good for putting up posters and charts. (See Resources for more information.)

I also need a small bulletin board or definite place for my memos, schedules, and other information. Sometimes I use the insides of cupboard doors for yard-duty schedules, times for speech and other pull-out programs, our district calendar, and other important notices.

Although this is a long list you really do *not* need a lot of commercial materials to have a wonderful classroom. (In fact, I find that I don't care for some commercial materials; to me, they have kind of a slick, plastic look.) What we need most as teachers is imagination, and children's art, writing, and sample work. And we need wonderful children's books!

Your Classroom Library

It is important to begin building a library of children's literature books and picture books right away. The books do not have to be new, but they must be carefully selected. A minimal investment at a library sale will give you a good start on your class library.

I had some pretty shabby and ill-equipped classrooms during the early part of my teaching career. During those years, I wasn't in a position to provide many new supplies or books. But a lot can be done with used books and free book posters from bookstores. A few well-chosen art prints are wonderful additions to classroom walls. Butcher paper illustrated with children's marking pen drawings can be used to cover cardboard boxes, to create "shelves" and display areas. And nothing is more beautiful than children's drawings, paintings, and murals.

I am fortunate now in the supplies and books I have available to me (most of which I have purchased over the years). But it has always been important to me to work to make my classroom come to life, and this can be achieved with almost no monetary investment.

Children's bookstores frequently have book posters and bookmarks available for teachers. These are free, good quality, and stimulate children's interest in reading. They are a good choice for room decorations and small gifts at the beginning of the school year.

Getting Funding

Our first-grade team, thanks to the brainstorm of primary teacher Laura Darcy, sells small snack packs of cookies after school one day a week. We use that money for subsidizing field trips and classroom supplies. We often involve students in the planning for these funds.

A Display for Next Year's First Graders

When I come into the classroom at the end of summer, I usually have one beautiful bulletin board ready. Most boards are blank, except for fadeless background paper and headings, ready for children's work and art on day one. But the large, central bulletin board display is complete, covered with a protective drop cloth from a paint store. This board is titled, "Welcome to First Grade! From Last Year's Class!" In June, my former first graders created this marvel by writing letters to incoming children, explaining what the upcoming year would be like. They also created wonderful art, showing off highlights of their own first-grade school year. I give the letters from veteran first graders to my new students on the first day of school. (See Figure 2–2.)

This bulletin board done by my former first graders is authentic, lively, and very welcoming. It is a big help for me in terms of getting the classroom ready. Looking at it lifts my spirits and reminds me why I'm in the classroom in the first place. Even more importantly, the letters and art are good planning and assessment tools for me! In June I can see each child's growth in writing and in the ability to organize and convey thoughts. I can assess growth in printing and in art as well. When children write these letters, they are also indirectly assessing me.

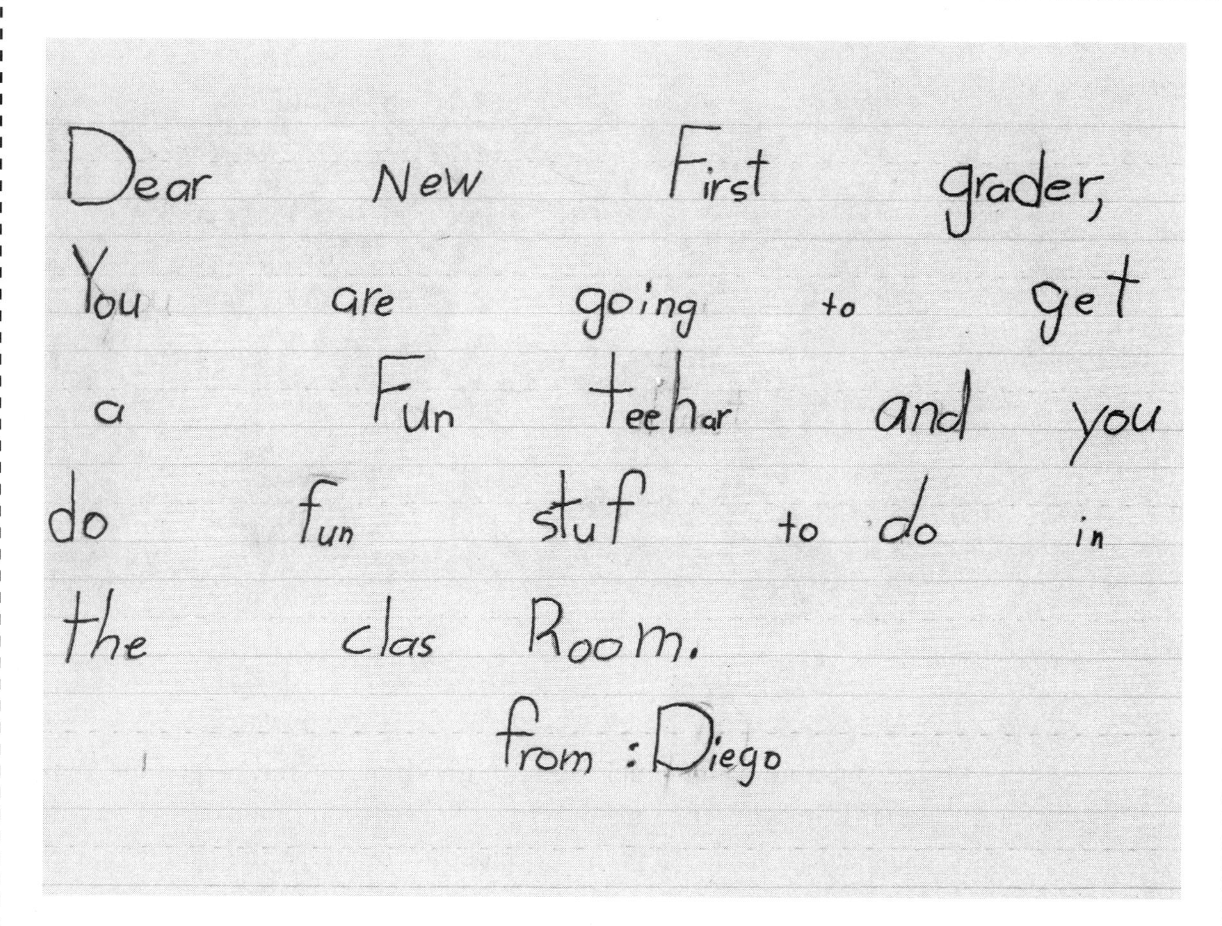
Dear New First grader,
You are going to get a Fun teehar and you do fun stuf to do in the clas Room.
from : Diego

Figure 2–2 *Letter from former first grader to incoming first grader*

I see what the children remember and value from our year together, and I get a good idea of how our time together went, from *their* points of view. These insights help me structure the year ahead with my new class.

Designing Room Arrangements and Organizational Systems

I had no idea that when it came time to be writing (and rewriting!) this chapter, I would have had to move my classroom of fifteen years, and that I would be setting up a new classroom myself. This certainly

Figure 2–3
Welcome bulletin board

has put a new and timely spin on my thinking and helped me analyze what is important to me in terms of classroom organization and management. *I* needed a plan! I decided to organize the things that were the most important to me first: our meeting area and our classroom library books and art supplies.

My mentor, Kay Goines, former kindergarten teacher and international specialist in children's literature, always says that our classrooms are autobiographical: they show at a glance what is important to us and reflect our personal philosophies and management ideas. Some important things for me are children's books, children's art, and children's work.

Here are some things I want to achieve as I set up my new room. These goals were also important to me in my former classroom:

- A comfortable feeling of space and movement: areas and some breathing space for us to easily move around. Easy access to exits. After years in the same classroom it is easy to collect too much stuff and lose this feeling of spaciousness. I have recently weeded out many materials and am beginning again!
- Room for us all to sit on the rug together for class meetings, stories, discussions, and some instruction. (In the days when I had a

room with no carpet, I used donated carpet squares from a local rug store.)

- Awareness of traffic patterns. When children work in small groups, or move from one area of the classroom to another, they could be intruding on each other. I try to set things up so that children can get around the classroom without tromping through another group's activities.
- Some well-defined areas: a place children can go to read big books; places to read classroom library books, play math games, build with blocks and Legos, or use puzzles or the dollhouse.
- A place for whimsy: I like to have "book advertisements" up in the classroom in colorful, changing displays. I pair a book with a corresponding stuffed animal or toy and run a line of these on a shelf across the classroom. Some pairings are *Madeline* and a Madeline doll; *Curious George* and a Curious George figure; *Tacky the Penguin* and several stuffed penguins; *Frog and Toad* and plastic Frog and Toad figures; *Where the Wild Things Are* and some wild things; and so forth. These are fun to change around, to use for enacting stories, and also to stimulate interest in specific books. Children *love* using these to "play" a story. (For more about this, see my book *Literacy from Day One*.)

Pat's Tip

Garage sales are a good place to find many toys and props to pair with children's books.

- Shelves, tubs, baskets, and rain gutters to hold quality books for children. (More about rain gutters on page 216). These shelves and containers also hold some of our published classroom books.
- Organized tubs, bins, baskets, and stacking trays accessible to the class. I want to foster children's independence by making materials

easily available to them. They have access to a variety of writing paper, construction and drawing paper, scissors, glue, marking pens, and other materials as the year evolves. At the beginning I limit supplies to writing paper and drawing paper.

- A place for big books: easel or big book holder, up in front at our meeting area, with a comfortable chair for me. This easel has a shelf for big books. (The shelf wasn't wide enough, so I taped on a long block from the big block area, using painter's tape, and now it is just right!) I also have a book rack for displaying a variety of big books.

Some children's book clubs have simple easels that can be purchased with bonus points.

- A large tablet of plain or lined paper for shared and interactive writing. I prefer the tablet paper with a light blue grid pattern. I can turn it sideways (longer space for writing) and still have light lines to use. I keep this on the big book easel. I have sometimes hung it on top of the whiteboard, using binder rings and hooks. Post-it-type chart paper is another possibility. It will stick right on the whiteboard or chalkboard. Recently I discovered I can hang things on the whiteboard with magnets. This gives me a lot of flexibility for brief displays.
- Whiteboard, whiteboard markers, and erasers. I need a large-sized whiteboard on the wall as well as two or three small, handheld whiteboards in different parts of the classroom. Magna Doodles also work well for writing brief notes, page numbers, a few words, and so on.
- Bookshelves or display areas for "overnight books" for daily take-home choices. (See Chapter 8 for more about overnight books.) When I did not have these shelves, I leaned books against the wall

under the chalk trays. Later I purchased rain gutters to hold some of them. (See page 216.)

- Place for children's coats, backpacks, lunches. I prefer cubbyholes to a coat closet, but of course I have to use the type of area that comes with the classroom.
- Shelves and tubs for math manipulatives. (See Chapter 12 for ideas for free manipulatives to collect.)
- Area for listening center: tape recorder and four to six head sets, book and cassette tape sets.

Pat's Tip

Children's book clubs have many good bargains on book sets and cassette tapes.

- Computer(s) and printer(s).
- Shelves for tubs or baskets of materials to be used at centers.
- Area to keep leveled reading books.
- Reading table (or other area, such as open space on the carpet).
- Art center with art materials, for example, an "art studio" (box or boxes) with papers, scissors, glue, and so on. (See Chapter 13.)
- Teacher desk and file cabinet(s).
- Shelves or cupboards near desk or teacher area for binders of frequently used materials.

Pat's Tip

Many businesses will donate used binders to schools.

- Desk basket and file folders of special materials for the week, such as children's weekly magazines or newspapers and special work or ideas.
- Bookends or other system for holding teacher's manuals.
- Pocket charts and chart racks. These are not crucial, but it is helpful to have two or three of varying sizes. These are also good room dividers and can be used to place materials within children's view, to organize a card game, and so forth. They can hold an art display or serve as backdrops for a play or creative dramatics. And they can be used to wall off a temporary area of the classroom for a variety of special projects. I keep a small pocket chart for lunch cards and one for our class members' names in alphabetical order. (I call this the Word Wall of Children's Names.) Pocket charts can be affixed to doors, walls, furniture, or on stands. When I have not had access to pocket charts, I have used large chart paper.
- Area on bulletin board for word wall words; extra sets of word wall words to use for games and for constant hands-on reference.
- Areas for a current mural, poetry charts, and jobs lists. (See Chapter 4 for more on classroom job ideas.)
- A place on bulletin board at meeting area for calendar and related materials.
- Area for educational-type toy clocks, large and small. Paper-plate clocks made by students can be kept here in a basket or box.
- Daily schedule on a whiteboard, on chart paper, or in a pocket chart.
- Bunny Planet—a nurturing area for a student to be alone for a while, take a brief timeout, recoup, take care of his own needs before rejoining group. This idea was inspired by the Voyage to the Bunny Planet trilogy, by Rosemary Wells (2003). (See more on this in Chapter 6).
- Time Away area or chair (stark) for a child or children who are not following classroom rules. (*Note*: The Bunny Planet and Time Away area could be one and the same.)

It can be helpful to make your own list of areas and materials you feel are important. Start with the basic, most important supplies first.

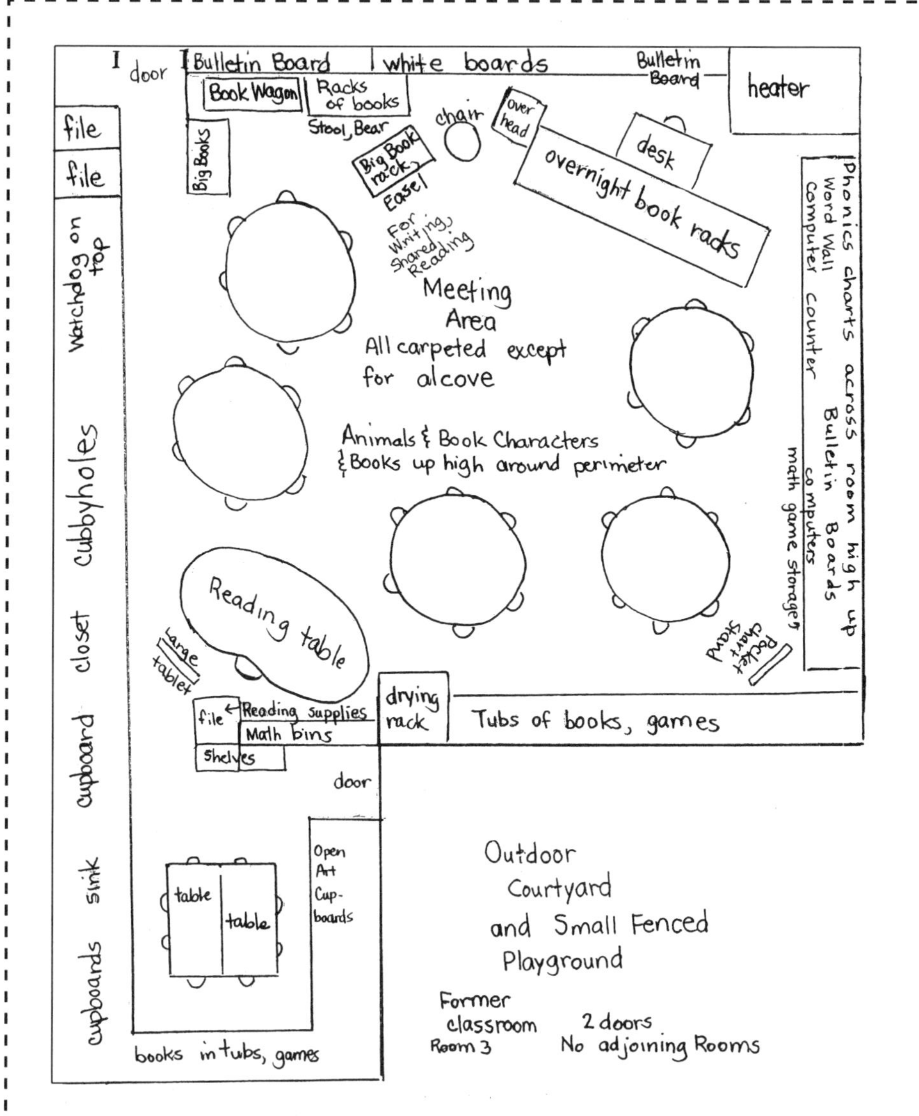

Figure 2–4
Sample room arrangment 1

Sometimes great materials don't work for a particular classroom, group of children, or individual teacher. Occasionally teachers give up or trade things that just don't fit their rooms or their styles.

Figures 2–4 and 2–5 show drawings of my classrooms (the one I recently left and my new one in another wing).

Strategic Seating Assignments

Although room arrangement is a little more difficult for me now that my classroom has round tables rather than rectangular desks, I make

Figure 2–5
Sample room arrangment 2

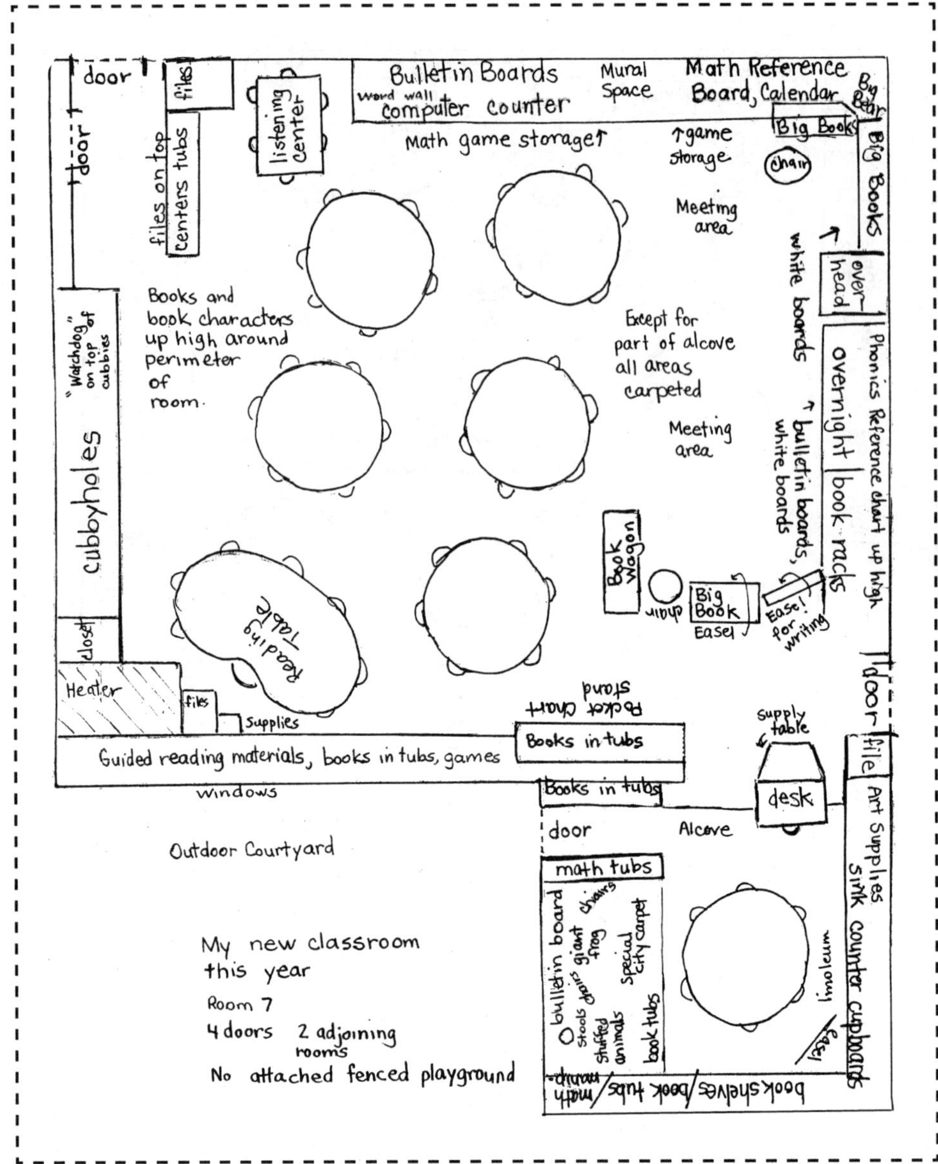

an effort to seat children so that they can all see the front of the classroom from their tables. I seat children on the outside ring of five tables. Seated like this, they can all see me. They can also see the white board, the overhead projector, word wall words, and each other. This gives us the option of working together on the rug, or at seats, both independently and as a group, during lessons or guided practice of new skills. Every table seats six children.

Storage

Each child has a bin that slides out from under the table. The bin and our classroom cubbyholes hold most necessary materials. Children have small plastic boxes that hold crayons and pencils. Each box has a large nametag on top. Boxes are placed in the center of each table, around a box of tissues. Because too much weight causes problems with our bins, some of the books we use, such as our math workbook, are stored in a crate under each large team table. Each child has a hanging file folder in the crate, and these materials have each child's name on the spine of the book. Ongoing books children are reading can also be stored here.

This year I used plastic crates for this extra storage, thanks to a brainstorm of my teaching partner, Joan Murphy. Last year I used file boxes with lids, all decorated with children's marking pen drawings. I would still be using these boxes—they were beautiful!—but I needed them when I packed to move to my new classroom. Plastic crates are stronger, able to withstand heavy use, and work better for holding file folders.

Other Types of Classroom Storage

In her book *Conversations* (2000), Regie Routman describes an over-the-chair pocket and directions for making it. I feel that these pockets would be essential for classrooms that lack a place for children to put personal items as well as school materials and books. I do feel fortunate to have built-in cubbyholes in my room. Stacked cardboard boxes or plastic crates can also be used to make cubbyholes if none are available.

In a previous classroom, I created team areas by moving rectangular table desks to form groups of four or six students. I placed these groups of desks, in a U shape, on the rim of the classroom meeting area. This created a center open space where we could share books and have discussions, as well as meet together to solve problems, innovate, and plan.

Partners

I like to have each child sit next to a partner at the *same* round table or adjacent desk. There are many reasons for this: Having a buddy can add to a child's sense of security and belonging. Partners can practice skills together, such as reading, and have time to discuss what they have read. They can help each other with math and science investigations, as well as ask each other for clarification about information they didn't understand. One of the main reasons I assign partners is to facilitate language learning. I try to put a struggling English language learner next to a talkative English speaker.

I take these things into consideration when matching up partners:

- Match middle-level students with other middle-ability students or students with lower achievement.
- Pair high-ability students with other high-achieving students.
- Match low-achieving students with middle-level students—preferably patient ones.
- Match second language learners in triads with a native English speaker and a bilingual child. If a triad is not possible, pair a second language learner with a student who speaks English fluently.

I change partners every six to eight weeks or so.

I do try to avoid partnering high-level students with children who need a lot of help. It isn't really fair to high-achieving children, and they often become impatient. The end result isn't fair to low-achieving students, either.

Making Provisions for the Solitary Learner

Although most children want a partner, there may be one or two who do not: some children like solitude and independence. I like to honor this and provide the opportunity for a child who does not want a partner to be satisfied and comfortable in the classroom as well.

An Easy Way to Change Classroom Seating

A simple way to change seating and see if your new seating plan works is to use magnets. Magnetic tape comes in rolls with adhesive on one side. A white paper strip covers the adhesive. This product is inexpensive and may be purchased from craft and sewing stores. It can be cut with scissors. Write students' names on the white paper on the magnetic strip using a permanent pen. Then cut the names apart. Place these little strips—your new room arrangement—on a cookie sheet, and move things around until you are satisfied with the way the grouping looks. This is much easier than moving children—or tables—until you get things right.

When I look at my seating chart, I ask myself these questions:

- Does every second language speaker have a partner support system?
- Do partners like each other or seem to get along with each other?
- Are high-achieving children sitting with partners who will challenge them, propel them to push themselves?
- Are floundering children going to get some partner help?
- Will middle-achieving children get the stimulus they need?
- Am I taking into account social needs and personalities, for example, the child who needs a patient friend?
- Will Jon be encouraged to speak because of interaction with a partner? Will sitting next to Elizabeth help Margo achieve more status in the group?

Regular magnets can also be used for your class seating system. Just use tape or pieces of computer labels to affix names to magnets.

Another variation of this idea is to stick class pictures and names on small magnets. This magnetic cookie-sheet overview of your seating assignments is helpful for a substitute, as well as handy for you.

Preliminary Organization

As you begin getting ready for the school year, it can be helpful to set up a small file box with folders. This can be a small open plastic file or a closed box with a handle. A cardboard box will work as well. Label the folders according to what you are thinking about and working on. Keep notes and thoughts in files in the box. Here is a sampling of file folders to create:

- Homework ideas and samples
- Parent notes
- Field trip ideas
- Classroom management and discipline ideas
- Room arrangement ideas
- Faculty meeting notes and other notes from the office (Weed this file out frequently.)
- District notes
- Committee notes
- A set of ten to twelve folders, one for each month of the year (Eventually, you may wish to have a file box for each month or two.)
- Class list
- Substitute folder
- Sponge activities: things to do in that odd spare two-minute time block
- Newsletter templates and ideas
- Things you *never* want to lose
- A folder for each major curriculum area: reading, writing/writers' workshop, literature book lists, math, science, social studies, English language learners (ELL), art, music, movement, health, PE, handwriting/printing, poetry.

Special Materials for the Beginning of the School Year

A chat with your school secretary will fill you in on what supplies to expect at the beginning of the year. In my experience, teaching on both the East and West Coasts, crayons, pencils, rulers, and a teacher plan book and grade book were provided, as were glue, tape, scissors, paper, textbooks, and some literature books. Many other items were available in one district, but not another. As we know, there is a great disparity in supplies, materials, and even the condition of the schools themselves, in districts all over the country. Given this, the first thing you need to know is what to expect *will* be provided for your classroom. Then you can figure out what *you* feel you need to have to begin the year.

Inexpensive Classroom Supplies

Many cities now have organized warehouses filled with materials teachers may purchase at a discount. They have names like Scrap and Re-Use. Most of these supplies are donated by businesses. Often there is a nominal membership fee, and sometimes the school or district will pay this charge. Other institutions of this type have no fee and charge by the bag or box of materials. It is well worth finding out about these places in your area before you invest in things for your classroom.

Some districts and schools have a budget for items for beginning teachers or teachers transferring from other schools or grade levels. Take a good look at your room and see what is there and what you think you need. It is possible that some of these things are in closets on campus and can be made available, or even ordered, for you.

Like many teachers, it has taken me *years* to gather some necessary educational items I now feel I cannot live without. A working computer, printer, overhead projector, and screen are real musts for me, but they are fairly recent acquisitions, as is a whiteboard. I did not have access to them for many years of my teaching career.

Here is a list of other items I feel I cannot do without in my first-grade classroom.

- Nontoxic, water-soluble marking pens—five sets (at least one set per team—more is great). I keep a basket for each table team with a set of marking pens, colored pencils, glitter crayons, and thin markers

- Plastic boxes with lids—one for each student to use for lunch money, pens, crayons, and pencils. I purchase the boxes; it would be worthwhile to see if your school, parents, or PTA could do this for you
- Sentence strips
- Educational clock (for showing children how to tell time)
- Oak tag or tagboard chart paper, 24-by-36-inch size
- Tablets of plain or lined paper, 27-by-32½-inch size (for pocket charts and pocket chart racks)
- Desk nametags (sentence strips can be used)
- Permanent nontoxic marking pens
- Crayons—set of sixteen for each child, plus lots of baskets of extras (I can scarcely believe it, but some teachers throw away their leftover crayons at the end of the year. It's worth asking, and letting people know if you would like a supply of old crayons.)
- Stacking trays for holding paper supplies (Cardboard soft drink trays work for this.)
- Manila file folders
- Electric pencil sharpener, preferably the kind that sharpens both large and small pencils (see Resources)
- Hole punch
- Three-hole punch
- Most of all, *books*—good-condition, good-quality children's literature. Of course books will necessitate bookshelves, book display racks, baskets and bins, and readers!

Other things I need:

- Math manipulatives
- Map of United States
- Map of the world
- Globe

- Puzzles and educational games
- File boxes or file cabinets
- Fun-Tak, clear plastic laminating paper, and book-covering plastic
- Phonics phones (see Chapter 9)
- Some 9-by-12-inch whiteboards

See Resources for more information about some of these items.

The Rolling Cart

An important investment to think about for your classroom (and your back!) is a rolling cart to keep in your car or somewhere in the room. I don't believe that we realize, as teachers, just how many pounds of materials we lug back and forth each day: books and game treasures from garage sales, student work, notebooks and portfolios, art supplies we have purchased, and so forth.

There are many kinds of carts. Some resemble luggage racks but have a larger base for stacking boxes or books. Others look like small suitcases or backpacks on wheels and have long handles. I believe in getting a good cart. My first one was very inexpensive, and it always collapsed like a camel when I put anything heavy on it. Whatever kind you choose, a rolling cart is an important purchase. It will help save your back and will remind you that you need to think about it before you blithely lift and carry things.

Some custodians are also helpful when you have heavy materials to transport.

Safe Climbing!

As well as a rolling cart, a small stepstool is also a useful acquisition. I see a lot of these at garage sales. Many teachers I know, and I am guilty, do a lot of climbing around in the classroom, standing on chairs, tables, even on the tops of cubbyholes and shelves. A stepstool is a healthy purchase.

Figure 2–6
Adrian writes about our custodian after watching him work.

Your School Secretary and Custodian

Two of your biggest assets in your school situation can be the school secretary and the custodian. Getting them on your side can make your life a lot easier. Since they deal with many people in the course of a day, it would ultimately be of great help to you to make their dealings with you as easy and pleasant as possible. I help children become aware of all the ways our school staff helps us. They love to make notes and drawings for our custodians and secretary (see Figures 2–6 and 2–7).

Teaching Responsibility

I feel that children need to be responsible in our classroom for using materials correctly, putting them away, and cleaning up their own

1-25
Dear Ed,
Your fish miss you. And I miss you.
From,
Martin

Figure 2–7 *A letter to our custodian*

messes. We always take about five minutes at the end of the day to pick up stray scraps and papers and straighten things up. I have always felt good about the fact that my children *do* take responsibility for our home away from home.

Find Out Where Your Students Are Coming From

One way to get in sync with your new class before school starts is to take a walk around the neighborhood, perhaps with a camera in hand. Take a look at everything you see with a child's eyes.

Once, as part of a university credential program, I was assigned the task of creating a photo journal of a student I was tutoring. I was to take photos of the boy's school, the block he lived on, and things he saw on the way to and from school. This included the types of buildings, businesses and services, open areas, signs, environmental print, and so forth. I mounted these photos on a long, thin strip of paper, folded accordion-style. (See Appendix, pages 394–395 for some ways to make and use accordion books.) Then I wrote captions to briefly describe each picture.

Even though personal aspects of the child's life were not photographed, nor was the child, I was astonished to see how illuminating this simple assignment turned out to be. I had a linear view of a day in a child's life: the things he would see and deal with on the way to and from home and school, the kinds of people, the different structures, the environmental print, the playgrounds (or lack of them), and so on. When this project was complete, I had a much clearer idea of where this little boy I was tutoring was coming from. I had seen his world.

If you do take photos of a child or your class, it may be important to get parent permission in writing. This is required in some school districts.

How to Do School

In first grade (and kindergarten and second grade as well), children are learning how to "do" school: how to organize themselves, listen and follow directions, work independently and cooperatively, and think creatively. They learn to get along with others and work and play with them. Children learn specific skills and many strategies and techniques. They are learning *how* to learn and learning about their own strengths and weaknesses in the job of acquiring knowledge.

Many children have spent a lot of mental and emotional energy on this rite of passage before they even arrive at the classroom door. Children talk a lot about dreams they have had before school starts. They also talk about things that matter most to them. Among the things children are most concerned with are learning to read and having friends. They also want to know they have a teacher who cares about them. We need to let them know that they do right away, on the first day of school.

CHAPTER 3

Celebrating the First Day of School

It's tricky to do a new thing,
Like go to first grade,
But then you go,
And you aren't scared so much,
And *then* you like it.
—Lilybeth

Greeting Your New Class—Have a Puppet in Your Pocket and Some Poems in Your Head!

My baby bear puppet is the best thing I've ever found to use when I'm welcoming my new first graders. The puppet is small, vulnerable, and looks so much like a real bear that no one is sure whether it's alive or not. I hold my free hand and arm over the place where the puppet fits on my hand and the children really think they are looking at a very tiny baby bear about 6 inches tall.

I bring the bear right out on the playground with me and pull it out of my pocket when I greet my new class. The little bear is the pied piper the children follow into the classroom on the first day of school.

This small creature captivates children and their parents. The bear hides under my arm, comes out for a peek, retreats, wiggles around,

Figure 3–1 *Children meet Little Bear on the first day of school.*

and so on. I encourage it to "be brave" and "get to know the new first graders." I tell it that it's "okay to be scared." I may ask a few children (those perhaps with watery eyes or a trembling lower lip) to pet it or tickle its tummy. Other children will have turns later. I put the bear up on a window ledge next to an even bigger bear. I do so in such a way that the children don't see me remove my hand, and the puppet opening is not showing. It seems important not to destroy the magic of the moment.

A little later in the morning, to break the tension and give us a chance to move around, I teach the children the poem "No Bears Out Tonight," using different intonations with each line. We enjoy reciting it together and acting it out.

No bears out tonight.
No bears out tonight.
No bears out tonight,
They've all gone away.
—Traditional

Find *Your* Way to Captivate and Enthrall

There are innumerable ways of meeting your new class. The point is to find one that is comfortable for you and helps children forget the big step they are taking—into your classroom! During your first few minutes with your children, help them to focus on something enjoyable and fascinating: a great poster, a giant stuffed animal, or a wonderful storybook. Books are always a good choice for me. Directing children to something of interest right away will help their nerves and, ultimately yours, too.

Relieving Parents' Minds—Outside the Classroom Door

When parents see their children interested and involved, it is easier for them to leave. I never ask parents not to come into the room; I just say a brief cordial greeting to parents at the door and then turn my complete attention to the children. Many parents leave at this point. The children enter the classroom and sit on the rug with me. I try to avert parental interaction by getting the children engrossed with me right away. (My attention can be on the parents or on the children, but not both. And for me, the children win!) There are teachers who enjoy having parents in the classroom for part of the day at the beginning of the school year. I'm just not one of them. Once in a while, a child becomes very upset when a parent is leaving. This reminds the rest of the students that maybe they should be upset, too. I try to avoid this "parting is such sweet sorrow" scenario. It can be contagious.

Parents who do come into the room typically watch for a while and then leave. This is a good thing, especially if it happens naturally and without fanfare. Many children do not notice parents leaving. Six inches of fur and two little beady bear eyes are a powerful draw.

The children and I talk about the little bear and I introduce some of the other classroom animals. I begin reading *Willy Bear, Little Bear,* or *Timothy Goes to School.* Almost before we know it, the children and I are alone in the room together and we're on our way to becoming a school family.

What to Do About Criers

Once in a while, there are children who cry when they come to class for the first time. Distractions are in order! It can be helpful to enlist these children's help with a plum job, such as passing out brand-new crayons and putting them on desks. Introducing them to classroom animals can work, especially the Biggest Bear, a truly gigantic teddy. I try to be sensitive to the moment and follow my intuition about each child.

Occasionally, if a child is upset and parents are still in the classroom, I may whisper to parents that I think it would be easier for their child if they were to leave.

"I Want My Mother!"

This year I had a child who held up beautifully until the time came for the flag salute. Suddenly the enormity of being in first grade hit him. He burst into tears and wailed, "I want my mother!"

I hugged him and heard myself saying, from my heart, "I want her, too!" He looked at me, astonished, and almost managed a smile. We got through a bad moment—a shared moment—and the situation was eased for both of us.

Greeting Each Child by Name

I strive to know all the children's names before the first day of school. I make a point to interact with some of them the previous year while they are eating lunch. The easiest way for me to quickly learn names is to study photocopies of last year's kindergarten class pictures for a few days before school starts. I make copies the previous June and refer to them a few times before the first day of school. Nametags can also be helpful.

Being able to call each child by name right away gives me a certain amount of confidence and helps the children feel comfortable. It also astonishes parents, who wonder how on earth that happened!

The Rug Area—We're a Contained Group, and There's Comfort in Numbers!

During the course of the first-grade year, when I really need children's attention, I call them to the part of the rug up in front of the classroom. Meeting here on the first day brings us all together immediately and gives me a way to see each child and take attendance. I have every child's name written on a tagboard strip or card. As I call a name, I show the corresponding name card. Many children enjoy trying to figure out these names before I say them. Often there are a few extra children who aren't on the class list and belong in other classrooms. Coming together like this provides an easy way to sort this out.

Name Cards—Our First Reading Experience

I make three sets of name cards and keep double sets in a pocket chart in our meeting area. These name cards can be used immediately for matching, for job assignments, to play a name game, to excuse children to line up for recess, and so on. One set of cards may be cut up and names can be spelled and reassembled like jigsaw puzzles. These name cards will also be used throughout our first month or so for finding specific letters, capital letters, certain sounds, and so forth. We will play with them in many ways. Names will be the first successful reading material for some first graders. (See *Phonics Lessons,* by Pinnell and Fountas [Heinemann 2003], for many more ideas about teaching with names.)

This name card session is also a good time to amend the cards to reflect nicknames, if the children prefer them. I always ask children what they would like to be called. Because I frequently have students from other countries, I sometimes have difficulty with the pronunciation of their names. We all practice names together. I want children to know it is important to me to use the names they want to be called and to say them correctly.

ELL Connection

I particularly do not want to Americanize children's names or change their names in any way. Alma Flor Ada writes about this experience, from a child's point of view, in her chapter book *My Name Is Maria Isabel* (1995). When Maria's teacher decides to call her Mary because there are two children named Maria in class, Maria Isabel feels as if she has lost her identity as well as her name. Not only has she lost the most important part of herself, Maria is constantly scolded for not answering when her new name (unrecognizable to her) is called. This book is available in English and Spanish.

Pat's Tip

If children wish to be called by a different name than the one listed on the roll sheet, I honor this, but in figuring it all out, I ask children what parents call them. Children can be pretty creative, as well as convincing. Years ago a child changed her name on the first day of school, and I didn't find out for weeks, until the parent asked, "Who is Lizzie?"

Putting Things in Desks or Cubbyholes

When the children seem somewhat settled, I have a few students at a time put things in cubbyholes. I place a Post-it Note with a name on it inside each child's cubby and put a little piece of tape on it. Later on during the first week, I make computer labels or sentence strips with names, for more permanent identification of each child's personal space. Usually there is a lot of movement the first few days, as well as the sorting out of nicknames, so it doesn't pay to do this too soon.

An Underlying Motive: Separate Children Without Them Knowing It

One reason for having children sit on the rug with me right away is to get them involved and busy. Another is so that I can view their reactions and responses to other children. Often during the first few minutes, as I watch children's interactions with each other, I see children who need to be sitting on opposite sides of the classroom. When I have children go to seats the first day, *I* choose their places and can easily and casually separate those who seem to need distance. This does help with class behavior. And it is much easier to *avoid* behavior problems than to acknowledge them and have to change a child's seat right away. Leaving a friend and moving to another part of the classroom can be disconcerting to a child during the first few days of school.

The reverse is also true. Some children really do need the confidence of sitting with friends as their first-grade journey begins.

Let's Get on with It and Learn to Read!

After a few preliminaries, as just described (such as taking attendance and getting coats and lunch boxes put away in cubbies), one of the first things we need to do, as a new school family, is to learn to "read." Children have heard for years that they will learn to read in first grade, and they want to get that out of the way so they can stop worrying about it and *do* it. This topic comes up immediately when I ask, "What do you want to learn this year? What are *your* best wishes about first grade?" (I feel that the idea of sharing these personal wishes is very bonding, and *my* wish is to have a bonded first-grade group.)

The most typical answer is the one Ricky gave: "I want to learn to read today." Usually children give variations of this answer. They also mention that they want to learn math. Some children say they want to learn to write. The answer they may or may not give is that they want to have friends. Most of them agree vehemently that they want to learn to read. What interests me about the reading answer is that it usually has a time limit. When new first graders say they want to learn to read today, they mean right now. So that's what we do. We learn to read right now.

Our First Shared Writing and Shared Reading Experiences

As the children tell me their wishes, I act as scribe and write their thoughts down on large chart paper. It is best to use 27-by-32½-inch tablet paper. I now place the paper horizontally so I can fit more words across and it is easier to read. (See *Interactive Writing: How Language & Literacy Come Together, K–2,* by McCarrier, Pinnell, and Fountas, [2000]). I prefer the tablet paper with a light blue grid, as I can use these light lines to organize and space my writing.

As I write, "'I want to learn to read today,' said Ricky," I point out a few things, such as specific words or letters. I don't expect to get a wish or a sentence from everyone so soon in the school year, so I sometimes add names next to sentences children agree are their wishes, too. Angel's original sentence then becomes amended to "'I want to learn to read to my baby brother,' said Angel, Ivan, Tatiana, and Willy." I try to have everyone's name somewhere on this new chart. Some years this evolves into a simple list of things children want to learn.

I do this activity as quickly as possible and condense the list if it is too lengthy. We can just begin this brainstorming session on the first day and then complete our First-Grade Wishes chart over a two- or three-day period. Children do not have a very long attention span at the beginning of the school year, and the *last* thing I want to do on the first day of school is make reading and writing boring for them!

After the chart has a sentence or two, we "read" children's wishes together. We talk about how, if you know what words say, that's real reading! We try to figure out what the words are on the chart, and then congratulate each other that we are real readers.

We Are Illustrators, Too!

When we illustrate our First-Grade Wishes chart, probably over several days, children use white drawing paper and marking pens or crayons. We trim these illustrations using scissors or by tearing away the extra paper around the drawings. Sometimes I do this part myself, in the interest of the fast completion of a new chart.

I place our masterpiece on a blank bulletin board that has been titled First-Grade Wishes and put up the illustrations all around it. This gives us an immediate first-day or first-week display that reflects our deepest feelings about why we are here in the classroom in the first place. We will reread our work and enjoy it many times. We will celebrate the look of it, our artwork, and the fact that we can read this chart together.

Figure 3–2
First-Grade Wishes list

Movement Is Crucial

Since beginning first graders need to move around a lot, we take stretch breaks, play Simon says, and do songs, nursery rhymes, and poems with movements. Frequent breaks are important at this stage of the game. I try specifically to go back and forth from tables to the rug so that children are listening, talking, moving, singing, chanting, drawing, and so on. This is kind of like cookies and milk: a little bite of this, a sip of that, and so on. I sometimes view the week as a sandwich. I have a pretty good idea of what I want to put in between the bread, but it might take me the whole week to get all the bits in there.

We Read What We Already Know

Nursery rhymes are great read-alouds for the first day of school. Two of my favorite nursery rhyme books are *My Very First Mother Goose* (1996) and *Here Comes Mother Goose* (1999). Both volumes are edited by Iona Archibald Opie and illustrated by Rosemary Wells. The text of these books is large, and the pictures are whimsical and very imaginative.

The children love to recite nursery rhymes they know and eventually choose a favorite to read together. In *Literacy from Day One*, I describe a beginning reading activity using the nursery rhyme "Humpty Dumpty." The children learn the rhyme, illustrate it in a little booklet, and "read" it on a chart where the words have mysteriously appeared. Then they practice reading their booklets. We role-play reading to parents in response to the certain question the children will be asked after school: "What did you do at school today?" The children practice asking the question *their* way, for example, "Hi, Sweetie, what did you learn today?" Response, from another participant: "Hi, Mom. I learned how to read! Want to hear me read 'Humpty Dumpty'?"

Our Readers Theatre Production

For our grand first-day finale, we make small drawings on sheets of overhead transparency plastic using nontoxic permanent marking pens. Then we have our own Humpty Dumpty show.

Figure 3–3
The children enjoy the "Humpty Dumpty" drawings they created on overhead transparencies.

The children run this show and enthusiastically read "Humpty Dumpty" together. We admire our reading, our illustrations, and our theatre production. By the time we leave for the day, we're on our way to becoming a close-knit, fun-loving, and literate community!

Making Reading Accessible to Children

Reading is a complex accomplishment, and we will approach it with many kinds of activities and experiences this year. I feel my main role on the first day of school is to help children relax about the idea of learning to read and feel successful with some beginning reading experiences. We play with a few ideas and enjoy some books and stories together. (Reading instruction is discussed more fully in Chapter 9.)

Back-to-School Shopping: Books!

When I do my own back-to-school shopping, I head for both the library and a children's bookstore. The best and most important thing

I can do for myself, and for my new first graders, is to have some wonderful new books that excite *me*, that I just can't wait to read aloud and share. This helps me fashion our first days together. I believe in reading aloud to children many times throughout the day, in between doing other curriculum work and other activities. The more time we spend like this, enjoying books together, the more we are on the same page, a bonded group, loving and learning through books.

Our Class Motto: Words to Live By

A story I like to tell right away sometime during the first day or first week of school is *Hickory*, by Palmer Brown (1978). I like to *tell* it because it is a long chapter book (too long for one sitting, especially at the beginning of the year) and also because it is out of print. By telling a specific part of the book, I can make a point about our first-grade classroom right away. I can also embellish this small portion of the book however I wish. We can all tell this part of the story if we know the basic idea:

Hickory is a small mouse who lives with his parents and his brother and sister, Dickory and Dock, in a grandfather clock. Hickory decides to move out of the clock, and out of the house, to a nearby meadow. On his first day in the meadow, he is almost killed by a cat but is saved by a small grasshopper named Hop.

The next day Hickory thanks his new friend Hop. She tells him that "here in the meadow we do what we can to help one another." The children and I decide that this is a good way to think about our classroom: "Here in our classroom, we help each other." This becomes our class motto.

I discovered the power of this little book by accident years ago, when I read it to a mixed group of first and second graders at the beginning of the year. We enjoyed the book over a period of several days. The day I finished it happened to be the day we had our first art lesson. One child finished her art project early, and sat in the middle of an island at her clean desk, with her artwork on top. There was a pile of rubble on the floor surrounding her. I asked, "Tracy, would you please pick up those paper scraps?"

And she responded, as you may have guessed, "They're not mine."

Inspiration struck. I replied, "But here in our classroom, we help each other."

"Oh," she said, and up she popped and cheerfully straightened out everything. I was flabbergasted and thought of all the times I had missed using *Hickory* or a similar piece of literature to help foster this kind of attitude. Throughout that school year, and since, I often heard children say, "Here in the meadow, we help each other; here in our classroom, we help each other."

Making Classroom Rules Together

An important activity for the beginning of school is deciding on our classroom rules together. As with the first-grade wishes, I write down these ideas for rules. To speed things up, I may write these ideas down on a piece of paper on a clipboard or on a transparency at an overhead projector. I read the children's rules back to them, and we decide on the ones we want. Later, on another day, I will invite each child to illustrate a rule, and I will take dictation on the computer. I will then put these rules and the illustrations where we can all see them, internalize them, and refer to them. Children have a lot more belief in rules if they have made them themselves. The rules may be modified throughout the year, as the need arises.

I do try to synthesize or combine these rules for a chart, using the ideas of my literature and classroom management mentor, Kay Goines. She has wonderful ideas for all areas of the curriculum.

One of Kay's classroom rules was *We never hurt anybody on the inside or the outside.* As a class, we discuss this idea and how it hurts people on the inside when we laugh at them, call them names, or do mean things. Another of Kay's rules was *We all clean up our places each day.* This sounds good to the children, too. I suggest something like *We all try to enjoy learning and learn as much as we can.* The wording varies from year to year, but children generally think this one sounds like a good rule, too. I do try to use the children's words and ideas.

With some help from the children, I created a piggyback song for our class rules, using a tune somewhat like the song "Ninety-nine Bottles of Pop on the Wall."

Never hurt anyone on the
inside or the outside.

Be a friend, and you'll have
  friends, you'll see.
Learn all you can in every way
  in every kind of subject,
Always be the best that
  you can be.

—PBD

We sing our song, illustrate our classroom code of behavior, and internalize it visually, kinesthetically, and in many other ways throughout our year together. I love to hear the children remind each other of our rules and talk about how we're going to treat each other.

This year the children came up with a more simplified list of rules:

- Follow directions.
- Listen carefully.
- Be a friend.
- Think and learn.

These rules led to our creation of the "Room 7 Super Star Song," sung roughly to the tune of "Muffin Man":

We do our best to listen, think, and learn,
  listen, think, and learn,
  listen, think, and learn.
We do our best
  to be as smart as we can be!
We are the Room 7 Super Stars!

—PBD

We sang this often, throughout the year, especially when we needed a boost to remember why we were trying to learn in the first place!

The School Tour: An Alphabet Hunt!

An important (sometimes urgent) activity in a first-grade classroom is a tour of the school, particularly the bathrooms. I read *Chicka Chicka,*

Celebrc
Da,

igure 3–4
Our class "Super Star Song"

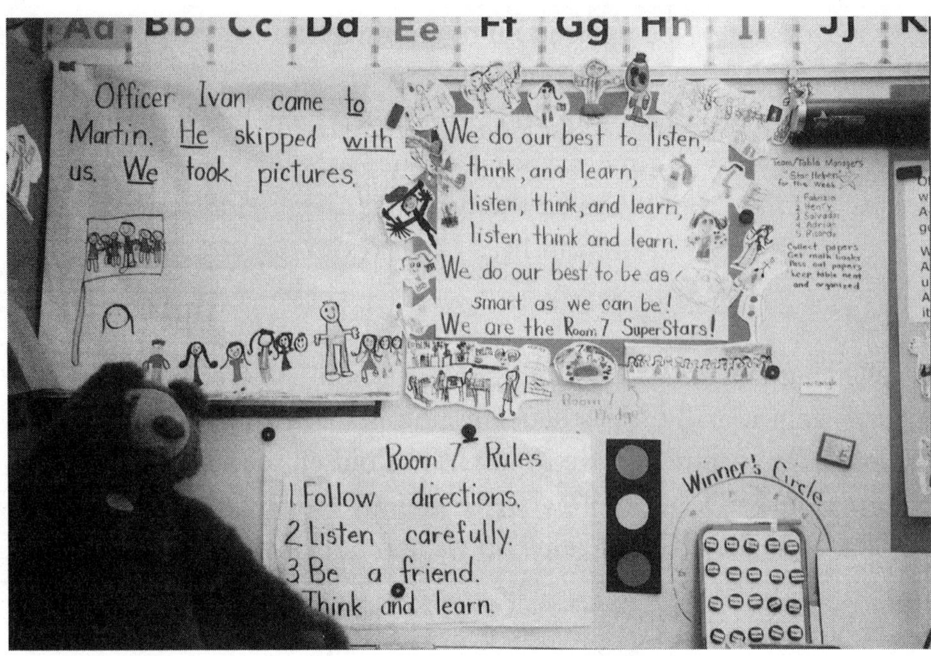

Boom Boom, by Bill Martin Jr. and John Archambault (2000). Then we take an alphabet walk.

Before we set off on our expedition, I show the children a whiteboard full of magnetic letters. We say the alphabet together and discover that there are spaces: some of the letters are missing. The children and I guess that some of the letters of the alphabet have gotten away and may be playing around in other parts of the school. We decide that we are going to learn about different places in the school and talk to different people who work here, and we are going to capture those letters!

I remind the children to keep careful track, like explorers and reporters, of the adventures we will have, the things we will learn, and the people we will meet. On our way out the door we find the letter *l* and decide that means we should walk in lines during our journey. We add the *l* to our magnetic board, and form two lines. (I find that one line drags on too long. For more about lines, see Chapter 4.)

I carry our incomplete magnetic board, and off we go to check out the bathrooms. There we meet the custodian, Jim Gillingham, who gives us a letter *b* that he has trapped. He mentions to the children how hard he works to keep the bathrooms clean for us. We talk about how the first graders will take care of the bathrooms, too. The children learn Jim's name and swear allegiance to neat bathrooms and washed hands.

Moving onward on our expedition, we check out the office, where we meet the secretary, who gives us an *s*, and explains her job. The principal comes to greet us, handing over, no surprise, the letter *p*. She talks about her job as well.

The children and I travel on to the cafeteria, where we meet the cafeteria manager. We receive information about lunches, lines, and behavior, and retrieve the letters *c* for cafeteria and *f* for food. By now, since it's almost time for recess, we investigate the playground and find the letter *p* on a nearby pole. We learn how to use the equipment and playground areas.

Figure 3–5 *Our custodian, Jim Gillingham, shares the letter* b *for bathroom.*

School Tour Follow-Up

When we come back to the classroom after recess, I use a clipboard to quickly write down the children's memories of the alphabet hunt. We check our magnetic board and celebrate that all the letters are there. We are great trackers! We all have an alphabet cookie to celebrate.

The children's words and memories of the trip around school will be part of our curriculum for the next few days. Again I will act as scribe for our shared writing activity each day. I will write down children's words and thoughts about our alphabet trip and all the places we visited. We will create a page for each place visited and each person we met.

Children will read and reread these adventures with me and will illustrate the pages. We will make a cover. This will become a class big book that we will cherish and share with our school staff.

The Gingerbread Man

An alternate activity to the alphabet hunt is looking for the Gingerbread Man. As described in *Reading, Writing & Learning in ESL,* by Peregoy and Boyle (2000), first graders in Buzz Bertolucci's new class

Figure 3–6
Shared writing: our alphabet hunt story

have just finished a shared reading experience with a big book titled *The Gingerbread Man* when a school cook enters the room and hands the teacher a note. This note is from the Gingerbread Man, who says he has jumped out of the book and is headed for the cafeteria. "Come and meet me," the Gingerbread Man taunts the class.

Of course, when the children get to the cafeteria and look in the oven, the Gingerbread Man is gone. A note in the oven informs them that they should check a different place. This goes on, much in the same vein as the alphabet hunt, with children going from place to place around school, meeting school personnel and becoming familiar with the lay of the land.

In this scenario, when the children return to the classroom, they find gingerbread man cookie treats. When I use this activity, I also plant a note from the Gingerbread Man with the cookies: "Ha, ha! You didn't catch me!"

Sometimes I use this idea with our alphabet tour, and leave a note from a letter that has escaped us. For example, when we came back to the classroom after our alphabet hunt one year, we found the letter *m* on my chair with a gloating note, "Ha! Ha! You missed me, but I came back to join my friends so I could make words!"

With both activities, children are introduced to their new environment and the important people in it. They also experience a work of literature in an interesting way and, I hope, will look forward to future literature books as a result.

Children's Literature Connection

The Alphabet Tree, by Leo Lionni (1990), is a great book to use to connect our alphabet trip to learning about letters and words. In this story, individual letters on an alphabet tree are tossed around by the wind. They band together to form words, and with the help of a caterpillar, learn to get those words together to say something meaningful, in a whole sentence. This book is a parable about the power of the written word. It also shows children there is strength in numbers and in working together.

Crucial Day One Curriculum: Time

One of the things I like to work on the first day of school is the concept of time. Children will never care more! Within the first hour of first grade, you will have heard the questions, "When's recess?" "When's lunch?" and "When do we go home?" innumerable times. The best thing to do is to whip out a large educational toy clock and proceed to teach time.

I show children how to tell time to the hour and explain that this is special knowledge they can take home and show off. I set up or draw a few small clocks to show them when we go to recess, lunch, and home. They can figure out if it is time for these activities by matching the small toy clocks or drawings with the classroom clock. If I have the feeling that mentioning going-home time may not be the wisest idea because it might upset some of my new first graders, I skip that time period.

Time is one of those concepts that should be reviewed often. This year I set up a daily schedule with little clocks attached and changed it every day. I think this helps keep alive the concepts we have learned and also helps with that oft-asked, very demanding question, "When's lunch?"

About the Bathroom and Bathroom Emergencies

My first-grade classroom has no bathroom. I ask children to use bathrooms at recess, but of course, not everyone follows this request. Some students are in such a hurry to play that they forget about using the bathroom. A few children avoid the bathroom when there are other children present. Some boys are uncomfortable about using the urinals and try to wait until they get home. I explain to first-grade boys privately that the bathrooms may look different than those at home, but they work just about the same: they should use them, flush, and wash their hands. For most children, that information is all that is needed.

When it comes to using the bathroom at recess, some children may not choose to do this, regardless of what I have said. I always feel that these children have a secret weapon: they can easily have an accident that requires a change of clothes and the cleaning of our classroom rug!

One way around this problem at the beginning of the year is to get to the bathroom a few minutes before recess. As children come out, I make sure they have washed their hands and so on.

I spend a lot of time reminding children to use bathrooms at recess, particularly the first few days. We talk about emergencies, and how if they have one, they should just take off and get to the bathroom right away, even if it is in the middle of a lesson. I clarify what constitutes an emergency. This works some of the time.

Despite these strategies, it is good to keep a sharp eye out for the bathroom dance, and direct any children doing it out of the classroom and into the bathroom immediately. A little later in the year, we have a sign language signal we use. (See Resouces for sign language book suggestions.)

Bathroom Pass

When children do need to go to the bathroom during class time, I ask them to place a bathroom pass on their desks. The pass is made from a margarine tub lid with a hole through it. The lid hangs from a piece of yarn. I keep two of these by the classroom door. In this way, I always know who is away at the bathroom. (It can be hard to remember who asked to leave class when you are in the middle of teaching.)

Planning for Recess: Helping Students Deal with Problems and Find Playmates

Recess on the first day can be tricky. Children aren't sure what to do out on the big playground or how to handle themselves. We prepare for this with literature and discussion.

Children's Literature Connection

Three wonderful books that help with the dilemma of how to get along out there in the play area are *King of the Playground*, by Phyllis Reynolds Naylor (1994), *Bootsie Barker Bites*, by Barbara Bottner (1997), and *The Recess Queen*, by Alexis O'Neill (2002). All of these books deal with bullies and what to do when someone is not treating you as a friend.

Before recess on the first day, we discuss possible playground situations and practice looking small, and looking big. We decide that looking big, with arms on hips, legs spread, and eyes staring right at the other person, is a good idea if someone is bothering us. Then we can be like Max, in *Where the Wild Things Are*, and stare right into their eyes "without blinking once."

I also inform the children that there are yard-duty teachers on the playground, and they are to go to them if they need help. Children can also help each other by playing together and being good friends. Reviewing games that can be played is a good strategy, too, and helps children figure out how to use their time.

I spend a lot of time on these strategies and on role-playing recess ideas and conflicts for the first week or two of school.

A Sampling of Other Activities for the First Day of School

This brief description of day one in my classroom is not sequential. There is a lot of "how to do it" business to be taken care of on the first day of school: how to walk in line, how to treat each other, how to make sense of what we are doing here. The second day, and beyond, we will settle into routines. But the first day is like no other: above all on our first day, I want children to feel the joyful pull of learning, the zest of acquiring knowledge, and the comfort and pleasure of being part of this adventure together.

CHAPTER 4

Managing Your Classroom and Motivating Your Students

Nothing I ever learned of value
was taught to me by an ogre.

From *Who Am I in the Lives of Children?* by J. T. Dillon

Children *really* need to know they matter to us personally before we can teach them anything. It is no coincidence that the teachers I remember warmly are also the ones from whom I learned the most.

Smiling is a first step in helping children feel they are in the right classroom. After walking children from the playground, I always stand at the door as children come in and greet each of them. I do the same thing when they leave at the end of the day. It's amazing the amount of information I can acquire about children as I watch them come into the classroom. In this brief amount of time, I can see who is ready to start the day, who didn't want to come, which children are having difficulties saying good-bye to their parents, and so forth. Once in a while I notice a child coming in upset, and I can quickly help with a diversionary tactic like giving him a job to do for me or starting a conversation. A child (the door monitor) holds the door open at this time. This helps let parents know we will soon be closing the door and getting down to the business—and joys!—of learning.

Rituals and routines play a large part in helping children feel comfortable. These step-by-step procedures are something to rely on and help children know what will happen next. When we systematically show students what to do, what we expect, and give them input as to how the classroom looks and runs, we help create a well-managed room and a safe place to be. This way, children will be feel good about being in first grade, and we will be on our way to a great year. I let my first graders know that this year we will *all* learn to be the best we can be!

Making Learning Goals Together

Another step for good motivation is to help students come up with their own learning goals. We make our wishes for the year and decide on classroom rules together (see Chapter 3). Having the room and materials ready is another step toward good management and success. In this way, we head off possible problems, and battles are won before they are fought.

Children's Literature Connection

Some children's books that reinforce beginning-of-the-year organization and school relationships are *Miss Bindergarten Gets Ready for Kindergarten*, by Joseph Slate (2001), illustrated by Ashley Wolff; and *Lilly's Purple Plastic Purse*, by Kevin Henkes (1996). (See Resources for more choices.)

Different Kinds of Plans

I have my lesson plans ready before the children enter the classroom; I don't believe in winging it. I find that I need different kinds of plans for teaching: daily lesson plans; weekly lesson plans; a yearly calendar roughed in with my curriculum goals, field trips, and special events; and an emergency plan: a box of materials and substitute notes in case of an unexpected prolonged absence. I also create a substitute folder, with such necessary information as a class schedule, names of children to count on for help, and names of those with special needs. Teacher stores carry substitute folders with spaces to fill in the information a substitute would need.

Daily Lesson Plans

When I structure my day, I try to balance activities that require sitting with those that allow children to have more hands-on time or the opportunity to move around. I may make a lesson plan for a specific subject if it's new to me, I want to prepare for being observed by my principal, or it's a lesson with difficult, tricky parts. Most of all, I visualize the lesson in my head, part by part, as if I were watching a silent movie. That way I can see the potential pitfalls and then avoid them.

If you do make a formal lesson plan for a specific subject, it should include the following:

- A description of your class or group.
- The objective for the lesson: Why teach this lesson? What is the concept or skill that will be learned? Connect this objective with standards or district goals. For example: Students will be able to _________.
- Materials needed.
- Procedures (four parts): Describe what you will say to introduce the lesson. List and number the steps you will take in the subsections:
  - Opening—Include an introduction/anticipatory set/bridge between what students bring to the task and what they are to learn.
  - Development—Include what you will say to move students from one phase of the lesson to another. Include prompts (questions) you will use to scaffold this learning.
  - Closing—How will you wrap up the lesson? How will you direct students' attention to what they are learning and have learned?
  - Follow-up or extensions, if any.

- Adaptations for English learners.
- Adaptations for students with special needs.
- Evaluations (two parts):
  - Of your teaching.
  - Of children's learning.

When evaluating the lesson, consider the organization and flow of the lesson and the clarity of your teaching. How did you elicit response from the students? How did you facilitate student self-discovery? What worked especially well? What would you change next time?

Weekly Lesson Plans

Lesson plans help me organize for the week ahead in every subject area. In my district, we use lesson plan books. We make certain these are on our desks every day and are completed for the following week before we leave each Friday afternoon. The office also has a copy of the following week's plans. (I do understand the need for this. I did some brief substitute teaching in a rough school district once and never saw a single lesson plan!) It's pretty hard to be a substitute without at least some ideas about scheduling and curriculum and some information about the class in front of you.

Pat's Tip

Make a lesson plan template on the computer. This template should include all the information that stays the same each week: times, general routines, and so on. To make my lessons current for the following week, I just have to add new page numbers or a few notes, yard-duty assignments, and information about a few new lessons. These lesson plans can be printed out weekly and pasted into plan books. (They could also be three-hole-punched and kept in a labeled binder.) Revising computer plans is much faster than rewriting set information every week.

Keep Lesson Plans Simple

A caution about lesson plans, and one I have learned the hard way: Don't make your written plans too detailed. It's easy to put in too much information when writing plans with a computer template. If you overdo it, your poor substitute will never get a chance to plow through all your notes. I am now writing plans more simply, with only essential information.

I keep teacher manuals for all programs on my desk, with my lesson plans. I keep extra content area materials in the cupboard next to the desk.

Plan Out Your Year

I keep a simple two-page yearly calendar in the front of my weekly lesson plan book. This way I can get a general idea about when I am teaching certain themes, any special events coming up, and so on. This helps me integrate curriculum and gives me an idea about when to order books, videos, and any other supplementary materials from the district or county library. I don't worry too much about sticking to this plan—it is meant to be a *tentative* idea of where we are going and when. I adjust it as the year moves on.

Substitute Emergency Box

This idea is the brainstorm of my colleague Colleen Quinn Malloy. Colleen was visiting family in Cleveland over a winter break. She was worried about getting back from vacation in time for school because of weather and airline problems. As she worried, she thought up the idea of having an emergency kit for her substitute. When she returned (on time), our first-grade team brainstormed together and came up with a group of materials for an emergency kit. The box had somewhat generic materials and was made to last a week. Some materials I included were

- Nametags—the conference-style type with a plastic pocket and elastic cord.
- A simple lesson plan for a week, somewhat roughly sketched in.

- A brief description of independent reading time (including expectations!) and whole group reading information.
- Brief notes on how I teach guided reading. I keep books for each group in a file at the reading table. This file also contains a list of children in each group.
- Information on continuing shared reading, at the easel on the rug, using a big book children have not yet read. (Keep one or two unread, just for this situation.)
- A hands-on math unit, such as All About Me. This was the beginning chapter from a math book. We had all skipped it at the beginning of the year because it was too difficult. Another suggestion would be to teach a specific contained unit, such as time, patterning, or geometry. These kinds of units do not depend as much on prior knowledge as some lessons do and are easier to slip into place for a week.
- An *All About Me* book for writers workshop. This is a simple autobiography booklet for each student to write and illustrate. The sample template was adapted from a booklet from a museum store. My other suggestion, and one I prefer, would be to carry on with writers workshop as usual, with children continuing to write in their writing notebooks.
- Directions for a self-portrait art project.
- Poetry to learn and illustrate. Poems focus on the All About Me theme. (See Appendix, pages 403–406 for some copyright-free poetry to use.)
- Lists of favorite games to play during physical education.
- Social studies and science big books in class meeting area, with Post-it Notes marking current study chapters.

It is fairly simple to put together a group of materials that could be used for a week in case you have a prolonged difficulty or emergency. Learning can be going on smoothly while the situation gets resolved. Our first-grade team members all labeled these boxes and let another team member know where the box was kept.

Keep Children Waiting? I Don't Think So!

I try my utmost not to keep children waiting between activities. I believe that leaving them sitting on the rug, or in their seats, while I go get something is a sure recipe for disruptive behavior. If I have forgotten something I really need, even 10 feet away, I may go get it, but I take the chance that it will be several minutes or more before we are again in a state of readiness to begin our lesson. A solution to this is to have a table or desktop where everything needed for the day can be set out in order, grabbed, used, and put back. This is sort of like an operating room setup, where all the tools are ready and in order (and we sure wouldn't want any waiting time there!).

I have several areas where I teach in the classroom, and I keep relevant materials in each place. I find it helpful to have a small handheld-sized whiteboard and whiteboard pens and eraser in each of those places. I keep a small tub of materials at the easel, where we meet on the rug for class meetings, shared reading, and writing. I set up my classroom so that the easel and materials at one end of this area deal with literacy activities. A wagon nearby holds books and other supplies. There is a chair for me. The bulletin board calendar area at the other end of this space has materials that pertain to our math studies. There is a chair for me there too. One of the materials I like to keep in my math teaching area is a Magna-Doodle Board. These are great attention-getting devices for reviewing or teaching tricky concepts.

Children face one direction on the rug when we are working on reading and language arts activities, and the other direction to face the math calendar board.

The guided reading table at the back of the classroom also holds materials for me: a whiteboard and pens, alphabet letters, magnet boards, and so on. The front table of children also has a small whiteboard for me, pens, and a few other items I might need.

With the room set up this way, I don't have to move far to access materials as I am teaching.

About Sitting on the Rug

This year I gave *all* my children assigned places to sit on the rug. (In fact, we made a map of where to sit that I used to reinforce this plan, as well as to incidentally teach mapping.) I usually do not ask children to sit in specific spots, but each group of children has its own needs. This year all students had a place to be where no one else was touching them or bothering them. I found this took care of the race to the rug and the raucous competition to sit near certain children or items. This type of seating map shows children that we mean business—*learning* business—when we are sitting together on the rug.

For circle time and class meetings, of course, children sit in a large circle or oval.

Counting off is a good strategy for the classroom, too. If each student has a number, assigned alphabetically by first names, not only will we know immediately if everyone is still with us on a field trip, but children can write their numbers on their papers. When papers are put in numerical order—by a number monitor—papers will immediately be in alphabetical order. The uses of this strategy are too numerous to count. The one thing necessary to make this idea work is to make sure children realize they must never call out or use someone else's number.

I do not rely totally on numbers to know that a child is present when we are outside our school setting. We have partners who look out for each other, and I count heads as well!

Transitions

Both in and out of the classroom, transitions from one activity to another can be tricky. I try to provide a smooth bridge from one activity to another. Sometimes we sing as we clean up, for example, "This is the way we put things away," sung to the tune of the "This Is the Way We Wash Our Clothes" nursery rhyme. Words to our song vary, but this sample has a motivational ending:

> This is the way we put centers away,
> Centers away, centers away,
> This is the way we put centers away,
> So we aren't late for lunch!
>
> —PBD

One of the tricks in making meaningful transitions to a different activity or place is first getting children's attention. (See Chapter 6 for some ideas for grabbing attention.) Many poems and songs are great ways to get children involved and refocused. Hookups (see pages 114–15) are another surefire method, as are unusual, interesting sounds that signal an end to an activity: wind chimes, a rain stick, an autoharp, a xylophone, and so forth.

Once we have children's attention, we can give them instructions. If they are cleaning up learning centers, they may all be working on this at once. However, sometimes we want just a few children at a time doing an activity or getting ready for dismissal: gradually getting lunch cards and getting in line for lunch, putting homework in backpacks, and so on. Here are some ways to avoid bottlenecks and have a few students at a time following an instruction or lining up:

- Those children who answer a question, such as "Name a word that rhymes with *bat*, may line up."
- Children wearing specific clothing types or colors may line up: "If you are wearing red, line up."
- Have children line up according to their birth months, the first letters of their names, their table teams, and so on.
- Choose children who have numbers from one to five, double-digit numbers, and so on. "If your number is an even number, get your lunch card."

It is fun coming up with riddles like this as ways to excuse children for lunch or dismissal. This is also a way to review concepts we are working on.

Teaching a *Giant* Amount of Curriculum

As generalists, first-grade teachers teach it *all*. This results in lots of content to be responsible for teaching, as well as many materials to keep in order. Generally, in a first-grade classroom, there is no downtime for teachers to put things away. We have no prep periods, at least in my district. We need to be well organized and have easily available places to put materials, or every day is a scavenger hunt. I freely admit that this is a tricky personal challenge. I am fortunate to be next door to Joan Murphy, a real efficiency expert, from whom I have learned some tricks on how to smoothly organize for ease in teaching.

Organization of Materials

Joan organizes everything in binders, using plastic page protectors. She labels binders clearly on spines as well as on front covers. She keeps these binders readily available on a small bookshelf behind her main teaching area. She has a binder for each area of the curriculum, where she stores relevant papers, worksheets, and ideas.

One of Joan's most frequently used binders is labeled "Originals." This is where she keeps all her original copies of everything, regardless of category or subject area. As a result, while I was searching through my files for things, trying to remember which heading I used for my folders, Joan easily put her fingers on anything! I am gradually adapting several parts of her system for my classroom.

Joan's On-the-Desk File

Joan also keeps a handy desk file, with a folder for each day of the week. Inside, she places daily homework, any papers specific to a given day, classroom magazines, and so forth. This is very helpful for a substitute, as well as for keeping the regular teacher organized.

Joan and I both keep small resource boxes for homework and other upcoming first-grade magazines and materials underneath our desks. I also keep a small box there with one or two specific art projects, ready to go.

Don't Plunk That Paper Down!

Now I am conscious enough, thanks to Joan, my organization mentor, that when I look at a paper from my school mailbox, I no longer just plunk it in a stack on my desk. I quickly read or skim each paper or flier and decide whether to throw it away, put it in a spot to think over, or put it where I can find it again. I keep undecided papers on the desk (usually for just a day or two).

My binder labeled "Important Things to Find" doesn't have plastic page protectors. I made pockets from 12-by-18-inch construction paper, folded in half. I three-hole-punch this doubled paper on the fold and staple the bottom. I also fold the top three or four inches of the top corner down (inside the folded page). This way I can see what is in the pocket. I make several pockets in different construction paper colors. (Similar plastic pocket folders can be purchased at stationery stores.) I label pockets and file important papers inside. Somehow this is easier for me than using a file cabinet. Some headings I use are

- Faculty Meeting Notes, Notes from the Office
- District Notes
- Grade-Level Meetings
- Possible Field Trips and Field Trip Info
- Notes About Upcoming Assemblies and School Events
- District Committees (labeled by committee)
- Reading Association Info
- County Library/Research Info
- California Teaching Association Info
- Weekly Class Newsletters (the *Braggin' Dragan*)
- Family Literacy Committee Notes
- Student Work to Save
- Student Referrals
- Emergency Form (copies of each student's form, listing allergies and other confidential student information)

I limit this binder to about ten or fifteen categories—just for things I may need to see again or find on a regular basis. (If this collection gets larger, a second binder is needed.) I also write dates and important notes down, right away, in my plan book and on the calendar inside the cupboard next to my desk.

I keep separate binders for parent conferences, assessments, and so forth (as mentioned). This system doesn't take much time. Best of all, it works for me!

Making Your Organizational System Fit You

I think the key to organizing is to make the system suit your personality, your learning and teaching styles, and your needs. I finally realized that I'm never going to enjoy organizing or want to spend a lot of time on it. I just want to be able to see things again without spending hours looking. On the other hand, there are people like Joan, who are good at organizing and also enjoy it. Her system fits her because it reflects ways she wants to spend her time, as well as the way she teaches. My system fits me because I want to spend my time other ways. I think we are at two ends of the organization spectrum, with lots of people and systems in between. The trick is to find your own system.

Going from One Place to Another: Getting Used to Lines

One of the first things we need to do as teachers is to get children in and out of the classroom: to and from the playground, the lunchroom, the library, and other places around school. Lines can be tedious, but they are a reliable way to accomplish this mass movement. Lines are also crucial in case of fire drills or earthquake drills and emergencies. We'd never get anywhere safely if we did it any other way!

There are a variety of ways to ask children to line up. I prefer two lines, just because one line drags on so long, but there are some teachers at my school who prefer one. I can't help noticing that following a one-line class in from the playground takes a lot longer than getting behind a group with two lines! I have tried single lines, as well as a variety of ways to assign double lines:

- A and B or Red and Blue lines, with children permanently signed up for a specific line (Children enjoy choosing colors or line names.)
- Boy and girl lines
- Team lines, with table teams assigned to certain lines
- Double lines in alphabetical order or by assigned numbers (See page 60 for information on assigning numbers.)

- Lining up by height—can be important on school picture day and for programs on stage

By far the easiest organizational system, I feel, is to have boy and girl lines. For one thing, children easily remember where they line up. I do, however, try out the long single line and double lines and give students a choice. This year's class preferred to have a line for girls and a line for boys, with assigned line leaders. Leaders were selected weekly. *Note*: Because of Title IX provisions, some schools prohibit boy and girl lines.

Sometimes there are tussles in lines and even pushing to be first or at the front. This is one reason to have assigned line leaders. We decided as a class that no one could save places or cut. However, we agreed that in case of a fire drill, we would merge just like traffic, into the easiest, quickest single line.

About Field Trips

One of the richest experiences to give children is to take them on field trips that enhance their classroom learning. (I still have vivid memories of a trip around San Francisco when I was a third-grade student!) Some of the trips we go on may be short walking trips around the neighborhood. Others are more involved journeys requiring a ride on hired school buses. We have also taken trips by way of BART, the Bay Area Rapid Transit system, operating from San Francisco to outlying areas, and city buses. Occasionally we have had parents drive. This entails some insurance paperwork to be filed with our district office.

Field Trips Build Community

It is important to take field trips as early in the school year as possible. This way you can get as much mileage as possible from them: connecting trip experiences with first-grade curriculum and building class community and friendships. Field trips give us common memories and bond us. They give impetus for class discussions and our writing and can relate to many of the things we do for the rest of the year.

Ways to Pay for Field Trips

Our PTA helps us with the cost of these trips. Our first-grade team, thanks to the entrepreneurial brainstorm of kindergarten and first-grade teacher Laura Darcy, sells cookies one day a week after school. We save much of the proceeds of this endeavor to go toward field trip admission fees and related special art and science materials. Other ways to pay for field trips are to write a grant, ask parents to contribute to the costs, and find out about possible scholarships available from field trip destinations. Our first-grade team has received theatre scholarships in the past, as well as a scholarship to a local hands-on discovery museum.

During the past few years, our first-grade classes have been fortunate to take field trips to the Laurence Hall of Science in Berkeley, California. Each February the museum holds a wonderful dinosaur exhibit. The children enjoy the dinosaur displays as well as related exhibits. They love climbing on the gigantic blue whale sculpture and other sea-life creations outside in the museum entrance area. The views of the San Francisco Bay Bridge and the silhouette of San Francisco seen from across the bay add to children's learning and enjoyment. In one day they have great science, geography, and related art experiences.

Children also enjoy shopping in and looking through a well-stocked museum store. Our first-grade team members use cookie money to afford materials from this educational shop to enhance learning in our classrooms.

The dinosaur exhibit at Laurence Hall of Science has been a favorite field trip for our students and teachers. Some other field trip possibilities are

- Zoo
- Aquarium
- Planetarium
- Teddy Bear factory
- Fire station
- Police department
- City hall
- Discovery museum or other type of hands-on museum

- Art museum
- Waterworks
- Post office
- Library
- Farm
- Train or subway ride
- Theatre production
- Airport
- Tortilla factory
- Bread factory
- Children's art exhibit at cultural center
- Park

Look around your own locality to spot likely field trip destinations. Sometimes several destinations can be combined. We sometimes take in the post office, library, city hall, and tortilla factory in a single walking trip. A visit to a local park combines well with a trip to a children's art exhibit at a nearby cultural center and to the local fire station and police department.

The Importance of Field Trips

Field trips are important experiences for students. They give children a chance to view their learning in a new way, through a more hands-on approach. It is exciting to leave school for this type of adventure, and this intensifies the learning and enjoyment. One of the things I have recently realized is that field trips are very important and worthwhile experiences for the parents who come with us. Many of our parents grew up in other countries and haven't had these opportunities themselves. They enjoy the trips as much as our children do.

Field Trip Planning and Safety

It is important to have enough adult help on a field trip. Parents enjoy going, and it is fun to share these experiences with them. At times, when space has allowed, there have been almost as many parents as children on our field trips.

In planning a field trip, there are many considerations:

- Choose a destination that maximizes learning, extends children's interests, and integrates with your curriculum.
- Milk the trip for all the learning possibilities: reading signs along the way, looking at geography, finding the way on a map, and so on.
- Use related children's books, fiction and nonfiction, to help prepare for the trip.
- Schedule the appointment for your group, both for school buses, if needed, and for the designated site.
- Fill out necessary school and district paperwork.
- Write a note to parents to inform them of the trip and get signed permission for each child.
- Arrange for parents to accompany your group (the number of parents may be limited by the company or place being visited or availability of seats on the bus. Occasionally space requirements are tight, and it is possible to take only one or two other adults.)
- Make nametags for children, with their first and last names, school address, and school phone number. These can be stick-on labels or hanging conference-type nametags.
- If children have school uniforms or special sweat suits, is a good idea to have everyone wear the same thing. Or have children wear clothing that reflects school colors. This makes everyone easy to spot.
- Bring a first-aid kit and a cell phone.
- Let the school cafeteria know ahead of time so that lunches are not planned for this group of children.
- Send permission slips to the office.

Planning Ahead with Your Class

There are also many field trip preparations to go over with children:

- Review rules and behavior.

- Choose partners; assign groups of children to specific parents, and give parents a list of group members.
- Keep a master list of groups and children in each group.
- Let parents know specifics of the plans for the day, for example, children will sit back in their seats on the bus, we will go through the aquarium in small groups, we will all meet outside at noon and have lunch together. (See Figure 4–1.)
- Instruct children not to leave their partners or adult group leaders.
- Instruct children to be safe, have fun, and learn as much as they can.

Field Trip Follow-up Activities

Back at school that day or the next we will discuss our trip. A field trip lends itself to lots of continued classroom learning, not just when we return to school but for several days. Some of the ways to link field trips to classroom learning are

- Planned class discussions that relate to field trip experiences
- Shared and interactive writing
- Children's independent writing during writing workshop
- Related art—sketching, torn-paper collage, paper sculpture, crayon resist (watercolor painted over crayon), murals, and so on
- Related musical experiences
- Class book
- Thank-you letters, if applicable
- Sharing of more related picture books and nonfiction books
- Photos of the trip: discussing them, writing captions for them, and putting them on a chart or in individual photo books (see Chapter 18 for more information about individual photo books)
- Class mural
- Class quilt
- Class presentation to another class, such as our book buddies class.

Figure 4–1
Informational note to field trip chaperones

Date

Dear Parents,

Thank you for coming with us on our field trip to ______________________.

We are going to have a great day!

Children have small pencils and tiny pocket-sized sketchbooks to make pictures or take notes of things they want to remember. All teachers and several parents have cameras so that we can have photos of our special trip!

The following are some rules and guidelines that need to be followed so that everyone will have a good safe time on our trip. We have already let the children know about these rules. Please let us know if you have any questions.

On the Bus

—The children must sit at all times. They need to sit with their backs against the seats. We will do some singing and talking, but children need to use quiet voices on the bus.

At Our Destination

—Children must stay with their parent leader and their group at all times.

—Children know that there is to be no running around, or making a lot of noise when we are indoors.

Lunch

—We will have lunch together at ____________. Children are to eat sitting down, in their designated groups. After eating, we will be sure all trash is thrown away. When the area is clean, children may play on____.

We will use restrooms after lunch. We will meet at ______ at __ p.m. and leave then to return to school. Back at school, children will return to the classroom so we can talk about our trip. You are welcome to join us!

Restrooms

—Please keep your group together.

Please make sure that when one child needs to use the restroom, they all go in and that they all stay in your sight. No child should enter a restroom without an adult, thus all children must enter with you.

Again, thank you for going with us today. We hope you have a wonderful experience!

The First-Grade Teachers

Class Jobs

Jobs help us do what needs to be done and *all* take responsibility for our classroom and our school. I have handled classroom chores several ways. Usually, at the beginning of the year, I ask different children to take care of specific tasks, such as opening the door if someone knocks, running an errand, putting out tubs for literacy centers, and so forth. When children are familiar with many jobs, after a couple of weeks in class, we get together in a class meeting and decide how we want to handle these responsibilities. Typically, we brainstorm a long list of jobs that need to be done. Then children decide whether to have semipermanent jobs that last for a month or even several months or weekly or bimonthly jobs.

Training a Team of Experts: Long- or Short-Term Job Assignments

An advantage to long-term job assignments is that children learn their jobs well and things work like clockwork. I find that when assignments are made for the week, it takes most of the week to remember to do the job without being reminded. Personally, I don't want to think about these jobs. I want the children to be able to handle them without input from me. For this reason I prefer to have children hold jobs for at least two or three weeks at a time. This year's class decided to keep jobs for a month. They were good at reminding each other about their chosen tasks.

I also have a few permanent jobs (see Chapter 10). These tasks need to be done well all the time; otherwise, organization, particularly for learning centers, is thrown off. There are a few children who handle these jobs well and do them all year.

My friend and colleague Peggy McNeil has a different way of handling classroom responsibilities. Her children take turns acting as Agent of the Day. One child each day takes care of all necessary jobs.

Job Charts

I have made a variety of different job charts in the classroom. One way is to create "helping hands" by asking children to trace and cutout their hands from colored construction paper. They label the hands with their names. (I need these hands to assess children's cutting abilities, so this task takes care of two things at once.)

The Helping Hands chart lists all classroom jobs. A child's cutout hand, or a pair of hands, is placed opposite the assigned job. I stick the hands on the chart using Fun-tak (see Resources) or blue painter's tape (a type of masking tape that is easily unstuck and reused). I move the hands around every couple of weeks.

Another job chart lists jobs on large tablet paper. I write children's names on Post-it Notes and move these notes to change jobs and keep

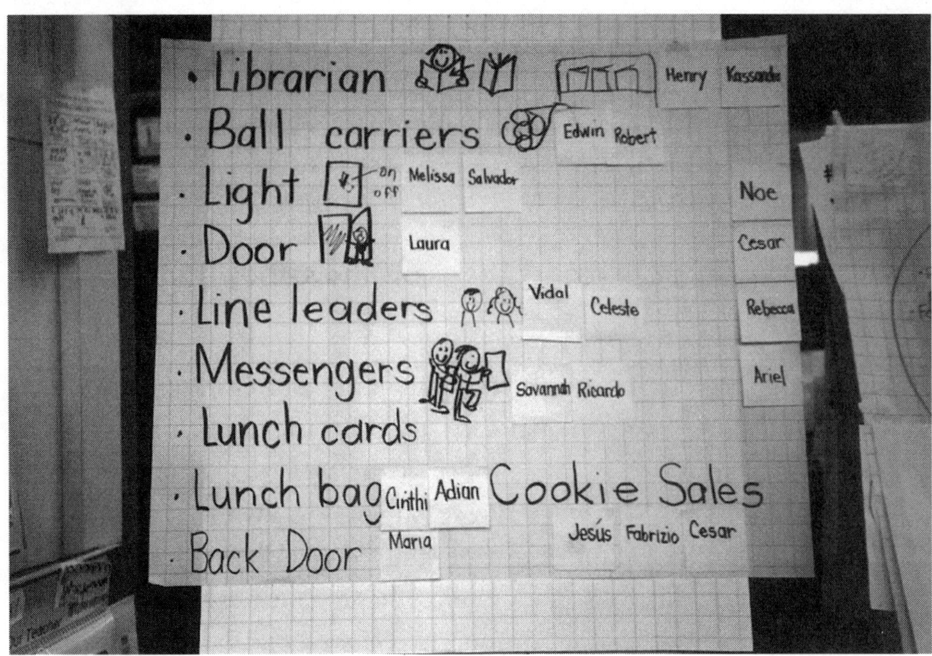

Figure 4–2
Job chart with Post-it Notes

the job chart up-to-date. There are a lot of commercial job charts, but I find it more fun to make our own. This way we can tailor everything to our own classroom needs.

Professional-Sounding Job Titles

Children enjoy coming up with professional-sounding job titles, such as librarians (for children who straighten and organize bookshelves), light technicians, and messengers or couriers.

Taking Care of Homework and Overnight Books

In the morning, while children are getting settled, debriefing, perusing books and magazines, and chatting, I am taking attendance. I do a quick check-in with each child to see that homework and overnight books have been returned. Children then put their homework on the "star place" at each table. (I affix a 3-by 5-inch card with a drawn star and team number to designate a "star place" at each table.)

I correct homework right at the star places, as I walk around, or in the case of more involved homework, when I have time during the day. The table captain, or star helper, at each table hands back the corrected work. If a child needs extra help, I go over the work right away.

A fast way to correct some homework (something like math problems) is to place two papers next to each other. It is easy to scan both papers. When answers are different, I pay attention and see which one is wrong. This works with homework because children were not sitting next to each other when they completed the papers.

Note: Some of my colleagues have homework monitors, who collect homework and put it in baskets to be corrected later.

Team by team, children return overnight books to selected bookshelves at the front of the room. Then one team chooses new books for overnight. Teams take turns, depending upon the day of the week.

When children have selected their overnight books, they write the titles on their book lists. I call each child by name; children tell me the title (some of them have to get help from a friend to find out the names of their books), and I record the titles on my class grid.

Meeting on the Rug

After our morning reading time, we meet on the rug. We sing our class song (see page 45). followed by a silent cheer, as we wait for everyone to come. After the flag salute, children take their places. We listen to a story or two and enjoy a poem. We read a daily message, often writing it together first. Phonics, reading, and language arts are taught at this time. We also make time for shared reading and writing. This is the large-group time in our reading/language arts program.

After recess, we have some time for word study, and then children have time for independent reading, centers, and guided reading. As I explain in Chapter 10, time for centers gradually decreases, and time for independent reading grows.

Guided Reading Book Baskets—Links to Independent Reading

I begin time for independent reading on the very first day. Children have time with a book they have chosen to look at the pictures, tell themselves the story, see what they notice, and so forth. This period is short at first, anywhere from five to seven minutes, with a brief time after for children to share something about a special book, if they wish to do so. After children have been in the classroom a while, are familiar with our routines, and have begun reading in flexible guided reading groups, I lengthen this independent reading time. Children meet with their guided reading groups and read leveled books from book baskets. These books have all been previously read during guided reading time and are now available for independent reading practice. Children gobble these up! As Salvador said excitedly one day, as he completed reading a story in his guided reading group, "I can read that! I can read that book! Put it in our basket!"

Figure 4–3 *Joey and Bridget enjoy a book together.*

Children may also make their own selections to read during this time from book tubs and bookshelves in the classroom. And they have plastic bags of photocopied practice booklets in their desks that they may read as well. I try to say very little and let children take the lead here. I want them to be propelled by their own desires to learn, not by demands on my part. I don't want to spoil their fun and excitement with books and reading.

Daily Class Schedule

Here is a copy of my daily schedule:

8:25 A.M.	Walk in from the playground. Children put things in cubbies. Attendance. Children put overnight books and homework on desks. I check this. Team by team, children put overnight books away. They pick new books and write titles on book lists and tell me titles. I check homework with children now or later in the day. Homework is placed on team tables on stars. Children read socially for about fifteen minutes—books of choice, with classmates of choice, or alone, if they prefer. Other days we bring overnight books to the rug for word games, title riddles, and so on.
8:50 A.M.–9:50 A.M.	We meet on the rug for flag salute and sing our class song. I read a story. We enjoy a few poems, then begin our reading/language arts block: morning message, shared reading. Whole-group reading and language arts. Some work with English language learners.
9:50 A.M.–10:10 A.M.	Recess.
10:10 A.M.–10:30 A.M.	Word study: phonics, word games, overnight book games, spelling and word wall words. Handwriting practice.

10:30 A.M.–11:30 A.M.	Children practice reading independently: small booklets, guided reading books from book baskets, other books of choice from our class library. This time for independent reading grows as the year goes on. Ultimately, it abbreviates the time for centers. I teach guided reading with leveled books during this period. Children are doing independent reading and centers, or as the year progresses, about thirty minutes of independent reading. We cut centers to a couple of times a week. Children may also be working on their writers workshop stories during part of this time. I also do some conferencing on independent reading during this period on some days. (The schedule is tight!)
11:30 A.M.–12:10 P.M.	Lunch.
12:10 P.M.–1:00 P.M.	Math story, calendar, math lesson: written work and manipulatives. Some days this period is slightly longer.
1:00 P.M.–1:20 P.M.	PE.
1:20 P.M.–1:50 P.M.	Writers workshop. Last ten minutes is for sharing.
1:50 P.M.–2:20 P.M.	Social studies, science, and ELD. (These times depend upon the day. Sometimes the schedule is rearranged and we have longer sessions.)
2:20 P.M.–2:30 P.M.	Recap day, sing, listen to another story, explain and practice the homework.

One day a week there is a longer period of time for social studies or science. Another day there is an art block. There is library time on Wednesdays. One late afternoon we have some free explore time.

Five-a-Day Papers

My colleague Joan Murphy creates a weekly paper she calls a five-a-day, because it has five brief review tasks for each day of the week.

The front of the paper is lined to create a vertical row for each week. There are horizontal lines separating four tasks in front, and one on the back, for each day. The front of the paper resembles a grid. The back is lined. (See Figure 4–4.)

The four daily problems on the front grid may contain a picture and missing letters to fill in, words to alphabetize, two or three math problems that reflect the class' current math learning, a few words to print correctly, and so forth. The back of the paper gives five sentences, one for each day of the week, to print correctly, with spaces and (later in the year) capitals and periods. This part of the page is also for handwriting practice. First-grade children's names are used in these sentences.

Joan's children do one section of each side of the paper right away when they come into the classroom every morning. She has a transparency of the paper, front and back, each week, and uses this to review relevant sections of the papers with her class daily. The five-a-day is a concise review of many skills. I like to keep my copies in a folder for each child and make the five-a-day a center time or independent work time choice.

These papers are one way to recap our week and can be sent home Fridays with the weekly newsletters (the *Braggin' Dragan*).

Star of the Week

Self-esteem is something first-grade teachers are always working on. Many teachers I know have a Star Student board featuring one child a week. This board or chart showcases a student photo or photos, sample work, drawings, and a paper written by the child. It is updated each Monday morning. I think this is a great idea. I used to do it myself, but when getting this board ready weekly began to take over my life, I decided to make a change. I was daunted by the fact that it was always a *stretch* to get that photo and get everything ready for the board each week. I was always worried about staying on schedule and making sure each child had a turn. And I didn't like the idea that many students (usually the ones who most needed this recognition) often had to wait for a turn. Even when a child finally got a turn, it was over with after such a short time—a week—with no more opportunities for stardom for the rest of the year.

Figure 4–4a
Sample five-a-day paper (front side)

Five-A-Day
Name
Monday
Tuesday
Wednesday
Thursday
Friday
make
have
did
pretty
children
a e i o u
b – g
f — n
h — s
b – y
f — r
5 +4
7 +2
6 + 4 = __
9 + 2 = __
5 + 0 = __
8 +3
10 +1
3 + 7 = __
11 +0
1 +1
6 + 5 = __
5 +5
7 +4
8 +0
2 + 6 = __

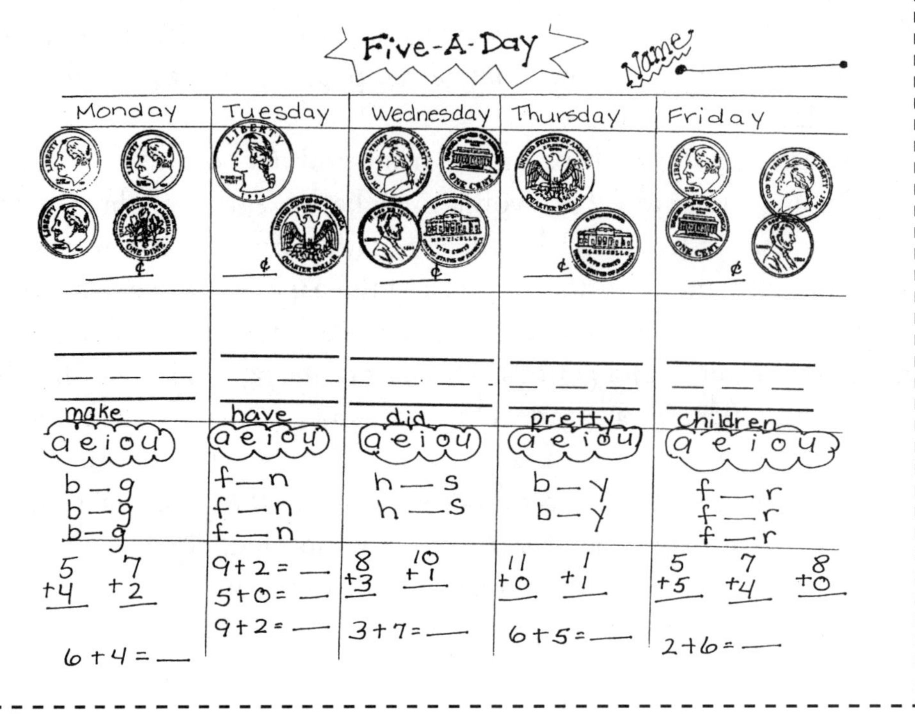

Figure 4–4b
Back side of five-a-day paper

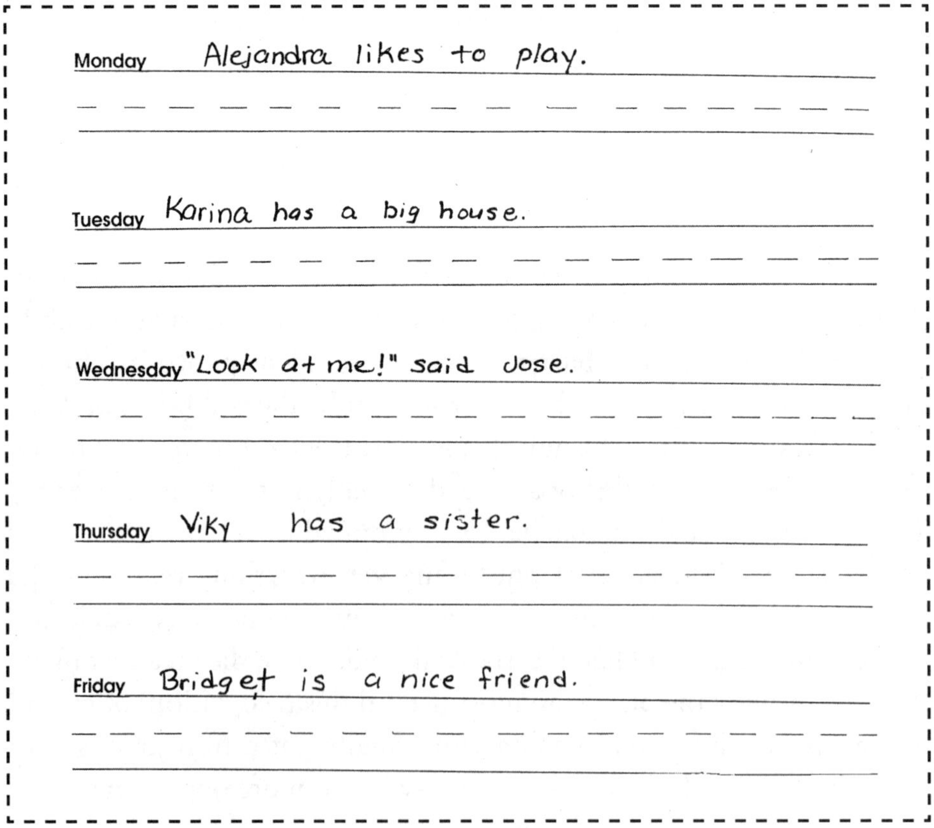

Monday Alejandra likes to play.
Tuesday Karina has a big house.
Wednesday "Look at me!" said Jose.
Thursday Viky has a sister.
Friday Bridget is a nice friend.

Our Stars

Instead of taking turns and featuring one star student each week, I now celebrate everybody at once, several times a year. I invite the children to fill out a star card the first week of school (see Appendix, page 375). The card features a photo (a small photocopy of last year's photo from the office book of school pictures, or a photograph I take). An alternative is for children to draw their own portrait in the small, framed area of the card. Students write their own answers to questions about their wishes, what they are good at, what makes them special, what they want to learn, and any other information they want us all to know.

When this year's class first created their star cards in August, many children had difficulty writing the things they wanted to express. I asked children to try to "write *their* way," putting down the information using any symbol system that worked for them. (See section on writing our way, Chapter 11.) Then I went around and penciled in, lightly, the things children were trying to say. I made these notes so we could make sense of the writing later and also to see whether students were writing some actual letters, sounds, or words that corresponded to what they wanted to say.

These star cards are made on regular copy paper and then mounted on construction paper colors of the children's choice. Children can add colored borders if they wish with marking pens or construction paper crayons. The bulletin board heading for this display is Our Stars. I add other photos I take of children working, reading, and doing things together and alone. This board stays up all year.

Assessments of Our Stars

Children have a chance to make star cards several times a year, so the exhibit stays fresh and meaningful. I also add new photos at random intervals. I save all the cards for each child, so that we can compare how we are doing. I believe this activity is a good assessment of each child's writing and drawing and will also clue me in as to how children are feeling about their progress and about school. I think the children also feel good about being showcased on the classroom wall. I bind these pages for each student at the end of the year, so they each have a personal star book. An alternative plan is to include these pages in the personal photo album each child makes. (See Chapter 18 for information on the photo album.)

There is no set timetable for changing this exhibit and no pressure on me to get it done each Monday morning, as with a Star of the Week board. If I am short of time, and can't update the whole board for a while, I just pop up a few new photos. This is an ongoing exhibit. I always know that all the children are having a turn, and no one is waiting. Everybody is a star all the time!

CHAPTER 5

Connecting with Families

The decision to have a child . . . it's momentous.
It is to decide forever to have your heart
go walking outside your body.

—Elizabeth Stone, quoted by Shelley Harwayne in *Going Public*

When I think about Elizabeth Stone's poignant quote describing children and their parents, I think about the faces I see in the doorway after school, when parents meet their children after a day apart from them. One parent, in particular this year, always greeted her daughter with wide-open arms and a joyful smile. The little girl propelled herself toward her mother as if she had been shot out of a cannon. This image reminds me that all day long, I am entrusted with something precious: our children and our future.

As we all know, being a teacher means being on, being at your best for the children in your class. It also means being on for their parents, too. On the first day, and throughout the year, parents will be scrutinizing your reactions to their children, hoping for a teacher who is kind, professional, good-humored, and teaches children well. You may be all of these things—of course you are! But parents, as well as children, need to see this to know this about you.

This is one reason I try to give it my best, always, as I greet my first graders on the playground each morning. I *aim* for a zippy walk

Figure 5–1
Cesar and his dad enjoy reading and writing together at a Family Literacy event.

and a positive attitude. I hope to be both chipper and kind as I greet my first graders and their parents. I strive to be my best self. When you interact with a cheerful demeanor like this, it not only conveys to parents who you are in the lives of their children but sets you up well for your day ahead.

I always spend some time—especially before the beginning of each school year and for a minute or two each morning—visualizing myself as a child in my classroom. This is one reason I keep my first-grade photograph on the classroom wall. I want the atmosphere in here to be caring and nurturing, as well as exciting and full of learning and accomplishments. Remembering how I felt as a first grader helps me to create the kind of classroom that would have helped me grow and flourish. This is what I want for my students. Of course, this is no substitute for an organized, well-planned day, but it *is* helpful to have a vision of the kind of classroom atmosphere you want to create.

Children may not remember what they learn in my class, but I hope they remember how they *felt* while they were here with me. And I hope these feelings and memories will help propel them through their lives with confidence and will serve them well!

Getting to Know Your Parents

You will probably meet the majority of your first graders' parents before school or right after the closing bell on the first day. Even parents who won't be available on a regular basis often make arrangements to bring their children to school at the start of the year.

After our beginning day of meetings and greetings, I try to protect my time, whenever possible, and keep it stress-free before school starts in the morning. This helps me stay focused so that I can give the best of myself to my first graders. Too many before-school activities and last-minute tasks set me up for a frantic beginning to the day.

Time for Parent Connections

I sometimes find it necessary to let parents know that I can only speak *briefly* with them in the morning as the children are entering the classroom. Responding to parent questions and concerns at this time can be an easy habit to fall into, and the result could be a whole group of parents who wish to ask you about something as the children are coming in and getting settled. (This is not a regular occurrence. I have had this experience with a few classes, and not others.)

I think what is really going on if parents clamber to talk with you is that they want this personal contact from their child's teacher. And some of them may have separation anxiety and be nervous about being away from their children all day. I explain as tactfully as possible that I need to be with the children now, and that I will be glad to see parents after school.

Unless I have a meeting, a tutoring session, or other commitment, I always try to make myself available to parents for a few minutes after the final bell. I say good-bye to every child individually each day at the classroom door. As the children head off, I check that they are leaving with parents or older siblings. This ensures that children go home safely and also provides a good opportunity for me to exchange a few words with parents. Some parents with questions or anxieties have a chance speak with me at this time. I can also share any immediate concerns and questions I may have.

In school situations where children are transported by bus, parent-teacher access is not as simple as this. Some regular form of home-classroom contact is very helpful in opening lines of communication and keeping them open. This is one of the reasons I send a classroom newsletter home each Friday.

The Class Newsletter: An Important Link Between Home and School

I send a newsletter home the first week of school, even if the week is only two days long. My *Braggin' Dragan* newsletter features highlights of the week. The title is apt: I want to sing our praises, *brag* about our accomplishments! The first item lists titles and authors of one or two favorite literature books I have read aloud during the week. Although I send some of these home as part of our overnight book program (see Chapter 8), I always dream that there are parents out there who will look for these books in libraries and bookstores and make them available to their children.

The *Braggin' Dragan* briefly notes our curricular focus for the week in reading, writing, math, and other areas. It often gives the words to a poem or song we are learning and provides ideas for things children could practice at home. If we have had classroom guests or an assembly, these are always featured, as are other special events. Figure 5–2 shows a sample *Braggin' Dragan*. Please keep in mind that these newsletters are meant to be brief. I include different kinds of information each week. (See the Appendix for a sample newsletter template that you could adapt for your own classroom.)

There is a place on my newsletter to indicate children's behavior, interests, and handling of school responsibilities during the week. To fill this part out, I just circle a number from 1 (terrific!) to 5 (needs to *really* work to improve). I rarely mark anything below 2 or 3, but there are times I feel it is necessary to do so. I might circle 4 or 5 and mark it "Thursday," and then circle 2 for the rest of the week.

I speak briefly with each child as I give out the newsletters each Friday. If there is an occasional, really low score or comment, I spend some time with the child, elicit some ideas for improvement, and write a small note to parents, such as, "James says he will do much better next week." This sets the stage for the week to come and also takes a little bit of pressure off James when he takes his newsletter home. His

Figure 5–2 *Sample class newsletter*

Joey ♡ Hooray for you, Joey!

The Braggin Dragan

Mrs. Pat Barrett Dragan - Martin School, Gr. I, Room 3

Week of October 29, 2001

Highlights of the Week:

READING: We read *LOTS* of poetry together. Children have their own bags of photo-poetry booklets to read.

GUIDED READING in small groups

LITERATURE: Special literature we enjoyed: *Happy Birthday Moon; Seven Silly Eaters.*

MATH: Addition. I am sending home math pages we have completed. Please review them with your child. Thank you.

*SOCIAL STUDIES: Coloring Book About America. We made the coloring book about America to sell so that we could buy books for Public School #89 in New York City. $1. per book.

*SCIENCE/ENGLISHLANG. (ELL) Children went to different first grade teachers 45 minutes daily to study science units.

*Please return this part on Monday.

Comments, suggestions, if desired.

I'm very pleased that Joey is so well we are working with him everyday So far so good

Child's Name Joey

Parent signature

We can read our little books!

Listens and follows directions. Pays attention during lessons. Tries hard to learn.

1 (2) 3 4 5

*Returns books, booklists, envelopes, homework, Braggin' Dragans on time.

1 (2) 3 4 5

*Gets along well with others. Better!

1 (2) 3 4

KEY: 1 = Outstanding
2= Very Good 3 = Satisfactory
4 = Needs improvement
5 = Poor; very unacceptable

parents know that he is already planning to do something to improve his behavior.

If a child has trouble focusing but is really trying to learn and not be disruptive, I may tell both parent and child that 3 is good for Ivan, and they shouldn't feel he needs 1s to be successful. I try to take children's learning styles and needs into account when I send this newsletter home. My intent is not to pin a child to the wall, but just to give parents a brief, holistic look at how things are going.

Children return these *Braggin' Dragans*, signed, the following Monday, so I know that the newsletters made it home. Often parents write comments or questions, which I answer quickly and send home right away. Behavior problems are usually much improved as a result of an immediate contact with parents. I always make sure I acknowledge positive progress immediately, with a note home that afternoon, or at least at the end of the week, depending upon the situation.

Occasionally a phone call or personal contact is necessary.

Although there are usually anywhere from three to seven different languages spoken by parents of my first graders, the majority languages are English and Spanish. I send home an English language newsletter on one side of the paper and a Spanish version on the other. I let the children know what information is detailed on the paper. In some cases, for example, if parents speak only Urdu, Hindi, or Tagalog, children will have to translate for their parents. The illustrations are another way of making information available.

Setting Up Routines for the School Year

It can seem like overkill going to this amount of work for just one or two days of school the first week, but I feel that it is extremely important to start this back-and-forth home-school network right away. I want parents to know there are many ways to be in touch with me: a written note, the school phone after school, a chat at the doorway after the final bell, an appointment, and so forth.

My *Braggin' Dragan* gives families an idea about what our beginning days are all about. The newsletter provides parents with information and early indications about children's difficulties, strengths, and weaknesses. It circumvents problem situations before they become habit. The newsletter is also a simple way for the parent to request a meeting. I may wish to ask for a meeting myself. Of course, the telephone is another option, but I find it difficult to make phone calls after our full school day, although I do sometimes call parents. I am sure it is a good option for many teachers.

Years ago, during a two-day-long first week of school, I experienced absolutely terrible behavior from a child I had felt was capable of being a responsible, energetic, enthusiastic learner. I was a little anxious when I filled out his *Braggin' Dragan* the first Friday and was not surprised when his mother was waiting to see me five minutes after the end of school. The mother, the child, and I sat down and talked about the boy's behavior and our classroom and school expectations. Jarvis was a model student for the rest of his time both in my classroom and in our school.

Had I waited before addressing the multiple problems I was having with this child, his behavior may have become set in cement and harder to change. As it was, he corrected his problematic behavior immediately, to my delight and relief! I generally find immediate improvement in at least one child after the first *Braggin' Dragan* goes home.

Making the Newsletter *Ours*

I have found that while children enjoy the *Braggin' Dragan*, it is important to me to help them feel that this is *our* newsletter to parents, not just mine. Each day before we go home, we sit on the rug together and review our day. (This is always a good idea. It helps reinforce learning, and it also reminds children of things we have done, so they can answer the question, "What did you do at school today?") This technique gives children some time to practice recapping and discussing events. It is a chance to practice summarizing and to develop vocabulary. These few minutes reviewing the day also give children a chance to choose things *they* feel are important enough to go in our Friday newsletter. Sometimes we make drawings and write down words together. This activity is helpful for English language learners as well as the rest of the class.

Children as Illustrators

Children also enjoy illustrating the *Braggin' Dragan* newsletter. Sometimes I do this myself; sometimes I invite a child or children to do the drawings. Occasionally I leave the illustration box blank, and children can illustrate their own copies of the newsletter for the week. We always give credit: the illustration box always says, "Illustrated by," and then features the children's names, in their own printing.

Solving a Possible Illustration Problem

A variation of the *Braggin' Dragan* format that works both for a newsletter and class stationery is to ask children to make small drawings

Figure 5–3
Sample class stationery

(about 2 or 3 inches high) to represent themselves. Have them include their names. Reduce these on the copy machine. Cut and paste these by hand, not computer, and glue them onto white copy paper to make a border. Draw a line for the border, leaving the center area blank. Make many copies of these illustrated papers to use for class notes or for your weekly newsletter. (See Figure 5–3.)

If you know you will *not* enjoy illustrating a newsletter each week, this is a good solution. Change the border to include any new students as they become part of your school family.

Newsletter Logistics

I use my notes from children's end-of-the-day recaps (daily reviews) to help me write the newsletter at home each Thursday night. I print out two preliminary copies of each side: one side in English and one side in Spanish. (It always helps to have an extra copy in case a drawing just doesn't work out.) I either do the drawings Thursday night or invite children to do them at school the next morning. I keep notes in a spiral-bound notebook, or on a paper on the classroom wall, so I know which children have had turns as graphic artists.

I make copies of our illustrated *Braggin' Dragan* either at recess or lunch and fill them out during the lunch period on Friday. Of course, if I made the newsletters on Wednesday, or after school on Thursday, I could fill them out Thursday night at home. This is a great idea, but it doesn't work for me. It's like planning what I'm going to wear days ahead of time.

Occasionally, if there is time, I fill these weekly reports out with children individually, but this does not seem to happen often. I *do* speak to every child when I pass out the newsletters, aiming for a brief, positive pep talk, or accolades, whenever applicable. I try to put a short, positive comment on the top of each note.

Clipboard Grid: A View of Our Week Together

In filling out the *Braggin' Dragan* each week, I use a simple one-page grid I keep on a clipboard (see Appendix). Each grid has a small box for each child, listed alphabetically by first name. I use one grid a week to note things like behavior, things forgotten at home, and so forth. I use shorthand symbols as well as anecdotal notes. It is easy to come up with your own shorthand. Here is a brief list of symbols I use:

- Tr—Tardy
- Ab—Absent
- T—Talking while it is the teacher's or another child's turn
- D—Not following directions
- P—Not paying attention
- H —Forgot homework
- B—Forgot overnight book (see Chapter 8)

- A—Aggressive behavior—hit or kicked someone, hurt somebody's feelings, and so on
- Heart or happy face drawing—*Braggin' Dragan* was returned on Monday
- Star—Highlights positive note(s), such as, "Bridget listened to Andrea's story and had good suggestions," or "Vidal helped Salvador read a poem," so I don't forget those things either!

These notes are not meant to be negative, but to give me an idea about how things are going for each child. I try to write these furtively, rather than make a big production out of putting a *T* or a *D* on the clipboard grid. The notes are for *me*, to enlighten my teaching and also to document what is going on. Occasionally I use them to show a parent a pattern of behavior. If I see a whole row of *T*s (talking), *D*s (not following directions), *P*s (not paying attention), and *A*s (aggressive behavior), I have a record of where a lot of *my* energy and attention is going in a given week!

I also write brief notes to myself, as mentioned above, such as "Upset a lot this week"; "Kicked Luis"; "Would not come in from recess"; or "Showed Keith how to do math problems" or "Helped Maria find her homework and book." These jottings help me understand what is happening, as well as give specific information to parents, when necessary. Of course, if a child is having a difficult week, it is very important for me to get in touch with the parent right away. A light touch is important here. I usually ask if something has been going on at home that might be affecting the child's behavior, such as the child has seemed overtired, a relative is visiting, a baby brother is in the hospital, and so forth. These things are important for me to know if I am to assist with the child's adjustment to school and facilitate school success.

There is a fine line here about how much to share with parents, especially if I do not know them well. I do not want a giant or alarmed response from home as a result of a child's minor difficulty or small misbehavior.

Children Can Evaluate Themselves

In addition to the *Braggin' Dragan*, children have the option of bringing home a *Junior Braggin' Dragan* that *they* can fill out to assess their own behavior and learning (see Figure 5–4). Students do not seem to

The Junior Braggin' Dragan

Dear Parents,

I have asked children to circle the picture that best represents how they feel they did in school this week. Children added written comments and other drawings (front and back) if they wished to do so. Children made their own decisions about how to fill out this paper.

I hope you and your child will enjoy talking about school.

Name______________________ Date:____________

I was terrific! I learned a lot!
I did some good thinking.
I got along with others.
I remembered my books and homework!

****

I learned some things.
I was pretty good to other children.
I remembered books and homework most of the time.

****

Uh oh! I'll do better next week!
I need to pay attention, think, and learn.
I need to not bother or hurt other children.
I need to remember books and homework.

Child's notes (optional)______________________

Figure 5–4
Sample Junior Braggin' Dragan

need this experience weekly. It seems to work better if they fill out *Junior Braggin' Dragans* once in a while—every month or so, or when children want to do it. I keep a stack of these handy, and it is an option for everyone each week, or whenever they choose.

School Phobias

I also ask parents to let me know, whenever possible, any information that may be important for me to know about their children. Sometimes children have fears, such as going out to recess or using school bathrooms. The child may be afraid of another student. Seemingly small events may disturb a child and result in school phobia or reluctance to come to school. Sometimes children just don't know what is bothering them or making them uneasy. It is crucial for the teacher to know if a child is reluctant to come to school, so that the problem can be solved.

I was a victim of school phobia myself for two or three months in the middle of first grade, when my little sister became extremely ill. She had polio and was in the hospital for several months. I vividly remember all those mornings I was afraid to leave home . . . I think I was anxious about what would happen to my family if I weren't there to worry about everybody! My parents worked with my first-grade teacher to get me past this difficult time. I have a lot of sympathy for children who go through this! (*And* for their teachers and parents, too.)

Children's Literature Connection

A wonderful picture book, *The Kissing Hand*, by Audrey Penn (1993), addresses these feelings of not wanting to leave parents. The solution for the "child" in the story (a young raccoon named Chester) is to carry his mother's love to school with him—a kiss from Mother Raccoon in the palm of his hand. The kiss is there, all day long, and rushes from his hand to his heart whenever the little raccoon thinks of it and needs it.

Back-to-School Night

Typically, we hold our Back-to-School Night early in the school year. We meet together in the evening in the multiuse room, and teachers are introduced to parents and children. Our principal gives a brief overview of our school, goals, objectives, and philosophy. Teachers return to classrooms, and parents and children visit. Our families may have several children in our K–5 school, so we have three twenty-minute sessions in our classrooms where we display materials and explain our first-grade program.

Children Teaching Parents

This year our first-grade team, Joan Murphy, Rebecca Coolidge, and I, decided on three different activities we wanted to share with parents. We worked with our students on ways to demonstrate these activities on Back-to-School Night. When parents came into the classroom, they had time to peruse photos and student work on the walls and look at a variety of our educational materials. Then children demonstrated how to play a reading game: putting out magnetic letters in alphabetical order, spelling word wall words, and so forth. Children showed parents how they could use dried beans or coins to count math sets and work out math problems. And then children sat on the rug with me to help demonstrate how to do a picture walk to get a sense of a story. Finally, we showed parents how shared reading works: we read a big book together.

When a bell rang, and a new group of children and parents came into the classroom, the same activities were repeated. The children and I felt their parents had a good time and learned a lot at school!

A Packet of Materials to Support Our Program

I prepared packets of Back-to-School Night materials ahead of time and placed them on children's desks. The handout included

- A cover page, decorated with small self-portrait line drawings of all children in our class—this was the children's contribution
- Ways to contact me: The packet was stapled with my business card, with my name, school name, and school telephone number, on top
- Welcome message: my philosophy, goals, and expectations
- Our daily schedule
- Directions for the letter games and math games demonstrated during Back-to-School Night
- Directions for taking a picture walk
- Tips on reading aloud to children
- A sample of printing we were learning: how to correctly form each letter of the alphabet

- Information about our overnight book program (see Chapter 8)
- Homework philosophy
- Any other information I felt it was important for parents to know

I mentioned in my letter to parents that I was looking forward to talking with them in depth about their children at our upcoming parent conferences. I also let them know that I would be available to meet with them sooner if there was something we needed to discuss before that time.

Special First-Grade Figures

I sometimes help children make large paper-bag, paper-plate, and construction paper facsimiles of themselves. These whimsical figures fit over backs of chairs to sit at children's desks, hold books and pencils, and show off some of the things we do during our time together. A similar project is to help children trace each other's outlines. They can add details with crayons, marking pens, or tempera paints and then cut them out.

Introductions, First-Grade Style

My first graders and I also practice, ahead of time in the classroom, how to introduce parents. We role-play this, with different children taking the part of the mother, the father, the teacher, and the child. This helps children feel comfortable during our evening event.

I always leave a sign-in sheet for parents and a separate one for the children.

Parent Conferences

In my school district we hold parent conferences quite early in the school year. These are intake conferences. We endeavor to learn as much as we can about children and their needs during these twenty-minute appointments. A second parent conference is scheduled in March or April. When necessary, at other times during the school year,

I have informal conferences with parents before or after school. Many parents are available for a few minutes when they come to pick up their children.

Here are a few tips for making parent conferences successful:

- Greet parents at the classroom door. Let them know you are glad to be meeting with them!
- Sit at a table together, rather than meet with parents at your desk. If possible, provide some adult-sized chairs.
- Invite the child to attend, unless you prefer to meet with parents alone. It can be helpful to have the child there if you do not speak the parents' language and there is no other translator available. I have had a lot of success using young children to translate. However, I am now able to speak with Spanish-speaking parents myself.
- If younger children are present, endeavor to have a tub of things for them to play with or do, such as puzzles, games, or older picture books. (Don't provide anything really tempting, like your brand-new puppet, because little children may not want to part with it when they leave.) The hope is that younger children will sit quietly with the parents. Often the older child can take a hand in keeping the younger siblings busy.
- Always begin with positive comments about each child. If the child is present, I like to provide her the opportunity to show off something she has learned, share special papers she has done, and so forth.
- Share a small sampling of student work.
- Give parents information about curriculum and goals for the year, and show them books and other materials you are using.
- Give parents time to talk about their children and express needs and concerns.
- I share our photo wall. This collection displays photographs of parents reading aloud to their children. I explain the importance of reading aloud to children and how we celebrate this together by building a photo wall of the children and their parents enjoying a

book together. I let parents know that I will be sending a Polaroid camera home for someone to photograph their child being read to.

- Share packets of ideas or materials for parents to use to help their children learn, for example, a small alphabet book to illustrate, a word book for collecting words, a sample of first-grade writing paper with a paper on how to form letters and numerals, and so on. I like to share with parents a small booklet of a story for the child to practice reading. I show parents how to read *with* children, supportively, slightly ahead of them, if a child seems to need this kind of support.
- Aim for a positive experience where parents learn about school expectations and your philosophy, and you learn special information about each child.

I always like to give parents something they can take home and practice with their children.

Celebrate the Child: Sharing Children's Work and Accomplishments

I do like to always have a special piece of children's work to share with parents during parent conferences. This work should be something I feel good about sharing and the parents and children will feel good about, too—something that celebrates the child! Thanks to my friend and second-grade teacher Eileen Woods, I learned a great idea to use: a cassette tape. Usually at the first parent conference, I will play a brief bit of cassette tape of the child singing a song we have learned or reciting one of the poems we are practicing. If children are beginning to read, they can read a story on tape.

I plan this surprise ahead of time with my first graders, and *they* choose what goes on the cassette. It is pure magic to see the parents' and children's faces when the brief tape is played!

When we have our spring parent conferences, I give each parent a cassette tape wrapped in a big bow! We listen to the child reading, and each family takes home a cassette tape with a song or poem from the beginning of the year and a reading excerpt from later on. If there is time, we tape other samples of children's songs, poetry recitations, and reading.

Figure 5–5 *Luis' mother listens to the cassette tape of his reading.*

If parents wish, they may donate a new cassette tape to replace the one they take home.

An alternative to the cassette tape, if your student has come to the conference, is to give the child the time to read aloud from a book being read in class.

What to Cover at a Parent Conference

Following is a list of things I want to cover during our first parent conference:

- Our curriculum: books and themes that will be covered, and so on
- Early reading and math assessments—what the child needs to know and will be learning
- Some ideas for helping children at home
- How to read with the child
- More about overnight books
- More about using the class camera to take pictures of children being read to at home

Parent Questionnaire

I ask parents to tell me things I need to know about their children, such as

- Early illnesses, accidents, any special problems
- Any information that could be relevant to the child's success in school
- Personality traits, special needs
- Experiences with literacy—Is the child read to at home? Does the child go to the library? And so on.
- Children's hobbies, collections, and special interests

Parent Volunteers

Parent conferences are a good time to speak with parents about volunteering in the classroom, going on field trips, and so forth. Here is a sample list of ways parents can be used to help with your class:

- Read aloud to students, one or two at a time, any book children choose
- Listen to a child read
- Repair class library or overnight books—at home or school
- Illustrate poetry chart—at home or school (a parent may illustrate the chart or do it with a child)
- Write with a child, using the technique of written conversations (see pages 246–51)
- Help a child practice printing, write a story together, or take a child's dictation to create a story
- Measure things with a child, practice telling time or counting money
- Math practice
- Use math manipulatives with a child
- Use a globe

- Cover new books with plastic covering
- Help prepare materials to be used in class
- Do an art or craft project with an individual child or small group of children, such as starch ghosts, leaf prints, or puppets
- Monitor a learning center
- Help a child with a jigsaw puzzle or other activity
- Go on a class trip
- Help during a cooking activity

I used to plan more elaborate ways for parents to help in the classroom, such as run a math kit center during center time or play a reading game. Unfortunately, parents frequently weren't able to come at the scheduled time and sometimes couldn't let me know this.

Parents have so many obligations, with many of them working outside the home as well as caring for younger children in the family, that I have found it easier to make volunteer work as flexible as possible. I now plan open-ended volunteer jobs—tasks that do not depend upon a parent being available at a specific time.

One of the most popular activities, from the children's viewpoint, is when a classroom volunteer reads to them, individually, from whatever book or magazine article they choose. Last year I had two faithful parents who came in and did this special job in my classroom. They read everything from an article on frogs in *Ranger Rick* magazine, to picture books and poetry.

Gaby became very involved when her mother, Sandra, came in to read to children. Gaby's idea was to keep a list of children to be read to. Gaby made the list, and she checked off names as children had their turns. She carefully kept the list herself, and was able to produce it for months (something I would never have been able to manage), each time her mother came in to read.

Homework Without Tears

Another activity that involves parents, or needs to involve them, is homework. Once, as a brand-new teacher, I was invited to a colleague's home for dinner. My friend Liz had a seven-year-old daughter who had math homework. The child found the work difficult and cried before dinner, through dinner, and was still crying and struggling when I left (as quickly as possible!) after dinner. I vowed to *never* be the cause of a similar scenario.

In my school district, first-grade teachers are asked to send home fifteen minutes of homework a night, Monday through Thursday. I find that my children are eager to have homework. They love the idea of being in first grade and getting that homework, like their big brothers and sisters. My goal is always to send home an easy math, printing, or word wall practice paper that everyone can do with little difficulty and no trauma! I try to send home work that gives additional practice for something we have just learned in class: a small booklet to read to someone at home, a math page similar to some math work we have just done in the room, and so forth. If a child is having difficulties reading the little booklet, I ask parents or siblings to read along with the child.

I also send home overnight books that children have chosen, so that someone in their families can read aloud to them. (See *Literacy from Day One*.) I am *really* happy when parents spend homework time (and more!) reading aloud to their children from the overnight books and other reading materials. I believe that homework should, whenever possible, be an enriching family experience.

Ways to Adjust Homework Assignments

If I see that a child is having difficulty with the specific homework being sent home, here are some things I can do:

- I can cut the paper into a smaller, more workable assignment with fewer problems.
- I can have the child practice with me for a few minutes before the work goes home.
- I can find a cross-age tutor (usually the child's third-grade book buddy) to work with the student for a few minutes on the homework paper (or a similar assignment).
- I can ask the child's reading partner or another child in our classroom to help him practice.

- I can practice the assignment in more depth with *everyone* before it goes home.

Sending home a simple first-grade homework paper gives children a chance to develop responsibility, complete a task, and return the paper the next day. This experience helps build good habits. I want the children to bring these papers back each day, completed, done to the best of their abilities. And I do keep track of who has forgotten the homework.

I ask each table to hold up homework, and then place it on the star place on each table. (See page 72.) I look at the homework right at the tables sometime during the day. If I see a child has had difficulties, we fix the paper together. Bravo! Success!

Homework Packets

I have colleagues who send home a packet of homework each week. I have avoided doing this for a number of reasons. I can tailor homework and match it to our school day better if I do it day by day. Sending home a packet is a lot of paperwork for me, all at once. Correcting it takes a bigger chunk of time. I prefer to correct homework briefly with each child every day.

Another reason I avoid homework packets is that I have heard parents talking about them. For many of our parents, English is a second language. Some parents feel overwhelmed with so many papers coming home all at once, in a language that is difficult for them. They want to help their children but need help themselves. Many parents in this situation wait until later in the week, hoping to get help from other family members or friends. And then when they *do* get help, the poor child and parent have five or six papers to do at one time.

I am sure that homework packets are a good choice for some people, but they do not work for me!

Linking Home and School Through Family Books

A great thing to do, periodically, to keep that home-classroom connection viable and strong, is to include parents in class projects. I like to make family books an occasional part of our homework assignments. I want homework to be a positive and productive experience, not one that drains a family's time together. I make sure that parents know that these family books will not be graded, just appreciated, shared, and cherished! Every child will receive a copy of our finished efforts.

I have found that it is really important to talk about what encompasses a family whenever the word is mentioned in class. One year I hurriedly asked children to draw pictures of their families for homework. To my chagrin and real sorrow, one child asked me, "Do we make pictures of all our family, like even the people who don't like us or love us anymore?"

Now, whenever the word *family* comes up, we talk about how a family can be a mother and a child, a father and a child, a grandmother, grandfather, and so forth. Children really need to know that there are all kinds of families, and they all count!

Types of Family Books

One family book I like to create with my class reflects the cultural diversity of children at my school, as well as the world. This book is called *Family Celebrations*. I ask children and their families to write about and illustrate a special day they celebrate together. We learn about many customs and other cultures as we share these stories, and this helps children appreciate their own traditions, customs, and families. (See Appendix, page 379–83, for a sample page template for this type of book.)

As Alma Flor Ada says in her book *A Magical Encounter*, "Children and youth should have access to the best of their culture and human culture. . . . Meaningful links between home and school are essential for children's well-being and full growth, while also increasing academic achievement" (2002, p. xiii).

I believe these family books are important ties connecting both parts of children's lives.

Another book that is very exciting for children and parents to write is the story about how the children got their names (see Figure 5–6). Also interesting are the stories about the names they *almost* received! These can be compiled to make a class name booklet.

An interesting riddle book can be made from photocopies of children's baby pictures. The child or family writes a riddle, and it goes on the page with the photograph. Children love to read these books, and they love to guess whose baby picture answers the riddle.

My friend Beverly Crosby Wallace helped children make books for their mothers by surreptitiously photographing mothers on Back-to-School Night. Photographs were cut out and attached to papers. Children wrote anagrams about their mothers, using their mothers' first names. They drew pictures of their mothers. Beverly compiled these pages into a Mother's Day book and gave each mother a copy.

My name came from my dad. I love my name. Mi nombre es bonito.

Por Danny

Figure 5–6
Page from family book about children's names

Another of Beverley's books was a family alphabet book, with a sentence or sentences created by each family, such as "Alice and Andy ate apples and animal crackers."

Children's Literature Connection

Before beginning our bookmaking experiences, I first like to share with children the picture book *Family Pictures/Cuadros de Familia*, by Carmen Lomas Garza (1993). In this book, Garza takes vignettes from her childhood and writes about them in English and Spanish, one memory on each page. The opposite page features a painting that illustrates and illuminates the written experience. This book evokes many memories and seems to help the children value and want to share their own experiences.

Another book I love to share with children is *Marianthe's Story: Painted Words, Spoken Memories*, by Aliki (1998). Aliki grew up in Philadelphia, in a Greek family. Her own childhood makes her very sympathetic to children who are learning English. This two-part story evolves around Marianthe's feelings about starting school as a non-English speaker. Her wise and patient teacher lets her paint to communicate things about herself. Mari's beautiful paintings give her status in the classroom and help the other children get to know her. Slowly, as English becomes clear, and words have meanings, Marianthe uses her newly acquired language to tell her life story in the "Spoken Memories" section of the book.

Aliki's book helps children learn that there is more than one way to communicate and more than one way to tell a story. This is an inspiring book for the many children in my class who are struggling to learn English.

Developing Family Books

When we plan our books about our families, we have a theme to unify our book, such as a special family holiday, recipe, or something children love to do with their families. Papers may have a heading, with room for the family's story and art, or a template may be used. A template may take up a single page or take the form of a booklet, with two or three pages. (See Appendix, pages 379–83, for some sample templates.)

Here is a sample template:

In our family we like to ________________.
We celebrate ________________.

Another template reads,

Here is my family.
Here is my ________________. (And so on.)

It can be helpful if there is a template for families to follow. This decision depends upon your knowledge of your own class. Homework directions, written in English and Spanish, invite parents and other family members to fill out pages however they like, with words, sentences, illustrations, and family stories. I ask children to draw their family members and to help write the stories about them. I like to give families a week or so to complete these individual pages or booklets. If too much time is allotted, it is easier for these to become lost.

This homework is celebrated and enjoyed by all of us, if the child wishes to share it.

Books may be brainstormed first by doing a class book, shared-writing style. We may use this template:

In our class we like to ________________ together.

List of Family Book Ideas

This year my goal was to create one home/family class book each month. Here is a list of possible ideas. Class books may be stapled with construction paper covers or spiral-bound.

- *My Family Book*—Introduces family members
- *Family Alphabet Book*—"Aa is for ________." These would be filled out by individual families in accordance with words important to them
- *My Name Book*—The story of a child's name, and the almost-chosen name

- *Family Favorite Recipe Book or Favorite Foods to Eat*—Includes the story about when these foods are eaten
- *Family Celebration Book*
- *Old Toy/New Toy*—Parent and child each choose a favorite childhood toy to tell about
- *Our Best Family Story*
- *The Day I Was Born*—What happened on the day the child was born
- *Our Trip to* ________ (grocery, library, flea market, anywhere)
- *Our Family's Favorite Things to Do*
- *The Funniest Thing That Happened at Our House*

Sample Letter of Explanation

Dear Parents,

We are making a class book about our families. You are invited to be part of it. You will receive a copy when we are finished and publish it.

Part of the homework this week is to gather information for our family book. Please talk with your child and decide on some of your family's favorite things to do together. The family you and your child write about and draw can include you and your child or children. You are welcome to include extended family members if you wish.

There is also a space for you and your child to make a picture. Your child can do the drawing, or you can do it together.

If your family chooses to participate, please return these papers by ________. I hope you will want to be part of our class book.

Sincerely,

____

Family Literacy Programs

One of the best things we do at my school is the Family Literacy Program for first graders and their parents. Colleen Quinn Malloy, Tonya

Singer, and I spearhcaded the program three years ago. Now our committee of six teachers, headed by Bridget Burke and Rebecca Fishman, plans long and hard to come up with relevant literacy experiences for children and adults. Some events are evening programs, while others are after-school meetings. We vary the time to accommodate the maximum number of families.

We have held these family literacy events for three years now and have experimented with different ways of organizing them. One year we held thematic evening events, with different centers each week over a four-week period. We gave four different sessions.

The following year we selected several first-grade children we considered at risk and invited them to attend after-school Reading Club meetings once a week with their parents. (See Figure 5–7.) This year we combined both approaches. We held four after-school classes for our at-risk group of children and their parents, then organized a culminating evening activity for *all* first graders and their families. Next semester, we will target kindergarten children and create a program focusing on their needs.

Planning the Events

After giving our district's beginning-of-the-year reading assessment, teachers submitted a list of children most in need of help with beginning reading skills.

Once we had a list of first graders we felt needed help, our committee met after school to plan lessons. We wanted each hour-and-fifteen-minute session to include time for families to read aloud together (we provided picture books in English and Spanish), a specific reading or writing focus, and time for parents and children to practice what had been taught. We included share-outs (brief sharing sessions) at the beginning and end of the meeting to provide a forum for feedback from everyone in the group. We broke up our sessions in such a way that children worked on specific skills with some of the teachers while other teachers worked with parents to explain these skills. Then children came in and celebrated what they learned, by showing their parents.

Here are some of the themes of our lessons

- Games for practicing beginning sounds, ending sounds, vowel sounds

Figure 5–7
Family Literacy Program invitation

Dear Parents,

You are invited to participate in a special Family Reading Club, after school on _______________. It will last four sessions. Dates are _______________.

Teachers, children, and parents will focus on fun ways to share reading and writing together. We will focus on ways to help children learn literacy skills.

Your child has been chosen for this program because he/she needs extra support in reading.

When: _______________
Where: _______________
Why: Your child will get the extra help she/he needs.
Your participation will inspire your child.
You will receive a free book each session you attend.
It will be a lot of fun.

Please return the bottom of this form to let us know if you can participate and, if so, to give us important information.

_____ Yes, I will be able to participate.

Do you need child care?

If so, for what age children?

Can you read in English?____ Spanish?____
(Not necessary for participation)

_____ No, I will not be able to participate at this time.

Child's name and grade: ________________________________

Parent's name: ________________________________

- How to blend words; how to use picture clues and other strategies
- How to take a picture walk
- Awareness of environmental print
- How to write down sounds we hear our way, without worrying about accuracy
- How to make lists and how to write down family stories
- How to make different kinds of books

We took a trip to the local library with parents and children and also held evening events with literacy centers. We role-played for parents some ways to work with children. We also brainstormed ideas together.

Our feedback from parents has always been very poignant. One parent said, "I was busy cooking, but my daughter said to me, 'Come and sit with me, Mommy, and let's write together like we do at school.'" Another parent said, "My son never came to me for help with his homework. When I would offer, he would just say, 'Oh, you don't know!' But *now*, he knows I *do* know. And now he does come to me for help."

Figure 5–8 *Adrian and his family work on a project together at Family Literacy Night.*

One father confided that he had lived in town for ten years but had not realized that he could use the public library. He was astounded by the amount of services, as well as books, available.

Celebrating Families Learning Together

Our evening programs in the multiuse room were open to all first graders and their families. Children and their parents played literacy games, made and wrote their own books, created family "triaramas" (folded three-dimensional scenes; see *Literacy from Day One*), enjoyed a movement word game, and best of all, read together on the couch or in the rocking chair at the reading corner. Eight different centers were set up, and children and their parents chose and experienced those that suited their own interests.

These Reading Club meetings have been the best possible partnerships with parents to help their children learn. A local foundation helped us support this program and provided a book for each family to take home every session.

CHAPTER 6

Helping Children Work on Discipline and Self-Control

Treat children as if they are the best they can be,
and you help them become the most they are capable of being.

—My adaptation of quote by Johann Wolfgang von Goethe

There are probably as many classroom management and discipline ideas as there are diets, and I have most likely tried most of them during my days in a first-grade classroom. The management and discipline approaches that will work best for you are those that mesh with your philosophy and your classroom goals. It's important to me to work toward a room full of happy children, working together and independently to learn as much as they can and be the most they can be. I very much want to create a classroom community where we are all pulling together and rooting for each other. This underlying philosophy helps determine the discipline and management methods I use.

Take Joy

For me, joy is the bottom line. I'm standing up for joy in the classroom. Without it, nothing we learn will be worth anything to us in the long run. Think of all the adults you know who know *how* to read, but would never read a book, let alone purchase one, or take pleasure in one. I don't think it's enough to learn things. The things we know and learn need to *matter* if they are always to be part of our lives.

Empowering Children

We all achieve more and work in more centered ways when we feel good about ourselves. One of the big jobs of a first-grade teacher is to help children become focused and centered and enthusiastic about learning. We need to encourage our students and cheer them on to succeed. When we use this kind of approach, many classroom management and discipline problems are taken care of before they happen. Children are empowered to work to try to get along, to strive to be successful. This is not to say that there will not be challenges!

As I reread these words, I recall a conversation I had with my mother recently, as I described the disastrous behavior of a brand-new student. She smiled and said, knowingly, "You haven't worked your magic on him yet." She helped me realize that this is what we do as teachers: we work our magic on children to help them succeed and feel good about themselves (as my mother had just done for me!). In the process, we show them what it's like to enjoy learning. We empower children to become can-do kids.

Getting Children's Attention

It is very important, right from the first bell on day one, to have a system or systems for getting children's attention. I explain to the children that it is my job to teach them, and that sometimes they will teach me, too! I let them know that when I need to speak to them, they need to be quiet as quickly as possible and listen. When it is their turn, the other children and I will listen to them.

We work on this together, and I time the children to emphasize the importance of my getting their attention quickly. I may say something like, "It took only ten seconds for you to get ready to listen this time. You broke your record!"

Once in a while, when I begin to speak, no one notices. Then I say, "Close your lips and look at me." The children raise their hands, put a finger over their lips, and turn their eyes my way. I count by fives until all the children are quiet and are looking at me. I ask my first graders to put hands down. I tell them how many seconds they took to become attentive. Then I go ahead with whatever it was that I needed to say.

I don't use this method frequently—only when it is absolutely critical that I have all children listening. But I do it often enough (a few times each week) that children remember what to do when I say, "Close your lips and look at me," and can do it quickly.

Teaching Students to Focus on You

I teach the children several ways to give me their attention.

One method I use is to say, "Listen," hold up my hand, and then wait. If this isn't enough, I might hold up my right hand and make a backward *L*. From the children's point of view, as they face me, this is an *L*. I say, "You need to *listen*." I might say, as one teacher I know does, "Look, listen, learn."

Or, I might start singing our class song (see Chapter 3).

My Turn and Your Turn: Giving Children Time to Talk

If children are slow to respond when I am trying to get their attention, I remind them that it is my turn to talk, not theirs. I do emphasize that their turn is important also. Occasionally, I may stop the group if a child is trying to talk and have everyone give his or her attention to the child who has the floor.

I *need* to get and keep children's attention if I am going to teach them anything. I also need to have a way of getting their attention fast in case of an emergency or important event.

Using Sign Language

My friend Kimberly Hock, a teacher in Millbrae, California, uses sign language both to access children's attention and to give directions. Kimberly explained to me how mystified her principal was when he observed her for the first time. He wasn't sure how she was controlling her class and how all the children knew to put things away, take out certain books and materials, line up, and so forth. She finally let him know that she was using sign language and had been giving all her instructions using this technique. (See Resources for some sign language book titles.)

The Importance of Getting Children's Attention

It is very important to have ways to access children's attention *quickly*. I may use several techniques throughout the day. I may flick the lights. However, the light switch is too far away from my usual places in the classroom for this to be handy for me. It can also alarm some children if the room is suddenly plunged in darkness. I may give a direction and then give team points for the fastest table or group to respond. Sometimes I say, "Freeze," or hold up a straight arm and two fingers for quiet. One of my most frequently used techniques is to lower my voice level. Speaking very quietly gets attention much faster than a loud voice, and is a lot easier on everyone!

I may clap a rhythm; children respond by clapping the rest of it. They can't resist! Sometimes I say, "Give me a 'shhhhhhhhh.'" Children repeat the "shhhhhhhh" exactly the way I have just said it. My favorite way to get attention is to begin a poem or a song. Children are joining in before we know it, and I have their attention when the song is completed. I love this, but it isn't the technique to use if you have a point you need to make quickly.

Hookups and Beyond

I have found hookups to be a great way to settle children down and help them become focused and centered. I learned of this exercise and several others through a Brain Gym® workshop I took with Sharron Patton, occupational therapist and Brain Gym® instructor. Sharron's presentation focused on the work of Dr. Paul Dennison, who developed this comprehensive movement-based program called Brain Gym®. Brain Gym® is a series of simple movements designed to enhance whole brain learning and make learning easier. To do one exercise, hookups, children cross their legs (while standing, sitting on the floor, or sitting at their desks). Then they either cross wrists or arms, or do a more involved crossing of arms by following these steps:

- Hold arms out, backs of hands touching.
- Cross one hand over another and clasp hands.
- Keeping hands clasped, turn hands under and up, so they are resting under chin.
- Put tongue on roof of mouth, mouth closed. Breathe deeply.
- Eyes may also be closed.

Children and I sit like this for approximately one minute. Then we uncross our legs and put our fingertips together. Next we move our hands up and down with fingertips touching. We call this spider pushups. This procedure isn't punitive. It is comfortable, and gives all of us time away—a brief interlude to recharge, refocus, and take a deep breath.

My first graders really like doing hookups. When the room is noisy, or children seem out of control, they often voluntarily do hookups and calm right down again. I find hookups helpful myself, when stress levels rise.

Literature Connection

For more about Brain Gym®, see the books *Smart Moves: Why Learning Is Not All in Your Head,* by Carla Hannaford (1995), and *Brain Gym®: Simple Activities for Whole Brain Learning,* by Dr. Paul Dennison and Gail E. Dennison (1992).

I admit to being somewhat skeptical when I first showed children this technique for settling down and focusing, but I have become a believer. And when all is said and done, how much havoc can a person cause if she is hooked up with arms and legs tangled, mouth closed, and tongue on the roof of her mouth?

After hookups (one minute in length, approximately) children seem much more ready to focus, pay attention, think, and learn.

Other Ways to Get Children's Attention

Here is a list recapping some ways to get attention from your first graders. I do try to emphasize the positive.

- I raise my hand and say, "Close your lips and look at me." Children put up one hand and put fingers on their lips. I time them, counting by fives.
- Say, "Give me a 'shhhhhh.'" I can vary the way we make this sound: long, short, wavy, fast, high, low (moving arm as we say it), and so on.
- Stand and wait, quietly. Sometimes this needs to be combined with other techniques, such as those above.
- Make an observation (be sure it is accurate and complimentary but not phony): "I never have to wait for Shannon. Thank you, Shannon." I'm careful with this method. If I use it, I try to do it for different children all the time. Otherwise, it can backfire and make other children angry with the praised child.
- Clap a pattern. Leave it unfinished. The children will complete it. This is great for developing rhythm, too.
- Begin a poem or song. Complete it together. This technique enhances oral language, as well as rhythm and rhyme.
- Flick the lights, click a clicker, shake a rain stick, or ring a little bell.
- Say "freeze," Say "thaw" after you have said what you wanted to say. Sometimes this method works well. On other occasions I find it somewhat chaotic. It depends upon the class, of course, but some first-grade children can get overly dramatic as they freeze and thaw.
- Give directions in sign language, as previously described. This method is like a secret code. Children feel very empowered if they can recognize what you are signing and are able to follow your directions.
- Give table or row points. I give the points and we celebrate getting them. I no longer believe in giving stickers or prizes for this. At the very least, it uses our class time and my money. At its worst,

it causes resentments. Children hate it when someone else gets a prize for winning and they don't! First graders seem very content just to get the most points or hear some words of praise.

- Sing or chant the directions, or give them as a rap. I use my own most well worn rap at the end of the day: "Chairs up, get your stuff, meet me on the rug!" Another rap I might use occasionally is, "One, two, three: Eyes on me!"
- Begin making motions, such as crossing your arms and touching your nose, and silently invite the children to mimic you, without sound. This is a little like Simon says, except that Simon doesn't say anything. At the beginning, so children notice I am waiting, I might just say something like: "Do this: (I put my hands on my shoulders). Do this: (I put one hand in the air)." Children silently copy what I do. They need to concentrate to do copy my movements accurately, and this helps them regain their calm and their focus.
- Do hookups. This Brain Gym® movement exercise helps children relieve stress, tune in, and focus.
- Begin reading a wonderful children's book, or start telling a story.
- Do a finger play.

Whatever methods you use to get children's attention, nothing works *all* the time.

Using Children's Literature to Focus the Class

I do try to accentuate the positive and avoid raising my voice. This way, when it *is* absolutely necessary to speak louder, I *really* get children's attention. I prefer to use a louder voice level as a last resort or for emergencies.

As suggested by Kay Goines, my mentor in so many ways, I like to integrate children's literature with the process of gaining and maintaining class control. I read Jane Thayer's book *Gus Was a Friendly Ghost* (1962) early in the school year. The book has a ghost protagonist who befriends a very self-centered, selfish mouse. The mouse doesn't listen when Gus tries to talk with him. Gus finally tells the mouse, "That's ENOUGH!" when the small creature is scaring the very sweet lady of the house.

After I have read this book, and enjoyed it with my first graders, I can raise my voice and say, "That's ENOUGH!" if I find it to be necessary. The children will know that I mean it, but they enjoy the fact that I am making a reference to a children's book we all enjoyed together. Sometimes we get a good laugh over this, at a time when we really need it. In essence, at these times, I am controlling my class through the words of a famous piece of children's literature and the children's love of that book.

A Treasure Chest of Discipline and Management Ideas

I have used a variety of discipline and management techniques throughout my teaching career and have found several that work for me. Of course, the strategies that worked for one class may not be effective with the next group of children. Different groups of children may need different approaches. A certain amount of experimentation may take place before I feel comfortable with the methods I'm using each year.

My Goals

My goals for children are to learn the most they can by thinking and making connections, paying attention, and remembering our classroom rules:

- We never hurt anybody on the inside or the outside.
- We do our best to listen, think, and learn.
- We clean up after ourselves every day.

The wording of these rules can vary by class, but this is the heart of them. The children agree on our classroom pledge at the beginning of the school year. (For more about making rules together, see pages 44–45.)

1-2-3 Magic!

I used a new approach this year that has greatly impacted my teaching in positive ways. It is based on the book *1-2-3 Magic: Effective Discipline for Children 2–12*, by Thomas W. Phelan, Ph.D. (1996). This method helps me to run my classroom well without being interrupted frequently to handle discipline problems. In the past I have used many different techniques to obtain the attention of my students and help them focus and learn, but this one is a hands-down favorite.

Stop Sign, Magnets, and Magnetic Whiteboard I have made simple adaptations to the discipline program I learned about in the book *1-2-3 Magic.* My system of using four color-coded behavior levels is simple and fast.

I keep a small (6-by-12-inch) cutout paper stoplight on the bottom of the large whiteboard in front of the room. It has a black construction paper background, with three circles glued on vertically: green, yellow, and red. On the chalk tray next to this display is a small (8-by-12-inch) whiteboard. I have written each student's name on the little board. Under printed names are magnets with names affixed with small squares cut from computer labels.

Figure 6–1
Cesar moves his magnet to the top circle (green).

I have written four rows of names, listing children in alphabetical order by first name. (I choose to use this small whiteboard and magnets rather than the chart and card pockets recommended in the book *1-2-3 Magic.*)

Moving a Magnet Marker If a child bothers someone else, or isn't paying attention, I say, "Move your magnet, please." If this is in the middle of something, I may just say, "Magnet." The child removes the magnet from the whiteboard and moves it to the green circle. Soon I can just gesture to the child to move the magnet, rather than my letting the whole group in on my request to Willy to move his magnet now. A second request to move the magnet will leave the child on the yellow circle—a warning. And the third request lands the magnet on the red circle, meaning the child must take an automatic five-minute time away from our group. The child who needs time away sits in a chair behind a bookshelf near the door and (I hope!) reflects and makes appropriate changes before rejoining our group.

A Walk and Talk with Me Those children who earn a time away during the morning walk to recess or lunch with the group, walk back with me for a little chat. I find I need to interrupt a child's recess or lunch only two or three times, even for the most disruptive of students, before the child realizes that his behavior isn't worth the consequences. If the time away occurs during the afternoon, I keep the child after dismissal for a few minutes to have our little pep talk.

Teacher and Child Safety Notes It is important for all of us, as teachers, to protect ourselves from any possible suggestion of impropriety. It is necessary for us to keep classroom doors open when meeting individually with a child, or to meet in a place where other people are nearby. I try never to see an individual child alone in an enclosed or isolated area. By the same token, I do make sure that any child having time away has returned to our group before we leave the classroom to go somewhere or are dismissed for the day.

Returning Magnets to the Winner's Circle I have had great success with the ideas from the book *1-2-3 Magic.* The system isn't punitive. Children are not scolded in front of their classmates, shamed, or embarrassed. I do not have to say much at all, because the system has been explained and children understand the way it works. After a brief time away, children put their markers back on the little whiteboard and rejoin our group. The return of the magnet to the small whiteboard symbolizes a child's opportunity to begin again. We have begun calling the little whiteboard the Winner's Circle.

Teaching Children to Pat Themselves on the Back Many Ways One of the beauties of the 1-2-3 system is that it defeats misbehaving for attention's sake. Children who aren't following classroom rules change their magnets but get very little attention. Children whose magnets are in the Winner's Circle receive pats on the back (they can give their own), clam claps (silent moving of thumb and fingers up and down), and other signs of approval. And we all talk about how good we feel when we are doing our best.

Smart Kids I recently attended a workshop called Smart Kids, written and given by Jean Blaydes. Afterward I showed my children her seal of approval: she says, "Kiss your brain," kisses her thumb, and presses it to her head. The children *love* this. My new child, who needs many signs of approval, said, "We could do this for 'Kiss your heart'!"

Time Away from the Group Children spend the five-minute time away in separate areas, never together, should two or more students need this experience at the same time. The rules the class decides upon together will determine whether students have to move their magnets. There is a lot of flexibility in how I run and enforce this program. I try to be consistent in my classroom but not punitive or vindictive. I want my children to succeed, and I would just as soon we don't have much time to even think about this behavior magnet board. I want it to be inconspicuous. My goals are that children try to think and learn, don't hurt anyone else, and don't do things that will prevent another child from learning.

Every child has two chances each day to start on the whiteboard: in the morning and after lunch. Children always have a new start to the day when they come into the classroom in the afternoon. (They also start again on the whiteboard after each five-minute time away.)

Time for the System to Work A child having extreme difficulties could have a new start each period, rather than twice a day. I almost went to this system with Gerald, a child who was having six and seven times away each day after hitting, pushing, attacking, threatening, attempting to argue with me, using bad language, and disturbing other children in a myriad of ways. I held off on modifying the system for Gerald, and within three weeks he made great improvements.

Although the *1-2-3 Magic* system took care of most of Gerald's behavior problems in the classroom, as the year went gone on, I found that occasionally I had to take other steps. For example, I recently had a long talk with Gerald after he slapped another child across the face at recess. I carefully explained that he must not treat other children this way, even if he is angry. When Gerald repeated the same behavior about half an hour later, I removed him from the situation, and he ate his lunch in the office. A phone call was made to parents, and a meeting was arranged. Because we are fortunate to have a grant with a local counseling group, this child is now receiving some additional help.

Conferring with Children and Providing Time and Materials for Student Response As we all know, no one approach works for everyone. There definitely are children who would be upset by this behavior magnet board system because they could not wait to talk about what had happened.

If a child is upset and needs to meet with me, I do it whenever possible. Usually there just isn't a chance to stop for a chat in the middle of a lesson, or when a whole group could get out of control if I were to go off and meet privately with one child.

My friend Marsha Oviatt, a school psychologist in Belmont, California, says that when we use behavior modification systems, like the stoplight and Winner's Circle, and take something away from a child, we need to provide replacement systems for that student. When a child is angry because of having to move a behavior marker or magnet, and perhaps feels this is not fair, the lack of opportunity to talk may be very upsetting. A replacement for talking, such as giving the child the chance to write (or draw) a brief note, can remind children what they wish to say to the teacher later, when there is time to talk. I believe that Marsha's idea of giving an upset child time to write a brief note honors children's needs for self-expression and gives them time to talk with the teacher about the problem and work out some solutions.

My first graders all have Post-it Notes in their desk bins. I now I ask the child to make a little note about what we need to talk about. Then I will go on with our lesson and check in with this student privately just as soon as I can.

You Don't Have to Be Perfect to Be Wonderful! I like to put a small sign near the whiteboard and magnet setup, or somewhere else in my classroom, with this optimistic message: You don't have to be perfect to be wonderful! I saw this bulletin board heading in my colleague Alison Appleby's room. This is a reassuring thought for us all. I hope this little reminder will help children's self-esteem and propel children toward better behavior. I think we all need to feel good about ourselves in order to be successful.

Giving Children Some Control I was recently explaining the stoplight and Winner's Circle program to Barbara Smailey, a counselor friend of mine. She said that part of the magic of the system is that each child has a personal magnet. Children can *choose* to move the magnet or not after an infraction. If they *do* move the magnet, they take responsibility for not having followed class procedures or rules. If a child chooses not to move the magnet we have a private talk later. Barbara said, "Children are empowered. They have choice—and control. They can think, 'Yes, I did that,' and move the magnet. And then they can work to get their magnet back on the Winner's Circle [after time away or after our lunch break]."

After I used this system for half the school year, I noticed that many children never had to move their magnets anymore. Children were very cognizant of the Winner's Circle. I heard them marveling, and saying things like, "Look! All our magnets are still in the Winner's Circle!" This was good incentive to keep everybody focused and keep magnets in a positive place.

The Bunny Planet

Voyage to the Bunny Planet is a wonderful three-volume set of picture books by Rosemary Wells (2003). In each of these books, the protagonist has had a terrible day and desperately needs a change of scene. Queen Janet, the bunny Queen, arrives and takes the little character to another world—the Bunny Planet—to have a special and personally meaningful experience. Then, after that interlude, the protagonist is returned to the place the story started, better able to handle the day.

I have always loved these books, and because of them, years ago, I created a Bunny Planet in my classroom. This is a place to get away and recharge. It is now close to the Time Away area, behind a bookcase in the alcove. I keep a variety of things in the Bunny Planet: a soft bunny puppet, a ball to squeeze, some books, crayons, and paper. I really do not differentiate which bit of space a child retreats to: the Time Away area or the Bunny Planet.

I learned more about this idea of time away from Barbara Smailey. She suggests that taking time out or time away is one way we take care of ourselves. We all need to take a brief time away sometimes. It is important for children to know that this is a positive thing for them to do. Barbara suggested that I let children pick some things to keep at the Bunny Planet, and that they may want to give the area their own personal name for it. (See Figure 6–2 for suggestions of things to keep at the Bunny Planet.)

Figure 6–2
Ideas for items to keep in the Bunny Planet

- Stuffed bunny
- Puppets
- Plasticine clay
- Rosemary Wells' books: *Voyage to the Bunny Planet; First Tomato; Moss Pillows; The Island Light*
- Puzzles
- Snow globe
- Magnets/magnetic board
- Magna Doodle
- Colored pencils and paper
- Teddy bear
- Books

A Variation of the Magnet Board

A variation of the magnet board strategy is to make a large chart with library pocket cards, one pocket for each student. Each pocket holds three cards: green, yellow, and red.

Much like the magnet board I use, a student changes the card (putting the top card, green, behind the rest) when so instructed. When a red card comes to the front, the child sits out recess or has another consequence. I found this system to be larger and more intrusive than the use of the small magnet board. Also, there were only three levels: green, yellow, and red. Green, rather than white, was the beginning level. The system was only changed once a day, so the students didn't have a chance to start over again. I felt that this larger-format system tended to *advertise* misbehavior. However, this card chart could be modified to reflect the lower-key magnet board system I use.

In the past, when I used the card system, I gave stickers to students who got through the day or week "on green." I now find that I prefer to *omit* stickers and focus more on verbal approval and on the magnet board itself. This is purely personal. I feel that stickers and similar rewards divert attention from what we are trying to achieve.

Team Points

Team points are another system that can be used to get children's attention and help them tune in to lessons and follow directions. When I give directions and children follow through, I use points on the board for the team or group of students that pays attention first. I kept tallies in the corner of the whiteboard.

One year this team points system was absolutely *crucial* in changing behavior. It just clicked with my class. I had an extremely difficult child who was quite defiant. At the beginning of the year he liked to spend a great deal of time under his desk. Although I tried a number of other methods, I found that giving team points was the way to change his behavior. He just couldn't resist them. When I calmly ignored his behavior, and began giving points to teams with all students paying attention, Blake would hustle out from under the desk and get ready to listen and learn.

Occasionally, when Blake was in our class, he would become so distraught when his team didn't win that the whole system seemed to backfire. This has led to my belief that giving the points is enough, and that stickers and other rewards aren't necessary.

Find Out What Worked Last Year

A good strategy when you are working to help children pay attention, be good to each other, and succeed in learning is to check with last year's teacher and see what was effective. Eileen Christopherson, kindergarten teacher at my school, confided to me that she had used a simple yet effective behavior system with Keith: a happy face (or the reverse) drawn on his hand at the end of the day. Keith still loved this system in first grade, where I added the additional straight face drawing for an up-and-down day of mixed success. Keith had acquired the habit of showing this behavior symbol to Mom at the end of the day. While I wasn't wild about this myself, I have to admit that it *did* work. All I had to do was gesture toward my hand, or mime drawing on it, and Keith snapped right back to attention, or to less disruptive behavior. Because I felt that this system might cause Keith some embarrassment as a second grader, I weaned him from it before the end of the year.

Behavior Contracts

I have also found behavior contracts to be good incentives for some children. When I first used this idea, as a brand-new teacher, Gerard and I set up one or two goals and I wrote them down on a behavior graph. At the end of the day, after we discussed and agreed on how he had done, Gerard colored the relevant square on the paper. I sent the graph home each day, and the parents signed it and returned it. We kept the graphs for a week at a time, until Gerard just didn't need them anymore. (See Figure 6–3.)

I have found since that time that some children need to mark their graphs at much more frequent intervals throughout the day, some after each period. The time for marking graphs can be lengthened, to cover all morning or the time between morning and recess.

With the help of Ed Fristoe, our school psychologist, I was able to successfully use a behavior graph last year with a frequently violent student. Willy was able to control most of his violent behavior and work on a secondary goal, working to pay attention and learn.

Name ______________ Week of ______________

Behavior goals:

____

____

Monday		Tuesday		Wednesday		Thursday		Friday	
a.m.	p.m.	a.m.	p.m.	a.m.	p.m.	am.	p.m.	a.m.	p.m.

Key: ☺ great! ☺ pretty good ☹ needs improvement

comments:				

parent signature daily

Figure 6–3 *Sample behavior chart*

Willy and I filled in this graph, or behavior contract, three times a day after a minute or two of discussion: after recess, after lunch, and before going home. His parents sent the paper back, signed, each morning.

In addition to this system, I used other strategies with Willy to help him improve his behavior. I do think that having a contract, discussing it, and seeing it filled in at regular intervals throughout the day really helped him be successful.

Positive Choices

Many of the ideas in *Positive Discipline in the Classroom*, by Jane Nelsen, Lynn Lott, and H. Stephen Glenn (2000), helped me reach a difficult student, such as one-on-one talks to show him I cared about his frustrations. As suggested by the authors, I used one- or two-word prompts to remind this new first grader, Daniel, of things he needed to do, such as "jacket," "book choice," "reading time," and so forth. I also made an effort to see things through *his* eyes, so I could understand his feelings and help him feel good about himself and succeed.

As the authors recommend, I gave Daniel some *choices* throughout the day. When he wasn't following through on work to be done, I reminded myself to speak in a calm and matter-of-fact manner as I asked him privately, "Would you like to finish that now, or do it during recess?" or "Do you want to stay with us for this shared reading lesson or practice the books in your guided reading basket?" Since this student believed himself to be higher-achieving than the rest of the class (and this was true in terms of his reading level), I needed to acknowledge this with him and help him get past resentment and behavior issues so he could learn.

If You Think You Can, You're Right Daniel was discouraged, and he needed *a lot* of hope and encouragement. I needed to continue working out ways to give him this kind of positive support. It was not until I wrote about Daniel in my seven-minute after-school log, and reread *Positive Discipline in the Classroom,* that I began to have a clear idea of what was going on and how I could help.

Upon reflection, I saw that one of the main things I needed to do with Daniel was to overlook a lot, and catch him doing things well. I made him a behavior card to take home each night. A positive note on the card each day helped him to do well the following day. (At times I caught Daniel's eye, and motioned as if writing on his card, to remind him that I was looking for that special comment just for him.)

Positive Choice Wheels or Spinners My goal was to keep giving Daniel choices, catching him when he exhibited or evidenced good behavior and positive attempts at learning. I also worked to create positive choice wheels with him. This is an idea from *Positive Discipline in the Classroom.* These wheels list eight to ten ideas in a circle divided like a pie—ideas that could be good ways *out* of an upsetting or problem-filled situation. Ideas range from apologizing or walking away, to playing with someone else, to starting over, to looking someone in the eyes and saying, "stop that," and so forth. (See Figure 6–4.)

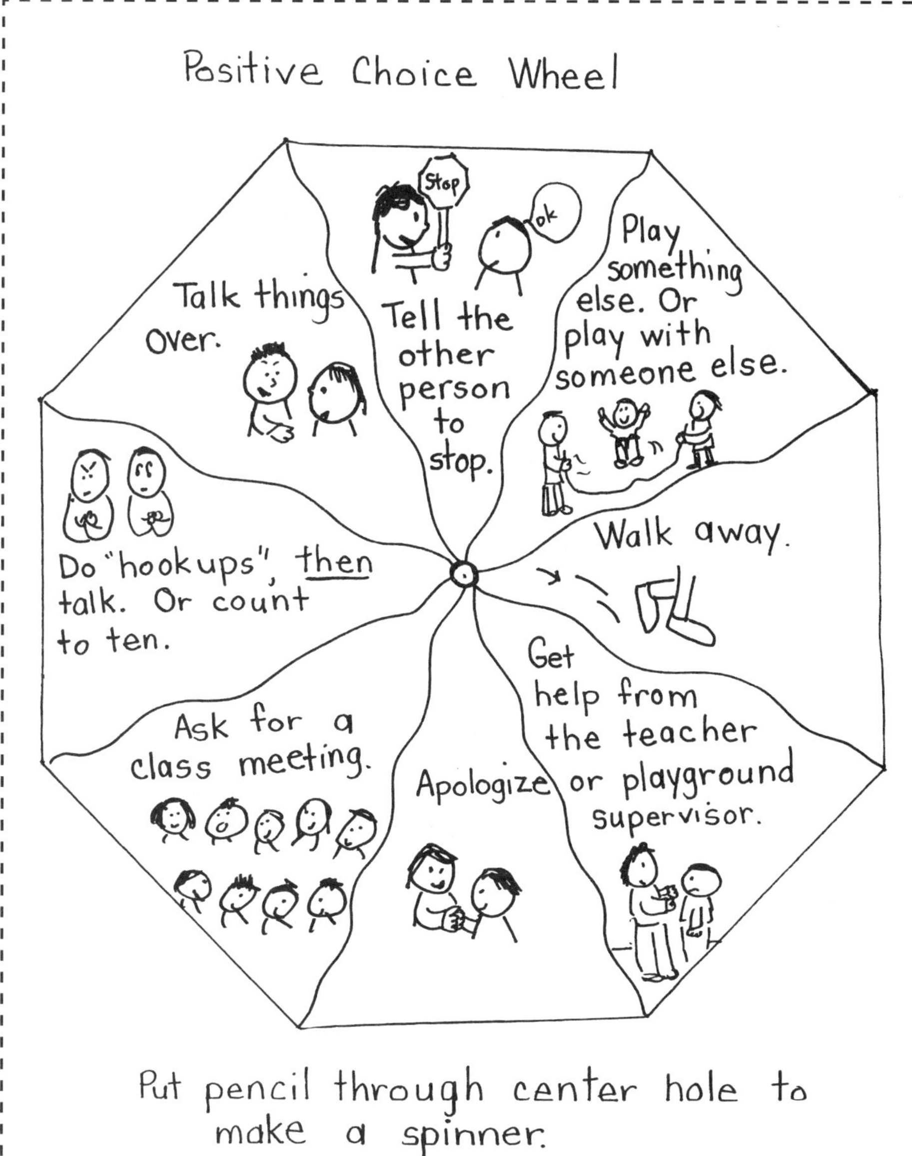

Figure 6–4 *Positive choice wheel*

Children in my class enjoy creating their own wheels, cutting out a circle template, with pie-piece areas for writing ideas. To make the wheel spin, children just twirl a pencil I poked through the center of the wheel. They may spin one or two times or choose a different solution on the wheel to try out when they are upset or angry.

When There Is a Problem, Create a Diversion! A great side effect of the positive choice wheels is that they divert children's attention from their problems, or their anger, and engage them in creative, positive decision making. It's pretty hard to hold onto anger when you have interesting choices to make! Children also enjoy making these wheels. When *they* create them, they are even more propelled to believe the wheels work to help them solve problems. I like to take one with me on yard duty as well.

Good Resources

There are many books on discipline and classroom management available. Some other books on positive discipline that I have found to be extremely helpful are: *Positive Discipline*, by Jane Nelsen and H. Stephen Glenn (1996), and *Positive Discipline: A Teacher's A–Z Guide,* by Jane Nelsen et al. (2001). Another good resource is *Building Classroom Discipline,* by C. M. Charles (2002). It is an overview of many different classroom discipline programs.

Some Days Are Just Difficult

No matter how experienced, well-organized, and good-humored you are, and what kind of management and discipline systems you have in place, there are going to be days when, for no understandable reason, everything goes wrong. Like Alexander, the protagonist of Judith Viorst's picture book *Alexander and the Terrible, Horrible, No Good, Very Bad Day,* you too may want to move to Australia.

Once, after a day of strange and bizarre behavior on the part of my first graders, I told the class I thought *I'd* move to Australia. They got my reference but convinced me it would do no good to move: it would all be "just the same there."

Mean Soup

When all else fails, try a bowl of mean soup. *Mean Soup* is a picture book written by Betsy Everitt (1995). The protagonist, a little boy named Horace, has a hard day at school. He goes home mad and stomps on a flower outside the house. Mom sees this from the doorway. She puts on a pot of water, throws in salt, and invites Horace to make soup. (Horace is lying on the floor. He doesn't want to make soup.) Mom yells into the soup pot. The water boils. She sticks out her tongue. Horace sticks out his tongue and yells and bangs on the pot.

At last Horace smiles. He and his mother stand side by side and wash away a bad day.

I keep the book handy, along with a wooden spoon and an empty pot. Once in a while, the children and I sit in a circle, pass the empty pot around, yell in it, bang on it, and make pretend mean soup. We can wash away a bad day this way too. And we know that some days are just like that.

CHAPTER 7

Our School Family

Creating Community, Managing Conflicts

Being together,
That's the key:
We all matter,
We're a school family!

—PBD

One essential job of a classroom teacher is to help create a sense of cohesion and a community where we all value each other and we all belong. Like any community, our school family will have its share of disagreements and problems. These conflicts are to be expected. That's the way life is. The important thing is how we deal with these difficulties. A positive approach gives us strategies that will benefit us throughout first grade and beyond.

The Watchdog and the Gummilump Box

As I drive to my mother's on a Sunday afternoon, I puzzle over the behavior of a few children in my class. I dwell particularly on Luis and try to think of ways I can motivate him to stop being so sneaky and so mean to other children. Just as I am at the height of my silent personal brainstorming, I drive by a collie dog lying on a wooden stand, about 12 feet in the air.

I do a double take and park my car. I find myself at a garage sale, and I realize I might have just found a way to motivate Luis and a few other students I am concerned about.

The stuffed collie—life-sized, realistic, and fairly reasonably priced—accompanies me to school the next day. It becomes our class watchdog and is appropriately named the Watchdog. It watches for all the *good* things going on in the classroom. The Watchdog wears a watch around its neck. As I made the watch of paper, I thought of the character of the same name in a book I've always loved, *The Phantom Tollbooth*, by Norton Juster (1963). Our stuffed collie stares down at all of us from the top of the cubbyholes. This seems appropriate, since when I first met this dog it was high up on a platform, scanning the neighborhood.

Figure 7–1
The Watchdog looks out for good things happening in our classroom.

Near the Watchdog, within reach of the children, is the Gummilump Box, a repository of treasured comments and compliments. As the Watchdog notices positive and wonderful things happening in our classroom—children helping each other, children reading together, students working hard to learn, and so forth—it *apparently* sneaks little notes of approval into the Gummilump Box. The children and I may put notes in there as well, about positive behavior, special learning—any compliment we wish to give a class member (or the teacher!). We read these notes aloud on the rug before we go home. There is great anticipation as we open the Gummilump Box each day.

I keep furtive little marks on a class grid to keep track of who has received notes. When this idea was first introduced, everybody got notes each week, some children more often, even daily. Children may stick some of these written comments on a Gummilump bulletin board

Figure 7–2
Celeste receives a great compliment from the Gummilump Box.

for us all to admire, or take them home, as they wish. The Gummilump notes really celebrate *both* the child receiving the compliment and the one who has written it.

If we are running short of time and I find on Friday that there are several children with no note, I may write a quick note from the Watchdog in list form, incorporating positive details about these students. I can quickly cut apart these comments so each child has something in the box. As time goes on, the Gummilump Box recedes a little in importance, and I do not make this kind of effort to balance things out.

The Watchdog and the Gummilump Box give us a way to acknowledge and appreciate each other. These little attention grabbers help affirm and change behavior, and they reinforce the idea of writing for a reason. Children may come to me for help with their notes, dictating them to me, or may write notes their way. As the year goes on, and children become more comfortable expressing themselves on paper, they take charge of writing their own notes.

Some days the Watchdog wears sunglasses so we can't see where it is looking. Our canine mascot may put in a personal note about something *it* is working on or even a note about me! On some occasions the Watchdog winks at me or whispers (only to me, of course) messages about specific children. The class can't hear these exchanges and children just have to trust me to relay comments correctly.

The week the Gummilump Box made its debut, Joey was thrilled to receive a note that he had "bin good" and another that he was becoming a reader. Christopher was glad to know he had been a good friend, and Marco enjoyed writing a note to praise Joan because she always remembered to bring things back from home. These notes bring to the children's consciousness things they can do to help each other, as well as themselves, as they strive to learn and get along in our school community. (See Figure 7–3.)

As the year progresses, and our routines become set, fewer notes are written each week. However, the Gummilump Box remains a place for input from the children, gives them a *real* reason for writing, and helps create an aura of anticipation and good feeling in our classroom. It goes hand in hand with class meetings to resolve problems and promote good behavior and a sense of community.

Of course, the only real item necessary for a similar classroom system is a box for comments. It is just more fun for me to do this as described.

Figure 7–3
Some Gummilump notes

Taking a Call on the Rabbit Phone

The Rabbit Phone, a tall stand-alone puppet that lives on a high window ledge, is a variation of the watchdog idea. In difficult moments, when I personally need to deliver a negative message, or even important news, I occasionally pick up the Rabbit Phone, hold it to my ear, nod my head, then relay the message—either aloud to the whole class or whispered to an individual child. Part of what makes this strategy successful is the children's willingness to suspend disbelief. There is a certain element of magic to messages from the Rabbit Phone, partly because they occur so rarely, and there is that hushed, strange wait time before we *all* find out the message. . . .

Class Meetings

Class meetings are a wonderful way to help us become a cohesive classroom family group. Once children are introduced to the idea of class

Figure 7–4
I pass on a message from the Rabbit Phone.

meetings to discuss concerns, problems, and ideas, they are firm believers in this system.

Often, as we walk in from recess, a child will ask, "Could we have a class meeting?" This procedure often just takes about five minutes. Children sit down on the carpet in a circle and discuss a problem: someone hit or "dog-piled" (the children's term for people running and landing on top of each other), someone pushed, kicked, or hurt their feelings, and so on. Other children have a chance to discuss the problem, and most of the time it is quickly solved. The main rule is that everyone who wants to contribute an idea or comment has time to talk. Meetings may be about a problem, a concern, or even a great idea. We modify and remake rules in our class meetings as we brainstorm together all year. I sit in the circle as well, so that I am part of the group, and facilitate running things. Often we end our days with class meetings.

We keep an ongoing agenda, a list of things we want to discuss at class meetings. However, I have found with first graders that it is sometimes easier to just have the meeting as soon as possible (usually right after recess or lunch) and solve problems right away. This takes only a few minutes. If children are upset, it is easier to handle things than wait. On the other hand, if we seem to be covering the same ground all the time, it is better to put the item on the agenda, wait, and have a more extensive meeting to resolve the problem.

A Symbol for Having the Floor

Sometimes in our meetings, we pass something around the circle, such as a starfish or small stuffed toy. This is a symbol to us all that the person holding the item is the one whose turn it is to talk. Children may choose not to talk as well, when the special object is handed to them. If so, they just pass it on.

Usually our meetings are whole-class affairs. Once in a while a little group may ask to use the alcove to discuss a problem of relevance to just a few children. I don't interfere, and I refrain from eavesdropping. The children seem content to be able to meet privately and resolve things this way. Sometimes I may ask them to tell me the end result of the conference, but most of the time they do not seem to need to report back to me. I am happy they feel they can solve problems on their own.

Hook Up and Cool Off!

Sometimes when children are upset, they may need my intervention. A cooling-off period is always a good idea before discussion. One technique I use is to ask the children to do one or two minutes of hookups while they focus silently on their problem and how to solve it. (See Chapter 6 for more about hookups.)

After a two-minute respite, I ask each child to briefly explain the problem. One child speaks at a time. Children are asked to give "I" messages when they talk out the problem. They take turns explaining the problem and tell what they think would solve it or would make them feel better. The participants decide on best outcomes, most of the time. Children can resolve just about anything when they learn these techniques:

- Calm down and cool off.
- Explain your side of the problem.
- Listen to the other person's point of view.
- Help think of a solution to resolve the problem.

Conflict Comes with the Territory

We begin learning conflict management and social strategies right away when school starts. We agree that learning conflict management skills will help us get along better and be happier in school. One way we approach this topic is through discussion. Another is through picture books and stories. Children's literature gives us experiences we can learn from without the emotional baggage of being embroiled in real conflicts, disagreements, and disputes. We can talk about a story and analyze it: How could it have turned out differently if the character had acted this way? What do you think the characters should have done? What was the point where the problem started—the moment that made the conflict happen or not happen?

We can draw the problem and different endings. One interesting way to make books showing a conflict and some different solutions is to use two sizes of paper: One piece 4½-by-6-inch piece is for drawing the problem. Stapled behind this paper are two or three larger pieces, 4½-by-12-inch. These larger pages are for drawing possible solutions to the problem, or different ways the problem could play out. (See Figure 7–5.)

Art and children's literature are great ways to help us explore conflicts and think of resolutions.

Figure 7–5 *We explore conflicts by drawing different solutions.*

Conflict Resolution Through the Arts

Russell Brunson, conflict resolution educator, has been part of a national project to teach conflict resolution through the arts. He is one of the authors of *The Art in Peacemaking*, along with Zephrun Conte and Shelley Mascar (2000). I met Russell at a recent County Art Education meeting at the San Mateo County Office of Education. Russell, an attorney, feels that art and literature can help create a language of perception that will help us understand problems and try to deal with them. With this approach, children learn why their conflicts occur. Communication is then a key for resolving problems peacefully.

Russell advocates group-brainstorming techniques, such as class meetings, rather than top-down telling, where the teacher tells the class how to solve a difficulty. When children get a chance to discuss problems and solve them, they learn strategies for taking responsibility for their problems and behavior.

The Art in Peacemaking integrates many conflict resolution techniques with the arts. Some examples are to share personal feelings about anger through drawings, poetry, mask making and role-playing. Children use the arts to help them figure out their own stories. (This program is sponsored by the National Endowment for the Arts and the Office of Juvenile Justice and Delinquency Prevention.)

One of my first graders, Bridget, recently used art and writing to express her recess conflict and the pain it caused her. She brought her paper to our class meeting, and it was a catalyst for discussion. Bridget's drawing and writing engaged children's interest and helped her devise a resolution to her problem. (See Figure 7–6.)

Literature Connection

Some professional literature titles for conflict management are *Teaching Conflict Resolution Through Children's Literature—K–2*, by William J. Kreidler (1994); *Talk It Out: Conflict Resolution in the Elementary Classroom*, by Barbara Porro (1996); and *A Teacher's Guide to Cooperative Discipline: How to Manage Your Classroom and Promote Self-Esteem*, by Linda Albert (1989).

Figure 7–6
Bridget's recess drawing

Community Building: Making a Class Quilt

When we become a class community, we nurture and support each other. We become a team. One way to facilitate this kind of bonding in your classroom is to create a class quilt together, with a quilt block for each group member. Here is how we do it:

You Need

Background paper, such as fadeless butcher paper
12-inch squares of construction paper, one or two colors that complement the background paper
9-inch squares of contrasting-colored construction paper that complement both background paper and the 12-inch squares (*Note*: Even numbers of each color will make the quilt more uniform. For example, orange background paper, black 12-inch squares, and an even number of yellow and orange 9-inch squares. Add paper scraps in a few color choices for accent.)
Glue or glue sticks scissors
A variety of paper scraps, or 6-inch squares of other colored papers
Optional: marking pens

Procedure

1. Invite children to pair up. Each partner picks a 12-inch square and a 9-inch square for the other person.

2. Children interview each other and design quilt blocks that showcase their partners: likes, dislikes, families, favorite things to do, and so forth.

3. Students cut or tear and glue colored paper (or create marking pen drawings) to design the blocks. This is done on the 9-inch square.

4. Glue the 9-inch square on top of the 12-inch square to make a quilt block and place blocks on background paper.

5. The group decides placement of different blocks, until you all like the arrangement.

6. Partners introduce each other to the group and show their quilt blocks.

7. Tape down the quilt blocks and you can all enjoy a class community quilt.

Quilts may be made reflecting all curriculum areas, favorite books, field trips, important events, and so forth.

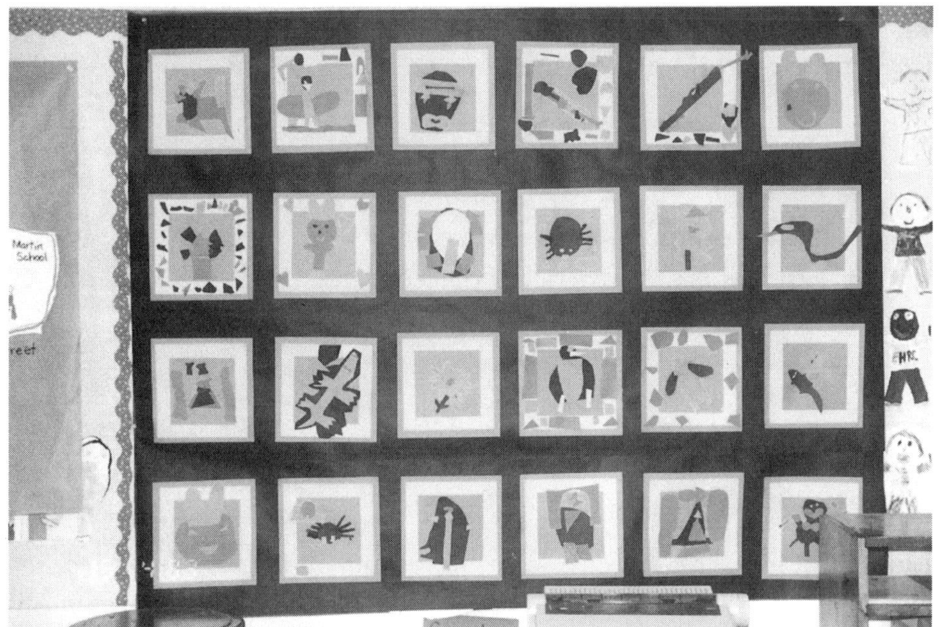

Figure 7–7
Cut-paper class quilt

T-Shirt Line

A variation of the class quilt idea is to invite children to pair up and design a T-shirt for each other. They may draw on colored construction paper using marking pens, crayons, or oil pastels. Light-colored paper works best for pens or crayons. As with the class quilt, partners introduce each other and share their T-shirts. Cut out the T-shirts and hang them from a yarn "clothesline."

Children's Literature Gives Us Vicarious Experiences

Many conflicts, misunderstandings, and difficulties arise, both with children and adults, because we simply do not have the vocabulary or experience of another approach. We are all trapped in those responses we know and have always used. Learning new methods and techniques for handling conflicts will help us gain and maintain friendships and have a positive, joyful year with each other. Children will also learn lifelong strategies for handling themselves and dealing with other people.

Children's books have always been crucial tools for me in teaching all areas of the curriculum. Here are some children's literature books that help children get along as well as resolve conflicts. (See Resources for a more extensive list.)

It's Mine! by Leo Lionni
The Quarreling Book, by Charlotte Zolotow
Let's Be Enemies, by Janice May Udry
Chicken Sunday, by Patricia Polacco
Six Crows, by Leo Lionni

Where the Wild Things Are

I like to begin our conflict resolution journey in first grade by reading *Where the Wild Things Are*, by Maurice Sendak (1988). This award-winning picture book begins with conflict: Max is in big trouble and is sent to his room without his supper. As the story moves along, Max sails away to the Land of the Wild Things and demonstrates great personal power: he is able to tame the Wild Things by looking into their yellow eyes "without blinking once."

We try this out, experimenting with a partner. Each partner gets a turn being the Wild Thing getting tamed, and Max the tamer, who becomes King of all the Wild Things.

This is an extremely powerful picture book: Max is safe and nurtured because he can and chooses to return to the place where "someone loves *him* best of all." But he also demonstrates great facility and success in handling himself in a strange new place: the Land of the Wild Things. (This is a great metaphor for the first day of school!)

Max is in a win-win situation, with a foot in each of two worlds: the familiar one where he gets in trouble but is well loved, and the strange new one he has found he can negotiate skillfully. Children can read in their own interpretations and be reassured: when our picture book hero triumphs, we do too!

Territoriality

Two immediate problems we have to deal with in the school year are the territoriality of the classroom and the territoriality of the playground (recess). Territoriality means we are all going to be sharing the same small space as well as materials: books, paper, pencils, art supplies, games, and so forth. And recess creates other stresses, because children have to deal with getting along out there alone on that big yard, finding something to do and someone to play with.

A positive approach is always good. Early in the school year we craft a list of things we can do at recess. We also talk about what we can do if someone is bothering us.

Room Seven's List of Things to Do on the Playground

- We could run around.
- We could play tag.
- We could run races.
- We could go on the playground equipment.
- We could play with balls, hula hoops, or jump ropes.
- We could tell somebody, "Let's play hopscotch."
- We could talk to another kid.
- We could hop, jump, sing, yell, dance.
- We could pretend to be stuff, like tigers.
- We could play a game, like duck, duck, goose.
- We could make up a game and do it with our friends.

It is also helpful to develop a troubleshooting list with children. *Note*: Lists like this take a few days or weeks to develop. It is worth spending time on these topics. Getting along at recess can be a factor in children wanting to come to school.

A sample problem list made by this year's class looked like this:

What to Do If You Have a Problem

- If someone won't play with us, we could play with somebody else.
- We could walk or run or hop or jump by ourselves. Our game might even look like fun to other kids and then they might like to play with us because we have good imaginations.

- We could say, "Don't do that!" if somebody bothers us. We could look powerful, like Max when he tamed the Wild Things.
- We could put our hands on our hips and make ourselves look big if somebody is bothering us.
- We could talk to the other kids if they aren't being fair or aren't treating us right.
- We could tell the yard-duty teacher if somebody won't listen to us.
- We could tell our teacher if we can't fix our problem.

Teaching Children to Take Care of Themselves

I frequently talk with my children about the need for them to take care of themselves. I tell them how important it is that *they* make sure they get the materials and feedback they need and even the help they need. For example, all of us in the classroom have probably experienced passing some work out to children and then finding out that we missed a student. Apparently several minutes passed one day when this happened to me, and I still had not realized that Andy was just sitting and not doing anything.

"What about your special paper?" I asked him.

"You didn't give me one," he replied (smugly, I thought), attempting to place the problem directly on my shoulders.

Several replies came to mind, but in this situation humor seemed to be my best bet.

"When were you going to tell me?" I asked Andy. "When you were old?"

Andy knew he needed to take responsibility for himself and so did I, but this seemed to be a way to handle things that gave us both a way to laugh, so we did. I gave Andy a paper and he quickly finished it.

I like to point out to children different ways they take care of themselves. I sometimes share a personal problem and how I handled it because I like to take care of *myself*. I find that time spent this way pays off, as children learn to take on the idea of ownership of a problem or difficulty. Sometimes in class meetings we brainstorm or role-play different ideas for solving a problem independently.

Now, as the year goes on, I hear children compliment each other on their problem-solving abilities. I sometimes hear a squabble, or a loud voice, followed by a call for my help. Then I hear, "Never mind, he took care of it himself."

"It's because we know how to take care of ourselves," Cassandra says.

And they do.

Hurting Someone Else

Hitting, kicking, or otherwise hurting another child is one way to get into serious trouble, both in my classroom and at my school—and in life! One of our main classroom rules (see Chapter 3) is that we do not injure other children or hurt their feelings.

In my classroom, and at my school, one of the things that is enforced after the school year is well under way is that a child must sit on the bench for part of recess time if there has been pushing, hitting, or deliberate injuring of other children. More serious offenses are handled with individual behavior contracts and other strategies.

My class is well aware of the bench rule for behavior that results in hurting another child. And we do remind each other often of our class credo: We don't hurt anyone on the inside or the outside. One day I broke that rule myself and inadvertently hurt a child's feelings when I misunderstood his behavior. As I apologized to Jeremiah, I said, "Oh, I am *sooo* sorry!" Hoping to lighten the moment, I said, "I'll sit on the bench at recess." Jeremiah forgave me, and he and the other children laughed, but another child, Joshua, was quite distressed to think I might sit recess out. "Oh, *you* don't have to sit on the bench," he said emphatically. "*I'll* sit on the bench for you." Such is the tenderness and love of a first grader. Teaching first grade is a humbling experience.

When a Child Is *Trying*, Keep Trying

I feel that it is important to keep working until you find a way to reach a child. As my friend Gloria Norton says, "I always think that *somebody* is going to be able to reach that student, and I want it to be *me*!" Gloria told a story about working with low-achieving sixth graders on reading when one student yelled in frustration and threw a book at her. He cried, "I'm stupid! When are you going to learn that I can't read?"

Her calm reply: "Never."

A few months later the same child came to her and excitedly confided, "Do you know what happened? Now I can read!"

A Note About Birthdays

Every child's birthday is acknowledged in my class, whether it occurs during a school break or not. Children who have birthdays when we are not in school just pick another special day to celebrate.

Students do not bring birthday food, but a birthday book for our class is a suggested option. Parents who do choose to give a class book in honor of their child's birthday may check titles on a class wish list first. I always put the child's school photo in the front of a donated book, along with a note about the child, including his or her birth date. The child puts the book, with ceremony, on our overnight bookshelf.

I always invite the birthday child to draw a birthday cake or a piñata. The child does the drawing on a small whiteboard, with a variety of marking pens. The class sings happy birthday while the birthday celebrant erases candles (or draws the breaking of the piñata!) and makes a wish. Each birthday child receives either a birthday pencil or a chance to pick something from the Treasure Box.

Treasure Box

The Treasure Box is *my* special collection: a decorated box filled with all kinds of small saved items: little toys, erasers, fancy pencils and pens, bells, and so on. I get many of these things at garage sales or flea markets. They may also be ordered from such places as Oriental Trading Company. (See Resources for contact information.)

I clean up these little items and pop them in the Treasure Box. In order to heighten anticipation and make this experience special, no one can look inside the box except the birthday child. It is fun for me to save small treasures to be used this way. I add to the collection throughout the year, so having a birthday late in the year is no disadvantage!

Our birthday celebration is short and simple, but it does acknowledge the child's own special rite of passage. In the past we took time for birthday cupcakes and juice, if parents chose to provide it, but the wear and tear on our carpets was terrible and all of this took up time that is increasingly precious and unavailable to us.

Since the majority of my children didn't have the luxury of birthday cupcakes anyway, this way of handling special days seems more equitable for everyone.

Naturally, whatever way birthdays are handled, the ritual needs to be done *exactly* the same way for each child. This is a good reason for carefully deciding on birthday procedures. They need to be something easily accomplished twenty to thirty-five times! Children look forward to the ritual you establish.

If children do not celebrate their birthdays, I call them aside on *other* days and offer them nonbirthday decorative pencils. I make no reference to birthdays at this time.

CHAPTER 8

The Beginnings of Literacy

Children's Faces Looking Up

Read aloud to children.
We must give them the best language we can find.
And the most exquisite, most beautiful language we have
is recorded in children's literature.

—Kay Goines

We can enrich children's worlds forever by introducing them to wonderful children's literature and the language of story and poetry. Children need to hear the sounds and flow of language. They need the opportunity to become immersed in the world of story and experience the magnificence and magic of quality picture book illustrations. This helps them learn to read and gives them reasons to *want* to acquire this skill. By listening to stories and experiencing them together, children become a bonded community, a group of learners with common experiences, reference points, and memories.

As we learn from Jim Trelease, author of the best-selling book *The Read-Aloud Handbook* (2001), when we read aloud to a child, we take the most important step of all in "raising a reader. . . . If reading to children were common instead of a rarity, we'd be facing fewer academic and social problems in this nation" (p. xiii).

As teachers, we need to help make books available to children, *both* at school and for overnight. We need to facilitate children being read

Figure 8–1
There is nothing like the magic of listening to a story.

to. Important ways to begin our literacy journey in first grade are to read aloud to children in class and help them have access to books they want to read in class and take home.

Overnight Books: Making Literature Available to *All* Our Children

Many children in our population *are* read to at home and *have* books available. However, a great many children lack these resources: books and people who are able to read to them. It is crucial that we level the playing field by giving all our children rich read-aloud and storytelling experiences. I believe that a powerful part of our work as teachers is to help make books and poetry and stories available to all the children in our classes, in school and at home. We also need to conference with adults about how to use these books, especially if people are not able to read or not able to read English.

In my book *Literacy from Day One,* I describe my overnight book program and many different literacy experiences that are an integral part of our curriculum. My first graders each take a book home every night for someone at home to read to them. *Literacy from Day One* details easy ways to manage this type of program and help children *and* their families have contact with literature.

Helping Parents Connect with Books and Stories

When I meet with parents at our first parent conference, early in the school year, I tell them about the overnight book program. If parents are not able to read English, I show them how to take a picture walk and talk about the story in their child's own language. Parents love this access to books and are very appreciative of efforts to bring books and stories into their children's lives. Many parents say things like, "I don't remember these books!" or "Where were these books when *I* was little?" They often mention that the whole family enjoys the books their children bring home. (See Figure 8–2.)

Figure 8–2 *Letter from parents about overnight book program*

Dear Mrs. Barrett - Dragan -

We wanted to let you know how great the overnight book program is. Christopher has actually learned to figure out words that he has not even had yet. He even surprises himself at how he can sound out new words. He brings home books that he enjoys & he'll read to us or we'll read to him. It's great that he gets to choose a book he is interested in and not forced to bring an assigned book from school for "homework"!

Hopefully this program will continue as he really looks forward to showing us how well he can read & we notice he has learned so much about all the animals, insects & dinosaurs he has read about.

Sincerely -
Mr. & Mrs. Jimmy Lew

Pairs of Books in Two Languages

In order to facilitate reading for parents who do not speak English, I have been collecting take-home books in Spanish and some other languages. I have several pairs of English and Spanish editions of the same book. Children may choose either or both of the books that are shelved together. We keep them faceout on our overnight bookshelves, one behind the other.

I'm now collecting pairs of books in other languages also, such as *Come Along, Daisy!* in English (Simmons 2003) and Arabic (*Eja, Dejzil!* 2002) and some other books in English and Tagalog. Children find it very interesting to compare the text in the paired books. This type of experience gives them a little taste of another language and culture. They can *see* the written language differences, which are quite pronounced. One child, Martin, was so excited about seeing Chinese writing that he looked at the Chinese book I showed him for days. He even wrote about the experience in his writing notebook.

The Excitement of Choosing Books

Children become so passionate about books that they hide them from each other (unfortunately) and must be stopped from leaping the tables when it's time to choose tonight's read. One of our class visitors, Linda Carlisle, a teacher from England, said she had never seen children so excited about picking books to read. "They *swarmed* those books!" she said, as she watched the children go back to their tables, write their titles in their book logs, and contentedly begin reading their chosen books.

By helping children have access to books both in and out of the classroom, we make it possible for them to become readers, become people who have active and real literary lives. We need to introduce students and their parents to the public library, in case they have not been there. Parents also need to be aware that through public libraries, they can borrow children's books and the tapes that go with them. This is particularly important for families who speak a language other than English at home.

And of course, we need to use the school library and make some of our own classroom book collections available as well. A lot can be accomplished with a minimum of books, although certainly a rich classroom library is something to strive for.

Building a Rich Classroom Library

Here are some ways to develop your classroom library so children have access to a variety of reading materials:

- See if you can borrow twenty to thirty books at a time, every three weeks or so, from your school library. If so, great! If not, use the books your students check out. Let children take their library book home overnight. Then keep library books in a separate place, such as under the chalk trays, leaning faceout. Allow children who *really* want to keep their library books themselves for a week to do so. Now you probably have about fifteen to twenty school library books left over that children may take home for overnight. It is especially important to keep careful track when writing down who is taking these books home, since your school library has signed them out to other children.
- Check out a number of public library books for extended teacher loan, if this service is available in your area. A note of caution: books are heavy! And you need to keep especially good notes on who has taken public library books home, since you are the one who is responsible for getting the books back on time and in good condition.
- Let colleagues, families of your students, and your own family and friends know that you are working to build up your classroom library. (When I was first trying to find some specific special books for my classroom, my husband, George, searched out a list of them and gave them to me for my birthday!)
- Purchase inexpensive children's book club books. Use points earned from your orders toward free book rewards.
- Attend library sales. Many quality children's books are available for twenty-five cents or fifty cents each. And they are already covered with protective plastic covers, and in most cases, are ready to send home.

Repair tears and damage first. Avoid severely damaged books and books you are not familiar with. Do study children's literature so that you have the knowledge to choose the best! Be selective. You can probably purchase enough quality literature books with a fifteen- to twenty-dollar investment to start your overnight book program. All you need to begin this program is one book per child and a few extras.

- Go to flea markets and garage sales. Often people, especially at garage sales, are willing to let books go for a minimal fee when they realize they will be used in classroom libraries.
- Swap books with colleagues. Visit and hold planned book swaps, or designate a special place in the teachers room for books up for grabs.
- Find out if your school district has a warehouse or other repository for books withdrawn from school libraries. Some of these older books are treasures!
- Write a grant to buy books for your classroom.
- Check with children in your own extended family. Perhaps they have books they have outgrown. Maybe they would be willing to trade books they no longer find interesting for a new book or a small number of books of their own choice. This can be a real win-win situation, but it needs to be handled carefully. There are special books that will always be meaningful to children. I believe it is important to encourage children to *keep* any books that are important to them.
- Check bookstores for sales, especially of remainders—books that haven't sold well and are sold at very reduced rates. Sometimes quality books are available. Peruse books carefully, and you are sure to find some special things you've been looking for. If you aren't familiar with a book, read it before you purchase it.
- Suggest to parents that children may enjoy donating a book from a teacher wish list to the classroom library to celebrate birthdays. If a child brings a book for the class, I put the child's photo on the inside cover along with the child's name, birth date, and current date.

Once you start building your classroom library, it is important that your first graders know what books are available and how books are sorted. (See pages 199–200.)

Book Field Trips

The public library is a wonderful place for a field trip. Children can get library cards, hear a storyteller, or listen to read-alouds, as well as check out their own books. It is good to help children become familiar with their local library. As part of our Family Literacy Program (see Chapter 5), we took parents and children to the library. Many parents from other countries had not been aware that they could use the library. And they were amazed at all the materials and services available!

Many children's bookstores have programs featuring visiting authors and illustrators. Often stores encourage students and classes to attend. These can be exciting experiences for children. It is worth checking with bookstores in your area to see whether children's programs are available. These can be excellent field trips.

In my school district we are quite a distance from any children's bookstores. I sometimes go to hear authors and illustrators myself, purchase a special book, and ask the author to sign it for my first graders. I let authors and illustrators know that my children are striving to create their own published books. Often when writers or artists sign a book, they write messages to my class, encouraging children to continue reading and writing!

Conferences and Other Contacts with Authors and Illustrators

I made plans just after September 11 to attend the annual Reading the World children's literature conference sponsored by the University of San Francisco. Because my friend Dr. Beverly Vaughn Hock is conference chair, I knew that Thacher Hurd would be in attendance. His book *Art Dog* was a great favorite with my first graders. This was a period

Figure 8–3
Sharing the Art Dog *mural with author-illustrator Thacher Hurd*

of time when my students craved many books about superheroes, and a dog superhero was also of great interest to them. My children *loved* Art Dog! Some of them were even convinced that they had seen him fly past our classroom windows, presumably protecting us by patrolling the skies.

I mentioned that I would be meeting Thacher Hurd at the conference and suggested to the children that they might wish to create an *Art Dog* mural for him. My first graders jumped at the chance and absolutely outdid themselves! Their mural was displayed at the Reading the World Conference, and I had the great pleasure of showing it to Thacher. I had my photograph taken in front of the mural with him so that I could bring it to school. And when Thacher Hurd signed the copy of a book I had purchased for my first-grade class, he thanked the children for the mural and drew a picture of Art Dog, paintbrush in hand, shouting "Touche!" (See Figure 8–4.)

The children were absolutely thrilled with the book, the drawing, and the special inscription. They loved the photos and all my stories about their mural. Although they couldn't make the trip to meet with Thacher Hurd themselves, it was as if he had visited our classroom and left something special behind. This whole experience meant a great deal to the children. And I think it made the idea of writing and illustrating a book a lot more accessible to them.

Figure 8–4
Special message from Thacher Hurd

Literacy Lights Up Our Days

In my first-grade classroom, we enjoy stories and poetry all day long. We weave books and stories and poems in and out of our class curriculum. Literature punctuates and illuminates our days. It's easy to fit in a short picture book as we stand in line waiting for the recess or dismissal bell to ring. (This is a good management technique as well as a suggestion for enrichment.) We can sing and chant poetry and songs on our way to lunch or as we clean up an art lesson. We discover a new poem on our way to the library and another after lunch. And, of course, we begin the day with a story, as we sit together on the carpet.

Through story we can take a trip into another time, place, or situation; we can even *become*, for a little while, another person (or creature!) as we live in the pages. Nothing enriches children's fantasy worlds like a great book. Words have spaces and places to tuck in and to live the story. Books give us the chance to learn about and see what it is like to be someone else. We can savor how words look and how they sound. We can take pleasure in the anticipation of discovering what they mean and how a story evolves.

Kay Goines

My literature mentor, Kay Goines, introduced me to the concept of an overnight book program in her University of California, Santa Cruz, Extension class. She also taught me about a myriad of quality children's books. She continues to be a major influence on me in this area. On my birthday this summer I spent a very contented day by her chair, listening to her read and discuss her latest picks from newly released children's literature books.

When I first met Kay Goines, in 1977, I was very discouraged with my own teaching situation. Many of my students spoke Spanish. At that time, I didn't. There were often speakers of three to five other languages in my classroom as well. I was attempting to learn Spanish to help me communicate with many children at my school who had limited English. I didn't realize it then, but I was also looking for a way to bond us as a group and create community. And I was searching for ways to create meaningful literacy experiences in my classroom—experiences that would bypass language barriers and capture us all. Through Kay Goines, I learned of many quality literature and picture books that do just that: transcend language difficulties and literally put us all on the same page, at least for part of our day together. These stories and poems give us beautiful language. They guide us and give us clues about how to live.

Kay Goines Says

When we read aloud to children, we help them see how to make good lives for themselves. We read to children so they know what it's like to be a human being. Books and stories teach us how things are for someone else. Story has been a guide throughout the ages. We need books about heroes: the kinds of heroes that make us feel we can be and do more, so we're not stuck with being less.

Kay's words and wisdom have guided me for most of my teaching career.

What It Means to *Love* a Book

At the time I wrote *Literacy from Day One,* a first grader in my class was so taken with a special book, *Avocado Baby,* that he chose it to take home almost every night of the school year. Oscar *lived* the story of *Avocado Baby* on a giant fantasy level. He later came back two or three times as a second grader to borrow the book. I always felt guilty I didn't give it to him, but it was the only copy I had.

Recently I visited with John Burningham, the author, at a book fair sponsored by the Bring Me a Book Foundation, Palo Alto, California. John had brought copies of *Avocado Baby* from England, where the book is still in print. I purchased several copies, including one for Oscar, but I wondered whether it would still be meaningful for him two years later. I found out recently, when I held a parent conference for Oscar's younger brother Cesar. The whole family came to the appointment. "I'm glad you're here," I said to Oscar, as I handed him a signed copy of *Avocado Baby.* "This is for you."

When Oscar saw the book, his face lit up like a beacon; his parents laughed and rolled their eyes. And Oscar spent the next twenty minutes reading the book to himself, to his younger brothers, and again, several times to himself. I really feel that the book will always mean something special to him and will always be a part of his life. And I assured Cesar that one day soon, when I had an idea about a book he especially cared about, I would have a book for him.

The Magic of Reading Aloud to Children

My first and most exciting goal in my first-grade classroom is to help children become passionate about books and stories and reading. To do that, I read aloud to them several times a day. It will not matter *what* reading program I use, or *how* I teach reading, if I do not ensure that books and stories are important to my children—an essential, crucial, part of their lives.

I begin reading aloud to my first graders as soon as we come together as a group on day one. I share the best literature available: literature I love, books that most likely will connect to the children's lives and experiences, as well as to our curriculum. (See Resources for some suggestions and many book lists.)

When I read to the children we have wonderful discussions and revel in words and ideas and illustrations. The books we find irresistible connect us as a school family. They enrich our time together and impact our lives. Those infrequent days when an assembly or other activity prevents us from beginning with a story just don't have the same rhythm, the same "starting the day together" feeling. On those days, everything feels just a little bit off.

I read to the children a number of times a day, sometimes more than one book at a sitting. I like to stop before the children are tired. I want them to crave more, not less, of a variety of literacy experiences. Children's capacity for concentration—their ability to relax and listen to a story—lengthens as the year progresses. They develop awareness of the rhythm of language, learn to rhyme, begin to play with words, and memorize poems and parts of stories they especially like. Memorized poetry is easy for them to read and gives them a way in to becoming accomplished readers.

Time spent listening to good literature also helps children focus and develop listening skills that will benefit them in all curriculum areas. And, of course, listening to picture books, looking at illustrations, and sharing comments are major ways for children to practice, comprehend, and strengthen oral language. They are also ways to convey information as well as teach ethics and moral values. Through story we see how other people handle challenges and live *their* lives. And the art in a picture book can bring children a museum experience between covers!

Reading aloud is an investment in the creation of readers. Children love stories, and the time spent this way is valuable beyond description. It teaches them that story is worth pursuing, investing in. Reading aloud to children lets them experience the end result of reading instruction—and lets them know that it is worth *their* efforts to learn to read and spend time this way.

A Book Reaches All of Us!

Once in a while I try to document, as closely as possible, children's reactions to a book I read. I do this when the children's response is intense or perhaps a bit unusual. Now and then I get an almost electric tingling up my spine as I read a book aloud. I feel as if this same sort of silent electric hum is coming from the children as well; then I *know* it's a book that is reaching all of us! A few of the books that have caused this response are *Where the Wild Things Are,* by Maurice Sendak (1988); *Goodnight Moon*, by Margaret Wise Brown (1991); *Lilly's Purple Plastic Purse,* by Kevin Henkes (1996); and *Angelo*, by David Macaulay (2002).

There are times when we laugh our way through a story, as with William Steig's book *Pete's a Pizza* (1998); *Martha Speaks* by Susan Meddaugh (1995); and *Chewy Louie* by Howie Schneider (2000). Sometimes we cry, as we did when I read *Charlotte's Web*, by E. B. White (1999), and *Stone Fox*, by John Gardiner (1988). I think that many books empower us, as we face recess on the big playground and other new experiences of first grade.

Overheard Overnight Book Conversation: Being Engaged by Books

One of the skills I've learned as a teacher is to become a good eavesdropper and a good observer. Yetta Goodman calls this kidwatching (2002).

Sometimes as the children choose overnight books and record their titles, I listen in on inspiring conversations. I recorded this dialogue verbatim in my spiral notebook the children call my Remember Book. (They have their own Remember Books, too!) I started documenting the conversation when Julian and Ricky had just chosen books for overnight and I heard them excitedly comparing titles:

Julian: I have reptiles too! We could study together!

Ricky: Yeah, we could read our books together! [*To me*] Could we read our books together?

Matthew: I need a reptile book, too!

Danny: I gotta get a turtle book!

Ricky: [*To me*] Could Matthew get a reptile book?

Julian: And could we read 'em together?

Four little boys were thrilled that they could read special books of choice together and learn about a topic they were really interested in. Other children scrambled to use this precious bit of early-morning time with friends and books they loved. It was inspiring to me to watch and listen to children interacting with books, enjoying illustrations and text, and experiencing the joy of sharing literature with special friends. And it was a great way to start our day together.

Providing Time to Read Books with Others and Alone

As shown in my class schedule in Chapter 4, I have two different timeslots planned each day for SSR (sustained silent reading), sometimes called DEAR time (drop everything and read) or, more recently, independent reading. One of these times, when we come into the room in the morning, is more social: children can read with a friend, in a group, or alone. The other time slot is later in the day. At this time children read by themselves. I tell the children that we are really lucky to have this time to read and practice. I remind Noe—and the other children (with Noe's permission)—that he couldn't tie his shoe a month ago, but he *practiced*. I stress that we have all learned things recently because we have done them over and over and gotten good at them.

Sometimes we call this special time with books our reading present.

The children know that when we are sharing books first thing in the morning, they are free to read wherever they wish, with or to whomever they wish. Some read to the classroom animals, particularly The Biggest Bear, the Giant Frog, and Caruso, our bear from Italy. Some children choose to read alone, others with a partner or a small group. A special choice they sometimes make is to read under the tables.

Where Are the Children?

One unseasonably cold April day, Sarah Jacobson, our speech teacher, came in to pick up a child and didn't see a single student. All the children were very much engaged in reading and discussing their books—underneath the tables! Sarah, always interested in what's going on with our class, just had to ask what was happening. On this gray and drizzly morning, it was warm and cozy on the carpet. I sensed that Sarah, like me, had an urge to crawl under a table and read with a friend. It took her a minute to spot the child she had come to literally pull out for speech. Sarah had just decided to have him come to her room a few minutes late, when he called out, from under the alcove table, "Luis isn't here today!"

Engaged by Books: The *Best* Thing

I feel that the best thing I can do in the classroom is to excite children about books and reading. The children *want* to read, they love books and stories, and so *their* big goal is to learn to read themselves. As Kay Goines expresses this crucial need for both books and *time* with quality literature, "We need to get our priorities straight. What is going to matter most in life, a phonics paper or a book we read?"

The Children Know What Matters

One of my first graders, Sabine, says, "Reading is for getting smart." The children talk a lot about this. They believe it. Ricky says that reading nonfiction is for getting knowledge and he bets I never had another kid who loved nonfiction and knowledge so much. His mother agrees! She said that Ricky never had any particular interest in reading until I began reading nonfiction books and making many nonfiction titles available.

Don't Neglect Nonfiction Books!

I believe we need to take pains not to overlook reading nonfiction books when we read aloud! This is a very important genre for children, and if they do not get time to experience nonfiction books early, it will be harder for some of them to get into them later.

Nonfiction books can be especially difficult for second language learners, until they learn something about the context and get some help with the specialized vocabulary. Prereading and discussing a nonfiction title before it is read to the group can set up children who are learning English so that the book is very accessible to them, too!

I like to bring in realia (real items) and magazine pictures to extend the meaning of these nonfiction books. For example, if we are reading about different kinds of trucks, I will meet first with ELL students and share truck photos, and some clear, simple information about what these trucks are doing. I'll bring in one or two small truck toys to share and discuss. We will go over the names of some different pieces of equipment and have a little time to get a jump on the content of the nonfiction title the whole group will enjoy.

Children's Thoughts About What It Means to Read

In early spring, around that time in the school year when children are really committed to reading, and have developed a lot of competency, I was very honored to receive a Celebrate Literacy award from the San Mateo County Reading Association of San Mateo, California. Winning the award was wonderful, and my children were very proud of me. Then I realized I had to write an acceptance speech. So, when I was wondering what to say in my speech, I asked the experts: my first graders. After all, one of our class mottos is *Here in our classroom, we help each other*. And these children were as involved as I was with the joys *and* work of acquiring literacy.

I wouldn't have missed my first graders' thoughts and ideas for the world. They gave me great insights about their thinking regarding books and literacy and learning. Their first response, very sensible, was that I should say, "Thank you for the award." Then they said, "Tell the people that we love books because you showed us how. And we don't write on them or tear them either. Like some other kids."

The children said, "Tell the people you helped us know how to read, and now we can read lots of things, and we're all getting knowledge. And we like stories. And we like the pictures. Tell them we love reading a lot."

CHAPTER 9

Reading Isn't Just Curriculum, It's a Miracle!

Reading teaches you lots of things.—Bridget

Reading gives my brain a push!—Darnell

You can learn to read when you are reading.—Gaby

You read, and you know!—José Manuel

I'm famous at my house for reading!—Esmeralda

When you know how to read you can read always.—Diego

—A compilation of some of my first graders' thoughts about reading

All year long, as we glory in knowing how to read, and getting good at it, I stress the purposes of our reading: we read this picture book because it's a wonderful story; the news so we know about whales migrating off our coast; the recipe so we can make corn meal muffins and eat them together. A favorite moment for me comes the day José Manuel drags a large plastic bag into the classroom, and says, "Teacher, this is a present for you!" He can barely lift my present, let alone carry it to school. He is out of breath and tremendously excited, and after I open the present, so am I. Inside the shredded and dragged plastic bag is a giant phone directory, all yellow pages. "It's so you can *read* it!" José Manuel says. "It's so you can read it and order us pizza!"

Clearly, for José Manuel, reading is about getting meaning from the written word, and I am happy.

A special and joyful goal of mine all year is to infuse reading into our entire curriculum and help my first graders connect meaning to the things we read. For most of my children, English is a second language. Typically, I have speakers of several different languages. They are very busy trying to make sense of the world around them, as well as learn to understand and speak English. Learning to *read* English is yet another difficulty.

I try to make our reading lessons as explicit as possible, by providing actual experiences and integrating reading and other content areas. I bring in photographs and children's magazines, share realia—interesting real items—and strive to make everything as clear as I can. The more I can help children connect reading to their own lives, and link it to their own prior knowledge, the more successful they can be. The written words will *matter*. Authentic purposes for reading are essential too, as José Manuel realized, when he thought through his pizza project and brought me the telephone book.

My Vision of Our Literacy Program: Children Have Got to Have It All!

I am always in awe of how much children can learn when they have good, all-encompassing reading instruction. Who knows what reading strategy, or combination of methods, will be the defining puzzle piece that makes reading clear and makes reading possible for a child? Children have got to have it *all*: read-alouds, shared and guided reading, phonemic awareness, phonics and word study, knowledge of high-frequency words, overnight books, literature circle discussions, and a writing program that supports all of this. Reading and writing are the push-me pull-you twins that enable children to crack code, discover meaning in the written word, express themselves, and soar.

Different learners will rely more on some of these elements than others, according to their own modalities and learning styles. But *all* the children need *all* the pieces to make learning to read—and learning to write—possible for them.

Our Reading/Language Arts Block

We begin with some very elementary activities: listening to stories, practicing alphabet letter names and sounds, learning to blend and segment words, learning to write, to form letters, and to play some games with our names and with titles of books we know. My reading schedule allows for a two-and-a-half to three-hour language arts block. However, aside from a strong focus on reading instruction during our reading/language arts period, I weave reading and language arts activities in and out of our days.

Our main block of time is very different at the beginning of the year. The plan changes as the year progresses. Early in the year, when children need to move around more, they learn to handle literacy centers and use them for about thirty minutes a day. As the school year goes on, time for independent reading gradually lengthens. Children come back from winter break more confident and able to do much more than they could just two short weeks before. Children take increased ownership of their independent reading. They are more involved in the books they have selected to read and think and talk more about what they have read.

Chapter 4 contains my sample daily schedule. Here is an annotated schedule for the reading/language arts block. If you just add "ish" to each time listed, you will have a better idea of how my day goes, for example, "Read-alouds, 8:50 A.M.-*ish*." Nothing is ever hard and fast.

8:25 A.M.–8:50 A.M.	Overnight books are returned and new book choices are made. Children read socially for about fifteen minutes: they read books *they* choose, with classmates *they* want to read with, or read alone, if they prefer. Other days we bring overnight books to the rug for word games, title riddles, and so on, as described in *Literacy from Day One.*
8:50 A.M.–9:00 A.M.	Children meet on the rug and listen to one or two stories. We enjoy a poem or two together. Often we read a poem we know together, shared reading style. The poem may be on an overhead transparency or on a poetry chart.

9:00 A.M.–9:50 A.M.	We begin our reading/language arts block: Write and read morning message. Shared reading using a big book or poem. Whole-group reading and language arts. Some small-group work with English language learners.
9:50 A.M.–10:10 A.M.	Recess.
10:10 A.M.–10:30 A.M.	Word study: phonics, word games, overnight book games (unless we already had time for this activity), and word wall words. Handwriting practice.
10:30 A.M.–11:30 A.M.	Children practice reading independently from small booklets, previously read guided reading books from book baskets, and other books of choice from our classroom library tubs and shelves. This time for independent reading grows as the year goes on. Ultimately, it abbreviates the time for literacy centers. I am teaching guided reading with leveled books during this period. Children are doing independent reading and centers, or as the year progresses, about thirty minutes of independent reading. We cut centers to two or three times a week, sometimes less. Children may also be working on their writers workshop stories during part of this time. I also do a little conferencing on independent reading during this period and jot down some anecdotal notes. (The schedule is *tight*!) With last year's schedule, I was able to spend more time conferencing during independent reading time. This year I use part of the guided reading time a couple of days a week to wander around and listen to children read independently and to talk with them about their reading choices.
11:30 A.M.–12:10 P.M.	Lunch.
1:30 P.M.–2:10 P.M.	Writers workshop (after math and PE). There is no choice about this time period. I prefer

having writers workshop in the morning, but a first-and-second-grade combination class this year impacted our schedule. First-grade classes were sharing children some of the time, thus we did not have a lot of flexibility with our schedules.

Phonics: A Great Tool!

As I mentioned previously, I believe fervently that in teaching reading, I first need to show the children *why* it is an important skill and enjoyable lifelong activity—by reading to them! Then, sometime after the story, or many stories, I can break down the learning and present phonics and word study lessons that children can relate back to some of the books and stories they know. Learning phonics, and learning about words, is easier for children and makes more sense if they have enjoyed the book and have experienced meaningful language and the story first.

English language learners especially need to have phonics instruction related to context-based activities if they are to get meaning from both oral and written language. We also need to link reading to hands-on activities such as readers theatre, mime, drama, singing, and drawing. This helps children who are learning the language get into it, internalize it, and make sense of it. (They also need this chance to have fun with language!)

Phonics is part of our literacy activities all day long, whether we are doing shared reading, doing guided reading, listening to a story, or reading a social studies or science big book. It is all melded together.

As my friend Beverly Vaughn Hock, professor of children's literature, says, "Teaching reading through isolated phonics—without the context of story, and some enriching activities—is like taking a trip without a map."

Phonics just doesn't sustain children's interest the way a story does. Story gives us *meaning* and evokes an emotional response. If I had needed to study computers in depth before I began word processing, I would be writing this manuscript by hand. My attention and focus just would not have been sustained unless I had first had some positive, *real* experiences with using a computer. I believe it is the same with teaching reading. We need some joy and meaningful experiences with listening to stories, talking about them, and connecting them to our lives. Then phonics and word study—tools for learning to read—will seem worth the effort.

A wonderful new program, *Phonics Lessons—Letters, Words, and How They Work,* by Gay Su Pinnell and Irene Fountas (2003), has terrific minilessons for phonics, using magnetic letters, picture cards, and other manipulatives. These can be whole-class activities, part of guided reading group time, as well as independent activities children do themselves at a center. The program comes with a binder of teaching resources. Everything is well laid out and easy to access. I find this to be a great supplement to any reading curriculum. The picture cards also help build vocabulary for second language learners.

When I teach phonics, I relate it, whenever I can, to literature, to things in the classroom, charts and poems, children's names, drawings, things that matter to us all. It is through *making connections* that things make sense. (Comprehension is so important. We aren't going to enjoy reading if we aren't getting some understanding out of it!) I also stress with my first graders that sounds and letters and words are magic *tools* for helping them read wonderful stories, like the one we just finished enjoying together. I believe that knowing this motivates my first graders to learn.

Children's Literature Connection

Children particularly enjoy stories that integrate a phonics plot line with phonics learning. Two books I especially like to use are *The Silent E's from Outer Space* by B. Preiss (1973), and *The War Between the Vowels and the Consonants*, by Priscilla Turner (1999). My class also likes to sing a song I made up for helping us learn both short and long vowel sounds. It can be sung roughly to the tune for "Humpty Dumpty."

The words are:

Five vowels in the alphabet: *a, e, i, o, u.* (we name vowels)
Each vowel says its own short sound: ă, ĕ, ĭ, ŏ, ŭ. (short vowel sounds)
Five vowels in the alphabet; some of them are long.
Each long vowel says its name: ā, ē, ī, ō, ū. (long vowel sounds).

—PBD

Phonics Reference Chart

I believe that children need a phonics chart they can refer to as they are learning sounds and accessing text. Our chart is a line of pictures and alphabet letters that goes across the front of the classroom. It reinforces learning whenever children look at it.

The chart shows each alphabet letter and a corresponding key picture. We learn the sounds and "skywrite" the motions to form the letters. Later on, we make literature connections and put a relevant book cover or drawing above each corresponding letter on the alphabet chart, for example, *Corduroy* and *Curious George* for *Cc*, *Madeline* for *Mm*, and so forth. Children can decide on and illustrate these drawings for our chart.

We can also add school pictures and children's names above specific letter cards. I build this multilayered reference tool *with* the children as we're playing with letter names and sounds. As we add on to our children's literature key picture collection, we create and illustrate an alphabet for the San Francisco Bay area: *bay* for *Bb*; *cable car* or *Coyote Point* for *Cc*; *Golden Gate Bridge* for *Gg*; *Transamerica Building* for *Tt*; and so forth. Now we have references that really give us help with our decoding and spelling. And our displays are full of beautiful child-created art, too!

Kinesthetic Practice of Letters and Sounds

At the beginning of the year when we learn *A* (letter name); *apple* (key word); and the "ă" sound, we stand and write the letter *a* in the air as we say, "A," "apple," and the short "ă" sound. We also have a motion we make for each sound, to help us remember. For the short "ă," it is taking a bite of an apple.

We use straight arms, draw in the air with two fingers, and skywrite the lowercase letter correctly. This is good kinesthetic learning practice and gives the children a chance to move and stretch as they look at the alphabet letter. It also helps connect physical memory, auditory memory, and visual memory of the letter name and sound to the chart on the wall. When children are writing, I sometimes see them making these motions as they try to figure out what letter they need.

Some of the children know these sounds and letter names and really do not need the practice. (They could be *reading* instead!) I do this activity in small groups with the children who *do* need it.

Relating Kinesthetic Practice to Handwriting

When we practice handwriting, we make the letters first in the air, making the motion and saying the key word, as just described. Children then write letters on their paper. In this way we make letters a three-dimensional experience and then practice them two-dimensionally.

When we are first learning letter formation, we trace over photocopied papers with large letters. We focus on one letter at a time. These papers are placed over pieces of aluminum window screen. I buy an inexpensive roll of this material at a hardware store and cut it on the paper cutter. I tape the edges with masking tape. We put the practice papers on top and trace letters with the flat ends of crayons. This has a great textured feel. (Pencils wear down too fast and don't have the same smooth ride over the bumps.) These screens are fun to draw on top of, too. Children enjoy this kind of handwriting practice. They also like to trace over the bumpy crayon letter with fingers to review the letter name and sound.

Figure 9–1 *Jesús practices printing with a screen under his paper.*

Also important for handwriting: Children need to hold pencils correctly. This is a problem because many children have been writing for some time by the time they come to first grade, and frequently they have gotten the habit of holding the pencil incorrectly. These habits are hard to change. As primary teacher Laura Darcy suggests, a pencil grip is a helpful solution. These are available at teacher supply stores.

Pat's Tip

Left-handed students find writing easier if they hold their pencils about 1/2 inch to 1 inch farther back from the pencil tip than right-handed children. (I did not know this until my university days.) I now know from my own experience that it *does* make a difference, both in comfort and legibility. I always seat left-handed children at left-handed places at tables, so that no one can bump their arms. Of course, at a round table, there is no left-handed spot.

Beat the Clock!

After I have introduced all the sounds (this takes several days), I set a timer and we see if we can complete the whole alphabet line, including letter names, key words, sounds, and motions, in five minutes, two minutes, or whatever time the children want to try for. Setting a timer helps us enjoy beating the clock, and gives us a finite, focused (and short!) amount of time for this activity. Racing the clock is fun, partly because we do it some days and not others.

Alphabet of Characters from Children's Literature

As the children are learning sounds and key words, we personalize our alphabet chart by adding the literature connections mentioned previously. We decide on picture books with titles or characters that begin with the target letters. I photocopy book covers, or children draw them, and we place these above the correct letter on the alphabet line. (Nursery rhyme characters can be used as well as picture book figures; or the key word could be a book title beginning with the target sound. Children can illustrate these as well.) Here is a list of some children's books I use to help us connect letter names and sounds with special stories that matter to us. Sometimes I have listed more than one book, in case one of them isn't available. I try to make sure the beginning sound of the book title or book character makes the correct sound of the targeted letter.

My children and I abbreviate this and say "Angelina," "Bootsie," "Cat," "Dogzilla," and so on.

Aa *Angelina Ballerina; Andy and the Lion*
Bb *Bootsie Barker Bites; Baby Beluga*
Cc *Cat in the Hat; Corduroy; Curious George*
Dd *Danny and the Dinosaur; Dogzilla*
Ee *Elmer*
Ff *Ferdinand; Frog and Toad Are Friends; Frederick; Farmer Duck; Flat Stanley*
Gg *Grinch*
Hh *Henny Penny;* Humpty Dumpty; *Hattie and the Fox*
Ii *Imogene's Antlers*
Jj Jack Be Nimble; *Jack and the Beanstalk; Julius, the Baby of the World*
Kk *Koala Lou; King of the Playground*

Ll *Little Bear; Lilly's Purple Plastic Purse; Leo, the Late Bloomer*
Mm *Madeline; Mike Mulligan and the Steam Shovel; Monster Mama*
Nn *Noisy Nora*
Oo *Oscar Otter; Olive, the Other Reindeer*
Pp *Petunia; Pierre; Pippo*
Qq *Quick as a Cricket; Quangle Wangle's Hat*
Rr *Red Riding Hood*
Ss *Sylvester and the Magic Pebble; Strega Nona; Snowman; Sleeping Ugly*
Tt Tigger; *Tough Boris; Ticki Ticki Tembo*
Uu *Ugly Duckling*
Vv *Very Hungry Caterpillar*
Ww *Willy the Wimp; Winnie-the-Pooh*
Xx Exit-Man (our own made-up character); *Axel, the Freeway Cat*
Yy *Yertle, the Turtle; Yankee Doodle*
Zz *Zomo the Rabbit*

Digraphs

Ch *Chicka Chicka Boom Boom; Chewy Louie*
Sh *Sheep in a Jeep*
Wh *Where the Wild Things Are*
Th *Three Little Pigs*

I hope these book covers, or drawings of favorite literary characters, are a memory jog or reference to help children remember the letter names and sounds. (See Figure 9–2.)

Overnight Book Games

We practice letter names and sounds as well as many different skills such as word families (onsets and rimes) through my overnight book program. (This program is described briefly in Chapter 8. See also *Literacy from Day One*.) I say things like, "Stand up if a word in your overnight book title rhymes with ________," or "Raise your hand if your book title has the sound you hear at the beginning of *Pete's a Pizza*." Children make up riddles, too.

File Folder References

Children have replicas of the alphabet key word chart on file folders at their desks. These file folders are personal reference charts. I make four different pages of things children are learning and duplicate them on heavy card stock. I glue or staple these pages to the file folders, front and back, to make first-grade "Cliff Notes." Here is a list of some of the items on the folders:

- Alphabet strip or chart: upper- and lowercase letters, showing key words
- Color words
- Number words
- Icons or drawings for left and right hands. (I outline *L* formed by left hand)
- Number line: 0–25
- Numbers by twos
- Numbers by fives
- 0–100 number chart
- Word wall words for the year, numbered, in alphabetical order

Folders may be individualized for each child with first and last names, addresses and phone numbers, and birthdays. These are things the children are practicing. This personal information is written on separate cards. These cards are affixed with tape rolls and covered with plastic contact paper. This way, the folders may be used again other years. I just remove the personalized information by taking it off the card, and pop on new information for next year's children.

This file folder can be a helpful reference chart for each child during language arts and math. It is also a privacy barrier that children may use if they wish to work without interference. Occasionally I ask children to use these folders or "set up offices" if they are doing an end-of-chapter math paper or other individual work. The folders reinforce things children will be learning in first grade and give them a place to look to find information they need.

Make Your Own Alphabet-Key Word Chart		Aa	Bb
Cc	Dd	Ee	Ff
Gg	Hh	Ii	Jj
Kk	Ll	Mm	Nn
Oo	Pp	Qq	Rr
Ss	Tt	Uu	Vv
Ww	Xx	Yy	Zz

Figure 9–2
Make your own alphabet key word chart

Introducing Our Word Wall— Words Are Treasures for Us to Use

A word wall is a collection of words, like a giant dictionary, that make up an ongoing display on a classroom wall or bulletin board. Children can use this collection as a visual reference point for words they will study, learn, and use all year. The word wall is a place to store and spotlight these high-frequency words, so that children can locate them easily. This structured wall or bulletin board keeps targeted words in sight *and* in mind.

Today, after eighteen days of school, we are kicking off our word wall activities with the opening of a wooden "treasure chest." I will share this treasure with the children as I pull the first five word wall words out of this simple wooden prop, one word at a time. I want to make this experience exciting and give children the feeling that something momentous has just occurred. Actually, it has. Being able to spell, read, use, and *own* five words is a big achievement!

The treasure chest isn't a necessity, of course, but I use this prop to make learning about words as exciting as possible. And I want to help children realize that words *are* treasures that enable us to express ourselves, communicate, and even think.

This year's class was completely captured by the treasure chest. They decided that we should bury it in the small school garden each Monday after pulling out our five new words and then dig it up again the following week. Usually, children are also very intrigued by the words we practice: *a, the, of, and, to*. They like the fact that the words are large in size and are mounted on different colors of paper. They are also intrigued by the idea that we can invent some games to help us learn to read and spell these words.

We need double or triple sets of word wall words so we can play with them and practice them. I keep them up around our shared reading and writing easel, and we refer to them as we write.

Visiting the Kingdom of Dictionopolis

Another time during the year I will read children excerpts from *The Phantom Tollbooth*, by Norton Juster (1993). In this classic chapter book, Milo, the protagonist, finds a tollbooth and a car in a mysterious box he opens. He sets up the tollbooth, gets in the car, and drives off to the land of Dictionopolis. Many unusual things occur in this country during his journey. Milo ultimately meets the King and Queen of Dictionopolis, who give out letters and words at a fair. The only thing participants need to do to keep these words is to learn to read, write, and spell them. When they can do these things, they get to keep the words forever! I explain to my students that when *they* learn to read, spell, and use the words on our word wall, they will get to keep them forever, too.

Ongoing Practice

We will add words to our word wall from September to April and will practice using and spelling these high-frequency words throughout the year. The word wall will be a constant reference on the bulletin board. Children will do a variety of activities as they locate words, celebrate them, and learn to write them. Today the children decide that they should play games with these words. Ariel's idea is that each table team should get to keep one word wall word for its very own. We decide we will think about all our game ideas and try them out.

The word wall words we use in my school district are on the high-frequency word list we use as part of our assessment three times a year. I add children's names and a few other words to the list. I also keep special word wall lists on hangers for important themes and events. We have word banks for holiday words, art words, science words, and so forth.

When I pull a new word from our treasure chest, we look at it carefully, noticing the letters and practicing spelling the word aloud. I print our words on copy paper and cut them out in such a way as to accentuate the configuration of tall letters, letters that fit on one line, and letters with tails. I then mount words on strips of colored construction paper. I use approximately five or six construction paper colors on our word wall. This helps differentiate words and facilitates our riddle work and the guessing games we play with words as the year goes on. When we are guessing words we're thinking of, the colored background is a good clue.

File Folder Reference Charts

Children also have laminated file folders at their desks with the same word wall words on them. For some students, it is easier to access the words if they are right in front of them, and they can put their finger right on the word. (See page 178 for more about these file folder references.)

Cut-Apart Words

As we talk about each word, we decide where it should go on the wall; I will put it up under the correct alphabet letter heading. I then print the word on a tagboard sentence strip and cut the letters apart. We figure out how to put the word back together, using a small pocket chart to hold the pieces. Children say the letter names and print the word on paper. I attach the little pocket chart showcasing the five words for the week to the whiteboard in front of the classroom and we use it in a variety of activities.

Magnetic Word Wall Words

I show children that we can practice creating our word wall words with refrigerator magnets as well as cut paper. I place small letter magnets, a steel cookie sheet or magnetic whiteboard, and large copies of word wall words at a center so that children can practice making and reading the words.

Literature Connection

I have learned a great deal about using word wall words, and about organizing for teaching phonics, through the book *Month-by-Month Phonics for First Grade*, written by Dorothy P. Hall and Patricia M. Cunningham (2002). As the title indicates, the book describes instructional ideas month by month.

Daily Practice

Hall and Cunningham list many activities for daily practice of word wall words. Using their book as a reference and adapting some of the activities, here are some things we do each day to learn our word wall words and help children to be able to find them on our reference bulletin board:

- Call out a word wall word and have children visually locate it on the wall. (As Hall and Cunningham say, children "glue their eyes" to the word.) I also tell children the color of the word (the background paper color) as a clue.

- We read the word together. We say the letter names and the word: "*T-h-e—the.*"
- We write the letters in the air and then on our arms. To write on our arms, we put the edge of our writing hands on the opposite shoulders, writing hand thumbs up. As we spell the word we tap our arms (as we say each letter) and move hands down as we name each letter. Then we write the words on paper. I do this in front of the children to model correct printing.
- We look carefully at the words, comment about whether there are tall letters, tails, and so on, and draw a crayon box or outline that just fits around each word.

The words for each week are always showcased in a pocket chart or corner of the whiteboard and take their places under correct alphabet headings on the word wall. We are all very conscious of finding these words in our reading. At my school we are fortunate to have class subscriptions to a first-grade weekly newsmagazine. After we read our magazine issue each week, children take yellow crayons and highlight any word wall words they can find. They love this word wall scavenger hunt.

Word Wall Puzzles

I like to give each student a cut-apart word wall puzzle each week, so that they can form word wall words with squares of copy paper. I create a paper with a space to put the letters and letters to cut out quickly. I ask my first graders to trace over each vowel letter with a red crayon. Children then practice moving the cut-apart letters around to make the words in the space provided on the paper or on their desks. They also have space to practice printing the words.

The practice paper I use (Figure 9–3 and Appendix) is similar to a sample page I saw in the book *The Teacher's Guide to the Four Blocks* by Cunningham, Hall, and Simon (2001).

I like using this paper because it is quick and easy for children to cut out the letters. It is faster and easier for me than making a set of letters for each child. I would have to pass them out, collect them, and then sort the letters later. With this activity, children are responsible for quickly cutting on the horizontal line and then cutting to separate

igure 9–3
Word wall practice paper

Cut letter boxes apart ← Print letters sideways, (tall size) | Words to Make ↓ | Print Words Here ↓

the letters needed to spell all five words. Then they write the words. This combination of forming words and then writing them solidifies children's learning. We can practice making new words as well, using these same letters.

I give each child an envelope to make in which to take the letters home and practice making their words. The children print the words to be practiced on the front of their envelopes.

A variation of this way to practice making words would be to use Hall and Cunningham's idea to make a set of letters for each child on tagboard or index cards. Vowels could be printed in red. Letter sets could also be photocopied on cardstock and cut apart.

Vary Word Wall Activities

There are many different activities we can do practice these word wall words. Another good reference is *The Scholastic Big Book of Word Walls* by Mary Beth Spann (2001). See also *Making Words: Multilevel, Hands-On, Developmentally Appropriate Spelling and Phonics Activities* by Cunningham and Hall (1994), and *Making More Words: Multilevel, Hands-On Phonics and Spelling Activities* by Cunningham and Hall (2000). The children and I really enjoy making up games together.

Here is a sampling of other ideas for learning word wall words. We do different activities each day.

- *Monday:* Introduce words. Spell them aloud and write them in the air and on paper. Draw a box to fit around each word. Attach the words to the word wall under correct alphabet headings.
- *Tuesday:* Spell the words, moving our hands down our opposite arms as we spell. Celebrate these words we are learning: Clap words. Snap and tap words. Whisper and chant them. Stretch out the sounds as we say a word; write words in the air and on paper.
- *Wednesday:* Write the words on a partner's back. See if the partner can guess the word. Write words on paper. Make up sentences using the words orally. Practice writing our word wall words.
- *Thursday:* Be a mind reader (Hall and Cunningham 2000). Children love this time to guess the word you have selected but not told them. Give children five clues about the word you have in mind. Children number their papers from 1 to 5. Children write a guess after each clue you give. By the last clue, everybody should have figured out the word.

  Here is the Hall and Cunningham list of clues, slightly adapted:

  1. It is one of the words on the board (always the first clue). It is ________. (Name a color. This refers to the color of the paper the word is mounted on.)

2. It has ________ letters.
3. It begins with the letter ________.
4. It ends with the letter ________.
5. It makes sense in the sentence: ________.

Word Wall Bingo

One of the activities I invented for my first graders is word wall bingo. I give children printing paper folded in thirds. Sometimes I give them a photocopied grid with nine boxes, with first-grade-sized lines printed in. The rules are

1. Choose and print *any* nine words from the word wall.
2. Use your best printing.
3. Practice reading and spelling the words if you finish ahead of the rest.

To play the game, I call out words at random, one at a time. If children have written the word I say on their papers, they circle the word with a crayon. To win, a child needs to have three words in a row, either horizontally or diagonally, and also be able to read back the words correctly. I choose an additional winner: the child with the best printing (printing I determine is better than mine!) or, some days, the most improved printing. I struggle to make sure everyone wins sometime.

Winners get their names written in a special winner's circle on the whiteboard. I draw a few cartoons, such as a blue ribbon or a crown, and write names there.(Children sometimes decorate the winner's circle.) I say, "The winners are ________ and ________!" And we all cheer!

In the past I gave stickers to the winners of these two prizes, but I have found that first-grade children tend to become very disgruntled if someone wins and gets prizes and they don't. It seems to be enough to acknowledge winners and put their names in a place of honor on the whiteboard or chalkboard. Other students do not seem to be disheartened by this, and all the children look forward to seeing their names up in the place of honor.

Some Word Wall Games

Here is a sampling of word wall games we play:

- *Beanbag throw:* Children take turns throwing a beanbag at a word wall. To get a team point, they must name the word they hit. For some reason this is a great rainy day activity.
- *Cut-ups:* I make word wall words on tagboard strips and cut the words apart. Each table team gets a set of letters. Each group works together to put the letters in correct order and read the word. A child from each group takes turns forming the word in a pocket chart and reading the word.
- *Scramble:* The children and I examine all the cut-up word wall words, which are reassembled in a pocket chart. Children close their eyes (good luck!) and I scramble one word. They take turns figuring out which word was scrambled and putting it back together correctly. Jesús, one of my first graders, invented a variation of this game. He decided we should hide the letters all over the classroom. In our final, modified version, scrambled letters to one word were placed partly hidden amid books on a chalk tray, while no one was looking. The child selected to be *It* had to find the letters and put the word back together.
- *Dog, Dog, the Word Wall Word:* This is a variation of a popular children's game, Dog, Dog, the Bone. To play this game, one child sits in a chair and the bone (or in this case, an index card with a word wall word written on it) is placed under the chair. The child who is the dog refrains from peeking and another student sneaks up and steals the word. When the child who took the word wall card is settled, the class chants, "Dog, dog, the word wall word!" The child sitting in the chair has three chances to guess who took the word. If selected or guessed, the student who took the word wall card gets one chance to read the word. Success means this student has a turn sitting in the dog's chair. If the child does not know the word, other students are called on to answer and take a turn in the dog's chair.
- *Rainbow words:* Children write the word wall on drawing paper using a crayon and writing the word with large letters. Then they change crayons and write the word again and again. Children say

and spell the word as they write and change colors after each completed writing of the word. Rainbow-colored word wall words result.

- *Painted words:* Children each use a small chalkboard, watercolor paintbrush, and about 1 inch of water in a cup. We say a word and locate it on our word wall. Children "paint" the word on the small chalkboard using plain water. Then they trace the word with fingers, trying to trace the word before it evaporates. If just a small amount of water is used, this doesn't damage the chalkboards.
- *Word Wall Seven-up:* Children love to play Seven-up. In this variation, each child who is *It* takes possession of a current word wall word printed on an index card. Seven cards are used per game. Other children sit with heads down, thumbs up. Children who are *It* touch other children's thumbs and leave a word wall card next to their hands. These children stand up when the signal is given ("Heads up, seven-up") and attempt to figure out who picked them. To get a turn as It, children have to correctly read and/or spell the word wall word, as well as correctly guess the child who picked them.

Rationale for Using Games

There are many pencil-and-paper games and activities that may be used as well. However, children also need time for active play, and combining educational activities with physical education games gives them the best of both curricula—an integrated learning experience! These types of games also give everyone some kinesthetic experiences with the word wall words.

Shared Reading

Shared reading is one of our first literacy activities. I read a big book, pointing to the words, and children enjoy the text and learn to read it with me. This shared reading time is a daily event, and a powerful one, as children interact with print, constructing meaning and enjoying the story as a group. We do shared reading throughout the year, sometimes reading large-print big books, poetry, and book excerpt charts that I make with the children, as well as overhead projector transparencies.

Shared reading and the idea of a book big enough for all children to read together came from the work of Don Holdaway (*Foundations of Literacy* 1984). He believed that schoolchildren would benefit from a nurturing reading atmosphere like the one surrounding the bedtime story at home.

When we have shared reading experiences, all children have success, and all have the opportunity to experience the material being read. They can grow in literacy in leaps and bounds and are not hemmed in by the level of the reading material or demands of expertise on their part. Children can relax and enjoy the story, learning easily and joyfully.

ELL Connection

Shared reading is an especially important activity for children who are learning English. They can gain facility in the language while being scaffolded by the group, as well as by the clear, visual illustrations. The pictures are a great help for making meaning clear. Children see the correlation between the story, the pictures, and the words, over and over again. This repetition helps them have a language to rely on.

Some Favorite Big Books

I choose my favorite big books for our first shared reading experiences. Among the books we read early in the school year are *Mrs. Wishy Washy,* by Joy Cowley (1990); *Mouse Count,* by Ellen Stohl Walsh (1995); *Sheep in a Jeep*, by Nancy Shaw (1997); and *Hattie and the Fox*, by Mem Fox (1992). I share the title and we look for the author's name. We take a picture walk and pretell the story we think goes with the illustrations. Then I read the story aloud, pointing to the words as I say them, using one of my many pointers. I especially like reading big books with repeating phrases or chants. We love saying story refrains together. I can't resist mentioning to my new first graders that they are *reading*—already!

Variations of Big Book Experiences

Another day during shared reading of the same story, I leave out words or phrases as I read, and the children fill in the missing parts as best they can. The group can figure this out easily as we read together. Sometimes I cover words with Post-it Notes, and the class figures out which words would make sense. Shared reading is really an enjoyable story game. We play scavenger hunt, locating words: "Can you find *fox*?" "How many times do you see *good grief* on this page?" "Which word rhymes with *sheep*?"

There are several ways for children to isolate and showcase the words they find:

- Point to the word or phrase with a pointer. It is fun to have a variety of pointers: commercial pointers, decorative garden sticks, unsharpened pencils with fancy erasers, and so forth.
- Place a wikki stick under the word. Wikki sticks are a commercial item sold in packages of assorted colors. They resemble small beeswax strips. When pressed on paper, they stick. Wikki sticks are a big attention-getting device because everyone wants to use them; everyone looks to see if they will stay in place; and everyone is looking at the targeted word! These may be placed under a word, to make a line, or formed into a circle or oval to isolate a word that way.
- Frames or masks cut from manila tagboard are also good for finding words. The frames are placed so that the word shows through the opening. I make the frame 4 inches by 7 inches with a 1-by-3-inch hole cut in the center. I add a movable Post-It Note to cover unwanted show-through text.
- Flyswatters (brand new, of course), with a rectangle cut out of the center, are great for framing words. Children love to hold these implements up to a word and let the word show through. They could also swat the word. I limit this, however, because it is a little hard on our books.

Other times when we are doing shared reading of a book we have spent time on, I say, "What do *you* notice?" This open-ended question gives children the opportunity to point out everything from a single letter *e* to words they know, clues they see in the illustrations, and so forth.

Literature Connection

A wonderful reference about using shared reading is the book *Perspectives on Shared Reading—Planning and Practice*, by Bobbi Fisher and Emily Fisher Medvic (2000). This book, written in two voices, has many strategies for using shared reading, as well as ways to organize for shared reading, applying techniques with groups and individual children, and how to use shared reading with a variety of texts.

Story Illustrations

Although we focus heavily on text, story illustrations give us much to discuss as we read big books: "If you could climb into the story, which picture would you crawl into, and why?" "Does the style of this illustrator seem interesting to you? Does it remind you of any other artist you know?" Children soon become familiar with the term *style* because we mention each of our own styles quite frequently. ("I knew this was Christopher's paper because of the style of the artwork, but we still need the name on top of the page." We also use the term *style* to refer to written work. "Hmm, this paper sounds like Christopher's style of writing." As Regie Routman says, "Style is the writer's voice."

We learn about different styles of artists and illustrators by sharing books together, as well as by viewing art study prints and having our *own* art experiences. (See Chapter 13.) Discovering the art media of each book is another adventure we puzzle over and often figure out. It really doesn't matter if we're correct in deciding whether these illustrations are cut-paper collage, airbrush, or watercolor. The *process* of noticing art, making comparisons, and relating our observations to our *own* experiences is the important part.

Acting As If We're Readers

Shared reading allows us to jump in and get busy reading right away. All the children have equal access to the text, because all learners are supported, whatever their reading abilities. Children nervous about learning to read find strength in numbers as they learn with the whole group. If children can't read yet, most of them don't realize it. This is a good thing.

These shared reading experiences enable the children to act as if they are readers. Reading along with me and with each other, they can soar into literacy competency without even being aware of it.

Big Books and Small Editions: Linking Shared and Independent Reading

I especially like to choose big books for shared reading when I have library editions or paperback copies of the same story. We read the big book first. Then, after rereading and enjoying the big book on another day, children can sit with a partner, share a small replica of the big book text, and practice reading a story they already know.

A related activity is to use these books at a listening center, so that children may further interact with the text while listening to the story. They can read along with the tape, and then even try reading without the tape, to themselves or with partners.

The Joys of Repeated Reading

A real delight, after we have spent a few days with a big book, is to see that the book becomes like family or a favorite toy—a valued item in our classroom, with a miraculous life of its own. Soon children can't wait to take over the pointer to showcase words they know, predict story happenings, and *read*. They laugh raucously, as if they have never heard these things before. Language skills are developing, and so is the ability to make sense of the written word. A lot of camaraderie builds up as children enjoy a story together, in groups large or small. The chance to spend time with big books they know and love is a wonderful literacy center activity for children. They also enjoy rereading stories we have written as a group, as well as reading interviews of individual children and other environmental print in the classroom. We may use the same big book for several days, and yet again many other times during the year. This is much like playing music CDs we like over and over. We replay the CDs because we like them and want to experience them again.

Rereading books we love is the best practice of all. The reading is easy and enjoyable. The experience propels children to want to *keep* on reading and make reading a permanent part of their lives!

Reading the Room

First graders also like to illustrate the large story retellings and shared writing papers that I write down for them on charts or tablets. The illustrations give clues and meaning to the words on the paper. These large tablet-sized pages can be hung on the walls, in sequential order, and children can read them again and again. They love to read the room. And they love having their own illustrations help make sense of the words on the wall. These are good word references, too.

I like to hang these pages in sequence in front of the top row of cubbies or from a wire or line hung across the back of the classroom.

Figure 9–4
Children love the camaraderie of shared reading.

Another easy way to put up stories and poems is to hang the chart or tablet paper from clothes hangers with built-in clips. These may often be obtained from department stores. Each hanger with clips holds at least two charts. I place charts back-to-back on the hangers. Children just turn over the hangers to read the other sides. These hangers may also be hung on pocket chart racks.

Other Types of Shared Reading Experiences

Once children get the hang of shared reading (just about immediately!), we can read many types of materials together, such as nursery rhymes and poetry. Children know the words; they have memorized them. Typically, we will learn a rhyme or poem and chant it, dance it, sing it, act it out, and enjoy it many ways together. Then, quite mysteriously, it appears in large chart form on the classroom wall, on poster board or manila tagboard. When this happens, usually after recess, someone almost always cracks the code and figures out what words these are. We all have a great "aha!"

We enjoy these poetry charts together and illustrate them, often by gluing on everyone's trimmed drawings to make a collage on the large paper. Before we make the charts, we have had many oral language experiences with the nursery rhymes and poetry. Then we have art experiences and create illustrations to illuminate the words. We talk about composition when we affix drawings to the charts. And then we share the reading and take pride in the whole experience.

Photo Poetry Charts: We Are the Stars!

Often our poetry charts are illustrated with large color or black-and-white photos of children in our class. I either make 8½-by-11-inch color photocopies at a local copy shop or make large black-and-white copies on the school copy machine. I cut and glue or tape these photos on the poetry charts with double-sided tape, after children decide on placement. They draw the rest of the chart illustrations with marking pens or oil pastels. These charts are very personal and very exciting for us to read.

I make sure everyone in the classroom is represented in photo poetry charts of their choice.

Oh, A-Hunting We Will Go!

This year's class fell in love with *Oh, A-Hunting We Will Go!*—a folksong retold by John Langstaff (1991) and illustrated by Nancy Winslow Parker. Children enjoyed the book so much they decided to bring things from home and act out the story. I photographed each scene as they assembled to catch a snake (using Henry's large toy snake), make a chorus for a brontosaurus, and so forth. We made a series of poetry charts of the song and illustrated them with the children's photographs and drawings. I later made a photocopy-sized replica of each photo chart, and children had their own illustrated books to practice.

Figure 9–5 *Children's photos make poetry charts come alive.*

"I Can Read" Binders

Another way we enjoy these nursery rhymes and poems is to have small photocopies of them. Each child has a special "I Can Read" binder. After we have enjoyed a poetry chart or nursery rhyme together, children love to illustrate their own copies of the poems and keep them in their binders. One day, a little girl named Lisa asked me, "Did you have a binder when you were a little girl?" When I answered affirmatively, she gave her binder an affectionate pat and said, "I'm keeping things in here from now on!" From such a simple act, a lifelong organizational habit may be born.

Children love taking their "I Can Read" binders home to show off the fact that they actually *can* read. To make these binders even more special, they decorate them with drawings or stickers, or slide in illustrated title pages. I am able to get binder donations from nearby businesses each year, so children get to keep their precious binders.

If You Can Sing Them, You Can Read Them

Some of my favorite materials for shared reading are songs. If we can sing them, we can read them! Reading songs they know is very empowering for children. It is easy to learn the words to songs when they are set to music—there is just something about music that carries us along and helps us remember. And when we already know the words to a song, we can *read* it as we sing! We added many songs to our "I Can Read" binders. (See Chapter 15 for more about reading music. See Resources lists for Chapter 15 for musical books to read and sing.)

Put the Story on the Ceiling

We can also use the overhead projector for shared reading, by writing the material to be viewed on an overhead transparency with transparency marking pens. Transparencies can also be made on the copy machine. Children may illustrate these projection sheets using the same pens. The pens come in many colors. These stories may be projected onto a whiteboard, a projection screen, a piece of white paper, and even the ceiling! Sometimes I aim the projector at the television set. (The black screen TV is the perfect size for projected math equations and illustrated story problems.)

Capturing Words and Other Tricky Doings

We also sneak projected words off of the chalkboard or whiteboard by "capturing" them with an 8-by-10-inch card stuck to a yardstick, or even a piece of white photocopy paper folded in half. Just reach up and get that word! After we read and practice a word we have seemingly removed from the whiteboard, we put it back.

Children love to use story and poetry transparencies on the overhead projector at centers. This special time to use the machine allows them to play with the story and control the story experience themselves. "Humpty Dumpty" takes on a whole new dimension onscreen, with the children in charge!

Another favorite overhead projector activity this year was to read retellings of *Pierre: A Cautionary Tale in Five Chapters and a Prologue,* by Maurice Sendak (1991). This class absolutely loved the story and couldn't get enough of it.

All these literacy experiences—reading aloud to children, shared reading, and having discussions about the story—also develop children's speaking skills. In addition, these activities help children concentrate, gain focus, and sharpen their thinking.

A Bridge to Reading: Photo Poetry Booklets

One of the best things about our shared reading using our photo poetry charts is that they *link* shared reading and independent reading. I was looking for a vehicle to excite the children about reading on their own and help them feel they could read. I realized that they were so positive about being able to read our big books and poetry charts that they needed their own miniature copies of these poems to keep and practice.

I made small booklets, each one with a poem we knew, by folding copy paper into four parts. These little booklets were easy to make. Each one featured the cutout small photograph from the big chart poetry title on the front and the words inside. I photocopied these and folded them. It was up to children to do the rest. I left some booklets on the top of each child's desk in the morning before school. When children came into the classroom, it was if the Tooth Fairy or Easter Rabbit had been there!

Children immediately began reading their photo poetry booklets, over and over, and were amazed that they knew how to do this. They

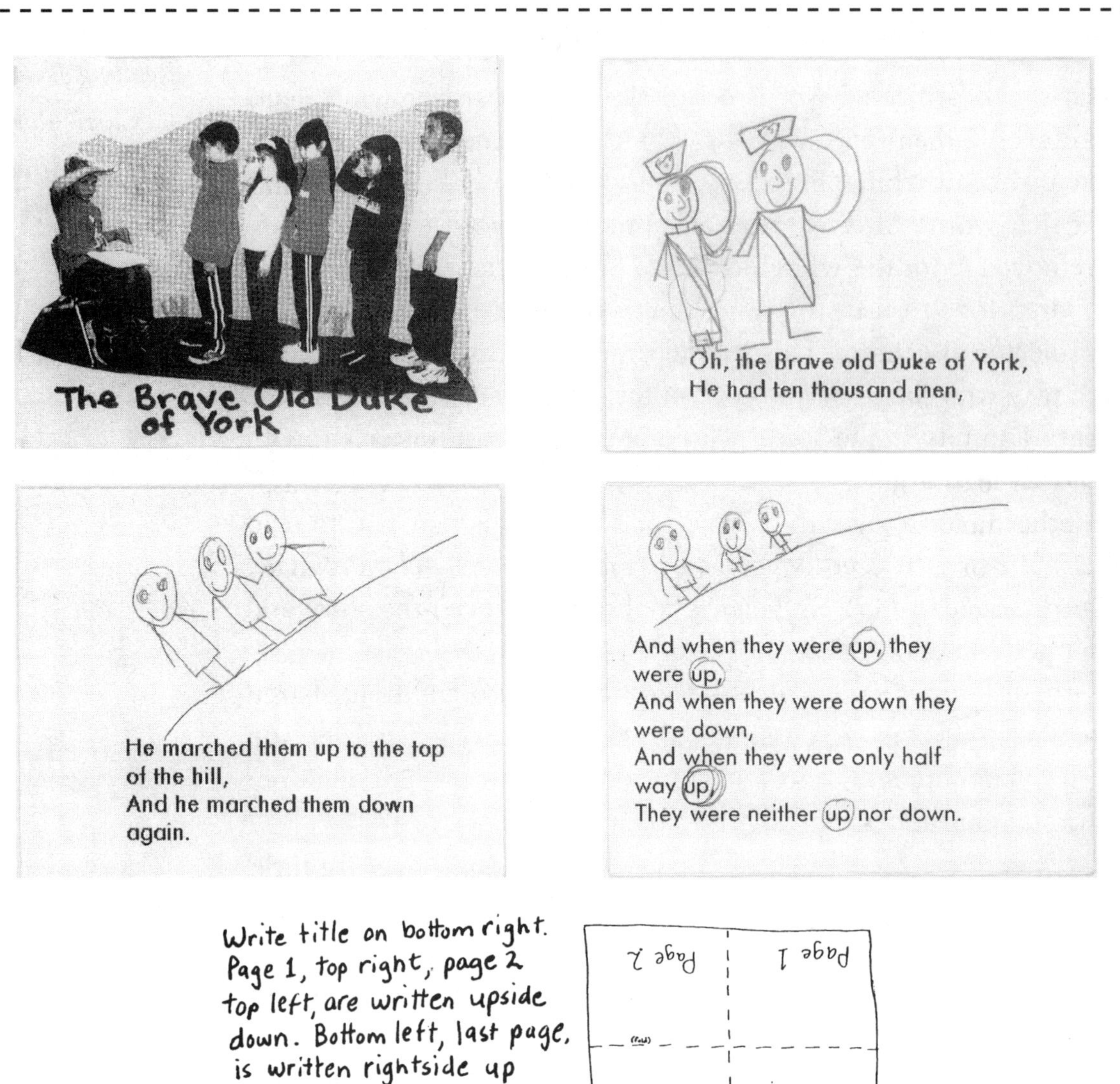

Figure 9–6 *Photo poetry booklet pages*

loved the photos and poems. After they read, they illustrated the booklets with their own illustrations if they wished, using pencils, colored pencils, ballpoint pens, or thin black marking pens. Before many days went by, each child had a collection of twenty or more small poetry booklets, all featuring children in our class as part of the illustrations. As our independent reading time grew each morning, children pulled their plastic bags out of bins and read and read and read. We added to these collections, periodically, for the rest of the year.

Launching Independent Reading

I recently replaced the words *DEAR time* (drop everything and read) and *SSR* (sustained silent reading) with the title *independent reading*. I want this to be a time when students are *really* reading books and materials of choice. I had begun to feel that this sustained silent reading period ended up being one big book browse, with not enough focus on the idea of really reading a book. And then another book. And another. . . . I thought maybe the idea would be more *clear* if we used a different name for the activity.

During this independent reading time, I want children to be reading. They have their social reading time when they come into the classroom in the morning. This reading period is for them to read alone.

I feel that our small photo poetry booklets and other easy reading materials help convince children that they can read, that reading is possible. I think these materials help children see what it is like to be a reader.

Just-Right Books

After the success of the photo poetry booklets, I began bringing little baskets of other booklets to each table and showing children how to choose just-right books. We sat on the rug together and I modeled how to choose such a book. Children practiced also. A just-right book has these qualities:

- It appeals to the child.
- It is in good condition.
- When a child begins reading, on any page of the book, she raises one finger for each difficult word that she can't figure out. If she raises five fingers (or fewer), the book is just right. If she raises more fingers, she puts the book back and tries out other books.
- It makes the reader feel good about reading!

As children become more and more confident in their independent reading, they begin using the labeled book bins on bookshelves to choose books they want to read. We practice here, too, locating books, removing them from the bin, and reshelving them correctly. As our classroom fills with readers, I spend time going from desk to desk, table to table, listening to children read, conferencing, sharing what *I* am reading. *Note*: I found I had less time for this with this year's schedule, so I devoted *some* of the guided reading time to it, one day a week.

Part of the power of independent reading is that *the child* makes the decision as to what book to read. And children can always change their minds about this, too, if something does not appeal after all, and pick something different.

Understanding Our Classroom Library Setup

I don't want this time with choosing and reading books to be a shelving-and-picking frenzy. I find it helps to suggest to children that they choose a couple of books and peruse them thoroughly before putting them back. One way to help children know how to choose books to read independently is to sort some books together. Most of the books in the classroom are already sorted in tubs and on shelves, and categories are labeled—for example, picture books about animals, poetry books, nonfiction books, and so on. However, I always seem to have books that need sorting and need to find a home. Children love sorting and deciding on categories and getting books organized. Each class needs a good book sort experience! Then children understand, from the inside out, how our classroom library is organized.

Figure 9–7 *Sorting books helps children understand our clasroom library organization.*

Watching a Love Affair with a Book

It is fascinating to watch children as they begin to be able to make sense of print on their own! One day I watched Cassandra choose *Green Eggs and Ham* for her independent reading book. I realized it was probably much too hard for her, but of course I would never have voiced that thought to her. I watched carefully as she struggled and persevered in her attempts to read this Dr. Seuss book. She read a bit of it to me, as I passed by her desk, but I didn't stay long. She seemed very self-involved and didn't seem to need or want any distractions. The only thought in Cassandra's mind seemed to be that she was going to read that book.

I watched Cassandra read *Green Eggs and Ham* every day for about three weeks. Some days I read a little of it with her, or she read to me. A few days she asked to take it home for overnight. By the end of the first week, she was reading the book fairly fluently and had read parts of it to some of her friends. All during the second week, she read it whenever she could, even taking it out for recess. When we went to the school library after lunch on Wednesday of the third week, Cassandra chose *Green Eggs and Ham* for her library book. I tried to be furtive, but I was so fascinated with Cassandra's intensity and deep rapport with this book that it was hard not to get caught watching her. I saw her walk back from the library (across a huge playground, and narrowly missing a pole) as she read *Green Eggs and Ham.* When we got to the classroom, all the children went inside. When I looked, Cassandra was standing outside the classroom door, still reading *Green Eggs and Ham.* All the children were in the room, and she was still outside, oblivious, reading this book.

It was a heart-stopping moment for me.

It truly is amazing what children can accomplish when they can follow *their* inner voices and work from their own great wishes and dreams.

Guided Reading

My first graders and I have had time for at least one read-aloud together and have done some shared reading and other whole-group reading activities. Most of the class is reading independently or engaged in literacy centers. (See more on this topic in the next chapter.) It is now time for guided reading, and five eager faces look at me from across the reading table. My first job is to convince these children they can read and maybe even to help them realize they are already reading!

Guided reading is a time for teaching small groups, or even individual children, to read books at their *instructional* reading levels. I determine these levels by taking a running record for each child. When they are reading at their instructional levels (92 to 97 percent accuracy), children have to struggle just a bit but can easily read the material with a short introduction and a little personal help from the teacher, if needed. (For more about about taking running records and teaching guided reading groups please see *Guided Reading: Good First Teaching for All Children*, by Irene C. Fountas and Gay Su Pinnell [1996]. Other great references are Regie Routman's book *Reading Essentials: The Specifics You Need to Teach Reading Well* [2002], and *On Solid Ground: Strategies for Teaching Reading K–3* by Sharon Taberski [2000].)

Guided reading is not round-robin reading, where children take turns reading parts of a story. It is not whole-group instruction with a lengthy skills-based introduction and twenty to thirty children reading the same story. In guided reading groups, children are spending their time engaged in the learning activity that will help them the most in their efforts to become literate: *reading*. Because of the instructional level of the text, there is some need for the child to use strategies to puzzle things out, but not so much difficulty that the text will be overwhelming. The text for each child is just right.

The group or child sits with me at a kidney-shaped reading table or on the rug. If we are reading on the rug, I give each child a small chalkboard lap desk.

I do a brief introduction to the book we will be reading, trying to get children involved with a minimum of time spent, usually three to five minutes. We take a picture walk together and get a sense of the story. If there are some unusual words in the text, I use them in my brief introduction so that the children hear the words in context. I point them out in the book or have the children locate them in their copies of the story. Children love hunting for words and finding them this way. The thrill of the hunt gets them on alert and set to read with more focus and drive.

We listen and look for patterns in the book and try to understand the way the book is structured. This helps children with their individual reading, too.

I sometimes think of guided reading as driver ed reading, because I get a mental image of my students driving and the instructor (me) at another set of controls, ready to help if needed. In this guided reading scenario, the children will be reading these books on their own, with me there to help. Before children begin to read, I ask them what strategies they can use if they get stuck.

As well as teaching children strategies, I think it is important to value and celebrate theirs—all the ways *they* make sense of text. My first graders and I keep an ongoing list. We talk about it and add to the list as we think of other things that work. It's fun to illustrate this chart, to give it another dimension.

Here is a list of sample strategies. Some of the ideas came from the children.

- Look at the book cover and the title. Think about what the title could mean.
- Look at the pictures. Take a picture walk. Tell yourself the story.
- If you get stuck on a word, think what word would make sense.
- Think about how the word looks. Think about other words you know that begin that way.
- Sound out the word.
- Get your mouth ready to say the beginning sound of the word.
- Blend: Make the first sound, the second sound, blend, and keep going. Let the word pop out!
- Find a little word you know inside the word you are puzzling out.
- Look for another word that looks like the problem word and has the same ending. See if there are any "word families" (rimes) in the word, like *ow* in *owl* and *cow*; *oy* in *toy* and *boy*.
- Skip the word you are stuck on; keep reading and then go back and put in the word that makes sense.
- Think about how *you* would write this if you were telling this story.

- Look to see if the tricky word is on the word wall or somewhere else in the classroom.
- Listen to other children reading, and "catch" the word when you hear someone else say it.
- Ask for help.

We isolate one or two strategies to focus on each reading time. Thus prepped, armed, and empowered, children then read aloud, quietly and individually. They point to or track each word as they read it. (*Note*: After progressing through three or four guided reading levels, tracking is no longer recommended, as it can slow down the child's reading.)

Reading with the Phonics Phone

I listen to all of the children read. Children each have a phonics phone to speak into as they read. This helps them to hear the sounds, blend, and figure out words. (See page 207 for more about phonics phones.) Phonics phones also cut out the noise interference of other children reading aloud. This helps some children concentrate.

I pass out the books in such a way that students are not all beginning their reading at the same moment. I want them to be on their own with this reading experience, with me available to make suggestions if they can't get past a difficult word or passage. When children complete the selected reading, they read it again. Sometimes I invite them to read to each other, or choose another child in class to go over and read to. My class is very receptive to this. Most children are honored if they are chosen to listen to another child read, and they are very supportive of each other.

We discuss the story briefly at the end of the guided reading lesson. This helps remind children that reading isn't just figuring out the words: it's knowing what they *mean* that makes reading worth doing!

Children may share with each other the word or words they are most proud of having figured out. They also share some of their thinking about the content of the story.

It is important that these guided reading groups are small—no bigger than six students, although I prefer a maximum of four. The children like reading this way. If I take too long with an introduction, a child is apt to say, to my covert embarrassment, "Can't we just read the book?"

Literature Connection

Leveled readers published by several companies for use in small, guided reading groups are crucial to my children's reading success. They can do it! They *can* read. Many children's literature books may also be used for guided reading if you know the reading levels of the books and can get sets of four to six books. See *Matching Books to Readers: Using Leveled Books in Guided Reading, K–3*, by Fountas and Pinnell (1999).

Flexible Grouping Is a Key

Guided reading groups are flexible. Children often move from one group to another. Frequently, one of my first graders will ask to read in another group. I always let them be the judge of what group feels the most comfortable. Sometimes children will choose to read in two different groups before deciding on one to stay with.

With small groups and leveled texts, success is within our grasp! My first graders have great enthusiasm and the satisfaction of completing the reading of many small books. I can tailor my reading instruction to the specific needs of each little group of learners. The children are *engaged* in reading, intense about it, and successful!

Here is a list of some activities I use as follow-ups to guided reading groups. (It isn't necessary to have a follow-up every day.)

- Sometimes we make booklets together using the same language structure as the story just read, with children contributing their own vocabulary and ideas. I type children's own stories for them on the computer and they illustrate them. They love these little books and keep them in their independent book bags to read again and again.
- I type up the story text ahead of time, and children cut it up and match it to the words in the book. A more difficult activity is to read the cut-up pieces and put the text in order *without* using the book as a reference. Children read this to double-check that everything is in the correct story sequence. This practices comprehension. When doing this activity, they are really rereading the story without pictures. I keep these story strips in a plastic bag with the books so that they may be used again.

- Children can make their own booklets (four-fold booklet, see page 198) using the same pattern used in the guided reading book. Students like to illustrate these and read them over and over.
- Children may also write their own story extensions or even prequels and sequels.
- Students love to go and read to someone else in class or even to a kindergarten child or teacher. (This takes prearrangement.)
- Make these books available for the children to read and practice by putting them in the group's book basket for independent reading time.

Word Study

Word study activities are also good follow-ups to guided reading groups. For some excellent minilessons and ideas, see *Words Their Way: Word Study for Phonics, Vocabulary, and Spelling Instruction*, by Donald R. Bear et al. (1999). See also *Phonics Lessons—Letters, Words, and How They Work*, by Pinnell and Fountas (2003).

Oral Reading Practice

One of the ways to help children gain fluency in reading is to help them *want* to practice reading. The children and I sometimes set up the puppet theatre as a television or radio station. Children love to practice reading so they can give shows to classmates. They especially love being the announcer or giving the commercial break.

Another activity that excites children is to use a microphone to read. An inexpensive karaoke machine can provide this experience. Just leave out the tape or CD, and the microphone will project the child's voice. Children who may not be motivated to practice reading get a boost if they want to use the microphone. Children practice reading first and then get turns reading into the microphone. They love to hear their great big voices!

Figure 9–8 *Children love to read into a microphone—great reading practice!*

Phonics Phones

Phonics phones are a way to facilitate "small voice" practice. These provide very quiet ways for children to read softly and hear themselves very well. Phonics phones are made from PVC pipes. One variety I purchased at the hardware store was a slightly curved piece of plastic. It was really a plumber's trap. As a child holds it like a telephone and speaks into it, he can hear his voice clearly. An even better phonics phone is made from a 4-inch piece of 1-inch-diameter PVC pipe and two curved elbows, one at either end (use a bandsaw to cut the pipe to the proper length). These can just be stuck together. This phone results in a much clearer sound. A third phonics phone possibility is a commercial product sold by the Candl Foundation in Huntsville, Alabama. This phonics phone is made from polished furniture grade PVC.

The phonics phone is a great teaching tool. It helps children hear words they say and read. It also helps them stretch sounds when they are trying to write. The phone isolates sounds and children can hear them a lot better than if they were just speaking without the phone.

See Resources (page 409) for more information on purchasing phonics phones from the Candl Foundation. Phonics phones are fun and motivating ways for children to practice reading.

Figure 9–9
Phonics phones help children hear themselves as they read quietly.

Children's Views of Reading and Reading Instruction

I work very hard to give children many different lively and meaningful reading experiences. One rainy-day recess in March, I decided to ask the children what *they* thought learning to read was all about. I told them I would like to take their ideas and their dictated paper to my students in the education class I was teaching at a local university.

The children thought this was a great idea. They gathered around the computer with me and dictated their thoughts. After much dickering and much discussion of ideas, they titled their opus:

> ***First Graders' Advice for Teaching Reading with Little Books and Lots of Other Good Books and Things to Read***

- We LOVE books, and we can all read now!
- We just like to read and read and read.
- We practice reading all the time and our teacher does, too. She reads Spanish good now, like way better.
- We sound words out. We blend. We go back when we don't get it.

- Sometimes we skip a word and go back. We figure out lots of stuff.
- We think what word makes sense, then we say it.
- We look at the pictures.
- We can find the word on the word wall and then we know what it is.
- You can read and read and then you get better at it.
- Maybe today you don't know, but tomorrow you'll get better and you'll know things.
- We explain it to the teacher when she doesn't get it.
- We can read all kinds of books: books with pictures, chapter books, ABC books, singing books, America books, horse books, more books with pictures, number books, Dr. Seuss books, star books, and everything.
- We read Valentines and letters, signs, math problems, word walls, spelling words, and things like "Don't run in the halls."
- We love reading a lot. It helps us know things. We practice and read a lot and we get to be good readers. And people read to us. And we write stories and letters and *everything!*

CHAPTER 10

Creating and Maintaining Literacy Centers

Kids like centers because we can figure out stuff we want to do there and then we get to do it.

—Jesús, first grader

Literacy centers are teacher-planned activities that children can work on independently. Small-group centers can be effective ways to give children choices about some learning experiences and give them time to move around, socialize, and take responsibility for some of their own learning. Centers provide a way for children to practice some of the skills and abilities they are acquiring. These literacy centers can take a great deal of teacher planning or be done more simply, with minimal preparation. They are *one* kind of meaningful activity children can be involved in while their teacher works with guided reading groups.

Rethinking Centers: My Personal Dilemma

I have been seriously rethinking and changing my use of centers over the past two years. I like having centers in place in my classroom. I take the time to show children how to use them, and I plan simple centers for them. But our time together is short. There is another activity I want children to be involved in even more than centers: independent reading. I begin teaching independent reading from our first day onward and provide time for it right away in my classroom. Gradually, as the school year progresses, I set aside more time for independent reading and less time for centers during our guided reading period. However, I try to provide for the children's free-spirited needs to play, invent, and explore materials through a free play time at another time during the week.

The bottom line for me is that I need children to have *time* for independent reading. I also need them to be able to work independently so I can concentrate on teaching guided reading groups. And I feel good about providing some free play time (separate from literacy centers), at least once a week, so that children can take charge of their own play and exploration. What I want children to develop more than anything is a lively, lifelong passion for learning.

The choice and balance between independent reading and literacy centers is a time crunch problem. There are some very good things about centers, but there just isn't room in my curriculum for sufficient independent reading time *and* prolonged center activities. I have taken a good hard look at centers because I want my children to get the best learning for the time they have available. I use centers more frequently at the beginning of the school year, when children are getting acquainted and also need to move around more. After our winter holiday break, I shorten time for centers, as our capacity for independent reading lengthens. I would much rather have children spend their priceless moments feeling the power, rush, and satisfaction of being able to *really* read a book than anything else I can think of.

Ultimately, my first graders work up to spending about thirty minutes or more a day reading independently, and perhaps as little as one or two periods a week involved with learning centers. I do feel my way with this and keep the centers up-to-date and ready to go—using center tubs, the pocket chart listing centers, and cards showing which groups of children go where. Even if center time is sparse, it is ongoing. The cards always let us pick up where we left off. Some days, centers are just what children need. And they *always* need some opportunities to wrap their minds around learning without someone else running the show!

Planning Literacy Centers

I plan literacy centers with the main goal of helping children focus on reading and writing. These centers have straightforward, uncomplicated titles and activities. Literacy or learning centers can be quite involved, with complex setups and management systems; they can also be done easily and simply. I have done all kinds of systems and setups, many of which kept my car in the parking lot very late on Friday evenings, while I figured out and organized centers for the following week. As a teacher who has spent time *tyrannized* by centers, I vote for the simplest and easiest of planning and management systems!

When I plan literacy centers, I envision a loose frame, or organization, around the materials that are grouped in tubs or set aside in certain parts of the classroom. Not only are simple activities and systems easier for me, they are much easier for children to handle. And when I plan *uncomplicated* activities, children have more opportunities to develop them further, explore the learning possibilities, and put their own spin on things.

Are Children *Really* Learning at Centers?

I have found that more involved centers often do not yield the results I worked so hard to plan: children may have their *hands* on materials and tasks, but do not necessarily have their *minds* engaged. They may feel rushed or unsure of how to proceed. They may be in a hurry because they want to move on to another center. (I do not make moving to another center an option anymore.) And children may not understand how to use materials at a center, even though a variety of suggestions and explanations have been given. It's like what happens when we give children an expensive, complicated gift and they play with the gift box. Children may not feel any ownership, or buy-in, since the centers were teacher-planned.

I believe children need to be assured they can explore and come up with some of their own learning goals and activities during this time at centers. Then when we come together and discuss our work, in a circle on the rug, we have a lot to share.

Sometimes observing children as they work at centers feels the same as taking days to shop for and cook a holiday meal and then watching it being demolished in twenty minutes. I find I just have to plan more simply, let go of some of *my* center goals, and give some of the ownership to the children. It's like saying, "Here are some great books and materials at this center. What can we learn here?" I find it exciting to be surprised.

If you have trained a classroom team of experts (see Chapter 4), cleaning up even the most horrendous mess is no problem. Children *want* to clean up, to know how to use materials and put them away, partly because they desperately want and need this kind of time to invent and explore. Another factor is that they want to be knowledgeable about materials and competent using them. This is the deal we make together: I show children—over a period of time—how to use and care for materials. Then I give them access to what they need; they take care of everything they use and clean it all up. They help each other achieve this. We also talk about ways not to make messes that are *really* hard to clean up. I point out that a long cleanup means less time for them to play.

Teaching Children to Use Centers *and* Practice Reading Independently

I start the children reading independently as soon as I can in the school year. I increase the time, little by little, so the independent reading time grows from five or seven minutes to a half hour or more. At the beginning of teaching children to use centers, I give them some independent reading time first, then train them in the use of one center. When they understand how to use this center, I teach another one, until I have explained several centers. The class needs to know how to use materials, what is expected at each center, how to work at the center and put things away. I also want children to know that unless they have an emergency, I cannot help them during this center time, since I will be teaching reading.

How to Get Help During Guided Reading/Center Time

Team or table managers, also called star helpers (see Chapter 4), are in charge of each center group. They are available to help and problem solve at centers during the guided reading time. Children are all encouraged to help each other as well. They take pride in this. I explain that sometimes children can help each other in ways a teacher can't. I also like to share my "best teacher" idea.

Who Is Your Best Teacher?

Trying to make my point, I occasionally ask children who their *best* teacher is—the teacher who will help them the most throughout their lives. They sometimes guess that I am talking about myself, or their parents, or their siblings. Usually, at least a couple of children figure out that I am talking about *them*! I explain that all of them are their own best teachers. They can help themselves better than anyone else can. All they need to do is try.

We talk about this idea frequently.

Introducing Centers

Each time a center is introduced, I explain it totally and go over the materials. We all participate in the center activity and clean up together. We role-play different problems and how to go to one of the team managers for help. We role-play successfully completing a center and cleaning up. And we role-play being in guided reading groups and not being interrupted! We also practice sitting in a circle at the end of center time, discussing problems and sharing our work and our learning.

Center Time Sharing

This end-of-center time for sharing accomplishments, problems, and work is what makes centers exciting. We sit in a circle so we can see each other as well as the things we want to share. I think this activity gives a stamp of approval to good thinking and gives children access to their classmates' ideas. Even five minutes for this pursuit can make a big difference in propelling children onward and validating both their work and their thoughts.

This center recap time is especially important for second language learners. Children have a lot more interest in expressing themselves when they are excited about learning they have just enjoyed. Because they share these experiences with others in the group, English language learners have increased ability to understand the language and participate in the discussion.

Simplifying Literacy Centers

I now plan for five, six, or seven somewhat generic centers. Some centers are kept in tubs to be set out (always at the same tables). Other centers, like our classroom library and listening center, are already in place. By figuring out set centers, I need to change things only a little and just update tubs or the listening center as needed.

I used to let children make their own choices at centers and even go to more than one center during this time block. However, I found that many children attacked center tubs like starving piranhas and were off to the next center as fast as possible. The room ended up looking like an after-Christmas sale. Things felt frantic, and I often felt that not much real learning was going on. Now I limit children to one center for each center period. They go to the centers as a table group or team. The team manager for the week is in charge of the group. If children have finished things they want to do at the center, they may read some of the additional books I have tucked into each center tub or choose other books to read from other places in the classroom. They clean up and put things away first, of course.

My centers pocket chart lists center groups by table team. Underneath the group number and list of students is the name of the assigned center for the day. Each time we do centers, I move the last team number on the right so it becomes the first number on the left. The other team numbers each move one space to the right. Every team number is now lined up with a new center activity.

If you organize your center groups by table teams, you need to remember that changing students' seats in the classroom needs to coincide with the beginning of each center rotation. Otherwise a child may be doing the same center twice in the same week.

A Sampling of Centers

Here are some of my main centers. As I mentioned, I make only about five to six centers available per center period. Some centers—the library and listening center—are always among the available centers.

Classoom Library Children read for enjoyment at this center! I always make sure some new books I have just read aloud are available. If these books are borrowed from the school library, children can check them out themselves the following library period. This familiarity with the stories helps them make good book choices when they go to the library. I also make sure to include fiction and nonfiction titles in our class library.

There are tubs and bookshelves (and rain gutters holding books faceout) throughout the classroom. Comfortable areas are set aside for reading. (See more about using rain gutters in *The Read-Aloud Handbook Fifth Edition*, by Jim Trelease [2001].)

Partner Reading Children read with partners, choosing from multiple copies of books. I keep a tub with double sets of books for partner reading. I also have single copies of books to be shared. I include books of many genres and reading levels. Children may sit side by side as they read together. They may sit in two chairs, next to each other (loveseat style), with one chair facing in one direction, and the other chair facing the opposite. They can hear each other read clearly when they sit this way. Children may also use phonics phones (see page 207) as they listen to each other read. Holding these pieces of plastic pipe, children can hear even whispered voices as they read. There is a bit of magic to using these phones, and this gives children impetus to read aloud together. I have different children model partner reading frequently. This reminds children how to make it work.

Sketchbooks We keep children's sketchbooks in labeled folders in a crate near this center bin. I organize folders according to center groups. It is easy for a monitor to put the correct sketchbooks in the tub for this center.

Keeping the right sketchbooks in this center tub is a job for a *permanent* monitor who gets it. This is a crucial organizational need, not a rotating, learn-as-you-go job. The sketchbook monitor needs to keep the target group's sketchbooks in the drawing tub, ready for use, and the rest of the sketchbooks in the crate file. It is unwieldy to store too many sketchbooks in the tub.

I make these sketchbooks from good-quality white drawing paper (twenty sheets of 9-by-12-inch paper) and a construction paper cover. I use a heavy-duty stapler; otherwise the sketchbooks fall apart immediately!

The sketchbook tub also contains a variety of art supplies, a good selection of drawing books, and some books with art prints. (See Resources lists for Chapter 13 for book lists of some favorite drawing books and art print books.) I ask children to use only one or two pages in their sketchbooks per center period. I also ask them to date their work. Of course, children may also write in these books as well as work on drawings and sketches. Many of them spend a lot of time perusing the books at the center as well.

Some ideas for art materials to keep in this tub are gel pens, marking pens, crayons, pencils and colored pencils, glitter crayons, and construction paper crayons. One package of each item is sufficient for a small center group. These materials are all kept in a basket or in plastic bags in the tub.

Listening Center Children *can* set up this center, but when they do, head set cords are likely to be twisted and tangled. I find it much easier to leave everything out, ready to go, on a spare table. When I don't have a spare table, children can use the listening center on the rug. I recruit another permanent monitor who understands how to set up this center.

The monitor keeps this center ready to go at all times: cassette tape, the tape player, and books set out on the table, with head sets on top of them. I ask children to follow along in the book as they listen to the story. Then they practice reading the story on their own or with another group member. Marking pens, crayons, pencils, and paper are available for follow-up writing and drawing. There is also a tub of additional books and magazines. Selections in the tub are changed frequently. The tape and books are changed after every group has listened to the selection, unless the book is a popular item and children want to spend more time with it.

An alternative to individual papers for listening center thoughts and responses is a stapled listening response booklet for each child. I use about twenty stapled pages, half with lines and half blank, for writing. The booklet has a construction paper cover. A monitor can keep the correct books at the listening center. I ask children to date their work.

I find I need four to six literature book copies for this center and one cassette. One way to acquire these listening tape and book sets is to use bonus points from children's book club purchases.

Pat's Tip

All the children are trained on how to use the tape player, but only *one* child may touch it during center time: the team or table manager for the week. (I have found that on those infrequent occasions when a tape player breaks, the cause has been two children competing to push the buttons at once.)

Dots color-code the push buttons on the player to help the monitor know what to do. A red dot means stop. A yellow dot or green arrow indicates rewind. And a green dot means play. If dots aren't available, color little bits of paper and tape them on the push buttons.

Some days at the listening center, I put on music and provide optional drawing materials. I vary the music from classical to such children's artists as Charlotte Diamond, Hap Palmer, and Raffi. I plug the head sets into either the record player or tape player, depending upon whether I have records, cassette tapes, or CDs.

Poetry Center This is a center where we enjoy poetry, rhythm, and rhyme. Poetry is one of our most evocative and versatile classroom activities. As Robert Frost, America's first poet laureate said, "Pretty things—well said—It's nice to have them in your head."

When I am teaching poetry to children, we begin with the wonderful oral language, and we learn to say the poem together. When we are familiar with the poem, we move to it, chant it, or recite it together. Only after the oral language experience will children be introduced to the written version on a 24-by-36-inch tagboard poetry chart. Because the words already live on the walls of their minds, the children realize they can read the poem. Later on they will illustrate it. The poetry center reinforces these activitics.

When they go to the poetry center, children illustrate three-hole-punched photocopies of the most recent poem we have learned. They read the poetry and keep the poem in their poetry binders. An additional activity at this center is to read the cut-up poem that I have printed on tagboard strips. Children may match the strips to the poem on the large illustrated poetry chart and then put the tagboard strips in order in a pocket chart.

Small versions of these poetry games are kept in envelopes with each poem printed in two or three different configurations on the envelope. Children put little tagboard pieces in order and read the poem.

The poetry center tub contains colored pencils and marking pens for illustrating poetry. It also holds a collection of poetry books for children to read, recite, and enjoy.

See the Appendix (pages 403–406) for several copyright-free poems, ready to be used.

Writing Center I have found that when children make their own books (see mini-book, Chapter 1), they can't wait to write in them. In his book *Making Books* (2002), Paul Johnson tells us that writing tasks are more successfully completed when children are engaged in the production of books. I keep a variety of paper, postcards, old greeting cards, and so forth at this center, as well as different kinds of pencils and marking pens. I make a few easy books that children are free to write in: simple list books (stapled paper scraps with a cover); simple four-fold books; eight-fold books from one piece of paper; and so forth. The center also has a stapler and loose papers (scraps of many sizes) so children may create their own books to write in. The items mentioned are *possibilities*. I do not make too many things available at the same time. I do not want to have so many papers and choices that children forget to write! Whenever a center feels frantic, I reduce the amount of choices there. The four-fold and eight-fold books are always a successful staple at this center.

Book Log Center This is another kind of writing center. At this center children are invited to use our book response form (see Figures 10–1 and 10–2) and write about books that are special to them. These book log papers have a space for illustrations as well. Children keep these book logs in pocket folders in the center tub. The tub also has a number of books available for reading.

Class Post Office Center This center is a variation of the writing center. Children need authentic opportunities for writing (and reading as

Name Bridget
Title Frogand Toad Together
Author Arnold Lobel

I red Frog and Toad
to geTher and That
made me Fell beder.
Cas it made me laF
So Frog and Toad WE Frensd Fore ver.

Figure 10–1
Book response (fiction)

well). An in-class post office is ideal to stimulate them to put thoughts down on paper.

I have a small cardboard box with dividers that I purchased from a stationery store. Another good source is Calloway House. (See Resources.) This box makes a great post office. It has dividers that form individual compartments—one for each child or every two children. These are labeled with all students' names. This is an easy literacy center. I provide many different kinds and sizes of paper as well as old greeting cards and postcards. A variety of pencils, pens, and stickers all add to the center.

A small stumbling block at this center is that some children feverishly scribble brief pictures and want to flood the mail system with

Figure 10–2
Book response (nonfiction)

these. As Postmaster General, I introduce the term *junk mail*. I require written messages and careful printing. Art is optional if a piece is to be mailed.

Occasional random checks can help reinforce expectations. I talk about this from the point of view of someone who is excited to have just gotten mail, but then can't read the sloppy message. When the center is on its way to working, postal inspectors can be appointed to take over monitoring the mail a little bit.

Word-Collecting Center Children *love* collecting words. I read them the chapter in Norton Juster's classic book *The Phantom Tollbooth* in which Milo, the protagonist, visits the Kingdom of Dictionopolis. One of the amazing things he sees there is a word fair. People are lining up to buy words they want to own. And the words are inexpensive: to keep a word, a character just has to learn how to spell it and use it!

Naturally, this center has a variety of dictionaries available. Many of these are picture dictionaries. There is a word-collecting book for each child, made up of pages of large grids, approximately four to eight boxes on a page (see Appendix). One goal for this center is to enjoy perusing the variety of dictionaries. Another goal for the center is to recognize, print, and illustrate words to learn and keep. I ask children to print the word of their choice first and then illustrate it before going on to choose another word.

During another part of the day, children enjoy playing a game we invented together: Teacher Versus Kids. In this game, children pick a word out of the dictionary, read it, and ask me to spell it. If I spell it correctly, I get a point. If a child (or group of children) catches me in a mistake, the class gets the point.

I use Teacher Versus Kids games to teach and review many concepts, from place value, to phonics, to any subject matter that needs some review. Children become very competitive, and the game perks up even reluctant learners.

A similar game, played by my friend Carole Larson and her fifth graders, is called Stump the Teacher. Carole's fifth graders meet together and select any word from a dictionary. They have several types of dictionaries to choose from. Before they can ask Carole to spell the word, they must figure out the pronunciation, as well as the definition or definitions. Then a child from the group pronounces the word. Carole spells the word and gives one definition. (Any definition from the dictionary is considered correct.) Carole's students are in awe each year. She has yet to lose a game. And her students have great vocabularies and dictionary skills!

Word Study Center—Phonics I use magnetic letters, pictures, and lessons from *Phonics Lessons—Letters, Words, and How They Work*, by Pinnell and Fountas (2003). The resource binder lays out a large variety of center activities.

Stamp-a-Word Center For this center, you need a set of alphabet stamps (see Lakeshore Learning Materials, Resources) and marking pens. I make stamp-a-word books by stapling a few "word collecting" pages. Children may stamp word wall words or spelling words (easily visible on the wall) or any words they like. Marking pens are much easier to use than a stamp pad and leave no mess. To stamp a word, students trace one alphabet stamp at a time with a marking pen and then press the stamp on paper. The alphabet set I use has dots, so children can use pens to connect the dots and trace over the letter stamps to make the finished words.

Read the Room Center It is helpful for this center to have clipboards (one per student), pencils, and scavenger-hunt-type lists of words or sounds to find. For example, a child may look around the room for words beginning with *b*, ending with *ck*, or having long *a* sounds. When students find a word, they write it down on the paper and then read it. This can be a good center when children need to move around. It can reinforce any phonics or word study.

Word Hunt Center This is a variation of the read the room center. Students have highlighter pens and copies of children's weekly newsmagazines. They look for and highlight word wall words or other words being studied. They also practice reading the magazines and discussing what they have read.

Television Station Center Children practice reading for a purpose at this center. A puppet theatre is set up, with a new sign reading "Television Station" covering the puppet show sign. Students at this center read books of choice and practice and practice. When they think they are ready, they read aloud on TV. One child may act as announcer. A great (although unnecessary) addition to this center is a microphone. (A karaoke machine with a microphone may be purchased inexpensively at a toy store.) This is a novelty center, but it makes reading practice fun and meaningful. The TV show may be presented at a class meeting or during center sharing time.

Big Voice, Little Voice This is a variation of the TV center. Children have access to the karaoke tape machine and microphone, as explained above, to help them practice their reading. They also have small phonics phones (described on page 207) for practicing reading to each other.

If a small gizmo makes it fun for children to practice reading and writing skills, I'm all for it!

Computer Center My favorite way to use computers in the classroom is to pair students up. (At centers, that means each computer has two children sharing.) Kid Pix is a wonderful program to use and provides children with many different art experiences. Pairs communicate as they explore a multitude of art media. I also like to use some reading and math games and easy word processing. Children enjoy recopying a sentence or two, or even a short story they have written. Then I print copies and they can illustrate their own stories.

Wee Deliver

Wee Deliver is a schoolwide program made available to schools by the U.S. Postal Service. It is an alternative, or in my classroom, an addition, to our class post office center. (To start a Wee Deliver program at your school, contact your local post office or call 1-888-332-0317 for a Wee Deliver starter kit.) Wee Deliver entails schoolwide effort and commitment. Each classroom needs an address, as does the office, the library, and other special places. Post office "employees"—upper-grade students—apply for jobs and take tests to become selected. Each student or school staff member who wishes to send a letter addresses mail with the correct address and return address, including ZIP codes. Then mail is picked up by upper-grade mail carriers and sorted and delivered by other post office staff. Mail is picked up and delivered twice a week.

Classroom Addresses and School Themes

Addresses can be created by students or faculty and can reflect a school mascot or other theme. At my school, Meteors is our theme. Classroom addresses reflect this focus. Addresses have such street names as Milky Way, Comet Court, Blastoff Boulevard, and so forth. Each wing of the school is named for a different planet. My classroom address, for example, used to be 3 Comet Court, Pluto, CA 01234. Now that I have changed classrooms, the address is 7 Stellar Street. Each classroom has a small mailbox, built by parents, to hold outgoing and incoming mail. Other equipment includes stamp pads and rubber stamps (all different) that reflect the school theme. These stamps were commercially made from drawings done by students.

Of course, this entire program could be modified. For example, stamps could be drawn on envelopes by students, or even printed or drawn on computer labels and then affixed to the mail. A shoe box makes a great mailbox.

The Wee Deliver program is a lot of work, but it is worth the effort. Children love it when the mail comes! And the program gives them real reasons and to read and write.

Wee Deliver Shortcuts

As much as I enjoy the entire Wee Deliver program, there have been glitches to work out. For example, the addressing of envelopes was taking a very long time for first graders, and I asked our third-grade book buddies to help us with this part for a while. One of the ways I eased this process was to devise a writing paper template. This photocopy has lines inside, with a place for the date, greeting, closing, and letter writer's name. The completed paper can be folded and taped or stapled. The reverse side of the photocopy has lines for the address, an outline showing the place for the stamp, and lines for the return address. This template helped children, but it wasn't enough. They still needed a way to access addresses of other people in school. So I decided to use our school pictures to make a photographic address book.

Photo Address Book

School pictures are taken early in the year. At my school, we get the type of pictures with little rectangular photos and children's names underneath. As soon as these class pictures are available, I photocopy them. I write the classroom address on the photocopies and keep these in a binder at the Wee Deliver center. Children can look up the addresses themselves. Some students still need help addressing envelopes. (Our postal service is quite strict and won't deliver hard-to-decipher mail.) But children *do* help each other, and the mail gets delivered.

The children came up with the idea of using the book of class photos and addresses as their own mug shot book. They look through it if there has been an unsolved problem on the playground. This helps them figure out the name of a child who has caused them difficulties at recess or lunch.

These photo address pages can be kept in a binder or folder, as described, or made into a permanent classroom display. They can be put up on a small bulletin board, under the chalk tray, or in some other accessible place for constant reference.

The Key: Keep Things Simple!

I have personally found that centers *can* be overwhelming, but it is possible to do them easily and simply. Teachers work too hard. This was brought home to me the day I took off school to have a root canal and had much more energy than I do when I teach all day.

As Regie Routman says in her book *Reading Essentials,* "You can't come to work each day enthusiastic about teaching if all you did the night before was grade papers. You want to be able to have dinner with a friend, go to a movie, read a book, cook for fun, reflect about what's just happened. We are not only role models for learning; we are role models for living" (2003, p. 202).

When we have interesting lives, and get to do some of the things *we* are passionate about, we are much better teachers. And we're happier too!

When I pare down the number of centers to five or six, just enough to accomodate all students in groups of four to six children, things are very workable. I believe in making centers easy to maintain and using them over and over again. Children are comfortable with the routines, and we can get things done! I no longer ask children to fill out papers checking off centers they have gone to or to turn in center papers to be corrected. I want to focus on guided reading while children are at centers, and I need to make everything else as simple as possible.

Each center tub or area has extra books, which are changed regularly, so that there is something to do if children feel their center work is done.

CHAPTER 11

Teaching Writing

From Scribbles to Authorship

Children's spontaneous quotes about their writing:

> *I got a pretty good story here!—Esmeralda*
>
> *My story is a good and funny one!—Danny*
>
> *Making the story is hard work, but it's fun!—Luis*
>
> *I love to write so I know what I think about stuff.—Cassandra*
>
> *Now* that's *a story!—Gaby*

Authors Day

It is a beautiful spring afternoon, and one my first graders and I have been looking forward to for months: today is our Authors Day!

The dismissal bell has rung, but children are still sitting at their places, with their handmade books and plates of cookies in front of them. They are expecting the arrival of family, friends, and other teachers and staff. Anticipation is high. Today is the day the children are going to read and share their own published books.

The time right after school is a good one for this special event, since many of our parents work morning and night shifts. Every child who chooses to stay has someone to read to: a parent, a grandparent or other family member, another teacher or staff member, someone else's parent, or me. Most children stay. The two or three who leave have

Figure 11–1 *Ricky shares his published book with his mom.*

planned their own events at home, with my help, and have taken their books with them. Some children have several books to share, others just one or two.

The atmosphere is very festive. Brothers, sisters, and other family members are listening to stories and admiring the artwork. Marek's mother tells her four-year-old that *he* can write his own books, too, like his big brother. Vanessa's older sister can't believe what Vanessa has accomplished. Parents are delighted and impressed. Everyone celebrates these wonderful triumphs.

Refreshments and Displays

As we planned our Authors Day, the children and I made many lists and had many discussions about how we envisioned our celebration. We decided to restrict our refreshments to an assortment of cookies to appease after-school hunger pangs. We do not want to spill food or drinks on our wonderful books! After all, our books and authors are the focus of this event.

The children and I began planning this affair early in the school year—the first day of school, in fact. As I describe my plan in *Literacy from Day One*, whenever I read aloud to children, I introduce the book, give the title, and say, as Kay Goines always said to her kindergarten class, "This book was written by ________, but the author couldn't come today."

Almost immediately after hearing me say, "The author couldn't come today," the children start grumbling. Robert asks earnestly, "Why does the person who writes the book not come?" This is my cue to let children know that people called authors write these books, and these authors might be too busy to visit them. I tell the children that soon they will be authors and illustrators themselves. *They* will sit in the author's and illustrator's chair to read their own books and share their own illustrations.

The Author Came Today!

Today, eight months later, book title charts line the room, announcing, "The Author Came Today!" Children shared pieces of 24-by-36-inch oak tag to make the charts. Every child affixed a tagboard sentence strip to the chart. Each strip lists a personal book title, as well as a small illustration and an individual photograph. I thought about inviting children to use a sentence strip for each published book but decided to ask children to choose one favorite among their own titles and use one strip each. I prefer limiting every first grader to just one sentence strip to avoid the competition aspect of our event and focus

Figure 11–2
Matthew reads his book to our third-grade book buddies.

Certificate

This is to certify that

____

is a REAL author and will write stories and poems and lists and wonderful ideas FOREVER!

SIGNED:____________________

DATE: ____________________

Figure 11–3
Author's certificate

on the celebration itself. The celebration is for all of us equally, as we take steps large and small on our road to literacy.

An additional benefit of making these visually exciting charts, aside from the fact that they are quite beautiful, is that the children love to read them and learn the names of their classmates' titles. Children also have many opportunities to read these published-by-children books, because an illustrated copy of each book (stapled, with a cardstock cover) goes into our classroom library.

This Authors Day event is full of glee, gloating, and showing off, as well as the pride of accomplishment. It does not last long—probably twenty to thirty minutes—but it is one of our best days all year. When children leave with their proud families, they carry with them the first edition copies of their published books along with certificates of authorship (see Figure 11–3).

But Can We Still Write Stories?

The day after our much-heralded Authors Day, the children were still elated—except for Gaby, who asked worriedly, the moment we entered the classroom: "But can we still write stories?" I assured her that we would and reminded the children that each of them could continue writing stories—forever! I heard more than one sigh of relief.

An advantage to having more than one Authors Day, if you can manage it, is that this event *really* whets children's appetites, both for writing and for sharing their writing. These first graders got an idea of what it means to be a published author and illustrator, and they wanted more of it! Without my saying a word, almost every child wrote and illustrated *at least* one more published story before the end of our school year together. I had to scramble to keep up with their efforts!

How to Begin

Every year I struggle with how best to help my first graders begin to write. I tell them that it took hundreds and thousands of years for people to figure out how to make marks that meant thinking and talking. I say it is magical to me that I can make a mark that means something important to me, and then someone else can read it and know what I feel and think. I tell the children that it took a very long time for people to learn this special secret, but *they* will be able to do this in first grade—right away, in fact.

The first thing we need to do, I tell the children, is to write things that are really special to us—and *we* get to pick what these things are! I tell them it is very important to me to be able to write things I care about, and that they will be able to do this, too.

ELL Connection

It is especially important for English as a second language learners to be able to choose what they are going to write about. As Stephen Cary says, in *Working with Second Language Learners* (2000, p. 71), "Writing from genuine need, writing from the heart, and taking that writing through editing cycles" are factors that are going to make a difference in children's growth as writers.

Writing Our Way

Children expect to learn to write immediately when school starts. This is the teachable moment, so, as I detail in *Literacy from Day One*, I like to have them jump in and begin.

I like to stress the mystery and magic and absolute wonder of writing with my first graders. I show them how our classroom animals practice writing their way at night, when we aren't in the room. I hold different stuffed animals in turn, and show how each one writes, starting with "scribble scrabble" from Caruso, our bear, who tries very hard to write. I hold an assortment of other toy animals, in turn, with marking pen in paw or claw, showing different styles and abilities, and in actuality, showing children different stages of writing development.

Writing Stages

I show the children different kinds of writing: scribble writing, making letters and pictures for words, writing even more letters to represent more sounds, and so forth. We talk about ways we learn. For example, when we were learning to walk, we didn't just take off and run around the block. (This image strikes first graders as absolutely hilarious.) We agree that now that we are writing, we are beginning to do it lots of different ways.

I end the demonstration by holding Spider Puppet and showing his way of writing—much more like the writing they will be learning to do. Spider, I explain, practices a lot when the other animals are asleep.

The children take this in but don't say much. They are thinking it over.

Greggie and the Great Invention

I want to empower my new first graders and arm them with stories as we begin to write. One of the children's favorite tales is the one I tell them about Greggie Larson, my friend Carole's son. When Greggie was about three years old, he discovered a great invention. He was watching his mother draw and write. On this day, Greggie took a pencil and paper and scribbled furiously, making lots of wild sideways marks.

Then he handed his mother the paper and stood in front of her expectantly, as befit the great inventor he was.

"What's this, Greggie?" Carole asked.

Greggie gave an impatient sigh. "The wind," he said. This very little boy had made marks that moved like the wind. He knew what those marks meant, and he expected his mother to know, too!

My first graders *love* the story of Greggie and the wind. It relieves them to hear of another child's successful tries at beginning writing, especially one younger than they are, with less sophistication and ability. Having classroom animals model the way *they* represent sounds and words also helps lighten things up for children.

When making plans to initiate writers workshop it is helpful to remember that writing has already been an important part of children's lives. Donald Graves, who revolutionized what we know about writing and young children, reminds us, "Children want to write. They want to write on the first day they attend school. This is no accident. Before they went to school they marked up walls, pavements, newspapers with crayons, chalk, pens or pencils . . . anything that makes a mark. The child's marks say, 'I am'" (Graves 2003, p. 3).

Discussion of Writing Topics and Shared Writing

Over the beginning weeks of school, the children and I spend a lot of time talking about possible writing topics and things we are good at. We talk about special things we have done that we want to remember forever. We make lists of things we know about and ways we are special. I regularly scribe for the children, writing down what they say on large tablet paper. They help me with the spelling, giving me letters, sounds, and words they know. This time for shared writing models for children an approach they can use when they write.

Our First Day of Writers Workshop

On our first day of writers workshop, I model a little bit of writing on the large tablet paper, or on the overhead projector, so the children can all see me listening, thinking, putting down the sounds I hear, and stretching words. I use the phonics phone (see page 207) to help me hear sounds. Children have phonics phones available too.

As a group, we read back what I have written. All this is done briefly, in just a few minutes, to rev up my new writers. Then I give each child a spiral-bound notebook and hope for the best.

Beginning Our Writing Notebooks

First I show the children how to put in today's date: our secret code. Then we raise our hands together, wiggle our fingers, and say a magic pledge: "We are going to do great things with these fingers and hands forever. We can make drawings, letters, words, and *stories*!" And off they go. The writing notebooks give children their *own* place for writing—the chance to try out expressing themselves through words and pictures and to learn to immerse themselves in this mode of self-expression and communication.

"I can't *do* this!" Joey says. "Come over and help me," he demands.

"Of course you can do it," I say as I scrunch down next to him. It takes a while to convince him, but finally he makes marks and we read them back together.

Carlos writes prolifically, long strings of letters. I compliment him and ask him what this says. "I don't know!" Carlos says emphatically. He just can't believe I'm asking him. "I can't read yet!" he tells me.

I explain to Carlos that he is probably the only person who knows what those marks say. When that doesn't work, I ask him what he *wants* those words to say. Now he remembers that they say, "I wish I had a little baby kitty and two doggies and I would take care of them always."

Carlos and Joey both have written something really important that they want to remember, and we are on our way.

Giving Support to Beginning Writers

I wander around the room, walking, stooping, kneeling, and sitting: watching children write and draw. I make supportive comments, help s-t-r-e-t-ch words, and listen to my neophyte writers. Joey is not happy with the phonics phone. He tells me he has ordered pizza, but it hasn't come. "This is a dumb phone," he says.

After children have been working for a few minutes, I sit with a few of them and we chat about their writing. I ask questions and try to give suggestions that will help children extend their thinking, illuminate their text. I want my first graders to know that I am really interested in their thinking and their writing.

When Edwin writes (with a mixture of letters and squiggles) that he taught his fish how to play dead, I genuinely have to know how he did that. I suggest that he write down this information, as it will be really interesting for his readers to know. In the course of listening to Edwin's training techniques, I am also privileged to learn how he teaches his fish to eat on command.

"I just say 'Go eat!' to them, and they do," he says.

Using a pencil, I lightly write down what children have written (as they explain their writing to me) so that we will be able to read their work on another day. This enables me to look back and see what the child does know: left-to-right direction of print, beginning sounds, ending sounds, capital letters at beginning of sentences, periods at the end, and so forth. When children are writing using their own symbols or strings of letters, this writing can be hard to figure out later without some kind of transcription. When I have the record of the child's explanation of what the writing says, I can also see if there is correspondence between the letters she wrote down and the words she spoke.

Just Get Them Writing!

The main thing with first-grade writers workshop, especially at the beginning of the year, and with second language learners, is to cajole children into getting something down on their papers. Sometimes I tell them that the words are in the paper. They just need to make *their* kind of marks or symbols and their words will be there.

An Overview of Our Editing Cycle

As children get things down on paper (squiggles, marks, letters, words, and sentences), they practice reading what they have written and read to me. I make light pencil transcriptions so *I* know. I type these, and children illustrate them and read them again. We keep these papers in

Figure 11–4
Crystal shares her writing with Banana Breath.

our writing folders (hanging folders for all our writing). A little later on in the year, children check that word wall words are spelled correctly when we have our editing conference. They also check for capitals and periods. I send them back a few times to make these corrections. They can get help from friends if they wish.

I type the final copy and give the child a cardstock cover. The cover is not stapled on yet. Children illustrate their stories using black marking pens, and I run off a copy for our class library. The original cover may then be illustrated with other media as well: glitter crayons, marking pens, and so on. A cover is decorated for our class library copy, too, and covers are now stapled on. Children love reading their own work, as well as books other children have written. We save some of these completed stories for our Authors Day celebration.

Day One Beginnings

At the end of our writers workshop on day one, we fold back pages and put the writing notebooks up on the chalk tray, leaning them against the whiteboard. (A few magnets keep notebooks from falling.) These beginning writing papers are wonderful to admire, and we celebrate!

A Visit from a Friend

Early in the school year, Banana Breath, my stuffed gorilla, pays a visit to read children's beginning attempts at writing. I translate for him, and he tells the group that their *brand-new writing* is his favorite kind of writing! This very real prop is a powerful stimulus. Children *love* to share with Banana Breath, who appears to really value their efforts and can listen to their writing attempts without fidgeting.

Some Children Converse as They Write

I believe it is important for children to be able to talk quietly with each other about their stories as they are working. This helps them develop their ideas and articulate their thoughts. (It is a good thing I believe in the importance of this, because it is almost impossible for first graders to get any writing done without chatting!) One day, during writers workshop, I hear an interesting conversation between writing partners as they work on their individual writing. I don't catch the beginning of the discussion, but this part is a *real* fish story:

"I eat little fish," Kevin says.

"I eat big fish," Martin says.

"I eat sea horses," Kevin replies.

Martin apparently decides not to pursue this discussion. Both boys resume writing, and that ends that.

My sense of this brief vignette is that these two little boys are benefiting a lot from being able to talk companionably as they write and draw. It is early in the school year, and they are just beginning to get the feel of being able to put to paper the sounds they hear, their way. They are getting the idea of what it means to be writers as well as readers. And they are learning that sometimes we don't know what we are writing and drawing and trying to say until we jump right in and do it.

Happy surprises awaited these two children. Before much time went by, both boys completed stories that were typed and published. I feel that one thing that led to their success was a classroom climate allowing them to confide, share, chat, and invent as they began learning to write.

I couldn't help noticing that neither child ever wrote about little fish, big fish, or sea horses.

Daily Writing Wrap-Up

We end our writers workshop each day by meeting on the rug to share and discuss how the writing went. I ask for volunteers to read something special they have written. Usually, I suggest sharing to one or two children as I see the writing evolving each day. I believe that this part of the workshop (usually lasting about five to ten minutes) really spurs children on. They want to share, and they may put a little more oomph into things the next day so they have something they can read to the group. Children get a lot of ideas from each other.

Interviews, Shared Writing Style

At the beginning of the school year, children interview each other, and I write down pertinent information on large tablet paper. This is a technique I learned from Hall and Cunningham's book *Month by Month Phonics for First Grade: Systematic, Multilevel Instruction* (2002).

At the beginning of the school year, one child takes a turn sitting in the interview chair each day while classmates ask questions. I print the children's words as I think out loud. I stretch words so they can see how I go about constructing print, for example: "Adrian likes to play with his hermit crab. He has a turtle. He likes to ride a cable car." We read these sentences together, and Adrian illustrates his page. Through these shared writing experiences, children learn to see what it is like to be a writer. And when we read their stories together, they learn about being readers as well.

Interactive Writing

After they grow comfortable with the shared writing experiences, children begin sharing the pen with me to write interactively on the same kind of large chart paper. My first graders love to illustrate these wonderful vignettes of what they think about and wonder as our year begins.

With my help with writing some of their thoughts, and children's use of the pen to write letters, words and phrases, and even sentences, we write about each other, tulips that will bloom in our garden, new baby brothers, and even advice to the president. The children's ideas flourish. We reread to see if we make sense and how the words sound. We check to see if our text conveys what we want to say. When the writing needs fixing, we figure out the spelling and fix it together, covering errors with magic correction tape, computer labels, or glue sticks and white paper scraps. I also show children how to fix things by just crossing out words or lining out mistakes.

I try to emphasize ways for children to fix or change things on their own papers when they write. By freeing children up to cross things out, I am also trying to suggest that they have another go at the word. This way no one needs to feel it is necessary to get it all right the first time around. I also show first graders my own first drafts, the messier the better, for these reasons. I show them a copy of a page that I don't think works, and demonstrate how I cut things up and put them in different order, even adding other ideas with taped-on pieces of papers.

For more on these ideas, please see *The Art of Teaching Writing* (1994) or *Primary Units of Study* (2003), both by Lucy Calkins.

Writing can be like a puzzle. Moving words around and thinking about them, deciding whether words say what we truly mean, is an exciting thing to share with children. I want them to know that I do this kind of thinking and modifying of my own writing until I am satisfied, and that they can do it too.

Shared and Interactive Writing Strengthens Our Individual Efforts

The beginning efforts of our writing journey—shared and interactive writing—live on the classroom walls on large pieces from paper tablets. They are a good reference for students, for spellings of words, sentence structure, capitals and periods, names, and so on. Throughout the year, with me as their scribe, the children tell many stories, make many lists, and organize their thinking as they talk about everything from the problem of playground balls on the roof, to favorite kinds of pizza, to the amazing transformation of our messy new caterpillars that are getting fatter every day.

These charts are read and illustrated, and read again and again. We love to read the room! Sometimes we send our writing charts to different places: for presents, to give our advice, and to glorify walls of offices and public buildings. Ultimately, I type many of these charts and the children illustrate the pages. These are made into booklets, and everyone gets a copy. We also keep a copy for our classroom library.

Shared and Interactive Writing: Additional Thoughts

As I analyze the writing we do, I now find that most of the whole-group chart writing I did in my classroom this year was apt to be shared writing, rather than interactive writing, because it takes more time to have children write interactively with me. Although I continued to do some large-group interactive writing, I preferred to use this method with small groups. Limited group size facilitates children having more turns to share the pen with me, short attention spans are honored, and we are able to get more writing accomplished.

For more information about shared and interactive writing, please see the book *Interactive Writing: How Language and Literacy Come Together, K–2,* by Andrea McCarrier, Gay Su Pinnell, and Irene C. Fountas (1999). Two other great references are *Invitations: Changing as Teachers and Learners K–12* (1995) and *Conversations* (1999), both by Regie Routman.

Word Wall Words

Our large shared writing charts help children know how to approach writing in their writing notebooks. Word wall words are another boost to scaffold writing. I teach five word wall words a week to extend our writing capabilities. Often we highlight these words on our shared writing charts and enjoy the scavenger hunts. The word wall words we practice and learn are not only on our word wall, but also on lists up at the large writing easel I use. We play word wall games and work with these words. We refer to them often and make them into familiar friends. As Regie Routman says, in *Reading Essentials* (2003), word wall words have to be *everywhere* and must be referred to frequently if they are going to be useful to us. (More about word walls in Chapter 9.)

Kinds of Writing Notebooks and Types of Paper

I have tried a variety of writing notebooks with my first graders: spiral-bound commercial notebooks and booklets I made by stapling many pages together using a heavy-duty stapler, for example. In the past I have tried stapling everything from blank pages to standard first-grade paper with a place for a picture on top. Last year I also ran off booklets of fifty photocopy-sized pages with standard first-grade-sized lines, which I spiral-bound. It is no longer possible for me to make these because of demands on our school copy machine.

I feel that the first-grade-sized paper, whether we use the commercial type provided or my first-grade-sized lines on photocopy paper, helps children with handwriting because it gives them more space to form letters. This size paper reinforces our printing practice. However, because the size of the lines is so big, children's stories are really spread out, on several pages. I think children have trouble connecting with the whole of what they have written. When they use full-sized first-grade paper, they also get in each other's way at their tables.

The commercial notebooks have small line spaces, more difficult for tidy printing, but a child's story and illustration can be seen at a glance without turning several pages. My feeling right now is that during our writers workshop, I am stressing the writing and the imaginative story. I am more interested in helping children see the story in its entirety when we are doing writers workshop than having them practice handwriting. We have time to work on legible printing during another part of the school day. (If I'm struggling to get an idea written down, I don't care about my handwriting!) Using composition notebooks or commercial spiral-bound notebooks, children can get a story and illustrations on a page or two. They can open these up for a two-page spread. This way my first graders can see it all, in one spot, and seem to find it easier to figure out what they have written and drawn.

What *Really* Matters

I think what *really* matters isn't the size of the notebook lines, if any, or whether first-grade writing is stapled, spiral-bound, or loose-leaf. What *really* matters is that children are cracking the code and learning to joyfully express things that really are important to them.

It is helpful to keep an accessible hanging folder for each child. The folder holds a variety of dated writing, with different kinds of papers, as well as the writing notebooks. Children can get their folders and decide for themselves what they will work on.

Empowering Children to Write: Bring a Treasure

One of the things I like to do to motivate children to write is to ask them to bring in something special from home—something they just can't wait to write about. When children bring *their* world into the classroom, they bloom! One morning, Frankie came to school full of repressed excitement, clutching a small brown bag. "Here it is," he said to me furtively. "Come over here and I'll show *you*, but nobody else." He waved me toward his desk and then toward the classroom floor.

We crawled under Frankie's desk together while the rest of the children put things in their cubbyholes and got settled. Frankie pulled out the treasure he had decided to write about and handled it reverently. "Look at this," he said, showing me a tiny white undershirt. "This is the little shirt I wore when I came home from the hospital." He put it gently in my hands, and as I held it, I could feel the power and reverence engendered by this little shirt. I could see what it meant to him.

Later that day, Frankie wrote about the shirt and ultimately published a wonderful story. When I read it I could really visualize newborn Frankie's trip home from the hospital. This was the first of many stories he authored.

We Try It All

As Frankie demonstrates, as children become more confident in their own ideas, they begin to express their feelings in their writing and tell about things important to them. Children try out other kinds of writing, too: letters, lists, and stories. Christopher writes a letter to one of our beloved custodians, who is ill, and Martin and others experiment with the First Steps template we learned about from Heinemann's Alison Mahoney when she came to visit our classroom. (See Figure 11–5.)

Name Martin Story Plan

Title: GO Back in Time Land

When	Who	What	Where	Why	Feelings
March sixth	Chris German Jose Kevin me	I saw The Bay Briu	Dinusor land	Bus	happy ~~sad~~

I saw the Bay Brij. Me, Kevin, German, Chris, Jose went on ~~the~~ bus at March sixth. We Felt happy. Dinuson land was ckool. and we went home we rid a Bus home I told my mother I had Fun souns like you had Fun yes i had los fo Fun.

Figure 11–5 *Story written with First Steps template*

A Special Time to Write

It is important to children that they have a writing time they can count on. They start working on stories mentally, saving them up to write down later. Lulu mentioned excitedly, as she came in from the playground one day, that she had seen dinosaur bones near the fence. "I think I'll write about it," she said. She spent a lot of time following up on her experience during writers workshop that week.

Karina confided to me that she had a problem at night because her little brother got up and went into her parent's bed. This left her alone in the bedroom. "It's the window," she whispered, her eyes wide and anxious. "It makes noises."

"You could just pretend it's your teddy bear fooling around," I suggested, grasping at straws.

Karina brightened right up. "Good idea!" she said. "I'm gonna write about it."

First Grader Bingo

One of the things the children most enjoy, after they gain some facility in reading and writing, is to play a bingo game they make themselves. I fold a large piece of butcher paper to make a square for each child. Each box is about 9 or 10 inches square. This is just a draft, so the size isn't important. Children think of interesting questions for a survey, such as "Has a pet bunny," "Likes the rain," "Plays soccer," and so on. We write a phrase in each box, until the butcher paper is full. This is like those get-acquainted "people bingo" grids teachers sometimes use at workshops.

I transfer all the information to a photocopy, with a box for each item (see Figure 11–7), and children move around the room to read their papers and have children sign boxes to indicate that those boxes describe them. This was a very exciting thing to watch as my first graders scrambled to read and write and talk with each other. They soon began networking and checking out each other's papers for ideas as to which child signed certain tricky boxes.

At the end of about fifteen minutes, most of the children had signed several papers and filled up a lot of their own boxes. "This is so much fun!" Martin said. "I could do this forever!"

I felt that reading and writing achievement took a giant leap that day.

Figure 11–6 *Children really get engrossed when they play First Grader Bingo.*

Likes snakes	Took a boat ride	Writes lists	Plays soccer
Has a pet bunny	Loves pizza	Rides a bike	Has a brother
Wears glasses	Best color: red	Sings a lot	Likes the rain
Likes to travel	Speaks Spanish	Likes to read	Draws and paints
Afraid of dark	Likes games	Has a sister	Has a kitten
Jumps rope	Likes the library	Likes to cook	Has a good friend

Figure 11–7 *Sample First Grader Bingo*

Written Conversations

A major new influence on my teaching of writing is the art of written conversations. This is a technique I have learned from Pat Gallagher and Gloria Norton in their book *A Jumpstart to Literacy—Using Written Conversation to Help Developing Readers and Writers* (2000).

I feel that this strategy is the most powerful and exciting new technique I have used in my classroom in a long time. As outlined in the aforementioned book, an adult invites a child to write, saying something like: "Would you like to write with me?" The adult then offers a choice of pens or writing materials. It is easier to follow the text of written conversations if two different colors or types of writing materials are used. Then the adult and the child write back and forth to each other, reading their words aloud as they write them. In this way, each of them knows what the words say.

Singing About Written Conversations

I created a small verse to familiarize the children with the process of written conversations. We sing my song together using a tune we invented. (Actually, our tune sounds suspiciously like "You Take the High Road, and I'll Take the Low Road".)

I write, and you write,
Then I write, and you write.
We take turns writing,
And we have fun!
—PBD

Piggyback songs like this one (new words made up for a purpose and sung to an existing tune) are a great way to celebrate new learning and to help concepts and facts stick in children's heads. In this case, it is meant to *celebrate* our time to write together.

Techniques and Strategies for Written Conversations

The technique for written conversations is one of very focused attention between participants and offers opportunities for intense, personal relationships, much the way an authentic verbal conversation does. My first written conversation in the classroom was with a child with whom I felt a lack of connection. Julian had just written a very interesting sentence about his toy soldiers, and I asked him a question on the same paper, using another pen color. (Of course, I asked him first if this would be okay.)

Julian and I wrote back and forth for several minutes and both enjoyed it immensely. I felt it was a turning point in our relationship and created a new bond between us.

I was tremendously excited to see what Julian could do with this writing idea. He seemed to really enjoy his personal time to write back and forth with me. This was a child who did not talk or express himself often, but he expressed himself very well on paper. This approach gave us a way to communicate. Julian gained some status in the class because of being the first child to get to experiment with writing this way with me. Never again did I feel a lack of connection with this child, and our relationship grew much closer.

Learning About My Students Through Written Conversations

I learn so much about my first graders through our written conversations. How else would I know that Ricky's uncle wrestled an eight-foot crocodile and took it to a wildlife preserve? (Ricky's Uncle Gabe, a wildlife specialist, felt that the reptile was in danger since the owner would only give it one chicken a day.) I learned that Esmeralda took her pretend puppies to the water slide and that Marek knew the Paul Bunyan and Babe the Blue Ox legend, really loved it, and had seen the statue in San Jose. Gaby let me know she was teaching her puppies to read their dog biscuit box. Julian wrote that his dog was brave and strong because it went to the "bafroom" outside alone at night. I was enchanted by these exchanges. (See Figure 11–8.)

The Impact of Written Conversations

I recently compared a lot of our written conversations to the children's writing notebooks. I feel that most of the notebooks lack the imaginative writing and passionate need to tell that I see in these conversations. The written conversations do what stories do—profoundly engage the reader and writer. I believe that the reason they are so compelling is that children know they have an immediate audience. When a child writes this way with me, I can respond that moment to the written words, feelings, thoughts, wishes, and dreams. And my little writing partner responds right away to me.

There are so many good stories in these written conversations. Some of the pieces are poignant; all seem powerful and intimate. I'm enthralled with the depth of the written responses from my first graders.

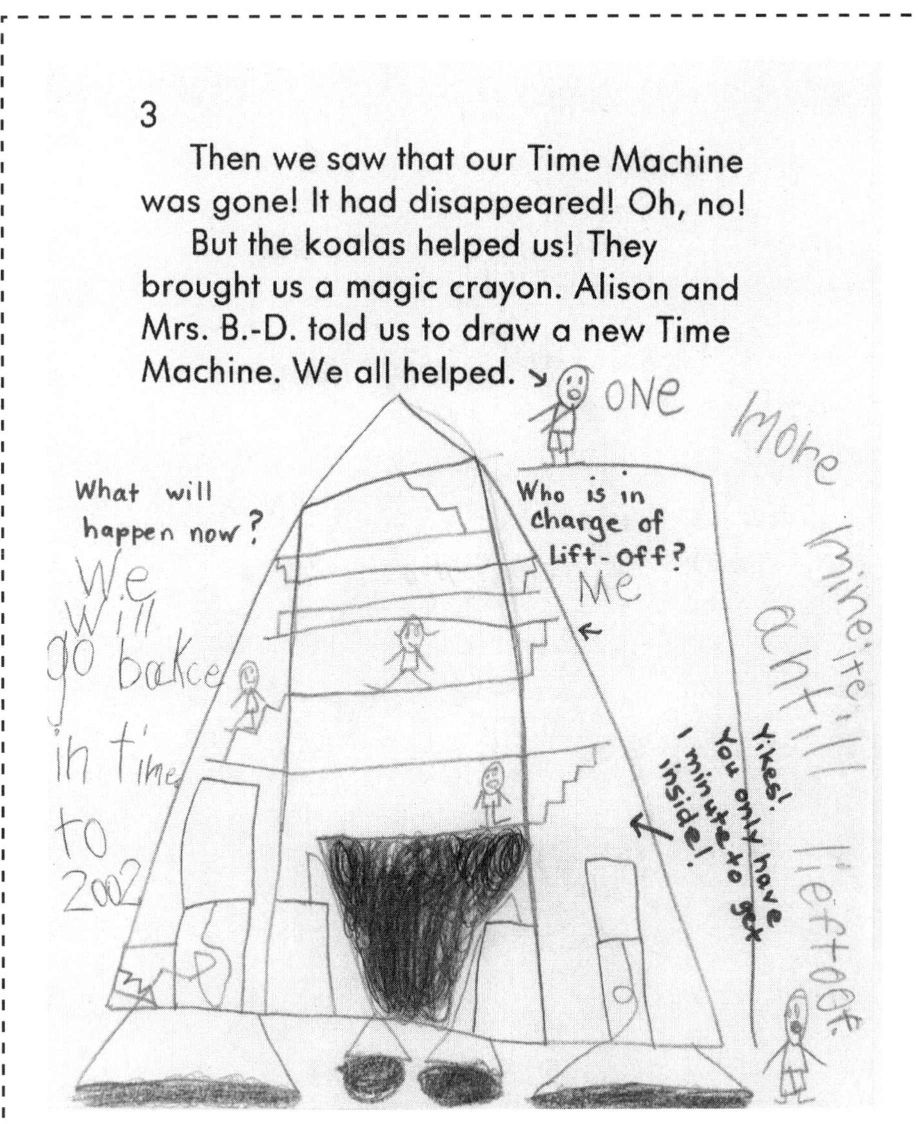

Figure 11–8 *A written conversation about a student's published story*

Touching Base with the Author

I asked Gloria Norton, one of the authors of *Jumpstart to Literacy,* and a friend of mine, whether she felt it was an appropriate use of the written conversation technique to use it in children's writing notebooks to help them develop their stories. She answered that there were no hard-and-fast rules, and as teachers we just use any and all tools we have, whenever we can make use of them. The technique of written conversations is a great addition to a teacher's repertoire of ways to help children write.

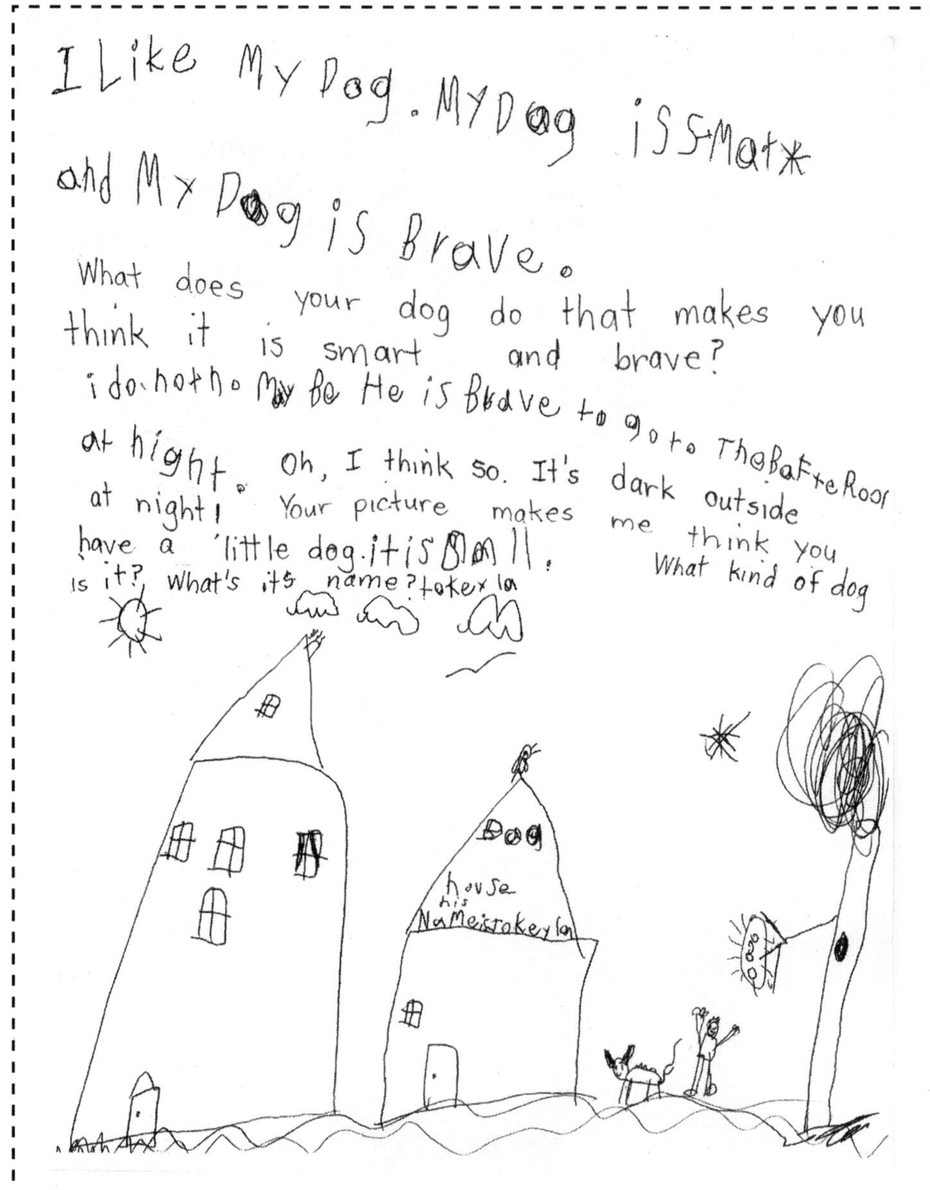

Figure 11–9
Julian admires his small dog—in written conversation form.

Written Conversations Can Be a Bridge

I have found that written conversations can also be a bridge to writing independently. One of my children, Willy, had a lot of difficulty writing during writers workshop. Quite frequently he lost his focus and got very little or nothing done.

I tried sitting with Willy and prodding him, writing to him, and helping him stretch words and put down sounds. This did not work awfully well. For one thing, no one else was getting any help or attention. And I found this effort with Willy to be something like that required for running a marathon. After just a brief time, I would be totally exhausted, and so would he. Through trial and error I discovered that if I folded a piece of copy paper into a small four-fold booklet and took dictation, Willy created incredible stories!

I wrote for him, and he just poured out a story, often completing one daily! Willy would reread each one with me effortlessly and then spend a happy interlude illustrating and rereading it.

Assessment

Written conversations are great assessment tools. They show graphically what a child knows about writing, as well as about concepts of print. I make a little T-chart for each child:

Knows/Uses	Doesn't Know/Use Yet

I go through written conversation samples and list things a child does and doesn't know. Here is a sample of things I look for: punctuation, concepts of print, beginning and ending sounds, short vowels, long vowels, blends, diagraphs, word families, and comfort level with writing.

Children's Literature: Another Way to Influence and Stimulate Children's Writing

Another thing that strengthens our writing efforts is literature connections. I read many, many books aloud to children during the course of the school year. It is the best and most joyous way we learn. In the beginning of the year, we enjoy talking about beginnings, middles, and ends of stories we have heard. This becomes part of the children's consciousness as we listen to and discuss stories. I also mention that all of the authors we love write about things *they* like, things they know about and are good at. We make lists—shared writing style on a large piece of tablet paper—of things the children are good at. These are *their* expert topics. We read them together.

Sometimes we make lists of what special authors and illustrators are good at. For example, the children agree that Kevin Henkes is good at "writing about kids and their friends." They think Eric Carle is good at painting and cutting papers and making pictures from them. It's a given that Maurice Sendak is the all-time expert on wild things and a wild rumpus! And they agree that Dr. Seuss is good at writing funny books.

As we begin our year of writing together, I love to ham it up, play with drawing and writing about things I'm good at, or even am *pretending* to be good at. If I can draw my picture and write about flying a plane to the North Pole, children get the feeling that the sky's the limit for them, too. Sometimes I tell my class that I don't know what I think until I write about it.

Some days during writers workshop, I give children blank paper and they make lists their way of their expert topics. I make one too. We have fun sharing these and in the process learn a little more about each other. I had no idea that Ricky was a turtle expert, Vanessa knew all about crayons and water slides, Danny had a lot of experience riding horses in Mexico, and Henry and Matthew were experts about baby brothers.

We steep ourselves, revel in the ways we are experts. We even draw ourselves doing or showing the things we know best. These drawings are trimmed and mounted on fadeless colored paper to make a large show-off mural titled "First-Grade Experts!" I type the children's words to put under their expert drawings. Confidence mounts as we celebrate ourselves.

Believing You Can Do It . . .

Writing and publishing with first graders is a process that takes faith and vision. Each year I cradle in my mind the belief that this really *can* happen: first graders *can* create readable, meaningful text—stories that deeply matter to them and are comprehensible to others. The surprising thing is that this can come about even if children begin the school year making unrecognizable marks and smudged hieroglyphics on their papers. A year is a brief time to go from illiteracy to members of what Frank Smith (1988) calls the Literacy Club. When you think about how long it took people to figure out this process in the first place, a year is really astounding.

I remember feeling at the beginning of the year that it was taking a long time to get things going. I remember thinking this during various other parts of the year, too! And I remember wondering if we *would* get to the place where the children could harness pencils and minds to communicate: to write their *own* thoughts and publish their *own* stories.

Next year I will look back and think often of our glorious Authors Day event and the children's genuine efforts to express themselves from their hearts in ways that were most truly theirs. Next year I will remember, and I will keep these vignettes in my mind as I begin again with another group of writers and illustrators.

CHAPTER 12
Math Matters

A few reflections from my first graders regarding what math is all about:

> *Math is puzzles.—Marco*
>
> *Math is figuring things out with numbers.—Joan*
>
> *Math is so I have five snacks in my lunch and I eat them all and now I have zero.—Christopher*

In his poem "Arithmetic," Carl Sandburg writes, "Arithmetic is where numbers fly like pigeons in and out of your head." This was just about my experience with math in school—these numbers were flying, and sometimes I never quite caught what they were all about. Listening to explanations and even seeing them modeled on the chalkboard didn't do it for me. I needed more concrete experiences, as well as time to express myself and explain my mathematical thinking. I needed the time and mindset to think as if I were a mathematician. Time was a crucial component for me because if I felt the least bit pressured, I became too *anxious* to think.

I find that most of my first graders have these same needs. They must have time to think about a problem and opportunities to use hands-on manipulatives, to draw the problem, or to use their own symbol systems or calculations to figure out solutions. They need opportunities to develop their own data and think of their own math problems. Working with partners or small groups can be helpful, too. Children need time to work on math concepts in depth, in a variety of ways. We need to slow down and give children time to process.

I believe it is more important for children to think through and puzzle over a few math problems thoroughly than to race through a number of problems.

What Will We Learn in Math This Year?

First-grade math encompasses a gigantic amount of learning material, from developing number sense, to recognizing numerals, to using them to solve addition and subtraction problems. Multiplication and division are beginning to be addressed at this grade level as well. The math curriculum also includes place value, geometry, measurement, telling time, counting money, making and understanding graphs, making patterns, adding and subtracting double-digit numbers, and so on. Many concepts are introduced and practiced at this time. Some material will be layered and practiced again in other years, or even again this same year.

The challenge with so much to teach is how to teach *in depth*. Children need math understandings that last them a lifetime, not a quick brush with many topics.

We Begin Our Days by Counting

Whatever math units we study, it is important that we integrate this learning into our everyday lives, both in and out of the classroom. Children need to see that there are *authentic* reasons we need mathematical knowledge and that math is something we use all the time. There are children who automatically do see everything in terms of mathematics. The rest need to have as many opportunities as possible to make these math connections. We begin by counting children each day as we walk in from the playground. We count girls and boys, decide which group has the most children, figure out how many more children there are in one line than another, and so forth.

We practice counting daily, for as long as seems necessary: by ones, twos, fives, and tens to one hundred. We practice counting backward, too. Sometimes we count in expanded notation format: "one ten and one; one ten and two."

Experiences with Math Tools

Children this age are capable of complicated, innovative thinking and very creative and clever ideas. They will be using sophisticated devices: calendars, clocks, number lines and charts, graphs, rulers, and geoboards. And they will be using symbols for numbers as well as for operations—greater than, less than, equals, plus, minus, and so forth—throughout the year. They need time as well as materials so they can *play* and understand what they are doing. And they need teacher support to help them move from concrete to abstract thinking.

Children come to school with a lot of intuitive understanding about math. *Authentic* math experiences in our school setting will help them connect math to everyday life. Math literature books help give children real math experiences as well. (See Resources.)

Math Literature

I believe children need access to a large number of math literature books—both fiction and nonfiction—to help them succeed in becoming numeric, or numerically savvy. Experiencing picture books and poetry with math themes will help make concepts clear and help connect math concepts to children's lives. Children can mentally play and compute as they listen to the stories, count with the pages, and puzzle things out. They are supported by the group and not put on the spot. Children can learn in a relaxed manner that lets them think. Repeated access to books that have been read aloud will help cement insights and learning. This is especially true for visual learners, who need to *see* things in order for them to make sense.

When I read Roger Duvoisin's classic picture book *Petunia* (2000) to my children, we enjoy Petunia the goose's mistaken assumptions as she endeavors to give wise advice (with a book under her wing). When she convinces Ida, the hen, that she has the correct number of chicks, Petunia has counted wrong. And there is an incorrect greater than–less than problem embedded in the text, when Petunia convinces Ida that six is *more* than nine, not *less*. We lift the problem from the book and figure it out together. Children see not just the problem and the solution—now they understand how silly Petunia's thinking really is. These insights lead right in to our own study of greater than and less than. Petunia's mistaken understanding of the concept subtly gives us *real* reasons that this is an important idea to understand.

Extend Your Math Program

As with many teachers in public schools, my district purchases programs for me to use with my students. I do use these materials, but I also add many math-related picture books, poetry, songs, games, creative dramatics, and other experiences. As with other curriculum areas, I use the *California Frameworks and Teaching Standards*. And I endeavor to integrate math with things that happen across our curriculum, all day long. This approach helps math make sense to children.

Counting Is Boring? Use a Story!

Counting by twos, or skip counting, is a skill I worked on intermittently this year. I confess to having become somewhat bored by it, and my usual rule is if *I'm* bored with a concept or learning task, certainly the children are, too! Recently, I tried a new angle on learning this skill and read aloud *Underwater Counting*, by Jerry Pallotta (2001). This is a counting book about even numbers. The secondary theme of this book is sea creatures, and there are many to count and learn about on each page. Fascination took over as I read this text and the children and I marveled over each new type of creature! We counted each page by twos and predicted how many ocean animals would be on the next page. We learned a great deal about fish and other sea life, skip counted each page, and thoroughly appreciated the experience.

Children enjoyed the pages further, counting them alone, or with a partner, when *they* read the book.

Another great math story for counting every other number is *Two Ways to Count to Ten,* retold by Ruby Dee (1990). This is an Ethiopian folktale with a twist, and the surprise ending helps children see the value of being able to count by twos.

This experience with both books has rekindled my interest in innovating ways to help children practice a variety of counting skills. I made skip-counting books with my first graders, and they drew their own items to count on each page, from two to twenty. We stapled these booklets and illustrated them, with the corresponding numerals on the bottom of each page. Children enjoyed practicing reading these as well as counting them. We kept these books in a basket to share and count some more.

"Oh, A-Counting We Will Go!"

A variation of this project is to teach the song "Oh, A-Hunting We Will Go." (This song is also a picture book retold by John Langstaff; see Chapter 9.) For our mathematical purposes, we change the words to "Oh, A-Counting We Will Go." My first graders and I developed several verses to sing and count.

When we make the counting book titled *Oh, A-Counting We Will Go!* we hade a page each for counting by ones, by twos, by fives, and by tens. This was an important integration of skills across the curriculum: math, singing and oral language, reading, and art. (See Figure 12–1.)

Counting Is a Crucial Skill

Counting practice is important for children who are beginning to learn math skills. The importance of a variety of math counting experiences cannot be overrated. Good practice with counting helps children develop number sense. It grounds them for the more involved concepts of addition, subtraction, and other skills they will learn this year.

Counter of the Day

In her book *The Young Child and Mathematics,* Juanita V. Copley (2000) suggests appointing a student to be counter of the day. There

Figure 12–1
"Oh, A-Counting We Will Go!"

Oh, a-counting we will go! A-counting we will go!
We'll count by one and count everyone,
And never let them go!

1 2 3 4 5 6 7 8 9 10 11 12 13 14 15 16 17 18 19 20 (Stop count after each child is counted)

Oh, a-counting we will go! A-counting we will go!
We'll count by twos and count our shoes,
And never let them go!

2 4 6 8 10 12 14 16 18 20 22 24 26 28 30 32 34 36 38 40 (Stop counting after reaching correct number of shoes)

Oh, a-counting we will go! A-counting we will go!
We'll count by fives and count high fives,
And never let them go!

5 10 15 20 25 30 35 40 45 50 55 60 65 70 75 80 85 90 95 100

Oh, a-counting we will go! A-counting we will go!
We'll count by tens to one hundred by tens,
And never let them go!

10 20 30 40 50 60 70 80 90 100

—PBD

are many things to count in a first-grade classroom: children's pockets, shoes, hats, noses, pencils, and so on. The child who is the counter distributes a set of stacked cubes so each child will have something to represent the item to be counted each day. Children turn in the correct number of cubes to the counting monitor: one cube when noses are being counted, a cube to represent each pocket if pockets are being counted, and so forth.

The counter monitor collects cubes and stacks them on the chalk tray with a picture or a label. We arrange cube stacks and counts for the week on the chalk ledge and reexamine them on Friday. At this time children take a good look at the visual representations of a week's worth of counting. They compare the different stacks. For example, the tower of shoes is higher than the tower of cubes representing noses. The stack that stands for pockets is tallest of all. They can also make predictions before counting: Which tower will the stack representing shoes be most like? Do they predict that the stack for eyes will be higher than the tower for noses? Which towers will have even numbers? Which will have odd numbers? And so on.

Graphing

We can easily turn our counting towers into a graph. I draw vertical lines around each stack and draw a box around them all. We label the stacks at the top of the box. We can easily see which stack has more items, which has less, and so on. Children enjoy filling in their own graphs on paper.

A different kind of graph, a variation of the vertical graph project, is a horizontal graph. Four or five blocks from our tub of building blocks separate the cube stacks representing things we counted. I line the stacks up on the left and draw a box around them. We add labels at the left of the cubes, to indicate what each stack means. Children can reproduce this graph on paper as well.

Stacking by Place Value

As the year goes on, I invite children to restack the towers by place value: hundreds, tens, and ones. They recount and figure out that the number representing pockets is six tens and eight ones, or sixty-eight.

Ideas such as this one bring the concept of counting to children's consciousness. This helps them think of the multitude of things they would like to count themselves. It also shows them some ways they can collect mathematical data.

Data Collecting and Making Graphs

Children become clever with data collection when they begin making up their own math problems and thinking of their own things to count. This leads to group and independent graphing ideas, as well as other kinds of mathematical thinking. For example, one day the children notice that most of the students are wearing red shirts. They decide

Figure 12–2 *Small groups work together to practice counting tens and ones.*

to make a graph. Students settle on one column for red shirts and one column for other clothing. They talk about their graph and the conclusions they can draw from it and all the things they notice.

Yes and No Surveys

Children can think of many questions that interest them: Do you like monsters? Do you have a pet? Do you like pizza? Do you like the rain? Do you play soccer? Many of these questions can lead to yes and no surveys. To answer a survey question, a child may check a yes or no box or give the survey taker one cube for yes and none for no. Survey takers may also use tally marks to keep track of yes and no answers. Then surveyors count the boxes, cubes, or tally marks. This data can be turned into math graphs. Information gathered may also lead to math story problems and math equations. For example, "Fourteen red shirts plus six shirts in other colors equals twenty," or "Eight more children have red shirts," and so forth. The point is to hook into children's unique curiosity and let them run with their own math ideas. Many of these inquiries can lead to family questionnaires and graphs and other projects.

These kinds of approaches help children *own* math ideas and enjoy thinking mathematically.

Edwin recently came to school with a survey he had thought of at home. He said he had worked on it "all night" until his father made him go to bed. Edwin was just bubbling over when he showed me his survey of yes and no answers to his question of whether the children liked to climb trees. "I like it that my brain gives me such good ideas," he said.

Edwin chose to record his survey answers by writing either "yes" or "no" (see Figure 12–3). Several other children thought making a survey was a great idea and made their own. Most followed Edwin's example, but one child used tally marks to record her responses to her survey questions. The children love going around taking surveys!

Counting Books and Stories

Some special counting books add to the fun. (See Resources for a list.) Some of my favorite counting books are *One Gorilla,* by Atsuko Morozumi (1990), and *Fish Eyes: A Book You Can Count On,* by Lois Ehlert (1992). Children love to munch as they count with *The M&M's Brand Counting Book* (1994) and *The Cheerios Counting Book* (1998), both by Barbara Barbieri McGrath. The children also enjoy Catherine Fallwell's book *Turtle Splash! Countdown at the Pond* (2002) and David Carter's pop-up book *How Many Bugs in a Box?* (1988). Another pop-up book that is fun to count with is *Cookie Count: A Tasty Pop-Up*, by Robert Sabuda (1997).

Pat's Tip

I have learned the hard way that the best approach for using a pop-up book with a class full of first graders is to hold the book myself and make it a read-aloud that *I alone* manipulate. Unfortunately, three minutes with a group of excited children, or even one careful child, usually results in a demolished pop-up book. I keep some brand-spanking-new copies that *I* handle and some slightly older books for children to play with. I keep a glue stick and tape handy and try to keep books repaired. When children have a few experiences making books with me, they better understand how these pop-ups are put together.

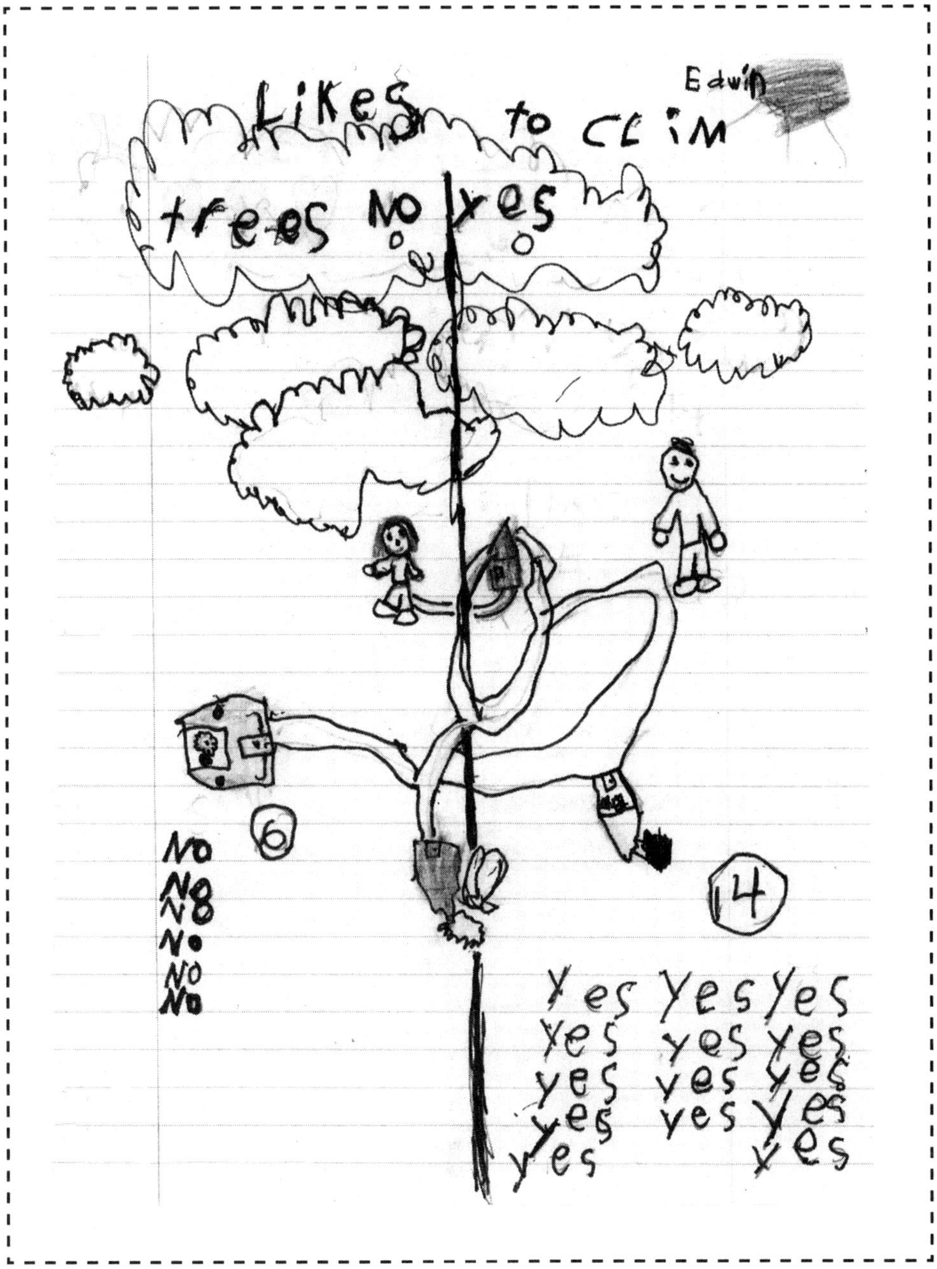

Figure 12–3
Edwin's survey

Our Own Counting Books

My first graders love to make their own counting books. One easy way to do this is to use an eight-fold booklet made from one piece of paper. (See page 6 for directions.) When these little booklets are folded, there is one page for the title and author and seven more pages for counting and for numerals and drawings.

Children also like to make pop-up counting books. This is a good class book activity. Put small numerals from one to twenty (whatever

Figure 12–4
(a) *One-box pop-up pattern;* (b) *three-box pop-up pattern;* (c) *sample math equation pop-up card*

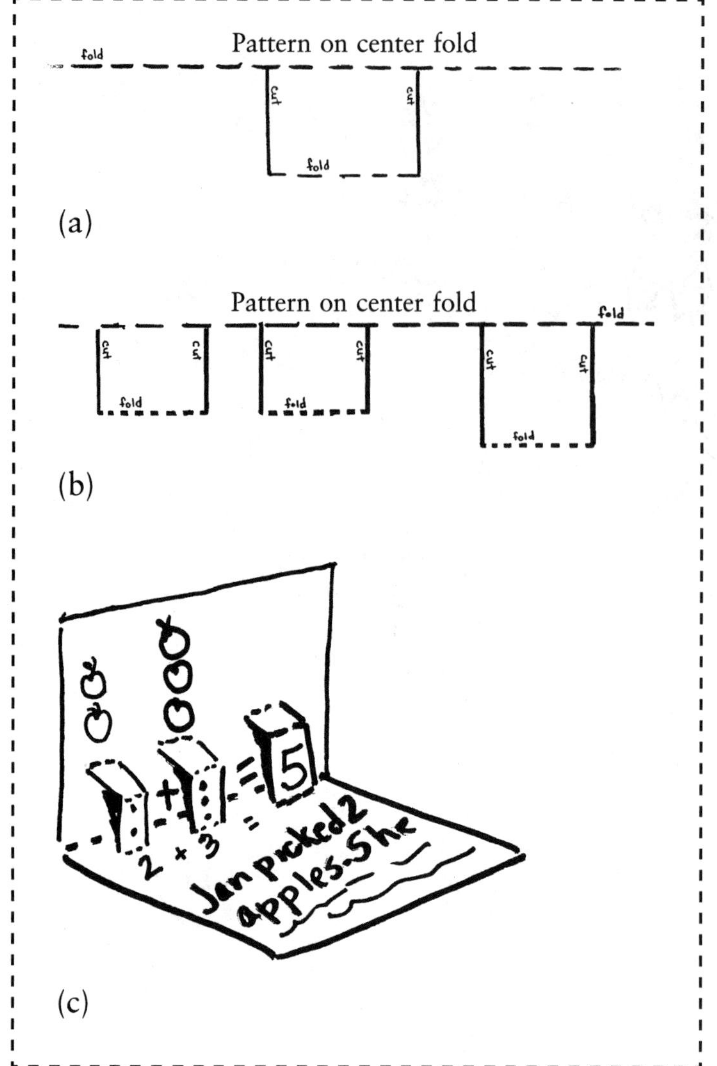

your class size) into a jar. Each child pulls out a numeral to illustrate on a 4-by-6-inch card or piece of paper.

Pop-up books are easy to make. Following are the directions for a one-box pop-up. A three-box pop-up is great for illustrating equations. (See Figure 12–4.)

You Need

9-by-12-inch construction paper, two pieces per book
White paper, 4½ by 6 inches, or an index card (I use 3-by-5-inch or 4-by-6-inch cards—whatever I can get my hands on.)
White glue or glue stick (I prefer a glue stick for this activity.)
Scissors
Marking pens or crayons

Procedure

1. Show children how to fold both pieces of construction paper in half the short way, one at a time. I call the short way a hamburger fold. (The long way is called hot dog fold and results in a longer, skinnier paper.) I believe this terminology for hamburger and hot dog folds came from Math Their Way workshops. It seems to make more sense to children than telling them to fold the long way or the short way.

2. Cut a pop-up box by making two slits, about 2 inches apart, about 2 inches long, down from the fold.

3. Bend the pop-up box back and forth, creating a fold at the bottom of the box, where the slits end. Push the box in, until it is inside the folded card. Press. This paper is the pop-up box paper.

4. Now glue the pop-up box paper to the cover (the other folded paper), one side at a time: First place the pop-up box paper inside the cover, folded edge against folded edge. Now children run a line of glue or glue stick along the bottom back side of the pop-up box paper, up one side to the top, and along the top, (gluing three edges only). Place this paper inside the cover, fold against fold, and press.

5. Flip everything over to glue the other side the same way: Run a line of glue or glue stick along the bottom back side of the pop-up box paper, up and around and back to the middle—three edges. Close the cover and press. Now the pop-up is ready for business!

6. Each child now has a card with a pop-up box. I ask them to make a small pencil dot on the front of the pop-up box. This is the place to add glue to attach items to be counted or the numeral representing these items.

This is the way to make a basic pop-up. Early in the year I make them for the children or give them a photocopied pop-up pattern to use (see Appendix).

Showing Off the Pop-Up Books

When making pop-up counting books, children may glue the numeral to the pop-up box with just a little dab of glue or may put a card with items to be counted there. If using a card, they would glue the numeral in another place on the page.

These may be put together as a class book (three-hole-punched and held together with loose binder rings or yarn). They may also be set out in order as a counting display. Use taped-on craft sticks to hold cards open. Or set these along the chalkboard or whiteboard on the tray and use small magnets to keep cards from falling or closing.

Other Counting Activities

There are many other activities for helping children practice counting:

- Working on counting with a partner
- Learning counting nursery rhymes and jump rope rhymes
- Enjoying counting songs and number raps
- Experiencing counting books (see Resources)
- Learning counting on—simple addition (for example, starting with three items, saying "Three," and counting on two more: "four, five")
- Learning counting back—simple subtraction (starting with, for example, five items, saying "Five," and counting back two: "four, three")
- Practicing counting backwards (There are many books for backward counting; one I like is Molly Bang's book *Ten, Nine, Eight* [2003].).
- Working with and counting movable sets of objects
- Partitioning or separating objects into groups or sets
- Putting two sets together to form a larger group, then counting that group
- Making a skip-counting machine

My Skip-Counting Machine

I was experimenting with pop-up book ideas and accidentally invented a skip-counting machine! This is easy and fun to make.

You Need

White or light-colored 12-by-18-inch construction paper (8½-by-11-inch copy paper; see pattern in Figure 12–5)

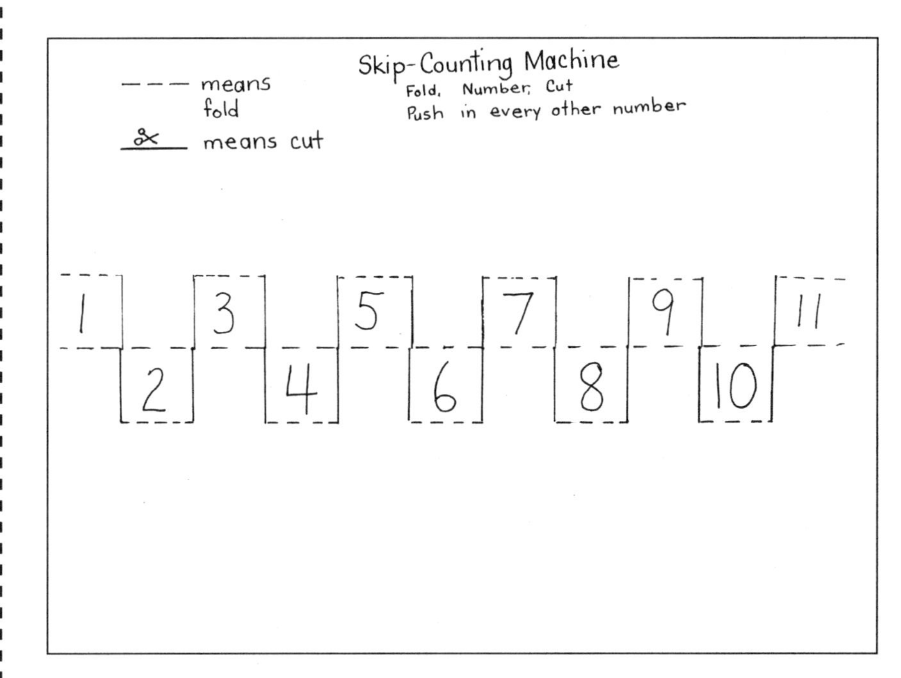

Figure 12–5
Pattern for skip-counting machine

Scissors
Pencils or thin-line marking pens
Rulers

Procedure

1. Fold the paper in half the long way.
2. Show students how to use the ruler to mark the folded edge in 1-inch increments.
3. Fold down the folded edge about 1 inch, to make a measuring fold.
4. Cut 1-inch-deep slits (I cut these down to the measuring fold) at 1-inch intervals all the way across the paper. These cuts become tabs.
5. Number each tab, starting with 1.
6. Beginning with the first tab, number 1, push 1 and *every other* numbered tab (1, 3, 5, 7, etc.) inside the folded paper.
7. Now the fun begins! The remaining numbered tabs (the ones still standing up) are *even* numbers. Children can use this small manipulative to help them count by twos.

8. Turn the paper to the backside, where tabs are not numbered, and number these with odd numbers, starting with 1 on the first tab sticking up. This time the odd numbers will show: 1, 3, 5, 7, and so on.

Children enjoyed seeing me make this prop and loved making their own skip-counting machines!

Other Ways to Skip Count

Another visual way to show counting by skipping every other number is to make paper chains of two alternating colors. Write all even numbers on one color and odd numbers on the other color in the chain.

We also act out this concept of counting by twos: Children stand in a line of ten or so, each one holding a number from one to ten. Beginning with the first child, odd-numbered children kneel down. This leaves even numbers standing. We count them. Then we reverse the positions of the children (even-numbered students kneel down) to count the odd numbers. Soon we are counting by twos to one hundred. We are playing our way to math literacy.

Give Children Freedom to Go Ahead

Not all students need repeated or alternate ways of experiencing math concepts such as those just mentioned, but it is important to use them for the children who just aren't getting it. First graders who do *not* need this kind of practice enjoy working on other mathematical concepts on their own. I have a wide range of "box-it" and "bag-it" math games available. (I owe many thanks to Kathy Ihle, at that time my instructional aide, for making most of them!) I also have a sequentially organized math kit for students who want to do advanced computations with this kind of kit format.

More time to practice making up their own math problems is another good alternative for students who are ready to go on. They can also make their own graphs. Card games are good practice for children. I also make such math tools as clocks, money, and other manipulatives available. Many math books are also on hand. I try to read math literature books at the beginning of math period each day.

Math Curse

Math Curse, an award-winning picture book by Jon Scieszka (1995), is the story of a child who cannot stop thinking about math and numbers, all day long, after having heard the teacher say, "You can think of everything as a math problem." We need to think like this too in order to capitalize on all the opportunities to integrate math into the rest of the curriculum each day.

This picture book, illustrated by Lane Smith, illustrates some of the many possible math problems that we are confronted with and solve almost without realizing we are thinking in mathematical terms—everything from organizing lunch to sharing birthday cupcakes.

The surprise ending of this book uses clever wordplay to solve the problem. The book uses a lot of the language of math but uses clever wordplay in Standard English in order to solve the problem and escape the math curse.

What Children Need in Order to Think Mathematically

If children are to access and develop mathematical thinking, they need good, solid math lessons, guided practice, and time to practice math problems and puzzles independently. They need the opportunity to visualize daily classroom occurrences as math problems and solve them. They also need to develop the mindset of leaving the math area of their brains turned on, not off. We never know when we might need to think through something mathematically!

I also think we need to lighten up and have some fun as we figure and puzzle our way to math competency!

Manipulatives—Great Stuff to Count, Move Around, and Stimulate Math Thinking

Manipulatives are an important way to give children concrete experiences counting and figuring out problems. I like to make sure each child has a plastic bag of craft sticks as well as a second bag with kidney beans and lima beans to use for counting. (Two colors of beans facilitate figuring out addition and subtraction problems.) Children store these materials in their desk bins. I keep other manipulatives readily available in dish tubs or plastic tubs with lids. Large plastic bags work, too. Here are some suggestions for math manipulatives:

- Seashells
- Washers, nuts, and bolts
- Unifix cubes
- Geoboards
- Pattern blocks
- Math tiles
- Clocks
- Buttons
- Bread tags from the supermarket
- Beads
- Clothespins
- Paper clips
- Pennies
- Old keys
- Fake jewels
- Colored plastic dots
- Marking pen caps

I always save the caps from lost or dried-up marking pens. These are colorful and fun to count as well as sort by color. Throwing a marking pen cap away is like throwing away a single mitten: when you toss one out, you inevitably find the mate. (Toss out a pen with no cap, and you'll find the cap within the hour!) I like to keep an old cookie tin full of marking pen caps. These are some of the children's favorite items for counting, sorting, and manipulating.

Time for Play

Children have such a great ability to play that their automatic response to hands-on materials is to fiddle with them and fool around with them. Children need time to play and have fun with any new materials like this before they use them for other purposes. They cannot focus on using manipulatives for counting or doing math until they have had a chance to use them creatively and play with them first. I want children to be thinking when they are using manipulatives. So, first we play. And then we use materials in more specific ways, such as number sentences, to help us learn.

Other Needs

As Marilyn Burns suggests in her book *About Teaching Mathematics* (2000), children also need access to plenty of counting grids so that they can explore patterns and other ideas as they work with math concepts. I now keep photocopied stacks of these papers so children have easy access as they need them:

- Blank hundreds grid
- Filled-in hundreds chart
- Number line, 0–25
- Pattern block paper
- 1-inch squares
- ½-inch squares
- 2-centimeter squares

Looking for Patterns

One of my favorite Marilyn Burns lessons, from her book *About Teaching Mathematics* (2000), uses a blank 0–99 math grid. This grid needs to be large enough for all the children to see. Marilyn begins the lesson by filling in all numbers from zero to twenty-five. As she does this, she asks children such questions as what number they think will come next and so on. She points to a blank square and asks them to guess what number will land there or asks where they think forty will land. Then she instructs children to look at the chart and think about the numbers. After a few minutes, children share what they have noticed.

First graders typically see patterns in rows and columns. With a little nudging, they can find diagonal patterns, odd and even numbers, numbers with both digits the same, numbers where digits add up to ten, and so on.

A good follow-up, as Marilyn suggests, is to give students copies of a 0–99 chart. Each child may work with a partner to find and color specific patterns.

Coloring the Patterns Activity

A related activity, also from Marilyn's book, is to provide direction strips in an envelope with 0–99 charts. Children work with partners. All children complete a paper and choose their own colors to show answers to the problems suggested on direction strips. Sample ideas for direction strips:

- Color numbers with both digits the same.
- Color all numbers whose digits add to ten.
- Color all numbers with a five in them.
- Color all numbers with first digits that are larger than the second digits.
- Color all numbers with a zero in them.

Children can also come up with and write their *own* direction slips.

Manipulatives and Story Mats

Another idea for math manipulatives is to make photocopies of reproducible thematic story mats and corresponding small pictures to use for counting. Children may color these, cut out the counters, and keep them in envelopes to help them work out math problems. (They may also use these for storytelling and to play with in many ways.) For example, children may use a prehistoric landscape mat with paper cutout dinosaur counters, or a mat of the solar system with cutouts of planets, stars, and even an astronaut or spaceships. Students can use these cut-paper manipulatives to create and solve their own problems, tell and write story problems, categorize objects, and extend their math learning in many ways. They enjoy socializing and playing this way.

ELL Connection

There is integration with other subject matter areas when children use the pictures and vocabulary for different types of vehicles, musical instruments, farm and city, and so forth. This opportunity to try out words and concepts is particularly helpful to second language learners.

You may make your own mats and counters, encourage children to make them, or use such books as Alison Abrohms' *1001 Instant Manipulatives for Math, Grades K–2* (1999). One of the things I like about using story mats and paper counters is that materials are inexpensive and easy to make for individual children or groups, as well as for math centers. Once children have the idea, they can extend their learning by letting their own creative juices flow. These materials give children the idea of creating something meaningful to them and then using the materials to take off creatively and imaginatively and come up with their own kinds of settings, math counters, and story situations. I send mats and counters home about once a week during the year, so that children have different sets of materials they can use to help them with their math thinking and homework.

These reproducible pages are a great way to send something meaningful home for children to work on. A math worksheet with a toy-room story mat and paper toy cutout counters attached is a lot more fun for many children than just a worksheet. Children may color a jungle mat, color, cut, and count animals, even write their own jungle stories, and so forth. Stapling blank papers to a math homework sheet gives children the opportunity to produce their own imaginative story mats and counters.

A Math Collage to Connect with a Special Experience

After a wonderful field trip to the dinosaur exhibit at the Laurence Hall of Science, in Berkeley, California, my first graders created a great cut-paper collage of the dinosaur landscape setting. We made dinosaur counters and child counters, individual and in sets, and taped them to pointers. To create the child counters, children drew themselves; we glued on cutout school photo heads and grouped children in sets. We attached these figures to pencils, yardsticks, and other pointers for working out our invented math problems. Children enjoyed creating story problems based not just on their new knowledge of dinosaurs and their environment but on their own trip to the museum.

We wrote down our story problems as fast as we invented them. I redrew this collage, made it into a booklet, and sent it home with counters and our story problems for further play and practice.

This same technique could be used for a trip to the planetarium, the zoo, and so on.

Manipulatives Help Make Many Concepts Clear

Hands-on materials are helpful for many concepts. For example, at the beginning of the school year, children were having difficulties understanding the ideas of greater than and less than. We colored story mats of a rain forest and cut out animal counters. I made a greater than (>) and less than (<) symbol for each child (this can be turned to indicate either greater than or less than). Children placed their counters on the

Figure 12–6
Maria shares her math problem using our dinosaur collage and a pointer.

story mat and worked out the problem, for example, putting five counters on the left and two on the right. They then had to decide on which way to place the symbol to make the sentence correct: 5 > 2.

After children understood how to use these manipulatives and story mat, I sent materials home in an envelope for students to keep for further practice and play. I sent home a letter requesting that parents help children to save both the story mats and the counters to play with and to use with future homework.

Make a Collection of Math Charts

I save a lot of the children's innovative work to put on math charts we can all enjoy. For example, after a trip to the zoo, Ivan wrote a great zebra math problem. The children all loved it, and, with Ivan's permission, we put it on a math chart.

Ivan's problem said, *I was walking down the street with my 47 zebras. We saw a garbage truck. Four zebras fell into the back with the garbage. How many zebras were left?*

Ivan balked only when he was invited to illustrate the story. There was no way he felt like drawing forty-seven zebras. I asked him if he would just make one and put it in a magic box. He was skeptical but drew one zebra and put it in a box I happened to find. On my way to yard duty, I left a note for Kathy Ihle, my instructional aide in the days when we had aides.

When we came back from recess, Ivan checked the box and found forty-seven identical zebras inside. Always skeptical, he said, "*You* did it!"

"You saw me on yard duty, remember?" I countered. I really don't know *what* the point of this was, except that it was a crazy, fun impulse on my part. And Ivan enjoyed illustrating the rest of his math chart and gluing on his forty-seven zebras.

Understanding of Number: Individual Assessments

I like to assess children's mathematical ability right away at the beginning of the year and periodically throughout the year. I do this through brief individual interviews. I have children count a few objects, tell me how many they have, hand me a certain number of things, make groupings of a certain number of objects, and so forth. I see whether they recognize numerals and can count on. For example, if there are two sets of objects, one with three, and one with four, a child who can count on would say, "Three," and then add on four more, saying, "four, five, six, seven," without starting all over again with the number one. Understanding of number is a foundation for addition and subtraction, as well as the basis for mental math and estimation and other higher-level skills.

Here are some possible brief tasks to have a child do during a math interview:

- Count objects
- Count on
- Recognize numerals—point out the numerals as you say them
- Write numerals as you say them
- Make sets of certain numbers of objects, for example, sets of six, sets of nine, and so on.

- Trade objects, for example, trade eight blocks for four blocks and four blocks
- Count by ones, twos, fives, and tens
- Answer questions such as, "What is one more than ________?" "What is one less than ________?"

I like to provide more difficult pen-and-pencil adding and subtracting tasks for children who demonstrate they can do more than what I have already asked.

This is helpful information for me to have as we begin our school year. I like to relay this information to parents at our first parent conference during the first month of school. Specific knowledge about each child's abilities helps me to be able to show parents a variety of ways they could work with their children to develop math concepts.

Math Reference Bulletin Board

As with the phonics reference chart (Chapter 9), I believe it is very helpful to build a reference board for mathematics and leave it up all year. We use this board as our daily tune-up after lunch each day, before we begin our math period.

We work with the items on this reference board all year long. Following are some of the things I put up as part of this display.

Daily Calendar

I use a literary calendar with a poem or nursery rhyme illustrated by one of the children. I print the calendar with permanent marking pen on a piece of 24-by-36-inch manila tagboard, with the calendar illustration on top, the calendar in the middle, and a poem or book excerpt at the bottom. Sometimes there is room for more illustrations next to the text as well.

Each month the class and I decide on a colored pattern for circling the days, for example, red, blue, blue; red, blue, blue; . . . . Each day we circle the date with the correct pattern color. We talk about the calendar: How many more Mondays will there be? Which day of the week

Figure 12–7
Math reference bulletin board

is Thursday? And so forth. We write important information in for specific dates, such as "Alejandro's birthday"; "Chinese New Year Assembly, 8:35 A.M."; and "School Holiday—President's Day." This helps us keep track of everything and shows the children *real* ways to use a calendar. A different child or pair of children illustrates our calendar each month.

Many teachers I know use a blank monthly calendar made out of poster board, with the days of the week written across the top of the boxes. Thematic paper cutouts, such as umbrellas or snowmen, have numerals written on them, and are hung on pins to show each day's date. These paper cutouts are available from teacher supply stores.

Place Value

Children learn place value all year long with our calendar. We keep track of the number of days in the school year. I have made a laminated chart with a box for each day of our year. When we do the calendar, we write the correct number in the box for the day. Then we add one straw to the pocket chart that represents the actual number of days we have been in school. The straw pockets are labeled, from right to left: "ones," "tens," and "hundreds." There is a place for a number in each pocket.

Every time we get ten straws in the ones pocket, we bundle the straws with a rubber band. We put this bundle in the tens pocket. If we have been in school eighteen days, our pocket chart will have one bundle of ten straws in the tens pocket and eight straws in the ones pocket.

We keep adding one straw a day and bundling each group of straws when we reach ten. The bundles of ten go into the tens pocket. When we get ten bundles of ten, we bundle them with a rubber band and put the bundle in the hundreds pocket. The number on the hundreds pocket is 1, and it represents one hundred.

If we have been in school 124 days, the chart has, of course, one large bundle of ten tens (with each set of ten rubber-banded) in the hundreds pocket; two bundles of tens in the tens pocket; and four straws in the ones pocket.

Keeping track of the calendar and the days in this way really helps place value make sense to children.

Small containers may be used instead of a pocket chart: different-sized milk cartons, cut down to short boxes, work fine, as do french fry boxes or Chinese food containers. I prefer the pocket chart because it fits flat on the wall, is easier to hang up, and saves me from looking for the right-sized boxes. This small pocket chart is a commercial product that I really value. Teacher supply stores sell all kinds of pocket charts.

The Date in Coins

The math board has many other daily references next to the calendar. I adhere real coins to a small cookie sheet using magnetic tape or Fun-Tak (see Resources). Magnetic tape comes in rolls and is available at craft shops. It is easily cut. Children may count different coins each day to make the same number as the calendar date.

Other Materials

Some of the other materials next to the calendar are:

- Clock with movable hands for practicing time
- Hundreds chart
- Blank hundreds chart for putting in the number of each day of school

- Skip-counting charts: by twos, by fives, by tens (This is usually a color-coded part of the hundreds chart.)
- Some addition and subtraction facts, as we learn them
- Patterns we have invented
- Flannel board with felt cutouts of numbers and items to count, such as pumpkins, stars, rabbits, and so forth

Beginning Our Math Program Each Day

When we come together for math each day, we meet on the rug after lunch. I read a story (usually one with a math theme) and then read briefly from *Emily's First 100 Days of School*, by Rosemary Wells (2000). This book has a page for each day, connecting math to ordinary school events in Emily's life. It helps reinforce for children that they have many math events in their daily lives, too.

We review assorted concepts using this book and our review board. Some of the ideas on this board are also on the file folder reference chart at each child's desk. (See Chapter 9.)

I introduce a specific lesson for the day, often using concrete objects first, in our circle on the rug, individually, or with partners. I frequently go over lessons using the overhead projector. I work with some children in small groups while other children who are able to work on their own or with a partner do so. When work is completed, children may go to math centers and use a variety of math games and manipulative materials or read and enjoy math picture books. They may make new math problems and try to stump each other. Sometimes we use this time to review the lesson using Unifix cubes or other manipulatives. Children work as table teams or with partners to find answers to a few problems.

Math Pop-Ups

Math pop-up books are great fun to make to illuminate addition and subtraction equations. They typically have three pop-up boxes: one for each addend and one for the sum or remainder. Children glue their equations to the pop-up boxes. They illustrate the math problems on the area behind the boxes and below the equation as well. They can write their math problem and paste it below the equation. The cover of the pop-up can have the title of the math problem, the name of the author-illustrator, and an illustration. (See pages 263–265.)

Math Murals

We created a new math board this year to showcase some of the things we were learning. Some of the headings on our work in progress were:

- Equation Station
- Addition Alley
- Tessellation Terrace
- Subtraction Suburb
- Place Value Place

We have fun thinking of things to put in each location.

Hundreds Day: A Place Value Celebration

One of our big events in first grade is the celebration of a hundred days of school. We call this Hundreds Day. We enjoy such picture books as *Miss Bindergarten Celebrates the 100th Day of Kindergarten,* by Joseph Slate (1998), illustrated by Ashley Wolff; *One Hundred Is a Family*, by Pam Muñoz Ryan (1996); and *100th Day Worries*, by Margery Cuyler (2000). Another favorite book, and one that extends our experiences about one of our picture book characters, is *The Wolf's Chicken Stew*, by Keiko Kasza (1989).

Place Value Math Machines

On Hundreds Day we make place value math machines and play with them. We bring in clean milk cartons, with tops opened wide. I cut slots for cards to go *into* the machine and *exit* and affix a slide for the cards to go down. (See Figure 12–10.) If they wish, students may decorate the machines with faux machine buttons and other details. I keep stacks of precut cards handy for math machine problems.

To use the machine, the children draw a number on a card, such as forty-seven. On the reverse side of the card, they draw (or paste on) four towers of ten cubes (four tens) and seven cubes (seven ones). A sheet of 1-centimeter squares may be provided to each student to use as cubes, to avoid all that drawing. We make cards to share, or children may have sets of their own.

Each card that slides down the math machine comes out reversed. To play, the children feed in the cards, tower and cube side up. They try to say the number represented by the picture before the card comes out the bottom slot. This machine may also be used for math equations. Print the equation and draw an arrow. Flip the card over. Draw another arrow and put the answer. Now, just feed the equation card into the machine, and the flipped-over answer will come out! Even though the children know how this works, they still think it is amazing. This makes a game out of practicing math facts. It can also be used in many other areas of the curriculum, for example, with words and their definitions.

Figure 12–8
Milk carton math machine

Figure 12–9
Diego makes a Hundreds Day sorting wheel, and shows off his hundreds necklace.

Other Hundreds Day Activities

Some other activities for Hundreds Day are to count to one hundred many ways, such as making necklaces to wear using one hundred large cereal pieces with holes in the center (all counted out by tens). Children like making headbands with adding machine tape, showing one hundred with tally marks. Sentence strips also make good headbands. Children can use small squares of colored paper and use stamp-type marking pens to "stamp" ten items on each paper square. Ten squares are stapled on each Hundreds Day headband.

Another activity is to bring in collections of one hundred items. We set these up as a museum and enjoy looking at them together. We also do a pizza-sized hundreds sort, for which we draw little items, ten sets in each pizza portion, until we have one hundred items. (See Appendix for the pattern.) Note: My photo shows a hoop framing the hundreds wheel. This is an unnecessary decoration.

CHAPTER 13

Ya Gotta Have Art!

The stronger the art program,
the stronger the academic result.
Art opens up the total mind to see.

—Dick Sperisen, Art Coordinator Emeritis,
San Mateo County Office of Education,
Redwood City, California

Nothing perks up a group of children faster than finding out that it's time for art.

In our diverse classrooms today, full of children with multiple language and cultural differences and wide ability spans, art is a universal language for teaching *everybody*. When children have the opportunity to draw, paint, tear, and construct, they learn great ways to respond to the world around them. And they have a joyful time using their imaginations as they play and create.

Through art experiences, all children make gains across many disciplines in vocabulary, cognitive development, and physical and social development. Students also experience personal growth and increased self-esteem and have the chance to learn about themselves. Art helps us all connect to our inner selves, express ourselves another way, and better understand what we think and feel and believe.

Art Is a Mandated Subject Area

In these days of high-stakes testing and worry over student achievement, it can be forgotten that art is a *mandated* area of the curriculum. It is a discipline to be taught in its own right. As with other subjects, art should be taught sequentially and developmentally so students can master skills and grow.

Artful Beginnings

From our first days together, I show children art techniques and provide time and materials for *them* to do art. We talk about and explore art prints, picture books, as well as our own artwork. I introduce and use specific art vocabulary, and we grow into it through both aesthetic art experiences and time to use art materials. One of the ways I feel like my best self in the classroom is when I am teaching art.

I want to teach in such a way that drawings and paintings, collage and crafts spill out of children in response to their feelings, their creative needs, and *their* ways of viewing and translating the world. I want this ability to respond to the world artistically to become a habitual way of reacting and feeling—something children can take for granted and rely on. I also want my students to have many varied opportunities to experience the deep joy of innovation, exploration, and creation.

Sustained Silent Sketching

As I describe in *Literacy from Day One*, I schedule time for sustained silent sketching for five to seven minutes each day. The children and I set something up to draw: a giant bear, Lego machines the children have invented, the flowers a child has brought in, two children modeling, a still life of stacked classroom animals, and so on. Children are *invited* to quickly sketch the scene. They are free to draw whatever they like during that brief time period: the setup in front of them, something else they are looking at, something from their imaginations, or a combination of things.

Figure 13–1
Karina sketches in the garden.

Sometimes I ask children to try out specific media, such as pencils, marking pens, or crayons. Most days the medium is their choice. I remind children that the part of the brain that specializes in speech is in a different area of the brain than the part that controls drawing. I explain that their drawings will be better, and they will have an easier time getting into their drawings, if they are silent while they draw.

Children draw for just a few minutes. They may leave their sketchbooks open for view if they wish or put them away. We take a two-minute walk-through and look at the sketchbooks available. Positive comments are welcomed. We always date these sketchbook pages.

Activities such as this emphasize the importance of drawing and give children a chance to hone their skills each day. I want these art skills, like reading skills, to become a habitual part of their lives—a part they take for granted and cannot do without.

Teaching a Sequence of Techniques

My art mentor, Dick Sperisen, is the Art Coordinator Emeritus at the San Mateo County Office of Education in Redwood City, California. He has developed a series of lessons for teaching art at every grade level, from kindergarten through high school. Dick's belief, and one I share, is that it is important to teach children a *sequence* of techniques, or ways to proceed in art, as well as giving them opportunities to do art.

For example, as Dick (a former basketball player) explains this, in a physical education class, a teacher or coach would show students how to dribble, pass, shoot a basket, feint, guard, and so forth. Players would then be able to put these techniques together their way to play in a basketball game. It's the same for art.

We need to teach children some simple basics and then provide them with time to *practice* what they are learning—time to put things together, try things out, innovate, invent, putter, and dream. Children who understand how to use art materials, and have experiences with drawing, collage, and painting, can carry these techniques with them throughout their lives. They own them. They can call up these abilities and use them whenever they wish, experiencing art separately or in conjunction with other subject matter disciplines.

As Dick explains, "There is no need to make elaborate plans for art lessons. Use the art media sequence of activities, and let art grow right out of the curriculum. Give youngsters many opportunities to use art to *respond* to what they are learning in other subject areas. Keep things simple."

The Sperisen Art Education Program

Dick's media-based sequential art education program is based on teaching children *bold* media activities first, such as torn-paper collage and crayon rubbings. These lessons are followed by experiences with finer, more detailed techniques, such as double-pencil drawing (pencils are taped or rubber-banded together), single-line drawing, and watercolor painting. This sequence mirrors the way children learn: First they develop large motor skills. After the chance to use and hone these skills, they develop more dexterity and small motor control.

Whenever possible I integrate these art experiences with other curricula and with award-winning picture books—literature with both beautiful art and text.

Dick's art sequence list was written for students in kindergarten through twelfth grade. I am abbreviating this to focus on the techniques and tools I teach the children in first grade. Simple explanations follow for some of these techniques later in this chapter.

Bold media activities

- Torn-paper collage; cut-paper collage
- Crayon rubbings (also called rub-overs)
- Drawing with hunks of paraffin (canning wax)
- Glue-line drawing
- Tempera painting washes
- Tempera painting with sponges

Detailed media activities

- Double-pencil drawing; single-line pencil drawing
- Double-crayon drawing; crayon sketching
- Double–marking pen drawing
- Watercolor and brush experiences
- Tempera and brush experiences

Set up an easel in your classroom so students can take turns painting.

Another good experience to include is construction of simple buildings and structures. See Chapter 14 for more information using these techniques.

Torn-Paper Collage

The number one art skill I teach children is how to make torn-paper pictures. We do a lot of cut-paper collage, as well. Children typically don't like to tear paper at first. I think that tearing makes them feel out of control, as if they're making mistakes. Seeing work of children's artists in this field helps children see torn-paper and cut-paper collage as accessible and important skills.

I love to share picture books by such renowned children's artists as Leo Lionni, Eric Carle, Lois Ehlert, Molly Bang, and Ezra Jack Keats. These are just a few of the many talented artists who make use of torn and cut paper to create their children's book illustrations. Some of my favorite books to use to highlight this art skill (as well as share wonderful stories) are

- Leo Lionni
  Frederick
  A Color of His Own
  Swimmy
  The Alphabet Tree
- Eric Carle
  The Very Hungry Caterpillar
  Animals, Animals (poetry)
  A House for Hermit Crab
- Lois Ehlert
  Chicka Chicka Boom Boom
  Snowballs
  Eating the Alphabet: Fruits and Vegetables from A to Z
- Molly Bang
  The Paper Crane
- Ezra Jack Keats
  The Snowy Day

Sharing the art of one or two picture book artists before an art lesson validates the use of torn and cut paper for children. It helps make the skill seem worthwhile and within the children's grasp. We talk about how to do torn and cut paper, as well as ways some of these torn- and cut-paper pictures fit the moods of the stories.

Tearing Practice I also have paper-tearing experiences right away, to help dispel children's reluctance to tear paper. We sit in a circle on the rug and tear newspaper strips. The children soon discover that paper is easier to tear in one direction than another. Paper has grain, like wood. Tearing in one direction can result in easily created strips; in another direction, little short, torn bits and pieces result. Sometimes we need strips, sometimes bits. The only way to know what we'll be getting is to start tearing and explore. I save all our paper pieces in a large bag or tub.

I always do this activity just before recess or a bathroom break. This way we can wash the newsprint from our hands before it gets all over everything. We will use these newspaper scraps later in the school year, to fill bags for scarecrow heads, self-portraits, and other creations. At the beginning of first grade, we focus on ways to move our hands to tear paper.

Apples and Pumpkins Soon after the newspaper-tearing activity, I show my first graders more about torn paper. A two-dimensional apple, pumpkin, or jack-o'-lantern is probably a good place to start, as is a self-portrait. Since a jack-o'-lantern is easier, I may begin there and do torn-paper self-portraits as a follow-up. Of course, children who do not celebrate Halloween or wish to create other objects are free to do so.

I begin this paper-tearing lesson by placing a large piece of oilcloth, or painter's drop cloth, in the center of the rug. This should be large enough to showcase children's completed artwork. Then I give children a paper shape about the size of a finished product. Usually this is about a 6-inch or 9-inch square of construction paper.

Pat's Tip

One of the best ways for me to provide paper is to *tear* some 12-by-18-inch paper or 9-by-12-inch paper in half for the children to use. Now that the paper is torn already, they don't have to worry about it anymore!

I explain to my first graders that the finished art is already in the paper—we just have to tear away the extra bits and pieces. This is a simplified version of Michelangelo's belief that he saw his completed sculpture in a block of marble, and just had to remove the extra marble to free the creation. This idea worked for him, and my simpler version seems to empower my first graders and give them confidence.

As I demonstrate tearing the shape—apple, pumpkin, and so forth—I tell children to watch my hands. I ask, "What is moving and turning the most: my hands, or the paper?" I accentuate the turning of the paper as I say this. I tell students I am "walking my fingers around the paper," as I turn the paper, tearing the edges as I go. We are all sitting on the rug together. I give children paper and invite them to try tearing a simple shape. I may make an error and say something like, "Oops," and "Oh, now I've got it!" as I'm tearing. I want all of this to be relaxed, upbeat, and fun—not an exacting task. There is no right and wrong way to do it.

Children clustered in a circle can see my evolving portrait, apple, pumpkin, or jack-o'-lantern. I place the jack-o'-lantern or object I am creating on top of an old book cover or newsprint mat. This mat protects the desk or rug as I work. I tear out other parts I need—several types of eyes, noses, mouths, stems, and so on—and try them out by placing them on the pumpkin. I may layer pieces, for example, a yellow triangle eye, and black eyeball, and so forth. It is extremely important that children have the chance to *play* with materials and try out different looks before they make anything permanent. After a few minutes of this, it's time to show children how to glue.

How to Glue with First Graders and Keep Sane I always point out to my students that I have paper on the table to protect my work area. They will have desk protector papers, too. I emphasize that we need to work on these papers, as the glue is hard to clean up. (At the beginning of our year, some children move these papers out of their way.)

I untwist the top of the glue bottle and squeeze out a *little* bit of glue. I glue the topmost layer (the eyeball) first, by lifting up one edge of the paper and squeezing a *little bit* of glue underneath. I push the paper down gently. I glue other bits and pieces in the same way—not moving a paper shape, but lifting up an edge and getting a little glue under there. I mention to the children that I think my project is more interesting to look at when parts of the paper are still sticking up. Things don't need to be cemented together as if a truck ran over them.

I don't tear or glue the whole thing when I am demonstrating. I set the paper aside, out of sight, so it doesn't interfere with children's own images—the masterpieces *they* will be creating.

Reviewing the Lesson Before It Starts Before I turn my first graders loose to create and glue their artwork, I recap the lesson and talk to them about cleanup. I hope they will come up with our procedures. I prompt and remind them: We will create special art, then put away good scraps in the table tubs (one plastic bin or cardboard soft drink tray per table). We will toss small and tiny scraps in the recycling bin. We will close the glue and wipe off the tops of glue bottles with tissue. I like to keep a box of tissues at each team table. Baby wipes are handy for cleanup also. Glue is stored in a small plastic basket, with all bottles closed and standing upright. And we finish by making sure that everything is picked up off the carpet.

I ask the children to spread their completed art out on the protected area of the rug (the part with oilcloth or a drop cloth) when they have finished. Children know that if they finish early, they may help clean up the carpet, help someone else, read, write, or even make a second project. Now I invite children to tear, and glue, and "do art." First they need to get their desk protector papers on their desks and choose materials.

I invite a few children at a time to select papers they need from the "art store." This is an area of the carpet where I lay out (or ask children to lay out) piles of paper choices available. I no longer put out pristine pieces of colored paper. I rip large and small construction paper in half or smaller, or at least tear off some edges to leave some pieces bigger. As I suspected, children are much more apt to try paper tearing if there is a torn edge on the paper to begin with!

Breaking How-to Lessons into Small Parts If this tearing and gluing lesson seems like too much for a class, I may do just a gluing lesson, giving each child the chance to practice gluing one piece of paper to another one without flooding a table, or an area, with glue.

Making Photographic Reference Charts Another time, after children have had more experience, I explain that I will be looking for children who are excellent paper tearers, gluers, and scrap picker-uppers, and I will be photographing them. I will especially be photographing their hands as they demonstrate these skills. I find and photograph these children, and I make these photographs into instructional charts. These classroom visuals help us all understand these techniques.

In subsequent torn-paper lessons, I can say things like, "Go and look at Andrea's photograph on the chart. See how she glues," or, "Look at the tearing chart and see some ways Joan and Efrain are tearing."

I strive to have a collection of charts with every child demonstrating something. These photo charts can be used for art lessons, for centers, for general literacy—even for how to correctly hold a pencil or turn the pages of a book. The charts can also be reminders, almost like billboards, for example, "Christopher says, 'Be sure to close the glue bottles!'"

We *Made* It! When the room is cleaned up, and all projects are on the drop cloth in the center of the rug (or sometimes, are right on the wall in front of us, or affixed to the whiteboard with magnets), the children and I sit facing the artwork and discuss it. We review our goals for the lesson, for example, to tear paper; to stick it down to make a collage; to do careful gluing; and so on. I ask them what they notice about our art, and we discuss everything of interest to us. This is the aesthetic-valuing portion of the lesson. This is a great wrap-up for all of us, but it is especially important for second language learners.

Figure 13–2
One of our many murals, with everyone's art included

After our session, I show the children how to be absolutely *stunned* by the greatness of it all: We close our eyes and then open them when I count to three. We look at and admire our floor or wall display of art! Often we put a lot of our work together to make wonderful murals.

This year, after our first torn-paper lesson, the children are beside themselves with the beauty and cleverness of their creations. We talk about individual pieces of art but also marvel over our whole art show. We have attached all our work to a bulletin board. (I put it up as children cleaned up the room and straightened out their desk bins.)

Karina claps her hands as she looks at it, and says, in a voice full of joy and awe, "We *made* it. We *made* it all!"

We take a bathroom break and then come back to the classroom to be surprised and awed once again.

In another lesson, we will do more specific aesthetic valuing, looking back together at the intent of the lesson. Then children will have a chance to pick out one or two art pieces that they feel demonstrate what we have learned, notice art in which they particularly like the tearing or the colors, and so on.

This type of lesson can often develop into a vocabulary or English language lesson.

ELL Connection

Once, after our first torn-paper lesson of the year, we placed our pumpkins and jack-o'-lanterns on a field of dark blue paper and moved things around until we liked the placement. I showed the children how we could overlap some pumpkins to make them fit more easily and look more real.

As we admired our mural, I began creating riddles about the pumpkins and jack-o'-lanterns: "I see twin jack-o'-lanterns with green eyes and jagged teeth." The children started making their own riddles too. Vocabularies expanded as well as our visual acuity as we celebrated our first torn-paper lesson. I mounted some of our "I see" and "I spy" riddles next to the mural.

Figure 13–3 *Children had a lot to talk about after creating their jack-o'-lantern mural.*

Crayon Rubbings

I love to show children how to make crayon rubbings of their torn- or cut-paper creations.

To make a rubbing, it's best to use broken crayon pieces with wrappers removed. Place a thin piece of newsprint or copy paper over the torn- or cut-paper collage. I show children how I hold the crayon piece by the *side* of the crayon, with my fingers and thumb, and rub over the blank paper. For a clear rubbing, it is important not to move the top paper. Children can help each other hold things, while one child rubs over the blank paper with a crayon. All of a sudden, the image appears. I remind children *not* to let go, but to keep rubbing. Crayon colors may be changed. Several layers of rubbing may be done. Usually first-grade children do not keep at this too long, but if they do, they can get a clear crayon image of the original artwork.

Extending Rubbings I used to think my creation was complete after I made a rubbing. Not so, as I learned from Dick Sperisen. We can add details to crayon rubbings with marking pens, by gluing on more torn-paper scraps, and even adding more crayon or oil pastel details. Years ago, I created an art lesson in *The Kid's Arts and Crafts Book,* by Patricia Petrich (my name at the time) and Rosemary Dalton (1975). In this rubbing lesson example, a child is taking a walk in the forest.

I created trees by doing a crayon rubbing over a variety of actual leaves, placed on a hard surface with the veins up. I covered this assortment of foliage with newsprint. A few passes with different crayons made a great combined leaf rubbing. A child or children could be drawn into the scene; actual cutout children's photographs or cutout magazine illustrations could also be added.

Once children know how to use watercolor paints, paint may be added to crayon rubbings.

A Favorite Resource If I could have only *one* (perish the thought!) art reference book, I think the one I would choose is *Paste, Pencil, Scissors, and Crayons,* by Gene Baer (1972). The author is an art teacher on Martha's Vineyard. In the winter, when the hoards of tourists have gone home, he and his family play with all kinds of materials and create new art lessons. I love his thoughtful tips and unique ideas, as well as his sense of humor. In one excerpt from the book, where he introduces the idea of rubbings, Gene Baer tells his students he has been practicing drawing leaves and has gotten really good at it. He proceeds to rub a crayon over a folded paper he has prepared ahead of time, and a leaf appears! It can take some children a while to figure out that he has just made a crayon rubbing over the leaf he has folded into the paper.

When I tried this boast, and rub-over, children's eyes almost popped out as they saw the crayon image of the leaf appear on the newsprint! When they figured it out, they thought it was a great trick. At the end of our rubbing lesson, I gave each child a leaf, piece of crayon, and some paper so the students could play the trick on someone at home. They were very happy about this experience, as they reported the next day, except for one child, who must have gotten a crumbly leaf. He said accusingly, "You know that leaf you gave me? It was *dead* by the time I got it home!" (I gave him a new leaf.)

See Resources for a few other art reference books I particularly like.

Teaching Drawing

Quite soon in the school year I teach drawing, often the double-pencil drawing I learned from Dick Sperisen. I tape or rubber-band two pencils together, one *pair* of pencils for each child. Then I put out something stimulating for the children to draw: a plant, a pumpkin, a stuffed animal, some toys, and so forth. Children love to model and to draw each other. I often bring things in that relate to something we are studying in another curriculum area, such as seashells, cars and trucks, or posters of butterflies.

Children have many ideas about things that they would like to draw too. We have fun setting up our drawing scenes together.

The Double-Pencil Grip: Quack! Double pencils are held with what Dick Sperisen calls the "quacking duck" grip: Grab the pair of pencils between thumb and fingers, with the index finger on top.

I invite children to look carefully and then draw with the double pencils, without removing their pencils from the paper. They are "taking a walk with a line." This technique really loosens children up to draw wild and free and create something quickly. When moving their double pencils without taking the pencils off the paper, they soon have papers in front of them that are covered with drawn lines. This is a much different result from a typical beginning first-grade drawing: a tight little picture in the center of an enormous white space.

At this point, children see lots of lines on their papers and may even be alarmed. So I tell them about Jerry Pinkney and share some of his books.

Children's Literature Connection

Jerry Pinkney is a picture book author-illustrator whose books have won Caldecott medals and many other prestigious awards. Children especially enjoy Hans Christian Andersen's story *The Ugly Duckling* (1999) illustrated by Pinkney, and *New Shoes for Silvia*, written by Johanna Hurwitz (1993) and illustrated by Pinkney. Typically, Jerry Pinckney's watercolors have a background of many pencil lines. In an interview in *The Horn Book Magazine* (March–April 1991), Jerry said that he purposely doesn't erase these lines. He feels that they add depth and dimension to his work. The lines also leave clues as to his thinking as he develops his art. I had the opportunity to speak with Jerry about this at an Otter Dinner for booksellers and other book lovers in Berkeley, California, in March of 2000. Jerry seemed pleased that his way of drawing before applying watercolor was of help to children in the classroom.

After they have created their double-pencil drawings, I ask children to really *look* at them. Something starts to emerge in their drawings. As Dick Sperisen says, "Many lines make a line."

I tell my first graders that many lines make a line we *like*, a line that *means* something to us. We find those lines we think are good ones and make them visible by darkening them, using pencil or dark crayon to bring them out of obscurity. (See Figure 13–4.)

Double-pencil drawings may be left as pencil drawings, or other treatments may be added: crayon, bits of torn paper, black crayon or marking pen outlines, watercolors, oil pastels, or tempera.

Double-Crayon and Double-Pen Drawings Double-crayon and double-marking pen drawings are similar to double-pencil ones—two tools are rubber-banded or taped together so that many lines are made quickly.

Glue-Line Drawings Before children make glue-line drawings, they create large pencil drawings on 12-by-18-inch newsprint or white drawing paper. For the next part of the lesson, they agree *not* to pick up or move their drawings. This project is best done at the end of the day so it can dry overnight.

Figure 13–4 *Double-pencil artwork with black crayon line and watercolor added*

When children's pencil drawings are complete, they redraw them with white glue lines. To do this, they open the glue bottle top and squeeze the bottle as they draw with glue over existing pencil lines. This is best to do with a few children at a time.

When children have redrawn all the lines, they leave the project flat on the table to dry. The next day, we will see that the pencil drawing has been transformed into a clear line of hardened glue.

At this point, the glue-line drawing is not finished. There are many possibilities for this project. Children may make crayon rubbings by placing a blank paper over the glue line and rubbing with a crayon. This makes a bold, clear rubbing. Other items may be added to rubbings at this point using a variety of media: crayon, oil pastels, torn paper, marking pen, watercolor paint, and so on.

Watercolors and Glue-Line Drawing Watercolor paint is especially effective right on the glue-line drawing papers. This is a great beginning watercolor lesson. The dried glue creates barriers to the paint. Instead of the typical first-grade watercolor painting, where the paint all mixes together to an ugly gray, in this case the glue lines keep paint colors separate, bright, and clear.

Watercolor Specifics Before children use watercolor paints, I give them very specific guidelines: They may not get up. They may not pick up their watercolor paintings. I will deliver clean water (I use a pitcher) and collect dirty water (in another pitcher, or empty half-gallon milk carton, with the top opened up).

Planning Our Art Schedule

I usually prefer to introduce paint a little later in the year. I limit art media to paper, pencil, pens, crayons, and torn paper for a while, until children are comfortable and know how to handle these materials.

I plan an art block each week: this time is set aside to teach children a developmentally sequential lesson. I use Dick's list of art sequences and curriculum from other subject areas we are learning to structure my lessons. For example, if we are studying the rain forest, I may use this curriculum as a suggested focus for our art learning. I use children's literature to introduce lessons and give them depth. Many picture books are very beautiful. Using them is like having a museum at our disposal in the classroom!

I also integrate art with other curriculum whenever possible and provide daily time for drawing.

Crayons

Children have in all probability been using crayons for a long time before they started school. We do many different lessons using crayons. One of my favorite lessons is to use crayons in conjunction with double-pencil drawing. This helps children *move* their arms and create larger, freer artwork. After making a large double-pencil or double-crayon drawing, children outline parts they like with crayon. They use crayon to fill in and add details. They outline the whole picture with a black crayon line. This is a way of helping children create without worrying about all those lines they want to erase. The lines they make are part of their process and show a lot about their creation. We want those lines in there to make the art interesting. They just need to darken the lines they want to keep prominent. Using black marking pen outlines on a crayon drawing really intensifies a piece of art. (See Figure 13–5.)

Crayons act as barriers in the same way that dried glue does in the glue-line technique explained earlier. When children watercolor their outlined crayon drawings, the heavy black crayon keeps different watercolor hues from running together.

Magic and Science Together: The Watercolor or Tempera Wash

A wash is a weak mixture of paint and water used as background on paper or to cover crayon or oil pastels. I use watercolors, or dilute tempera paint before this lesson to a very watery consistency, about half paint, half water. I generally prepare two or three watered-down tempera paint colors in margarine tubs or plastic bowls. I introduce the idea of water resistant and waterproof materials: raincoats, umbrellas, and so on. The children and I talk about how water is not absorbed by these materials.

It is easy to paint a dilution of tempera and water over crayon. This is called crayon resist. The trick is that the crayon must have several layers of color in order to have enough wax buildup to repel the paint. The children and I explore with sample crayon drawings I have prepared and talk about what happens when we add a watercolor wash

Figure 13–5
Bernadette's crayon drawing with black crayon outline

to crayon colored lightly, colored with several layers of crayon, and colored more heavily.

Canning Wax: A Great Drawing Tool

I share with children the idea of crayons containing wax, which repels water.

I show more about wax by drawing heavily with a chunk of paraffin or canning wax. I purchase this 6-by-8-inch block of wax from the grocery store and cut it up at home into rough cubes or wedges, using a serrated knife. I don't want the canning wax pieces to be too small; they should be a size children can hold onto.

As I draw with my hunk of canning wax, on white paper, the children are dismayed that nothing shows. They are convinced I don't notice this, as I blithely draw. *Then*, I show them the magic of a wash by painting over the invisible wax. I use a large paintbrush, going across the paper in long strokes, left to right, left to right, until the paper is covered with color. The white wax drawing underneath, repelling the paint, emerges from nowhere!

An important step for you to take before having students paint a wash is to double-check, with your own heavily layered scribbles of crayon on scratch paper, that the paint is diluted with enough water so that the crayon will not disappear for good. If this happens, just add a little more water, and try the mixture on your own sample again.

When you are teaching how to paint a wash, it is best to monitor it yourself, with just a few children at a time. Have children come to the sink area or a table covered with protective paper. (I use pieces of oilcloth, or even a cut-up, opened-out garbage bag. Plastic drop cloths are also very inexpensive.)

Demonstrate again how to apply the paint, going across the paper and painting over the crayon *one time only*. Be sure to stay with children as they paint their wash over the crayon on their papers. Ideally, the entire paper should be covered with paint.

If you turn your back, you can be sure children will apply several layers of diluted paint, "scrub-scrub" fashion, and end up with a vanished crayon drawing, and a scrubbed, beat-up-looking painted paper! Young children just cannot resist. The appearance of a wax or crayon

Figure 13–6
Want-ad designs

drawing when paint is applied is magical. They want to see it happen again and again. And of course, it just does not work well, except for the *first* application of paint!

Want-Ad Designs and Watercolors

Another idea I have used for years comes from the work of Jenean Romberg and Miriam Rutz's classic book *Art Today and Every Day* (1972). This idea is to create designs in crayon on the want ads from a newspaper. The grid layout of the newspaper gives structure to the work.

I teach children seven basic design symbols to use to create many designs on the newspaper. These symbols are: dot, half circle, circle, loops, spiral, line, and triangle. When all designs are colored, and the crayon looks dark enough, children may paint over the crayon with a wash. (See Figure 13–6.)

Shaving Cream and Food Coloring

An alternative to a wash is my concoction of shaving cream and food coloring. This mixture accomplishes the same thing, adding painted color to crayon or even marking pen drawings. It is actually simpler and faster than watercolor or diluted tempera paint. On the downside, the results are not very predictable, but that is half the fun of the activity!

I use shaving cream and food coloring occasionally, when we need a lift, need color to enliven crayon drawings that just didn't quite gel, or want an eclectic art experience. This is also a great thing to do on a day when everything is going wrong and we desperately need a light moment—or perhaps a magical one!

Before using shaving cream and food coloring, children color with crayons or marking pens. I prepare blobs of white shaving cream on sturdy paper plates, one big blob per plate. A shaving cream squirt slightly bigger than my fist is sufficient for about four children. I arbitrarily squeeze drops of food coloring into each blob of shaving cream. I use two or three drops of each food color per blob, resulting in multicolored blobs.

Children can get out their desk protectors (manila file folders), open them up, and put their crayon or pen drawings on top of them. They can apply a small blob of shaving cream and food coloring to their drawing with a crumpled up paper towel, or scrape the mixture across their pictures with a 3-by-5-inch index card. (They should scrape *around* marking pen drawing areas because nonpermanent pens will smear when wet.)

This shaving cream mix takes only seconds to apply and dries almost instantly. Children should scrape the mixture across their papers thoroughly, as a buildup of shaving cream will just soak into the paper or come off on someone's clothing.

A note of caution: Although this mixture dries instantly, and is easy to use, it *will stain* clothing and hands, especially the blue color. However, I find that when forewarned of pitfalls, children can use the shaving cream and food color mixture quickly and deftly, and they are delighted with the colorful and unpredictable results.

This should be obvious (but apparently it wasn't to me): *Never* leave the shaving cream and food coloring out unattended. I actually left some around, and children claimed they thought it was something they could use at the centers. Before I noticed them using it, my first graders went through a year's supply of materials and invented color combinations never seen before or since. I count myself lucky that most of the materials landed on the paper.

Teaching Children How to Handle Materials

If you are new to teaching art, it could seem overwhelming to worry about the mess involved! This is easily handled when we realize there are ways to break down every activity into workable pieces. And another factor is that we can teach children how to be responsible, how to clean up. They need many specifics and practice with little parts of the process at a time.

Children *love* art and will want to have the art experiences again. I always begin my lesson with details about how we will clean up and tips on using the materials and tools. I reinforce this at the end of the lesson, before time to clean up. And then children *do* clean up. I take an occasional deep breath but remind myself that they have been taught the specifics of cleanup, we've practiced it, and they realize that they must take care of messes and materials if they expect to have these kinds of lessons again.

Children are magical. They can change *everything* into *anything*! They just need materials and ideas of ways to use them, time, and encouragement. They need the chance to stretch and fulfill themselves with all kinds of art experiences.

I believe that for all ages, art is a way to play and invent, a way to express ourselves and communicate. We need it the way we need the sun and the moon and the stars, food, shelter, family, love, and friendship.

CHAPTER 14

Making Social Studies, Health, and Science Come Alive Through Literacy and Play

Whatever the country of your birth
You are a citizen of Earth.
Whatever the color of your skin
All its peoples are your kin.
They are your kin and you their brother,
So live in peace and love each other.

—From the picture book *I Love My Love with an A,* Diana Ross

If you opened the door to my classroom this afternoon, you would see a myriad of colors and bits and pieces of all kinds of items: cardboard, buttons, varieties of papers, foil, craft sticks, and many other things. If you didn't know better, you might even think this was junk. Children can be found down on a plastic drop cloth on the carpet, amid this sea of materials. A few are at tables. They are all working intently together to create a three-dimensional city.

I can see many houses, apartment buildings, and a bicycle shop. There are three churches, a police station, and a fire station. I spot several stores. Somewhat haphazard lettering proclaims two of them to be ice cream stores. There are bent cardboard flaps cut from boxes, tall and short paper towel rolls (cut to different heights on the paper cutter—by me, of course). There are marking pens, glue sticks and glue bottles, pieces of construction paper, and wallpaper strewn about as we work. The mess is no problem: we know how to clean it all up efficiently.

We are in the middle of a social studies unit about neighborhoods and cities. We are learning about our own community in South San Francisco, as well as our state, our country, and our world. And we are carrying this knowledge over to our *own* project as we create a community on the classroom floor. We don't just want structures. We want to create the type of neighborhood or city that makes for a better world.

Children's Literature Connection

We share such children's literature books as *The World That Jack Built*, by Ruth Brown (1991), a takeoff of the nursery rhyme "The House That Jack Built." The book stimulates a lot of discussion about caring for the world around us. Another special book is *All in a Day*, by Mitsumasa Anno (1999). It shows us cultural diversity and gives us a glimpse of what children are doing all over the world as we go through our own days and nights. When we read *The Little House*, by Virginia Lee Burton (1978), we realize that cities change: a house may start out in the countryside but end up many years later in the center of a large, crowded city.

Integrating curriculum with literature and active learning is an all-encompassing way to teach. I am using an urban planning theme to link our research and experiences from social studies curriculum to art, music, math, science, and of course, reading/language arts. When we teach in this way, children are readily able to learn and make connections. They have *lived* the concepts and understand them from the inside out.

Checking Out the Neighborhood

My first graders and I have taken a photographic walking trip around town. We had snacks at a local tortilla factory, after watching tortillas being made on an assembly line. We visited the post office, the old city hall, and the library and sketched and drew several old historical buildings. We also visited a fruit and vegetable market, a grocery store, and the fire station. We took pictures of buildings, ate ice cream, and learned about businesses, services, and facilities in our local area and beyond.

In the days after our trip, we had many discussions about the needs of a community and the people and businesses that help fill these needs. We used interactive writing and art to create a book about South San Francisco on large tablet paper. We illustrated our masterpiece with our photographs and drawings. We also created a class quilt, with yet more drawings of businesses and community structures. And we made a long panel with portraits of people who do important jobs in our town. Some of our artwork ultimately went on display at the public library.

Construction Strategies

The class has been introduced to a variety of art and craft strategies for putting buildings together, and now each child is creating a structure important to the lives of the fictional people in our fabricated town. When buildings are completed, and the room is cleaned up, we will sit together on the carpet and analyze and admire these structures. Children will have time to explain the function and importance of their creations.

It may take two, three, or even more sessions to complete our buildings. The whole project looks elaborate, but buildings are just cut and torn construction paper structures that have been glued to circles of paper towel rolls so they can stand up. Different heights of paper rolls are used, depending upon the height of the buildings.

We stack the buildings when we clean up, and put them away until our next construction session. Scraps may be cleaned up now, or we can pick up the messiest of them and just loosely fold the rest up in the drop cloth. This large, inexpensive piece of plastic captures all the bits and pieces of materials until we lay it down again another day.

City Planning

When the buildings are completed, we will begin the most important part of our thematic unit: city planning. We will add roads, stoplights, mailboxes, and other necessary services. We will move things around, discussing and giving the rationale for our decisions, until we have created a neighborhood that works for us. We may add parks and perhaps a hospital and pet store. We may put buildings on a large piece of butcher paper so that we can add streets, highways, and bridges. I never know details about the end result: this all depends upon the pint-sized architects and city planners in my classroom.

We say things like, "Do we really want the school so far away from those houses? Where shall we put the supermarket? Do we want the stores that close to the zoo? Where should the airport go? Is there anything missing that we really need?" There is never one right way or one right answer. We learn so much from the questions.

We make changes in our city as we create more roads, buildings, bridges, and other structures. We learn that sometimes, just as with real city planning, it is too late for some decisions because existing houses and roads make new growth and change more difficult.

Project Variation

A quicker way to do almost the same lesson, if time is a factor, is to have children work in groups to create joint scenes of three or four buildings. These may be showcased on large construction paper, 18 by 24 inches or larger. Details may be added. Each group may present its project, and the collection of building scenes may be grouped to create a community.

City Planning—Quick and Easy

Another alternative, fast way to plan a city or neighborhood with first graders is to use a piece of butcher paper or fadeless paper the size of your bulletin board. Put the paper down on the floor or on top of a large table.

Give children construction paper and access to books and magazines with buildings of all sorts for reference. Invite children to create, cut, and paste structures, and place them on butcher paper or fadeless paper background. They can also use marking pens. Discuss and move buildings around before attaching them with glue or glue stick. A better idea is to attach them with Fun-Tak. (See Resources.) This material is not permanent, so changes may be made.

Children may wish to complete the neighborhood by adding roads and other details with crayons or marking pens. Paper scraps could also be used, but more time is needed for this media. With just a little planning, the background paper may be turned into a neighborhood map.

Children's Literature Connection

See *My Map Book*, by Sara Fanelli (2001), to add concepts to your map experiences. The book features all kinds of maps, including "a map of my heart." Another children's book to use for this unit of study is *Roxaboxen,* by Alice McLerran (1992) and illustrated by Barbara Cooney. This picture book is a memoir of a town created out of the imaginations of the children who played there until they grew up.

Figure 14–1
Our neighborhood grew and grew, just as real ones do.

Integrated Themes

Working under this thematic umbrella of town and city, I am able to integrate a lot of other curriculum into our social science unit. Thematic organization enriches the learning experiences for my students. We learn poetry and songs about cities and towns and share a variety of literature, both fiction and nonfiction. We read our social studies big book together. We do several art projects and spend a lot of time reading and writing. There is a lot of time to talk and plan together. We always make sure to sketch our city, both when it is in progress and when it is finished. These drawings, or city time lines, make a great sequential display. Like *real* cities and neighborhoods, ours changes over time.

Using all kinds of materials, the children work metaphorically to create places to live and work, just as their ancestors did many years ago and their families are doing today.

Children need these concrete experiences. They learn best when they are actively involved in the learning process. At a recent science inservice, first-grade teachers in my school district were asked to describe a science lesson remembered from our own elementary school experiences. The only lessons the group recalled and described were those with projects, or active learning. These were the kinds of activities where we were able to manipulate objects, to fiddle and experiment with things, and had been given the chance to analyze and see for ourselves the results of our experimentation.

The Literacy Time Machine

Active learning is crucial to our success in social studies, science, math, and other curriculum, too! Access to a large number of picture books and nonfiction is also highly important. Literacy brings richness and knowledge to our study. It provides, as nothing else can, information, feelings, and the closest thing we have to real experiences. Our books are time machines that take us to other places, other times, and even into other well-lived lives. They help us learn about our world, as well as the world of nature and the things and creatures in it.

Books we have been reading, both in our read-aloud group and independently, are available to children as they work. Many of our books have social studies themes and are listed in California's *Literature for History–Social Science K–8* document. I have added to this book list, and I keep many of these children's literature books in a special book rack accessible to my first graders. (See Resources for a list of some children's books I use.)

Depending upon the class, this project emphasis may be on creating either a neighborhood or an entire city. Sometimes when we build a city, we create a harbor and a bay as well. Often this is made into a big city port. We may also construct an airport.

When we build a port, I especially like using literature for the creation of all the possible boats and ships a port could contain. *Big City Port*, by Betsy Maestro (1984), is a wonderful resource. It reminds me of my excitement in seeing the different kinds of ships at the Port of San Francisco when I was a child.

A Port Extends Our City Scene

In creating *our* port, children make boats from construction paper and cut them out. They label the type of boat or ship they have created. I sometimes draw different types of boats and ships to make a reference chart for the children. Other times I make overhead transparencies from *Big City Port* and other books, so that children have something to look at while they are creating their own seagoing vessels. If time allows, my first graders can collect magazine and newspaper photos of different kinds of ships to make their own collage reference tool.

The water for the ocean or bay is easy to make, and it holds the boats and ships upright. We use pieces of 12-by-18-inch construction paper in shades of blue and green. We make accordion folds by folding one edge of the paper up about an inch and a half. (The exact measurement is not crucial, as the water level varies!) We press the edge of this fold, then turn the paper over. We say, "Fold up, flip; fold up, flip. . . ." We fold and flip until the paper is full of zigzag accordion folds. (This is the same method we use to make paper fans.) I show children how to hold the center two or three folds and make about an inch-long snip, from the top of the folds down, with scissors. When they spread the accordion folds out slightly and fit their ship or boat into the snipped area, the ship will stay upright. We really do enjoy making waves and putting our port together.

Figure 14–2 *Our city and port and sea-going vessels*

Displaying Our Creation

There are several ways to display this beautiful creation of city and harbor. The first time I did this project with children, I had a class of thirty-three first graders. Even without taking up any of our floor space with an art project, the classroom was very crowded. Children could barely make it to the door to line up without jostling each other. However, after we created this city and port (which took up a third of the classroom floor space, most of it in the center of the room), we were all so proud of our creation that we wanted to leave it up for a while. (This was the children's vehement wish.) For two weeks, my first graders made it to line and everywhere else in the classroom without bumping a thing! After school each day, our room was filled with relatives large and small, admiring our masterpiece. The children made sure that nothing was touched or destroyed.

My husband, George, made a special trip to visit our city and port. He was amazed at the detail and depth of the project. "Just think," he told the children. "The bananas you had in your lunch today might have come through a port like this one!"

There was silence and nodding of heads. "Well, we *know* that!" Abraham said. "Our teacher told us that!"

I had read the class the nonfiction book *Bananas: From Manolo to Margie*, by George Ancona (1990). The book shows the growth of bananas, and has photos of their whole journey from a plantation in Honduras to a grocery store in North America. This class loved the book and had certainly absorbed the information!

Logistics of Classroom Cleanup: Remembering the Custodian

Even if you have a fabulous custodian, and we *do* at my school, this kind of display can be a problem when the room needs to be cleaned. Children picked up around the city and port so that our custodian did not have to do it. However, although nothing was said, I realize that this was very inconvenient for him. I'm thankful he enjoyed the whole project so much that it was not a real problem. However, the next time I taught this unit, I made changes to take care of this potential difficulty.

The Neighborhood or City Center

One year when we did this project, we completed buildings, roads, and other structures, as previously discussed. We did our city-planning part of the lesson and created a complete city or neighborhood. Then we put it all away! We kept all of the pieces in plastic tubs. Children spent center time, as well as rainy-day recesses, re-creating their city or neighborhood scene. All the things we made became toys we used to cement our learning as we played.

A variation of this playtime activity, later in the year, was to build a castle, using castle blocks from a museum store. We created our own surrounding countryside and other details.

Over time I have taught several variations of this neighborhood and city project. Often we have made maps, just using butcher paper or fadeless paper and crayons or marking pens. Sometimes we have added stand-up figures attached to paper rolls just the way we created our city. Here are some variations that have worked well:

- Classroom map
- Playground map
- Map of our school

- Little Red Riding Hood's forest, including her house and Grandma's house and the story figures
- Map of the area where the Three Little Pigs live, including the Wolf's house and story characters
- Snowmen on an ice floe. We use a block of Styrofoam, paper cups, cotton batting, and felt scraps to create snowmen floating past a city. (This is a great project to use with the book *The Snowman Who Went for a Walk,* by Mira Lobe [1984].)

Assessment of the Project: A Class Poem

Before and after our creation of a city or neighborhood, I assess children's knowledge by helping them create a class poem or *synopsis* of their understandings about neighborhoods, towns, and cities. I sit with children on the carpet, clipboard in hand. "Tell me about a neighborhood (or city, depending upon our lesson focus). What do you know?" I write down everything the children say and read it back to them. Then I ask, "Do you want to make any changes or add to what you have said?" I reread the "poem" aloud when the children feel it is complete.

I make a large-font computer printout of our final poem, and we put it on display on a bulletin board. Of course, we make illustrations and put them up as well.

Comparing the two different class poems (the one done before the unit and our culminating poem at the end of the unit) is always rewarding for me. I see such conceptual development, growth in vocabulary, and *smug* satisfaction!

The children also acquire cooperative learning skills through this project, which is probably more complex than something they could accomplish individually. The city or neighborhood comes to life through the efforts and passion of the whole group.

Flat Stanley

Of course, sometimes we long to travel beyond our community. This year's class planned a trip to Australia—not for themselves, but for a storybook character. The children listened to *Flat Stanley,* a chapter book by Jeff Brown (1996). Stanley is flat because a bulletin board has fallen on his head. He has many adventures, even traveling in an envelope to visit a friend across the country. The children created our version of Flat Stanley and sent him off to Australia in September with Henry's parents.

Julio and Maria Martin were good sports about our request to take Stanley with them. They photographed Flat Stanley enjoying many activities on their trip. A favorite event for our class was the arrival of a large package from Australia—a care package for Henry and for all of us. Henry's favorite item in the parcel was the photo of Stanley in Melbourne, half in and half out of the coin telephone money slot during a phone call home to him.

Check out Flat Stanley on the Internet for many similar ideas.

Guided Imagery

When Henry's parents sent books about Australian wildlife, I read them aloud, and then the children and I took a guided imagery trip to the area. Students closed their eyes while I described the scenery and our experiences. They could add to the telling as well, if they wished. Some of the children seemed to feel they had really been in Australia and knew a lot about the country. And we all benefited from some "time away," just as we all do on a real vacation.

Interactive Writing: A Flat Stanley Escapade

My first graders enjoyed creating their own Flat Stanley story on large tablet paper, dictating the story to me and helping me write it. Our tale told of Stanley's adventures in Australia with Henry's parents. Henry, Jesús, and Robert created the three-dimensional paper airplane

Figure 14–3 *Our shared writing tells about Flat Stanley's trip to Australia.*

on which Flat Stanley flew home. We attached this plane to the story chart, along with the photos from Australia, and of course, the cut-out of Flat Stanley.

Our Flat Stanley character continued to look for other adventures, and he did appear in and out of stories the children voluntarily wrote during writers workshop.

KWL Chart

Another activity I often use at the beginning of a new unit is the KWL chart. I scribe for the children as they list what they know (*K*); what they want to know (*W*); and what they have learned (*L*). We add to our chart frequently during the course of our unit of study.

Dental Health/Teeth Theme

One of the themes, or learning units, commonly addressed in first grade is dental health. This is of great interest to children this age because they have lost or are beginning to lose baby teeth and acquire permanent teeth. Another reason for addressing the topic at this time is that children are developing the coordination and small motor control to brush and floss their teeth correctly. This makes first grade the perfect age to teach children about their teeth and stress the importance of taking care of them.

When teeth are loose, children wiggle and jiggle them constantly. Many cannot leave them alone and want to share every detail of the experience with you. Children know intellectually that their teeth will be falling out, but this can be an unsettling process for some of them if their teeth hurt or if they see even a spot of blood. When a child tells me about a tooth hurting, a light touch is called for. I usually explain that the tooth will stop hurting soon. Sometimes I say something like, "This is your tooth's way of saying good-bye. Soon it will fall out and you will have a brand-new permanent tooth."

When teeth fall out, we celebrate. Considering the fact that it is possible for a six-year-old to lose as many as eight teeth in a single year, this could mean a lot of time out for celebrating, so we make our celebrations brief. We clap and say a short tooth rhyme I wrote for these occasions: "Hooray! Hooray! ________ lost a tooth today!"

The child goes back to the sink for a swish, a drink of water, and a plastic bag for the tooth. The really important time at the sink is for looking in the mirror to check out the new look with the tooth missing.

To save time and alleviate fears, it can be helpful to do a short, brief, informational lesson right away in the school year, explaining about teeth and how they will fall out and be replaced by permanent teeth growing in. I like to set up the whole celebration procedure at this time and put pertinent information on a chart by the sink. Children can illustrate this important document. I keep "tooth bags" (snack-sized plastic bags) available in a large plastic bag or envelope attached to the chart. There is a permanent Sharpie pen available for writing names on plastic bags. (Small-sized plain white envelopes may also be used, but these make it harder to see and admire the tooth!) Tooth saver necklaces are a new commercial item that is lots of fun to have available. (See Resources.)

Here is a sample tooth chart:

What to Do When Your Tooth Falls Out

- Go to the sink and swish.
- Take a drink of water.

Figure 14–4
Jesús shows off his tooth and his new look.

- Put your tooth in a bag. Put your name on the bag, and put it in your cubbie to take home.
- Check out your new look.

Our illustrated chart stresses the important details and gives children strategies for taking care of things by themselves.

Dental Connections

It would be a shame to miss all the curriculum connections afforded by the highly charged moments of losing teeth.

I keep a cutout construction paper bag on an easily reached bulletin board or cupboard door. Next to this tooth bag I put a plastic bag with pins, thin black marking pens, and small pieces of paper. A child may put a name and date on the paper (and a drawing of the tooth!) and pin this to the "tooth bag" on the day a tooth falls out. Transparent tape (rolled backward to make tape rolls) or Fun-Tak (a gumlike adhesive) may be used instead of pins.

This tooth bag may also be made into a chart. Just attach everything to poster board or large manilla chart paper. The completed chart can be hung on a wall or hung from a chart rack, using binder rings or a clip-type pants hanger.

Graphing is another way to integrate this tooth business with ongoing curriculum. This is another activity a child can do independently on the day a tooth falls out. I make a simple graph with the name of each child in a box across the bottom (alphabetically, by first name). Then I write numbers up the left side of the graph. I demonstrate and help with the first few teeth, but children soon get the hang of this and are able to color in one box per tooth, working from the bottom up. This graph gives us a visual to check out the status of classroom teeth! It also reinforces how to graph and how to use math for *authentic* reasons that are important to us.

We also have a graph for new teeth coming in!

Children's Literature About Teeth

I read many books about teeth, the tooth fairy, and legends from all over the world. I especially like Lucy Bate's book *Little Rabbit's Loose Tooth* (1988), because Little Rabbit discovers she has "a window in her mouth." Children are intrigued by this image. I also read several folktales and stories about teeth and what happens to them after they fall out. Since many of my children are from other countries, they have a variety of different stories to tell. It is interesting to me that many cultures have legends and folklore about the loss of teeth. I also find the endurance of tooth folklore fascinating. In my experience, listening to children in other grade levels who come back to visit me, children believe in the Tooth Fairy long after they have stopped believing in Santa Claus.

Children's Literature Connection

It's a good idea to keep a supply of picture books about teeth, since losing teeth is a frequent event. Some books I like to use are *Andrew's Loose Tooth*, by Robert Munsch (2002); *Throw Your Tooth on the Roof: Tooth Traditions from Around the World,* by Selby B. Beeler (2001); and *Tabitha's Terrifically Tough Tooth,* by Charlotte Middleton (2001).

Why Celebrate the Loss of Teeth?

I believe that losing a tooth is a rite of passage, or important life event, and as such, should be celebrated. This can be an exciting experience, and sometimes an upsetting one. It is important to support children going through this, particularly with the first tooth. Losing a tooth is a sign of growth and change: children never look the same after this happens, especially when new, larger permanent teeth grow in.

Losing teeth also provides important *real* reasons for reading and writing. There are even songs about this event, such as "All I Want for Christmas Is My Two Front Teeth." The experience is memorable enough that many adults remember the loss of first teeth and have special stories to tell.

Creative Writing About Teeth

My friend Julie Fox, a teacher in Pleasanton, California, celebrates the loss of teeth in other ways. She integrates the entire lost-tooth phenomenon with creative writing experiences. Julie's class keeps track of the number of teeth lost and has a tooth writing project every time they have lost ten teeth. They write incredible stories of the teeth they lost and what happened to them. Each time they hit twenty-five teeth lost, they have a tooth party and eat pudding, applesauce, and Popsicles and enjoy tooth storybooks. They sometimes watch a tooth-related video, such as *Arthur's Lost Tooth*, by Marc Brown. Julie says that their entire curriculum revolves around teeth on Tooth Party Day.

She has to discourage children from wiggling and pulling on teeth so that they can have a tooth party sooner!

A Tooth Pop-Up Book

One of the tooth-related activities I like to do is to give children a small pop-up booklet, shaped like a tooth, to write in and illustrate. If children wish, they may attach a small picture (or even their tooth!) to the inside pop-up box: a drawing of a tooth, a self-portrait showing a tooth missing, and so forth. (See Figure 14–5.)

Teeth and English-Language Arts

Oral language and poetry may also be linked to the lost-tooth phenomenon. I wrote a simple poem to share with children in my class.

Figure 14–5
Tooth pop-up

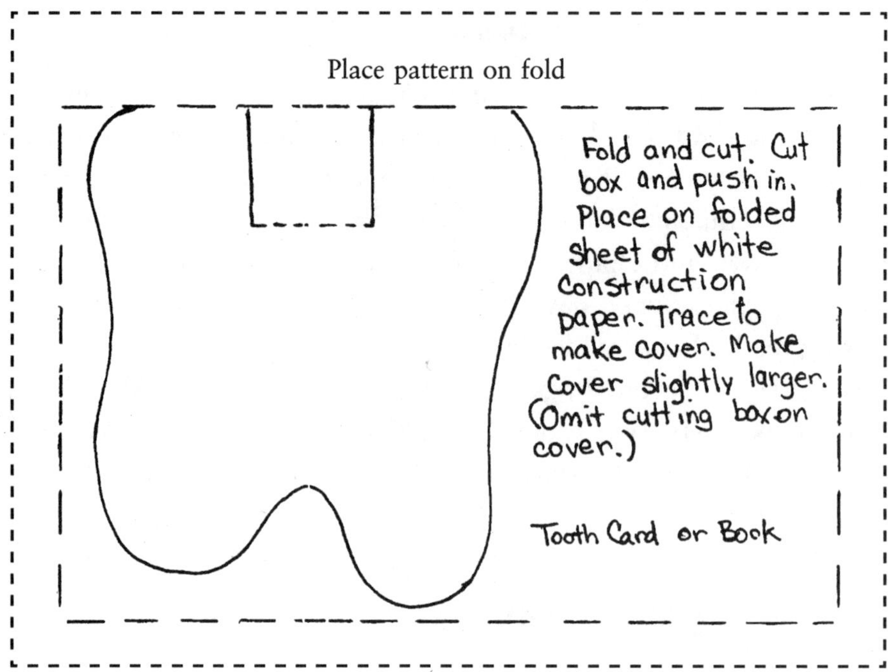

Any child's name may be plugged in instead of Tom. This is a good reading/oral language activity for those frequent days when teeth are loose, and it gives brief, valid attention to the child having this experience.

> *Tom's* tooth is loose,
> It cannot stay,
> I think he'll lose
> A tooth today!
> —PBD

It is a good idea to make your own tooth curriculum plan early in the school year: decide how you are going to handle things when teeth fall out. I have even had this happen to children on the first day of school, so there is no time to waste! The point is that children will lose teeth multiple times during the school year, mostly at the least convenient moments. Whatever you decide to do for the first child who loses a tooth should be repeated again for each child, each time. So it is really important to design activities that children can handle independently and that do not take up a great deal of class time. I aim for a brief festive moment and then a return to whatever we are doing.

Learning About Dental Care: The Brushmobile and the Tooth Lady

I teach about teeth throughout our first-grade year. This is a topic worth teaching in layers, or spirals, so that concepts become clear and children grow in understanding. First graders need time and reminders to develop good dental health and nutrition. I generally teach my thematic unit on care of teeth in February, nationwide Dental Health Month.

There are different resources available across the country. San Mateo County, California, where I teach, sponsors a Brushmobile that comes to schools. Children may visit the Brushmobile, see a short video on brushing and flossing, and brush their teeth in the sinks available. (Generally there are sixteen to twenty sinks per Brushmobile.) Brushmobile personnel give children instructions about their brushing and flossing techniques. They also give children extra help, if needed. Each child gets a toothbrush, toothpaste, and floss.

We are fortunate, at my school, to arrange for first graders to have a visit from Gina Lazzari, the Tooth Lady. Gina is a former parent who works as a dental hygienist. When she visits our first-grade classes, two groups at a time, she brings a large model of teeth and a giant toothbrush. She demonstrates brushing, and children are better able to see how this should be done.

There is time for discussion of tooth care, good foods to eat, and when to brush. We also discuss flossing. The highlight of Gina's program is her flossing demonstration. She chooses six first graders to participate, while the rest watch. Five children stand close together while Gina tucks a long pink cloth beneath their heads, poking it in at their necks, until only heads show. Their heads represent teeth. The pink cloth transforms children's necks and shoulders into gums. Another child wields the large toothbrush, gently, to demonstrate how to brush. With Gina's help, the child then uses large-sized green yarn (mint floss) around each "tooth" to show children how to floss teeth.

Our Tooth Lady's grand finale is a piggyback song with words she wrote to the tune of "Old MacDonald." The children sing it vigorously as they make motions to go with the words.

Old MacDonald had some teeth,
e-I, e-I, o!
With a brush, brush here,
And a brush, brush there.
Here a brush, there a brush,
Everywhere a brush, brush.

Old MacDonald had some gums,
e-I, e-I, o!
With a floss, floss here,
And a floss, floss there.
Here a floss, there a floss,
Everywhere a floss, floss.

Old MacDonald kept his teeth,
e-I, e-I, o!
With a smile, smile here,
And a smile, smile there,
Here a smile, there a smile,
Everywhere a smile, smile,
Old MacDonald kept his teeth,
e-I, e-I, o!

—Gina Lazzari

A piggyback song, as mentioned near the end of Chapter 11, is one in which an existing tune is given new words. Gina explains to the children that Old MacDonald was a real person. He lived to be more than one hundred years old and kept all his own teeth.

The Tooth Lady gives each child a toothbrush and toothpaste and a good understanding of how to care for teeth and gums. The first-grade teachers at Martin School look forward to her visits each year, and the school takes care of the cost for us.

I especially enjoy Gina's visits because her son Tom was my student in first grade, and Gina uses posters he has drawn as part of her presentation.

Other Dental Health Resources

Another good dental health resource is the Colgate Bright Futures, Bright Smiles Kit. This set of materials contains posters, a video, and a package of toothpaste for each child. There are also leaflets for children to take home. Classroom teachers may order these kits free of charge at *www.colgatebsbf.com.*

Butterflies and Other Living Things

Watching butterflies emerge from chyrsalides is one of the most miraculous experiences I have ever had in the classroom, and I think the children feel the same way. I began using this thematic unit several years ago, ordering caterpillars from Insect Lore, by calling 1-800-LIVE BUG. I had purchased a butterfly kit from a local store. Many companies now sell this item, but the kit can also be purchased from Insect Lore by calling the above number.

I loved teaching this unit at the beginning of the school year because children were so excited: they invited brothers, sisters, parents, and everyone else they could find into the classroom to see our caterpillars metamorphose to chrysalides and then butterflies. Now I teach this unit toward the end of the school year, because it is a culmination of our science curriculum. I have tried to replace the beginning-of-the-year butterfly excitement with an ant farm unit.

I find that it is important to include the children in all areas of the thematic butterfly unit, including placing the order for our painted lady caterpillars. First, we plan the best days for our caterpillars to arrive, making sure that there are no large blocks of time when we will be missing from the classroom. (If caterpillars were delivered during Spring Break, we would miss some of the action!)

After we decide dates we want our caterpillars to come, I make the telephone call, with the children present. I make sure children are aware that these small caterpillars first hatch from eggs and are then sent on to us.

When the caterpillars arrive, they are in a small container with a lid and air holes. These tiny insects rest on a bed of mashed-up food (leaves) that looks a bit like green peanut butter. We handle the caterpillar container only briefly. Then we place it on a shelf where we can all see the changes that will be taking place. Once, when I taught this unit, we passed around the container frequently, and the caterpillars did not metamorphose. I have felt sorry about that error ever since!

Shared Writing

There is great excitement when our caterpillars come! I wield a pen and write down the children's thoughts and feelings on large chart paper. We read back our ideas together. Children illustrate the chart and we tape on cutout drawings that illuminate our thinking.

Children then begin their caterpillar/butterfly science logs on this first day. My colleague Colleen Quinn Malloy designed the log. The booklet contains about fifteen stapled pages, with a construction paper cover. There are spaces for two days of observations on each page. Naturally, we do not want to handle these small insects, so we estimate the probable length of each caterpillar. Using a magnifying glass helps us determine this information. Usually these caterpillars measure anywhere from about 1/8 of an inch to 3/8 of an inch long. Children draw the caterpillars in their science logs. They also write information: things they notice and find interesting. (See Figure 14–6.)

I often turn this caterpillar experience into a learning center, with several magnifying glasses, a variety of drawing materials, and many fiction and nonfiction books about caterpillars and butterflies. In this learning center, children have more time, in a small group, to enjoy this experience.

Some books I have particularly found to be helpful in teaching this unit are *Amazing Butterflies and Moths* by John Still (1991), with photographs by Jerry Young; *Where Butterflies Grow,* a picture book by Joanne Ryder (1996); and *Young Naturalist Pop-Up Handbook: Butterflies*, by Robert Sabuda and Matthew Reinhart (2001). Please see the Resources for names of other books I have found to be particularly helpful with this thematic unit. I like to use a mixture of fiction and nonfiction books.

We Use All the Arts to Learn and Wonder

As with other thematic units, this one on butterflies is extended and enhanced with art, music, writing, poetry, and other experiences. The children love this poem, adapted from *Millions of Cats*, by Wanda Gag:

Hundreds of butterflies,
Thousands of butterflies,
Millions and billions and
Trillions of butterflies!
—adapted by PBD

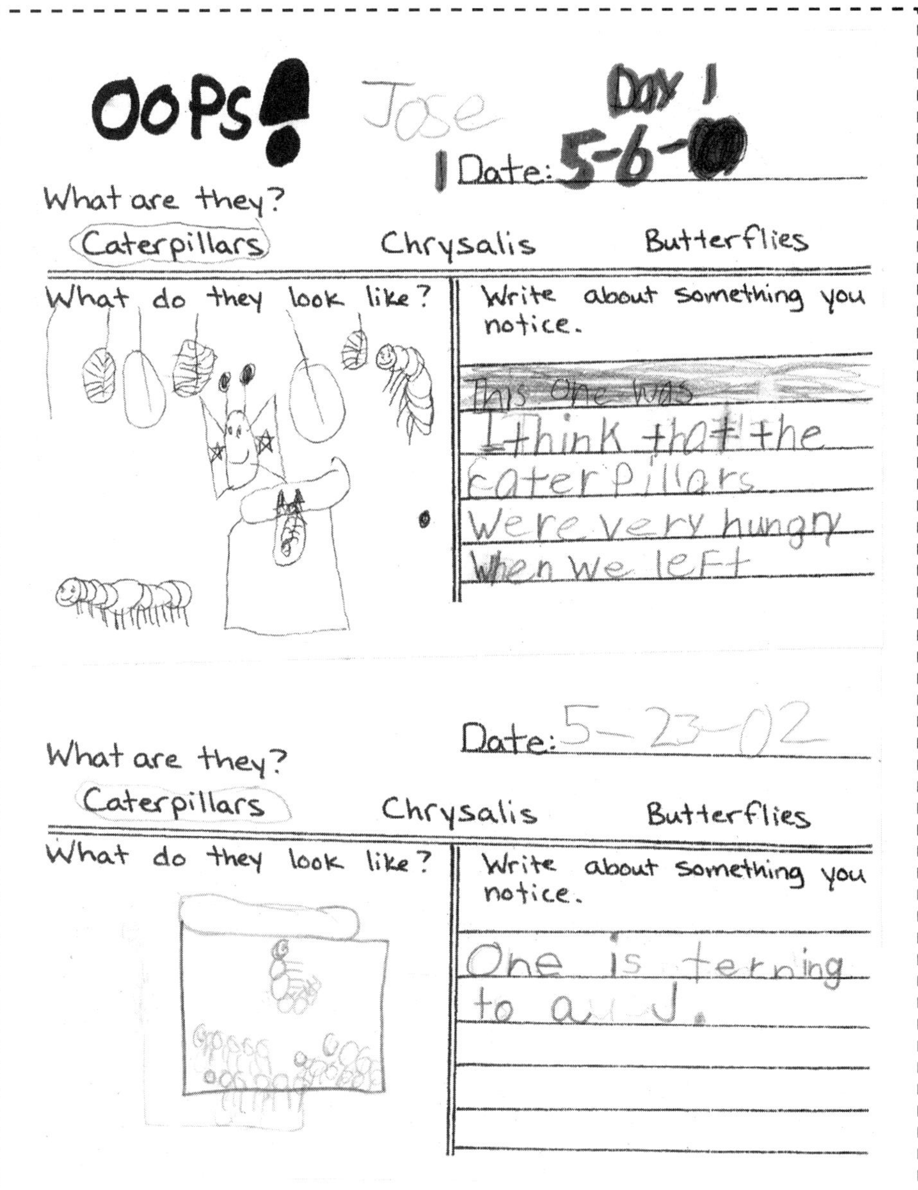

Figure 14–6
Jose's science log entries

Children also enjoy making a butterfly pop-up book (see Appendix). The booklet can be turned into a butterfly puppet when children stick a finger or two through the pop-up box. Children enjoy decorating these with crayons and a mixture of shaving cream and food coloring (see Chapter 13).

Three-Dimensional Butterflies

One of my colleagues, Laura Darcy, developed a wonderful butterfly art lesson. Using crayons and watercolors, children were invited to create giant butterflies on 18-by-24-inch paper. These were cut out when dry and overlapped on a bulletin board in three-dimensional positions. The crayon lines created borders for the watercolor, so that the color remained clear and true.

Releasing Our Butterflies—One of Our Most Beautiful Experiences!

Children approach our butterfly unit with reverence and awe. I believe this becomes a metaphor for learning about and respecting other living things. To accentuate this feeling, we frequently recite one of our favorite poems, "Hurt No Living Thing," by Christina Rossetti:

Hurt no living thing;
Ladybird, nor butterfly,
Nor moth with dusty wing,
Nor cricket chirping cheerily,
Nor grasshopper so light of leap,
Nor dancing gnat, nor beetle fat,
Nor harmless worms that creep.

Our favorite day comes when butterflies have emerged from their chrisalides and it is time to release them. Although we realize that our

Figure 14–7 *Giant crayon and watercolor butterflies*

butterflies will not remain in the area, we are aware that they tend to hang around for a few days. We have a beautiful garden at school that is the perfect place for us to release our butterflies.

We bring flowers, especially carnations, for the butterfly good-bye. Children may also bring sketchbooks and drawing materials if they wish. We could release our butterflies by opening the butterfly box, but that is problematic, since we assembled it well. Children take turns putting either a finger or a carnation into the butterfly box, for a landing platform. The butterfly rides out on the finger or flower, pauses, then takes off into the air. This is repeated until all five butterflies are released. These are stunning moments for us all. We draw for a few minutes, watch the butterflies that linger in our garden, then return to the classroom to talk and record our feelings together. Then we turn our thoughts into a class poem.

Butterfly Poem

To make our class poem, we gather on the rug together. Children share their thoughts and I write them down as quickly as I can. (Sometimes I do this on the computer; it's faster and easier to read.) When all the children who wish to contribute have expressed themselves, I read the poem back to the class. Often we reproduce this group poem in large

Figure 14–8
It is a magical moment when we watch our butterflies fly away.

type on a chart or bulletin board. We illustrate our experience, our words. I give children notebook-sized copies to illustrate and keep in their poetry binders. This last activity culminates a very satisfying experience for us all.

Thematic Teaching: Clarity for English Language Learners and *All* Learners

In my school district, we group children by language ability for one period a day. During that time we teach leveled English language classes. Learners at the first two levels of English proficiency are grouped together, while more experienced English language learners are in other groups. In addition to this specific language time, we teach English language instruction throughout the school day by using specific techniques such as providing realia (actual items), photographs, and picture books and teaching poetry, chants, and songs. This is just good teaching for *every* primary-aged learner to help make meaning become clear. Using this way of grouping for language instruction, the second language learners who are just beginning to speak English do not have to compete with children with much greater proficiency in order to express themselves.

There is a myriad of information about teaching English language learners in the following professional literature books: *Reading, Writing, & Learning in ESL*, by Suzanne F. Peregoy and Owen F. Boyle (2000); *Second Language Learners*, by Stephen Cary (1997); and *Working with Second Language Learners: Answers to Teachers' Top Ten Questions,* by Stephen Cary (2000).

Making Connections: Science, Social Studies, and ELL Instruction

At my grade level, we plan together as a group to integrate some science and social studies with our ESL program. We also teach thematically and make connections with other curricula.

I begin today's English language/science lesson with a science big book, introducing a unit about how things move. The big book is very visual. The large photos give everyone, even children with little English proficiency, an idea about what we will be studying and investigating. The text shows children doing the same tasks *we* will be doing. We also use songs, stories, and chants to teach oral language development as well as comprehension.

Today we have several items to use in our preliminary investigations of how things move: each child has a paper, pencil, string, small block, a craft stick, and a piece of drinking straw. After a brief discussion, the children experiment with these materials.

As the children move from the rug to tables, and begin tentatively fiddling with the items, a sense of play and adventure takes over. It is amazing to see the way fun and involvement get language going. The children are *intensely* interested and involved in this activity and want to talk about it. Their language is supported by the vocabulary and concepts in the big book we read and looked at, our brief discussion, and some picture cards.

Sitting together in a circle on the rug after our "lab work," we recap what we did: We spin a block with string the way Robert invented, build a stick and paper ramp or incline to slide blocks down, as Olivia did, and blow through straws, as Deyanira discovered, to make the paper move. I take a pen and write down what the children say. They help me write letters, sounds, and words they know. We also share the pen to *draw* the different discoveries the children made.

Figure 14–9
Group play and investigation stimulate creativity, thought, and language.

We all had fun with this lesson, internalized some important science concepts, and made strides in acquisition of the English language. The children's attempts to express themselves were all honored. Indeed, children outdid themselves, trying out materials, making predictions, drawing conclusions, and talking about it all. They took a lot of risks in their play and explorations. The excitement this engendered helped propel them to take risks with language and try to express what great things they had figured out, both orally and with written language and drawings.

The spirit of investigation was in us all as we spun cubes with strings to turn them into tops, flung straws threaded with string across the classroom, blew papers and pencils, and created our own paper ramps. There just wasn't time to be worried about our language or lack of it; we were too busy investigating and expressing ourselves.

We capitalized on our love of fiddling with things; we investigate all kinds of materials throughout our science units.

Multisensory Communication Is a Key!

I believe that a focus on *all kinds* of communication and the willingness to try to communicate with each other in many different ways are keys for success in helping children understand curriculum. These are also important factors in facilitating children's acquisition of language. I experienced these ideas in a slightly different way in my own life, growing up.

From the time I was a very tiny child, my mother was totally deaf for speech. The best way to communicate with her, other than using some sign language and looking at her so she could lip-read, was to say things another, simpler way, *show* her, or even draw or write what we were trying to communicate. The more things my Dad, sister, brother, and I tried, the more successful we were at making ourselves understood.

I feel this is another key with second language learners: we, as teachers, need to try many modalities to make meaning become clear—drawings, mime and creative dramatics, music, and art. Also helpful are translations from students (or the teacher!) who speak the native languages of children in the group.

My mother sped up the process of understanding what we were trying to say by being very clever with words, a good guesser, and most of the time keeping a kind of playful, solve-the-puzzle attitude about it all. Although we didn't always succeed, we tried to be flexible and creative about our attempts to communicate with her. My mother is fun to interact with. None of us wanted to miss out!

As time went on, I saw each of my mother's little grandchildren, as they grew old enough to communicate, gently turn her face to look at them when they talked. I witnessed each of them spontaneously tell her wonderful stories, all with both words and pretend sign language, which she added to and embellished verbally. It would look something like this:

Toddler: [*Talking a little, doing pretend sign language, moving hand or hands expressively and purposefully*]

My Mother: [*Speaking as she signed*] Oh, no! Really? Then what happened?

Toddler: [*Nodding, smiling, and going at it even more enthusiastically, moving hands rapidly*]

My Mother: [*Inventing even more involved and creative imaginary conversations and affirming child's efforts to communicate*] That's the best story I've ever heard!

None of us in the family had any training in any of this at that time—sign language, lip-reading, or working with the deaf—but we tried many things. And we all felt that these inventive and creative efforts by very small children to communicate with someone they loved were amazing and beautiful to behold.

On the other hand, I have seen people outside our home, mostly adults, speak painfully loudly to my mother when she didn't hear them, expressing exasperation with her lack of understanding. I have seen people repeat things the same way countless times, with more volume each time. And, of course, she still didn't get it, because it was physically impossible.

I think that sometimes we treat our second language learners in similar ways. The above descriptions are metaphors for what happens to second language learners in some classrooms. I had a few of these kinds of frustrating experiences myself in an elective art and culture class at a language school in Mexico. I am thankful for these memories now because I have an idea of how second language children feel in the monolingual classroom. At least, I know how this second language adult felt!

If I, as the teacher, just talk and talk, repeat myself over and over, and then talk even louder, children who don't speak English *still* aren't going to have any idea what I am saying. The children don't have enough experience with English to understand me unless I scaffold this learning with other strategies and techniques and a lot of provisions for hands-on learning.

CHAPTER 15

Making Music

You can teach things with music
that you just can't teach in any other ways.

—Charlotte Diamond, musician and songwriter

Charlotte Diamond is one of my music mentors. I have heard her perform, and I use many of her techniques, as well as her books and tapes, in my classroom. I have other music mentors as well. Among them are John Langstaff, Raffi, and Hap Palmer. When I listen to their tapes or CDs, or hear any of these people give a presentation, I leave in the most joyful of moods, eager to share what I have learned with my first graders.

If you play a musical instrument, this will enable you to provide wonderful classroom experiences. If not, there are many CDs and videos available to help you teach music.

Music is an evocative, often moving experience. Through music and rhythm, we convey and learn so much. Music can be a hook for hanging onto facts and concepts. It can also help resurrect a day or lesson gone awry. Music gets us away from a problem, and possibly out of our left brains as well, and into the right hemisphere. Songs and other musical experiences take us on a rhythmic journey, where we can participate, imagine, dream, create, and express ourselves. Music is truly magic!

Music is very closely related to dance. Children learn a lot about how to control their bodies through music and movement. These are some of the most natural ways for children to enjoy themselves.

Wind ribbons are a great tool to use with music and dance. Use the paper cutter and chop 2-inch wide pieces from unfolded crepe paper. Give a folded piece to each child to unfurl, run with, and use to dance and sing. These strips are wonderful for windy days and are a great indoor activity as well. (See Figure 15–2.)

I always try to remind children not to go near the water fountain with these wind ribbons. The crepe paper dyes make a terrible mess when wet.

Wind ribbons may also be made by cutting strips from a plastic tablecloth or drop cloth.

Figure 15–1
Salvador sings his heart out.

Figure 15–2
Andrea and J.J. move and swirl their wind ribbons.

The Way to Teach a Song

Charlotte Diamond uses what she calls the echo technique to teach her songs, signs, gestures, movements, and musical games. In this method, she sings a small portion of a song, and the audience echoes this part of the piece. In this way children can easily learn songs and rhythms.

Charlotte often teaches American Sign Language *with* the music, as she says signs are much easier to learn along *with* the music, rather than separately. Signs and gestures engage us all physically and are of special help to kinesthetic learners, who really need to feel things in this way as they learn.

Charlotte has produced several audio CDs as well as books for teachers. (See Resources.) My class this year particularly liked *10 Carrot Diamond* (1985) and *Charlotte Diamond's World* (2000).

Props are another big part of Charlotte's repertoire. For example, when she sings "Singing in the Rain," she twirls a large decorative yellow umbrella. "I Am a Dog" calls for a headband with felt dog ears attached. And for "I Am a Bubble," she blows bubbles with a bubble wand and small bowl of bubble soap.

Charlotte suggests that the bubble soap, wand, and song are especially great for a difficult day. Children (and their teacher!) can blow sad, mad, and grouchy feelings into the bubble wand. The bubbles come out and pop, often dissolving difficulties and putting a happier face on things.

These props, as well as the music, are an easy way to get children's attention, especially on days when this is problematic.

Charlotte believes that music helps us all to leave the world a little bit better than we found it.

Music is great for getting away, for learning and memorizing some curriculum, such as math facts, as well as for fostering good feelings and cooperation. Children are quick to respond to music and rhythm and rhythm games. The sight of a prop, or the sound of a few bars of song, can signal an end to an activity or an invitation to be at the class meeting area as quickly as possible.

John Langstaff

Another of my music mentors is John Langstaff. He has had a long and distinguished career in music education and is also the author of twenty-five children's books. One of his tales, *Frog Went A-Courtin'*, is a winner of the Caldecott Medal. John Langstaff has many musical cassettes and audio CDs for children. Two CDs we especially enjoyed in my classroom this year are *Songs for Singing Children* (1996) and *John Langstaff Sings the Jackfish, and Other Songs for Singing Children* (2002).

One of my most memorable experiences has been to attend the Children's Literature New England Conference held each summer and be part of a group of more than two hundred participants singing and dancing and spiraling outside into the moonlight, all of us led by Jack Langstaff.

Music and Memory

According to a *Newsweek* article written by Sharon Begley (July 24, 2000), scientists believe the human brain is wired for music, and that music enhances some forms of intelligence. People can typically remember or recognize the words to hundreds of song lyrics, but can recall only a small number of prose or poetry passages. It appears that music enhances memory, and helps us hold onto pieces of information. I do not know how these statistics were obtained, but I do believe the hypothesis that we are much more able to remember words, facts, and information when they are set to music. When I want to recall the names for colors, or the order of colors in a rainbow, I sing a song or two that I learned in kindergarten long ago.

Linking Music, Literacy, and Art

I find that music and rhyme are very important ways to help children learn to read and enjoy reading. If we can sing something, we can *read* it! I use a lot of musical picture books. (See Resources). We learn the song first and enjoy it together. We magically find that when the book appears, we can read it! Musical books and songs are great staples for listening centers, as well as for whole-group read-alouds and sing-alouds.

I find it important to *make* music-related reading materials for my children to read during their beginning independent reading times. After we enjoy a song together I make music charts, as I did for "Oh, A-Hunting We Will Go!" (see Chapter 9). We sing and read and track the words together on the charts. Then we illustrate them.

Often these song charts evolve to become musical murals. We showcase the words to a favorite song somewhere on the mural paper, and add cut- or torn-paper or paint illustrations to illuminate the words. These are *multiart* activities!

As an important follow-up to these experiences, I make a four-page booklet with the words to the song. (See p. 197, Chapter 9). Children find they can read these song books because they can sing the words. It is an astonishing revelation for many children at this age to pick up something and discover that they are able to read it! I leave space on each page so that children can illustrate the songs themselves. We add these special pieces of illustrated literature and song to children's own independent reading bags at their desks and read and sing them over and over.

Music helps improve self-image and empowers us all to enjoy, learn, create, express ourselves, and grow. It helps us to succeed and then succeed again.

Musical Resources

Another way we make music is with rhythm instruments: sticks, triangles, maracas, xylophones, tambourines, drums, and so forth. These can be purchased from school supply stores. They are also easy and fun to make. We enjoy making a variety of sounds, too, and we can sing along with our own rhythms.

Here are some simple musical instruments to create in class.

You Need

- Paper plates—assorted sizes
- Staplers
- Beans, popcorn kernels, pebbles, rice—an assortment
- Straight pins
- Masking tape
- Paper tubes of assorted sizes
- Marking pens or paint for decorating instruments

Procedures

- *Tambourine*: Place a few dried beans, popcorn kernels, rice, or pebbles on a paper plate. Cover the plate with a second paper plate and staple the edges. Decorate with marking pens. Hang paper streamers or bells on plates if desired. Shake and make music.
- *Rhythm stick*: Tape one end of a paper tube. Add a few of the materials listed above for a tambourine. Tape the other end of the tube. Decorate and shake. This is a great rhythm stick.

- *Rain stick*: For a more involved instrument, a rain stick, cover index fingertips with a "wrap" of masking tape to cushion them. Now push a few pins into the seams of a paper tube, all the way around. Tape one end of the tube shut, and add a few dried beans and other materials, as with other instruments. Tape the other end closed. The beans and other items will make great sounds as they fall through the pins inside the tube. This is called a rain stick because it does sound like the rain. You can change the sound, depending upon the number of pins you use and the variety of items you put inside.

Here are some other easy ways to make a rhythm band, using things you already have (or can cheaply get from a secondhand store or flea market):

- A large pot to bang on with a spoon to make a drum
- Two pot lids to clang for cymbals
- Two spoons to jingle together for castanets
- A ring of measuring spoons to shake for tambourines
- Two wooden spoons to bang together for rhythm sticks

Rainy-Day Help

A great rainy-day activity that incorporates music, dance, and drama is to put on a record or audiotape and have children dance and move spontaneously. When you stop the music, students freeze in position. This gets rid of *a lot* of energy. The activity is a good one to draw as well as to participate in.

Music is an important curriculum area. It is also one of the ways we have the most fun.

CHAPTER 16

Physical Education

Play Everything!

When you teach PE make it skill-based,
nonthreatening, and fun.
PE class might be some kids'
only success in school—
the only time they really feel good about themselves.

—Peggy Merin, former PE teacher, kindergarten teacher

My first graders think *PE* means "play everyday," or "play everything." These are good guesses, because children need play (movement education, as well as creative play) on a daily basis. These opportunities to move, run, stretch, and play games enable children to keep mind and body in balance. PE relieves stress and helps children develop good self-concepts. It provides fun and excitement, too.

Physical education, games, and interacting with friends are all reasons some children *want* to come to school! When it's time for PE (daily), my children chant, "Hooray! Hooray! We get PE today!" They love this time and look forward to it. As Matthew said spontaneously one afternoon, "PE is good for kids from the inside out."

PE is a much overlooked and important area of the first-grade (and all school) curriculum. Many adults in our population would not live such sedentary lives if physical activity had become habit when they were in school. PE is a subject that is sometimes omitted when time is short. A twenty-minute physical education period each day is mandated in California and many other states.

This time for movement helps children get everything tuned up and working together. Many experts believe students do better academically when they have these physical education experiences. I *do* know my first graders are happier if they get this stimulating time for fun and for noncompetitive, cooperative learning. And we seem to get a lot more accomplished when we come back to the classroom after our PE period.

Giving Children PE Skills to Practice

There are many PE skills typically addressed in kindergarten and first grade. Children love to practice these on the playground. Spending time like this can also give their recess time some focus. We all know children who wander around out there on the playground and don't know what to do with themselves. This year I made a list of these PE skills taught *with* my first graders early in the school year in order to give them ideas about some things they could be doing at recess. And of course, we practiced these skills in our PE program, at another time in the day.

First-Grade Games and PE Practice

What are some ways we can get from one space to another? We could try

- Walking
- Hopping
- Jumping
- Running
- Skipping
- Galloping
- Sliding
- Running backward

- Walking in a crossover pattern: left hand or elbow touches right leg; right hand or elbow touches left leg
- Turning and twisting

We could play

- Tag
- Hopscotch
- Jump rope
- Throwing, catching, bouncing, and dodging a ball
- Kicking, rolling, or stopping a ball with our feet
- Soccer
- Hula hoops

Children told me these things and we added them to the list:

- We could imagine and pretend to play all kinds of games.
- We could act out a poem or a song or a story.
- We could walk or run all the way around the playground.
- We could do all kinds of things on the PE apparatus.

I kept this list by the classroom door and reviewed ideas periodically with my first graders before recess. Of course, they kept adding ideas! This type of information empowers children. Giving them things to do on the playground cuts conflict considerably and gives students more chance to succeed and have fun.

I like to reproduce lists like this one on charts or pieces of large tablet paper and invite children to illustrate them. This makes the text even more accessible to them. My first graders are creating works of art as well as text to read and help us remember!

Some other skills children practice at recess or during PE times are

- Learning a variety of games
- Taking turns

- Taking care of PE equipment
- Being good sports and playing fair

My colleague and friend Peggy Merin is an expert in physical education. She taught it as a subject to K–6 students and now uses her knowledge to teach other teachers, as well as her kindergarten children. Peggy says PE should never be omitted from the school day.

Maximizing Participation

Children need both individual experiences and time to play games and learn with the whole group. Peggy says the main thing about teaching PE, like most areas of the curriculum, is to avoid *wait time*. "We want the least amount of waiting time and the greatest amount of participation," Peggy says. She takes this into account when structuring all her PE activities.

Lots of Equipment Means No Waiting!

As Peggy suggests, the more equipment we can use for PE, the more we cut out the time children spend waiting for turns. Double-ball dodge ball is much more fun and exciting than playing the game with a single ball. We can also cut our class in half, use smaller playground circles, and play games in smaller groups. When we practice catching this way, we use many balls. One child takes charge of one circle and I work with the other group of children. Everybody has a chance to get involved.

We have balls to throw, bounce, catch, dribble, and spin. We have enough jump ropes that we get a lot of time to try out jump rope ideas. If children get tired of jumping individually, they join a jump rope game with me.

Figure 16–1
Henry practices jumping rope

Noncompetitive Kickball: Don't Keep Score!

Another important point Peggy Merin stresses is teaching the children noncompetitive activities.

A good example of this noncompetitive way of teaching PE, with a minimal amount of time to wait for a turn, is Peggy's way of playing kickball. First graders all want, and need, chances to kick the ball. They don't need to be on a team that gets the most points—just the chance to play and practice. So, with Peggy's way of playing the game, half the class is up, and the other half is in the field. Peggy pitches or rolls the ball, to maximize children's chances of kicking it. The fielding team helps the kickers by catching the ball quickly, so that more kickers have turns in a short amount of time. As soon as everyone on the kicking team has had a chance to kick the ball and run the bases, the teams reverse positions: kickers take the field, and the other children now have their turns to kick.

This is a very cooperative way of playing. Children are also practicing and learning PE skills. As Peggy says, "Nobody needs to keep score!" *All* the children win when they all have turns, enjoy a game, get some exercise, and help each other succeed. Everybody roots for everybody else!

Only Teachers Create Teams!

It is highly important that teachers, *not* students, create the groups for team games. Nothing is more devastating than being picked last—over and over again. As teachers, we can appear to be *randomly* assigning teams, while we quickly and subtly create balanced teams with a variety of strengths and weaknesses. We can also just number-off students and get a random mix of team members.

Our Optimum PE Time

The best time for PE in my classroom seems to be about an hour after lunch. We have had a story, finished math, and need a break—physically, as well as for water and trips to the bathroom. Usually children take care of these needs quickly, so we can head out to the playground. Sometimes, however, we play games or do exercises while we wait by the bathrooms.

The time waiting for the children to finish in the bathroom and at the water fountain can be profitable in many ways. We have conversations. We play little games, sing songs, and recite our favorite poems. An all-time favorite activity used to be to talk with one of our beloved custodians, Ed Malacarne. Ed always cautioned the children against using one particular drinking fountain for many drinks of water. This fountain frequently overflowed and had not yet been fixed. Ed's way of warning the children off was to ask them not to use the fountain because his pet fish lived in it.

"We don't see any fish!" was the children's logical and usual response. Ed always explained, tongue in cheek, that his fish were invisible, and that this variety was the best kind of pet. My first graders bought into this bit of folklore because it was appealing to them and because they all loved Ed.

When Ed took a long leave of absence due to illness, the children sent him get-well notes. Many of them wrote to him about his fish. Most of them told Ed his invisible fish were fine, but the fish missed him. A few children wrote that he shouldn't worry: *they* themselves were taking care of his fish and also cleaning the bathrooms for him!

Ed's stories were something we all looked forward to every afternoon. The children also liked to play *their version* of Simon says while they chatted with Ed and waited for each other. Some of the fun of this was that Ed would mime the actions in the background.

Simon Says—Our Style!

In this game, children lined up on the wall around the corner from Ed's fish fountain. At first I would start the game and give the Simon says directions. (In the *real* game, if you do a motion without hearing "Simon says," you are out and can't play. In *our* game, no one is out. The game just continues because we all want to play.)

Our game evolved to the point that the children were in charge. Each child leader took two or three turns giving directions. Of course, we *all* soon saw that *their* directions were much more involved and imaginative than mine!

I finally realized that having children take charge of the game resulted in much more imaginative play: being an airplane landing in the fog, climbing out of a really hot volcano, dancing ballet onstage, and so on. I also realized that children were imaginatively modeling for each other and were also using and grasping very involved vocabulary.

On many days our PE program took this focus, and the children took charge of vocabulary and imaginative play without really realizing the depth of their learning! In actuality, we got no farther than the wall outside the bathroom doors, but in our minds, we had visited zoos and rain forests, landed aircraft, and flown into space and around Jupiter! Some of the books we had read and loved contributed to our imaginary play. We visited Max and the Wild Things, danced Peter Pan with Amazing Grace. We sailed with Tough Boris, the pirate, ate green eggs and ham, and climbed a beanstalk with Jack. We had a very real break from academics, one that I believe spurred children on to increased focus and attention when we returned to the classroom. I know *I* felt revived by these moments of fun!

Integrating PE and Other Curricula

Because time is short in our school day, we often integrate PE curriculum with other subject matter, as just described. Another reason for integrating curriculum is that connections make learning much more powerful and meaningful.

Many of Peggy Merin's PE lessons have double goals and objectives, such as learning high-frequency sight words and practicing specific physical movements at the same time. For example, in one activity, Peggy uses Fun-Tak (see Resources) or tape to affix targeted sight-word cards (for example, *the*, *of*, *on*, *with*, and so on) to the playground fence. As her children run by her, in a large circle on the playground, she calls out different movements for them to practice: "gallop," "slide," "walk," "run," "hop," and so forth. As her students pass the fence, they pick a card, read it, and hand it to their teacher. If they do not know the word they have chosen, they find out what it is. Then they carry the word card around the circle for another go. Children love the game. They are playing as they learn in two different disciplines at once.

A Multiple-Goal Mindset

The mindset needed for creating this type of lesson is to think of a physical skill to be practiced and blend it with another kind of learning goal, such as adding two numbers or reading a sentence. Peggy asks herself, "How else could I teach these skills so the activity would be more fun?"

Another of Peggy's integrated games is sorts. Children move around the play area (indoors or out) as they group themselves in a variety of different categories of their own choosing. Children can become partners or form a group if they share a certain characteristic, for example:

- Same color of socks
- Same birthday
- Same birth month
- Same name
- Same favorite food
- Same shoes
- Same hairstyle

This is a good get-acquainted game for the beginning of the year. It gives children the chance to do a lot of talking and develop their vocabulary and oral language.

Connecting Writers Workshop and PE

When we come in from our PE period, it is time for writers workshop. Some of the time, children write about games and playground experiences. I have recently made children separate PE response logs they may use if they want to write about PE. These are available all the time, but ideally, children write an entry every week or so. This writing is dated and illustrated and enables children to visually track their physical growth and abilities and their feelings over the first-grade year. They have a remembrance of how they felt and their own response to personal struggles and achievements.

After this PE journal time, children may meet in a circle to voluntarily share their feelings and their work. Sometimes there is a good flow of ideas as children support each other in their difficulties. They are empathetic and encouraging. This activity helps build personal confidence, as well as class community. This circle time in my classroom recently resulted in an amazing outreach program organized by three little girls.

An Outcome of PE Sharing Circle: Children Helping Other Children!

During one sharing circle, or class meeting, this year, three first-grade girls realized that some children were having trouble skipping. Bridget, Karina, and Cassandra decided to talk with these children on the playground and see about helping them learn how to skip. I overheard some of the preliminary planning for this idea but pretended ignorance and stayed out of it. (After all, I wasn't consulted. And the girls had their program all figured out.) An alternative would have been for the children to discuss this at a class meeting, but the girls handled things their way.

The end result of the children's plan was that Bridget, Karina, and Cassandra voluntarily spent several recess periods helping other children with PE skills. The three girls took several children in hand over a number of recesses, until the group *all* felt good about the five boys' and two girls' newly acquired ability to skip.

I do not know exactly who instigated these learning sessions, but they went on with great enthusiasm, and everybody seemed happy with the results. Best of all, my first graders took responsibility, made a plan, and had fun helping each other!

The Importance of Knowing Our Goals

That true anecdote about my students' outreach program points out an important fact: Children need to know what it is they can and should be learning. This knowledge helps them launch themselves toward those goals and help other children succeed as well. I am really proud of my three junior PE instructors. I am equally proud of the children who worked with them to learn a necessary skill. Most of all, I am amazed that they all pulled it off!

Inventing Games

About once a week, children take playground equipment out and use it for free play. This is what Peggy calls free exploration. I'm always amazed about the inventiveness and the depth of children's play. One day recently a little group of children used hula hoops to make Venn diagrams, like the ones we had been learning about in math. They created a game by throwing playground balls through the hoops, which other children held in the air. Students assigned points for throws going through the hoops. The balls that went through the center of the Venn diagram hoops earned more points.

It's great kidwatching on the big playground when my class is out with the playground equipment!

Top PE Activities

I asked Peggy to tell me her top PE activities. She gave me this list:

- *Dodge ball* with more than one ball. Use foam balls. They can be purchased very inexpensively, and they don't hurt if they should accidentally hit a child in the face.
- *Relay races*. Children are divided into four or five teams, a short distance from each other. (More teams means more turns for everybody!) Children learn the basics of a relay: You stand in line, perform the task for your team, such as run to a wall 20 feet in front of you, tap the wall, run back, and then go to the end of the line and sit down. The first team to perform the tasks wins. You can tell which team is first, because everyone is sitting down.

  Peggy's favorite relays are seasonal and crazy toy relays. She provides items for children to run with, catch, and throw. Some of the items Peggy provides are mini-pumpkins, unbreakable Christmas ornaments, and rubber chickens, plastic eggs, and spoons. Children *love* to run with rubber chickens on their heads, and watching them is great fun too!
- *Wacky relays* are another favorite of Peggy's. To play these, Peggy sets up piles of PE equipment at a short distance from the relay lines. Every team has the same pile of equipment in front of it, tucked inside a hula hoop to keep it from rolling. One example of an equipment pile is a hula hoop with a jump rope, a beanbag, and a play ground ball tucked inside.

  Peggy calls out the same directions to each relay team. Directions may be something simple, like, "Go get the ball. Run back," or they may be very involved, like, "Jump rope two times, throw the beanbag up and catch it two times, bounce the ball three times, and run back to tag the next person in line." Directions may be different for the second person in each line, and the third, and so on. This is a great game for practicing listening skills.

If you have a class with second language learners, keep the directions clear, simple, and exactly the same throughout the relay. Place second language learners toward the back of your relay lines so they have a chance to hear the directions several times, watch how things are done, and process the directions.

- *Snowball toss* is a favorite indoor game, played either in the classroom or the multiuse room. Each child makes a snowball from a piece of recycled paper. The teacher forms two teams, and hangs a string of yarn across the room. Children toss their snowballs back and forth over the "net."
- Peggy also likes to set up *PE learning stations*. Each station has a 9-by-12-inch card with directions. Cards are spread out over an area. If this game is played outside, it is a good idea to have little rocks to weight the cards down. About eight stations are needed. Children travel from station to station, moving clockwise. They follow the directions on the station, for example, "Do four jumping jacks." They do not change stations until signaled to do so.

  Peggy instructs the children as to *how* to move to the next station, for example, sing as you move; gallop; sneak; walk backward. Peggy also includes some silly stations invented by the students. One station is for resting and for looking around at things going on at all the other stations.

Professional Resources

Peggy hardly needs reference books or other resources, since she is so well versed in PE, but here are a couple she recommends: Hap Palmer records and videos, such as *Learning Basic Skills Through Music* record or CD (1969) and E*arly Childhood Classics—Old Favorites with a New Twist* CD (2000).

Peggy also recommends the book *You'll Never Guess What We Did in Gym Today! More New Physical Education, Games and Activities* by Kenneth G. Tillman and Patricia Rizzo Toner (1991).

I recently took a workshop from Jean Blades, and recommend her book *Thinking on Your Feet, 100+ Activities That Make Learning a Moving Experience!* (2000). Jean gives a great workshop and references the multiple intelligences work of Howard Gardner (see *Frames of Mind: The Theory of Multiple Intelligences* [1993]). She also refers to Paul E. Dennison's learning program Brain Gym®.

Peggy's Top Advice

Peggy recommends to new teachers that they ask their school district for copies of both the state PE framework and the district's materials, so they know what they are expected to be teaching. She also advises, "If a game or activity isn't working, *stop*. Do *not* make the children endure a mistake!"

I believe this is great advice for all our teaching in all curriculum areas.

Peggy's advice to me: "Whenever you can, involve first-grade curriculum when you teach PE. Use easily obtained props to hold interest. Learn and have fun!"

CHAPTER 17

Assessing Your Children, Evaluating Yourself

I'm doing great, 'cause I can read now.
And I read to my baby brother.

—Kevin

We are continually assessing children every day in our elementary classrooms, both formally and informally, as we listen to them talk about and show us what they can do. We are also assessing when we write anecdotal notes about what we observe, when we take dictation before and after a field trip, as well as when we give district-mandated and state-prescribed tests. When we fill out our standards-based report cards, we are assessing children as well.

I want children to feel they take an active part in this ongoing evaluation process. I want them to know what our classroom goals are and have some special goals of their own. It's important that children have time to discuss with me how they are doing. I believe that students need to be *energized* by our assessments and propelled by them to make even more positive progress in learning.

When we fill out our Friday *Braggin' Dragans* and *Junior Braggin' Dragans* (see Chapter 5), children have some input on the assessment process. We also confer at other times.

One day in early spring of last year, a day when I was scheduled to give formal district reading assessments to children individually, I was brought up short by a child's enthusiasm for real reading and then his total deflation when he took the district reading assessment with me. This experience left me with a pain in my heart, and the very strong belief that we need to be very sensitive and careful when we assess children: we must honor what they have learned and avoid diverting them from achieving positive learning goals by giving them experiences that discourage them, label them, or emphasize things they cannot yet do. Whenever possible, we should avoid giving children assessments that are out of their learning context and stick with materials they have used in class.

Darnell's Story: "I Can't Wait for Reading!"

Now that they are familiar with our classroom routines, and our year together is under way, my first graders come into the classroom and get right to it, reading from their personal book bags every day. I don't say a word—they just dive right in. One day, as Darnell opened one of the books he had stored in his book bag, he said to me with great passion, "I just can't wait to get to school every morning, so I can read and read and read!" I was as excited as he was as I listened to him.

Figure 17–1 *Diego and Darnell find much to share as they read together.*

As the children read and peruse books, I wander, watch, and listen to them read. Sometimes I make brief notes on a one-page grid with everyone's name or in a notebook. Sometimes I confer with children. I bring along with me a book I'm reading in Spanish and read it some of the time. After all, I'm a learner, too. The room is beautiful to behold: the children are truly engaged with books of all kinds.

While I was conferencing with another child one morning, I furtively watched Darnell and saw him read and enjoy at least two books! As I observed him, he talked with great excitement to his reading partner about what he was reading.

Later in the day I called Darnell over to work with me individually. I needed to give him a district-mandated reading/phonics survey. One page of the survey had five letters on it in large print: five short vowels. Darnell became nervous, anxious, and just didn't get it. After a struggle, he could correctly give the sounds of three of the isolated short vowels. This part of the assessment was followed by two rows of short-vowel words. It took him quite a while, but he blended eight of the ten short-vowel words, struggling, sweating, and demonstrating great discomfort. The success of this endeavor did not come easy. I have to stress that I do teach a great deal of phonics, most of it *in the context* of things we are reading and writing. But Darnell was being asked to decode phonics without context. I believe that it was so easy for him, as a *real* reader of books, that it was hard. He just couldn't get into the mindset to do it. And his anxiety truly made it impossible.

I was as big a wreck as Darnell as I listened to him struggle. It was truly painful, especially when I remembered the joy and enthusiasm he had shown earlier in the day, when he had spontaneously talked about his love for reading. I *really* didn't want this child to feel that he was in any way lacking, so I went over and got one of the books he'd been reading on his own. We had a great book conversation and a lot of fun talking about our favorite parts of the story. I mentioned to Darnell that he seemed to know all of the ten short-vowel words and five sounds from the test, as well as many, many more sounds and words when he was reading the books. He looked at me in a very penetrating way and said, "It's just too tricky doing all those letters all by themselves." (Not to mention boring, I couldn't help thinking!)

I feel that Darnell definitely knew those sounds on the test, but there was no payoff or motivation for him to figure them out. I'm not going to curl up on a cozy chair in my living room, drinking tea and enjoying reading strings of letters. The task I was asking Darnell to do was by no means one he would be doing in a real-life situation. I believed that I needed to assess him as he read books of personal interest to him.

Assess Students Using *Real* Classroom Materials

I found out much more about Darnell's reading abilities when I listened to him read books he had chosen than I ever did through the test of word lists and isolated sounds. This literacy assessment was genuine and full of the excitement and success of real learning. Truly, Darnell could hardly contain himself; he was so excited about what he could read. And I knew just how he felt, because I could hardly contain myself either, when I saw his skill and excitement.

Children love the personal attention of being able to have a one-on-one conversation with their teacher. When I listen to a child read, talk about the book, and share ideas, I feel that I am creating a positive experience that moves the child much further along in reading than if I were to just circle letters and sounds she knows.

Keeping Perspective About Testing

I believe it is important to keep a level head about testing and remember what *really* matters in our classrooms and with our students' learning. If we keep *our* perspective, it helps children deal with tests and learning tasks in healthy ways. Children can help us keep a positive attitude, too!

One day, near the end of the year, I had to give a district reading test to my children. They really struggled with it, and it was hard for me to watch. But as the children finished, my heart soared. I saw several students take the scratch paper I had put on their tables, fold four-fold booklets, and start writing and illustrating their own stories. I felt that for these children, writing had become an irresistible and automatic activity whenever they had some time to use as they wished. My first graders hadn't let the difficult task they had to do bother them. *They* had a handle on what really mattered!

Matthew even chose to write about tests and evaluations during writers workshop. He took it very seriously and enjoyed the whole thing. Matthew titled his story, "I'm My Brother's Teacher." He composed some of the story by himself, at home. Matthew wrote, over several illustrated pages:

> I had this idea to make my brother learn really good, so I got a paper and then, he was laying on my bed and then I writed a letter and then I said, "Could you say 'I'?" and he said nothing, but then a few seconds later he said "I".
>
> Then I writed a letter and I said, "Do you know 'D'?" And then like two seconds later, he said "D"!
>
> Then I did six more letters and then he did them good! Here is the paper I did with Ethan."

Matthew showed me his test: a list of the letters he had tried out with Ethan. The paper was covered proudly with checks and stars.

Ethan was two months old. Matthew wrote a whole series of books about him.

Other Tools for Assessment: Anecdotal Records and Portfolios

When my children are reading independently, I keep dated anecdotal notes in a grid on a clipboard, as well as in a spiral-bound notebook, with a few pages for each child. I read back positive notes to the children as I write them.

Children also have portfolios of their work in reading and math, as well as art. I begin this whole idea of portfolios by sitting on the rug with my class. The children put their first names on file folders and help me sort these alphabetically. My students really catch on to alphabetization this way.

ABC Order—A New Idea!

I believe that when we hear information in story form, it captures our interest and imagination. After a story, we may care about things that meant nothing to us before hearing it. I like to tell children the story about how putting things in alphabetical order was invented. According to Roger von Oech, in his book *A Whack on the Side of the Head* (1998), a Greek librarian (in the second century B.C., which means nothing to first graders) was trying to think of a more efficient way to organize and retrieve thousands of manuscripts. Then he thought of using the alphabet and invented alphabetization for the world.

We talk about this story and imagine all the things we can think of that would be a mess without alphabetical order!

I keep portfolio file folders in a box or plastic crate for each subject (by alphabetical order—the children are now believers!) I save some work from each child, weekly. Children frequently have a chance to add special papers to their files as well. They can find and refile their folders because the idea of alphabetical order makes sense to them.

These portfolios are a good overview of how the year is going for each student. The files are also helpful to share at parent conferences and special needs conferences for students with learning difficulties.

After hearing my story about the invention of ABC order, I noticed that children enjoyed using this system in their own lists and writing center booklets. Once, when I was looking for a child's page to write down a note about her reading, Cassandra looked over and said, "Why didn't you put those in alphabetical order so you could find them?"

Oops. I had to admit that would have been a good idea.

Evaluating Yourself

Life can make a lot more sense looking backward. I find that the best thing I can do to get an idea of how I'm doing in the classroom is to follow the advice of Kay Goines and write a seven-minute log after school each day. Seven minutes isn't much time to commit to, which is the reason it works. Many times I write far longer than seven minutes. As the daily jottings accumulate, I see patterns forming, and both children's growth and their problems become clear. I gain more understanding about individual children and also about my handling of things. This habit of writing daily informs my teaching more than anything else I could do. And kidwatching is the best assessment of all.

Observations—Evaluations of Your Teaching

You are going to have observers in your classroom throughout your career, from principals and school district personnel to parents, colleagues, and most probably, student teachers. Most adults find it a little unsettling to have someone evaluating them as they teach. However, being well prepared each day helps with some anxiety.

Harriette Shakes, professor of reading, social studies, and student teaching at San Francisco State University, is a former principal from Palo Alto Unified School District. She gives her student teachers tips on how to prepare for observations. Harriette advises her student teachers:

- Tell the children in your class that someone is coming to "watch *me* teach and *you* learn."
- Give the children a little information about the person who is coming, for example, "Mrs. Shakes is my supervisor from the university."
- If you are in the middle of your lesson when your guest arrives, look up, smile, and say, "Welcome." If you are not in the middle of a lesson, and this is a first visit, introduce your guest to the class. (*Note*: Some principals and supervisors prefer not to be introduced or acknowledged.) Student teachers may find out this information ahead of time.
- If introductions are in order, introduce your supervisor or principal to the class yourself, rather than have your master teacher do this. When *you* do the introductions, *you* have control of the situation, not your master teacher.
- At the end of your lesson, when children are occupied with your master teacher, you may wish to go over to your supervisor or principal and personally point out a few things you would like him to see in the classroom.
- Have a copy of your lesson plan available in case your supervisor or principal wishes to see it.
- Enter into the spirit of the evaluation process. You may even find that this helps you enjoy the experience.

CHAPTER 18
Saying Good-Bye

Our year together was coming to a close.
We trooped outside, bubble soap bottles in hand,
and made our final circle as a first-grade family.
"On your mark, get set, go!"
We pulled our wands out of the bubble soap,
made pictures in our heads,
and together we blew our wishes into the sky.

—End-of-the-year celebration in my class

Around May each year there is a poignant feeling in the classroom, as the children and I realize that our time as a special school family will soon be over. My first graders, now grown tall and full of new accomplishments, will go on to second grade. I will begin again in August with a new group, amazed each year about how small the children seem and surprised about where we need to start to begin *our* learning journey.

When this time comes in May, followed by the frantic days of June, I look around the classroom at my first graders and marvel at all they can do, the changes they have made, and the self-confidence and abilities they display. And of course, I think about how much I will miss them. I believe that we have spent more time together in meaningful interactions than many families and friends do.

Figure 18–1
We blow bubbles and wishes into the sky.

During this time of year, some children begin acting clingy, exhibit unusual behavior, or indicate in other ways that they need more of my personal attention. I finally realized one day that a factor in some of this acting out was our impending separation from each other.

Special End-of-the-Year Celebrations

In the last weeks of school we recap our year together: sharing memories, redoing some favorite experiences, rereading special books, singing favorite songs, and patting ourselves on the back as we acknowledge all we have learned. There is always a final rush to do things we had decided we wanted to do as a group.

First-Grade Photo Albums

An end-of-the-year project we all enjoy is making a final souvenir: our own photo albums. I take many photographs all year and always get double copies so that I can share them with the children. I give each child several photos he or she is featured in and give the children time to choose some of the group photos. Children are free to trade pictures if they wish.

To make the photo albums, I photocopy a variety of photo-album-page templates on colored cardstock, using 90-pound paper. (This is approximately file folder weight.) Stacks of these album pages are spread out on the rug by color and template. All pages have lines and a boxed space to place a picture.

Children choose colors and page organizations they like. I show them how to fold transparent tape backward to make tape rolls, and they attach chosen photos to their album pages. (We don't use glue sticks for this, as glue might end up on photos.) Then the fun begins: First graders write *their* versions of the experiences shown in the pictures. (See Figure 18–2.) They assemble their books in an order meaningful to them, and we make cardstock covers. These are stapled, three-hole punched and threaded with yarn, or spiral-bound.

Star cards created throughout the school year (see pages 77–80) are also included in the photo albums.

Children love visiting each other and showing off their photos and album pages as they write. There is a wonderful feeling of sharing and community. We're all part of these memories! This is a great way for us to recap our year. I tell the children that I hope their writing will be as special to them in later years as the photographs are now. I sug-

Figure 18–2
Photo album page

gest that they save these albums in a safe place. Since they may live to be quite old, even one hundred years old or more, as time goes by they will enjoy seeing how they looked, what they thought, and how they wrote when they were very young.

Of course, I realize that children of this age have not yet developed sophisticated concepts of time. However, I cannot resist suggesting to my students that they take good care of these remembrances of first grade, so they *will* have them when they are older.

We staple on manila file folders or colored cardstock papers for photo album covers. Children think of names for their albums and write their titles with marking pens. Cassandra calls her album *The Mystery Book*. I wonder what she means by that but hesitate to ask her. Some things should remain personal. Besides, I like the mystery of it all.

There are a large variety of photo album titles. This delights me. These children have learned to think independently and to write what *really* matters to them!

We Celebrate Literacy

Another festive day at the end of the year is our Celebrate Literacy Celebration. This is a combination of events, highlighted by Authors Day, a special time for children to read their own published books. As with last year's Authors Day, described in Chapter 11, as well as in *Literacy from Day One*, we invite families, our principal, and other friends to share our writing. Children take home their own books at the end of the day.

This year we also give a readers theatre presentation of *Pierre: A Cautionary Tale*, by Maurice Sendak (1991). We have three alternating casts, as everyone wants to be Pierre, the father, the mother, or the lion.

For the final event of our Celebrate Literacy afternoon (this year held the hour before the end of the school day), we share our *Photo Poetry Book*. Children have illustrated their chosen poems with cutout photos and drawings, but this is their first look at the completed booklet. Faces light up as children see finished pages and listen to favorite poems. (See Figure 18–3.)

Children can't wait to read these, share poems they know, and see each child's selected way of illustrating the text. We read and chant the poetry together, and I give each child a copy of our compilation of favorite poems.

Children take these poetry books home when school ends, but for the remainder of the year, they *love* reading them together in groups of their own choosing.

This book becomes something like a yearbook, since each child's photograph and artwork is in the book. I am hopeful that children will read these books over the summer, strengthening their skills by enjoying reading again and again well-loved and memorized text.

Second-grade teachers tell me that the children bring these books to school frequently and practice rereading, memorizing, and sharing

Figure 18–3
A page from our Photo Poetry Book

Figure 18–4 *Children enthusiastically read Photo Poetry books together.*

the poetry with their second-grade classmates. I know that the children practice reading these at home. As one child, Amber, said to me proudly, "My daddy says I'm so good at reading this book, I don't need to read it to him anymore."

Summer Work Envelopes

These mini-celebrations help recap our year and ease our leave-taking. Another activity I believe helps with separation is the summer envelope program. In planning our summer envelope program, I send a note of explanation and four white business-sized envelopes home with each child. (See Appendix, page 402, for sample letter.) I ask parents to return envelopes stamped and addressed with children's names and home mailing addresses.

I explain first to the children, and then to families, in my note, that I have enjoyed my relationship to each child and wish to continue it over the summer by sending home summer work, play ideas, and small surprises. The project helps me feel connected to my first graders over the summer. I believe the children feel the same way. This eases the transition to second grade for all of us. And children have a lot of fun getting personal mail.

When I receive the stamped envelopes, I collate them into mailings by weeks. I select special work, with an eye to open-ended, fun activities that will support reading, writing, and math skills.

I also send a simple note (the same note is reproduced for each child) and some tiny surprises. It is important to take into account the postage requirements when sending little things in the envelopes. I had to add postage before I began taking this into account. The surprises also need to be flat so that they can go through the postal machine.

Some good envelope enclosures are

- Stickers or stars
- Tiny plastic rulers or stencils
- Bookmarks
- Photographs
- Paper sunglasses
- Balloons
- Postcards

I shop for these items at dollar stores, stationery stores, and garage sales. I also save publishers' bookmarks and postcards from conferences and children's bookstores. The easiest way to have special things to send in summer envelopes is to keep a box for these items and drop things in it all year.

Children's Literature Links

When I write my summer notes to children, I include brief book lists: titles and authors of some new children's books that they might enjoy over the summer. I mention something about my own reading, writing, and drawing, so students know these are ongoing activities for me, too.

Summer Work Ideas

I vary the work for each mailing. I send two work pages (photocopied front and back). Each mailing has math and reading/language arts work, with art ideas on the other side. I include my home mailing address so children can write back to me if they wish. Here is a list of sample summer work ideas:

- Additional class photos (photocopied) with space for children to write captions or stories
- Math mazes
- A favorite poem, with space for illustrations
- Small math flash cards to cut up and practice with
- Math problems, math quilts (see *Patchwork Math I, Grades 1–3*, Scholastic editor Debra Baycura 1999])
- Pop-up books to make (directions and photocopied page or booklet; see *How to Make Pop-Ups*, by Joan Irvine [1988])
- "Read and draw" pages (For ideas, see *Drawbreakers—A Drawing Book That We Start and You Finish*, by Klutz Press [2001]. Other books of this type include *The Anti-Coloring Book* by Susan Striker (Series) [2001] and *Mark Kistler's Draw Squad* [1988].)
- Make-it-type pages where students must read and follow directions, for example, origami, paper planes, or puppets, and so on.

Literature Connection

Some other books I use as references for summer work ideas are *Kids' Paper Airplane Book* by Ken Blackburn and Jeff Lammers (1996); *Easy Origami* by Dokuohtei Nakano (1994); and *The Muppets Make Puppets! Book and Puppet Kit: How to Make Puppets Out of All Kinds of Stuff Around Your House*, by Cheryl Henson et al. (1994).

Here is a sampling of art ideas to suggest to students:

- Ask your parents for a photograph of yourself (or photocopy) that you can cut out or trim; draw the rest of the setting and adventure.

- Draw your best play activity or game ever.
- Draw yourself with your favorite literature character.
- Draw your best friend and something you like to do together.
- Sketch your family/house/favorite toy or game.
- Draw yourself at the library choosing a *great* book. Then go to the library and make your drawing come true!
- Draw a favorite animal.
- Draw your favorite toy. Draw yourself the same size as the toy, playing with it.
- Draw your best invention, or creation, made with paper, Legos, blocks, craft materials, and so on.
- Invent a *famous* drawing.

Choosing Materials for the Summer Envelopes

Although I want to help maintain skills learned this year, I try to send summer work that is fun and motivating. I want children to be excited, not in hiding, when the mail arrives! And I certainly don't want to send anything that will mar the memory of our year together.

End-of-the-Year Notes

One of my final projects each year is to ask the children to write to the second-grade teachers, sharing any information about themselves they wish to mention. These are generic notes. Children write "Dear Second-Grade Teacher," rather than to a specific person. I use these letters as my end-of-the-year writing assessments. They are also a personal evaluation for me. As with our bulletin board for next year's class, these letters give me a feel for how the year went for each of my first graders and what each child found to be important.

When school begins I put these letters in a basket in the faculty room. Interested second-grade teachers may pick out the notes from children in their new classes. (See Figure 18–5.)

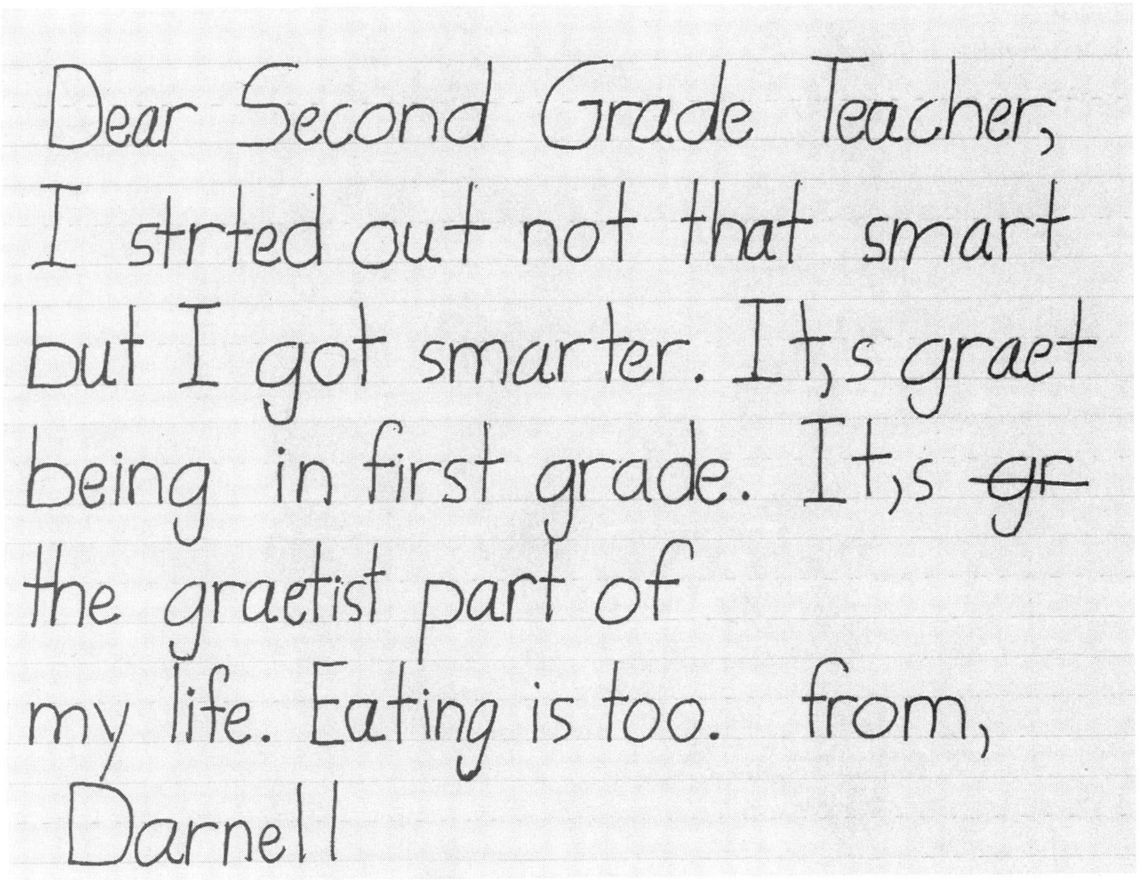

Dear Second Grade Teacher,
I strted out not that smart
but I got smarter. It,s graet
being in first grade. It,s ~~gr~~
the graetist part of
my life. Eating is too. from,
Darnell

Figure 18–5 *Darnell's note to the second-grade teacher*

Wrapping Up Your Year

There are a few other things to do to wrap up your first-grade year: Plan the second-grade class rosters with the other first-grade teachers, balancing behavior problems, ability levels, English language learners, and children with special needs. Cumulative folders need to be done for each child. These are kept in the office in file boxes. Your school principal will most likely have an end-of-the-year checklist for you, letting you know what must be packed and put away in your room and how to get the classroom ready for summer.

I'm never quite ready for the school year to end. But my family reminds me that I'm never quite ready for it to start either!

Figure 18–6 *Cassandra can't wait to give me this flower.*

One day, as I was leaving school quite late and very tired, I was enthusiastically and energetically greeted by a little group of first graders playing on the outdoor equipment. Although I had just seen them a few hours before, these children were absolutely beside themselves when they saw me, calling, waving, and coming over to talk with me. One child had been waiting for me and brought me a flower. It struck me that as teachers, we are very fortunate: not many people in this world get a greeting like that in their jobs or even in their lives.

I talked about this with my friend and colleague Julie Blair. "I know what you mean," she said. "The children are always so happy to see us. Being a teacher is the next best thing to being famous."

APPENDICES

Name: ____________________ **Overnight Book List:** Write down your title every day.

Star Card

Name ______________________________

I want to learn ______________________
____
____

I'm special because ____________________
____
____

I'm good at _________________________
____
____

Teacher's Name ______________________________

Child's Name ______________________________

Week of ______________________________

HIGHLIGHTS OF THE WEEK

READING:

Literature Books Enjoyed:

A Poem We Are Learning:

WRITING:

MATH:

SOCIAL STUDIES, SCIENCE:

ART/MUSIC/PE:

*Listens and follows directions.
Works hard to learn.
Pays attention during lessons.

1 2 3 4 5

****

*Returns books, book lists, book bags, and homework on time.

1 2 3 4 5

****

*Gets along well with others.

1 2 3 4 5

****

KEY: 1 = outstanding;
2 = very good;
3 = satisfactory;
4 = needs improvement;
5 = poor/unacceptable

*NOTE: Please return this part Monday, with comment, suggestions, if desired:

____

____

____

____

____

child's name __________________ parent's signature ______________________________

This grid can be used for overnight book checkout; behavior notes; anecdotal notes on reading, writing, or math; class list; or testing/assessment records.

Children's Newsletter Template

Dear Parents,

I have asked children to check the box that best represents how *they* feel they did in school this week. Children added written comments and drawings (front and back) if they wished to do so. Children made their *own* decisions about how to fill out this paper.

I hope you and your child will enjoy talking about school.

Name: ______________________________ Date: ________________

I was terrific! I learned a lot!
I did some good thinking.
I got along with others.
I remembered my books and homework! ☐

****

I learned some things.
I was pretty good to other children.
I remembered books and homework most of the time. ☐

****

Uh oh! I'll do better next week!
I need to pay attention, think, and learn.
I need to not bother or hurt other children.
I need to remember books and homework. ☐

Child's notes (optional): ______________________________________

____

____

____

____

Family Book Template

In my family we

___

___

___

We like to

___

___

___

___

___

A Special Day in Our Family

Family Celebration

Special Family Recipe

How we celebrate when we eat this food.

Then and Now: Favorite Toys

Child's favorite toy story

Story of family member's favorite toy when younger

Story Template

The Itsy Bitsy Spider

Illustrated by

The itsy bitsy spider
Went up the water spout.

Down came the rain
And washed the spider out.

Out came the sun and
Dried up all the rain,
And the itsy bitsy spider
Went up the spout again.

Humpty Dumpty

Illustrated by

Humpty Dumpty sat
on the wall.

Humpty Dumpty had
a great fall.

All the King's horses
And all the King's men
Couldn't put Humpty
Dumpty together again!

Reading Response Log

Name ____________________

Title ____________________

Author ____________________

Ideas for Using *Brian Wildsmith's Amazing World of Words*

I have found the book *Brian Wildsmith's Amazing World of Words*, published by Millbrook Press, 1997, to be one of the most engaging books I have used in my classroom for helping children learn language skills. Although the book and the lessons I have developed are useful for all my first graders, these techniques seem particularly helpful for second language learners.

Children enjoy the colorful illustrations in the book. Wildsmith uses lavish double-page spreads of different habitats and settings, tabbed for student reference. Categories include space, desert, ocean, mountains, jungle, town, transportation, market, farm, wildlife park, dinosaurs, school play, playground, and an index. The top border of each double-page setting details small line drawings of objects from the large picture. These small rebus pictures are labeled. The ocean scene, for example, features many kinds of ocean life, as well as a variety of ships and even a lighthouse. The border at the top displays small, colored, labeled pictures: dolphin, octopus, puffer fish, fishing boat, sea horse, shark, shell, submarine, whale, scorpion fish, ferry, jellyfish, submersible, seal, lighthouse, butterfly fish, seaweed.

In effect, the book can be used as a reference tool and doubles as a categorized dictionary. Following are some ways I use this book with children.

(continued)

Collecting Words—A Great Literacy Center!

Children love collecting things. I find it powerful, especially for second langage speakers, to give children word-collecting booklets so that they can *save* words they want to remember. I provide copies of Wildsmith's book to use, as well as a variety of picture dictionaries, pens, colored pencils, crayons. My only request here is that I ask children to write just one word they want to save at a time, in a small box in their booklet of grids. After the word is written, they "read" it, and then illustrate that word. In this way students can look back and read what they have drawn and written. See Appendix p. 393 for blank word collecting page.

I monitor this closely so that the children do not just forget the intent of the project, and mindlessly write or draw. This tends to happen at first.

If children just copy a variety of words, or just make drawings, they do not have everything they need to be able to access "their words," and their efforts don't yield much success in developing language and vocabulary.

It is important to allow time for children to practice reading the words they have collected, and to share their efforts. I want children to realize that they are creating a collection that they can save and use for years to come. They are building visual literacy as well as language and drawing skills.

I use this as a literacy center in my first-grade classroom.

"Gatefold" Habitat or Setting

Another technique I teach my first graders is how to make a "gatefold" paper, and then create a habitat or setting. Rebus drawings and labels are then added to these creations.

I use 12-by-18-inch paper for this project. I prefold these for my students and then teach them how to fold them. They can't miss. The lines are already there! First I bring the top corners of the paper together horizontally and make a small crease (about 1/8 of an inch) in the middle of the paper. I open the paper, and then fold each edge in to the middle using my crease as a guide. This creates a gatefold: a three-part paper, with left and right sides folded in to the middle. When the paper is opened, there is room for a habitat scene, and many rebus drawings.

Children choose the habitat or setting of their own special interest, Outer Space, for example. They label their closed gatefold with the title of the world or habitat and then illustrate it.

When this booklet is opened, there is room in the center area for a large habitat drawing. The left- and right-hand sides can be used for drawing and labeling rebuses of items included in the main drawing.

(*continued*)

Children get very engrossed in creating these gatefolds, and the project can last for days. They may make a collection of these and keep them in a box or folder. The gatefolds may help a child retell a story, sequence events, as well as develop vocabulary. Children working together may extend each other's ideas.

Categorization

I also love to use this book to teach categorization. Children can use the template I have developed to write down two or three categories of their choice, such as zoo and toys, and then collect appropriate words and pictures. They can also use the book to have their own scavenger hunts of specific sounds they are practicing, such as long-vowel words or words with *ph*, or *ar* sounds.

Of course, this book may be browsed and just *enjoyed*! But I like to invite children to use it to play with and choose words they can take pleasure in learning and knowing.

Categories			
Zoo		Toys	
elephant		car	
		doll	

Layered Booklet

Create an easy-to-make booklet for children to use for their categorized word collections. Cut light-colored construction paper in half to make pieces 6-by-12 inches, or use copy paper and cut it in half the long way. About three to four papers are needed per book.

Lay out papers so that they are overlapped with about an inch sticking out as shown. Fold papers to create even more pages.

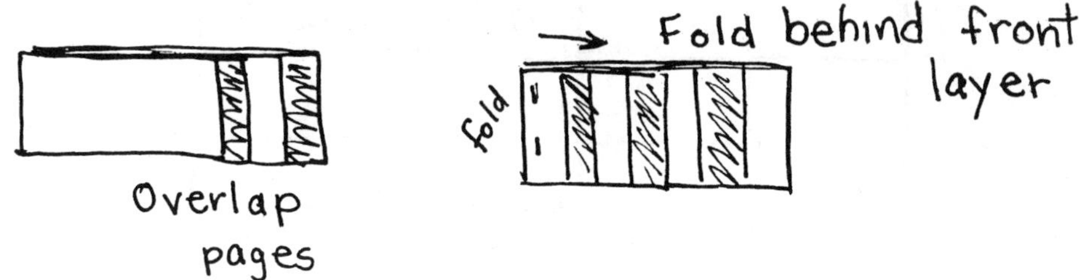

Staple at the fold. Students have a booklet in which to keep their categorized word collections.

Name ______________________ Collect Words

Little Books

Good for holidays and celebrations, miniatures of art from study prints, favorite art ideas, collections of kinds of marks, textures, and so on.

You need

2-by-18-inch paper strips—white construction paper
2 covers per book: colored construction paper or poster board, 2-by-2¼ inch
yarn, ribbon, or string

For decorating books: marking pens, crayons, or colored pencils, paper scraps, magazine pictures, beads, sequins, buttons—assorted materials
glue, scissors

These can be hung, tied closed, etc.

1. Have students fold the paper strip accordian-style (in half, in half again, then fold the ends back to the middle). Refold, back and forth, back and forth.

Add a cover at each end.

2. Fold strip to form 2-inch booklet. Glue on the front and back covers.

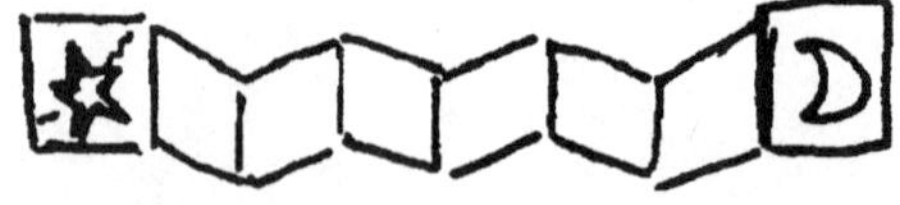

Little Books

3. Decorate booklet with all kinds of materials. Three-dimensional materials may also be added; booklet won't close all the way, but that is no problem. It will be very interesting visually.

4. Book may be tied closed with decorative ribbon, yarn, or string. A strip of holiday garland or other interesting item may be tucked into the yarn closure for a festive look. Books may be hung to display them, instead of tied closed. These may also be tied closed, then hung as a Christmas tree ornament.

Marbleized Paper (Simplified Suminagashi)

Great for Making Books, Reports, Art Backgrounds!

You need

A pan slightly larger than paper to be marbled
Water at least 1 inch deep
Construction paper (white or colored; or copy paper)
Boku Undo Marbling Kit—available from the following supplies for $12–$15:

Nasco, Art Dept.
901 Janesville Ave.
Fort Atkinson WI 53438-0901
1-800-538-9595

Dick Blick, Creative Arts Catalog
PO Box 1267
Galesburg IL
1-800-447-8192

Kinokuniya Stationery and Gift
1581 Webster St.
San Francisco CA 94115
1-415-567-8901

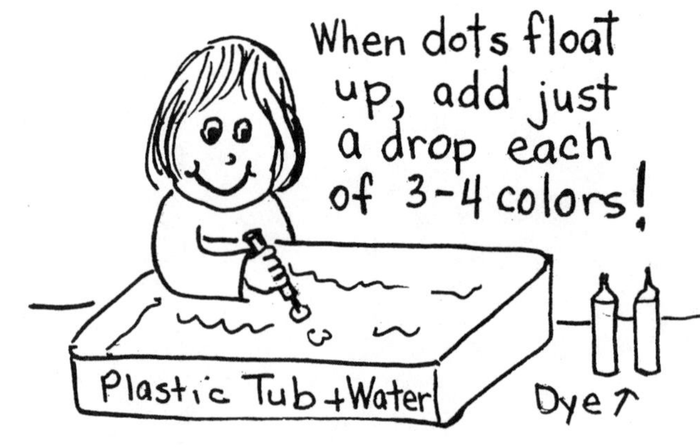

Marbleized Paper (Simplified Suminagashi)

1. Decorative paper marbling is very simple, and the Boku Undo Kit is nontoxic. (Ink will stain, however.) Drop a cardboard circle (several come with the kit) into the pan of water. Use a brush or pencil to push the circle down. When it floats back to the surface of the water, gently squeeze a drop of colored ink (eight colors come in the kit) onto the circle. Use as many colors as you like. The kit has very good directions for this entire procedure.
2. Fan or blow on the surface of the water, or draw in it with a stick or brush to create designs in the ink.
3. When the design is ready, carefully lay a piece of paper on the water. The ink design is transfered to the paper. Lift the paper off. Place it on newsprint and let it dry. When dry, papers may be pressed under a stack of books or ironed with a warm iron.

Note: Marbleized papers may be used for book covers and for creating a variety of books, including the eight-page minibook, accordian-folded books, and pop-up books.

Story Plan Template

Name: ______________________ Story Plan Title: ______________________

Who?	What?	When?	Where?	How? Why?

Pizza-shaped sorting wheel

Butterfly Pop-Up or Puppet

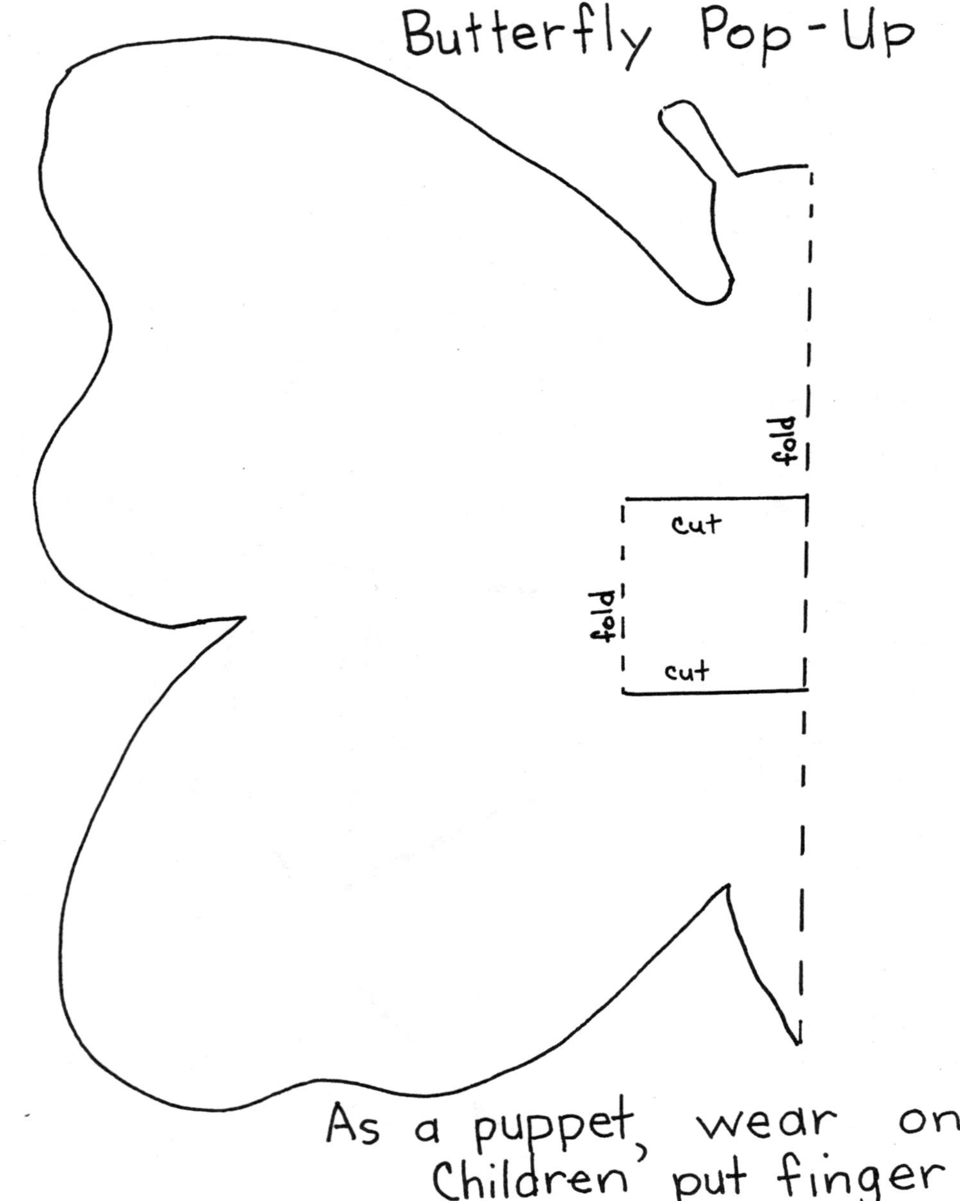

As a puppet, wear on a finger–
Children put finger in pop-up box.

Butterfly Science Log Template

Date: ____________________

What are they?

Caterpillars Chrysalides Butterflies

What do they look like?	Write about something you notice.

Date: ____________________

What are they?

Caterpillars Chrysalides Butterflies

What do they look like?	Write about something you notice.

Summer Work Program

Dear Parents,

I have enjoyed teaching your child this year, and I hope we can keep in touch over the summer. I would like to send a note and some work and project ideas four times over the vacation period. Since children *love* to get mail, and there will be small surprises in the envelopes, I think this would be fun for all of us.

I am sending four envelopes home. If you would like your child to be part of my summer mail program, please address the envelopes to your first grader, stamp them, and return them to me. I will mail them at intervals over the two-month period.

I'll need the envelopes by the beginning of June, if possible, in order to get everything organized.

I hope your child enjoys reading, and listening to read-alouds, as well as many other enriching experiences during our time away from school. Have a great summer!

Sincerely,

Copyright-Free Poetry

Here is a sampling of poetry to use in the classroom in many ways: on poetry charts, in booklets, in pocket charts, and on poetry cubes made from covered and decorated boxes (see *Literacy from Day One* for more information). Children love to recite and enact the words. They can learn many poems during their year in first grade.

We are the words in your mind, your mind,
We are the words in your mind.
When you are asleep,
When you are awake,
We are the words that no one can take,
From your mind, your mind, your mind, your mind,
We paint pictures and thoughts in your mind.

—Anonymous

*

My poem sings in my heart,
My poem lives in my head.
My poem makes pictures just for me
To see when I'm in bed.

—Pat Barrett Dragan

This poem can be sung to the tune of "The Farmer in the Dell." For a different sound, try singing it to the tune of "The Brave Old Duke of York" or "Swing Low, Sweet Chariot."

*

Weather

Whether the weather be fine
Or whether the weather be not,
Whether the weather be cold,
Or whether the weather be hot,
We'll weather the weather
Whatever the weather,
Whether we like it or not.

—Anonymous

*

Apples, peaches, pears and plums
Tell me when your birthday comes:
January
February
March
April
May
June
July
August
September
October
November
December

—Anonymous

Note: Children may stand when it is their birthday month, raise their hand, or otherwise indicate it is their birthday time.

*

(continued)

This is the day
They give babies away
With a half a pound of tea.
You open the lid
And out pops the kid
With a five-year guarantee!
—Anonymous

*

The moon is very, very old.
The reason why is clear:
It has a birthday once a month,
Instead of once a year.
—Anonymous

*

Sally go round the sun
Sally go round the moon
Sally go round the chimney tops
Every afternoon!
—Anonymous

*

The sun came up,
A ball of red
I followed my friend
Wherever he led.
He thought his fast horse
Would leave me behind,
But I rode a dragon
As swift as the wind.
—Chinese "Mother Goose" rhyme

*

Algy Met a Bear
Algy met a bear.
The bear met Algy.
The bear was bulgy.
The bulge was Algy.
—Anonymous

*

No bears out tonight,
No bears out tonight,
No bears out tonight,
They've all gone away!
—Anonymous

*

I asked my mother for fifty cents
To see the elephant jump the fence.
It jumped so high, it reached the sky,
And didn't come back till the
Fourth of July.
—Anonymous

*

Way down South where bananas
grow,
A grasshopper stepped on an
elephant's toe.
The elephant said, with tears in
his eyes,
"Pick on somebody your own size."
—Anonymous

*

I Eat My Peas with Honey
I eat my peas with honey;
I've done it all my life.
It makes the peas taste funny,
But it keeps them on the knife.
—Anonymous

*

Four Seasons
Spring is showery, flowery, bowery.
Summer: hoppy, choppy, poppy.
Autumn: wheezy, sneezy, freezy.
Winter: slippy, drippy, nippy.
—Anonymous

*

I'm Glad the Sky Is Painted Blue

I'm glad the sky is painted blue,
  And the earth is painted green,
With such a lot of nice fresh air
  All sandwiched in between.
—Anonymous

*

Happy birthday to you!
Squashed tomatoes and stew;
Eggs and bacon for breakfast,
Happy birthday to you!
—Anonymous

*

Five green and speckled frogs,
Sat on a speckled log,
Eating some most delicious bugs,
Yum, Yum!
One fell into a pool,
Where it was green and cool,
Then there were four green speckled
  frogs,
Ribbet, ribbet!!!
—Anonymous

*

Caterpillar

Brown and furry
Caterpillar in a hurry,
Take your walk
To the shady leaf, or stalk,
Or what not,
Which may be the chosen spot.
No toad spy you,
Hovering bird of prey pass by you;
Spin and die,
To live again a butterfly.
—Christina Rossetti

*

One, two, three, four, five,
Once I caught a fish alive.
Six, seven, eight, nine, ten,
Then I threw it back again!
—Anonymous

*

Wiggle Waggle, Wiggle Waggle

Wiggle waggle, wiggle waggle,
  went the bear,
Catching bees in his underwear.
One bee out, and one bee in,
And one bee bit him
on his big bear skin!
—Anonymous

*

Johnny drew a monster,
The monster chased him.
Just in time,
Johnny erased him.
—Anonymous

*

When Jacky's a very good boy,
He shall have cakes and custard.
But when he does nothing but cry,
He shall have nothing but mustard.
—Anonymous

*

Baby and I were baked in a pie,
The gravy was wonderful hot.
There was nothing to pay
To the baker that day,
So we crept out of the pot.
—Anonymous

*

(*continued*)

How Many Days
Has My Baby to Play?

How many days has my baby to play?
Saturday, Sunday, Monday—
Tuesday, Wednesday, Thursday, Friday,
Saturday, Sunday, Monday.

—Traditional nursery rhyme

*

The more we get together,
together, together,
The more we get together,
The happier we'll be.

For your friends are my friends
And my friends are your friends,
So . . .
The more we get together,
The happier we'll be!

—Anonymous

*

Cut letter boxes apart ←	Print letters sideways, (tall size)	Words to Make ↓	Print Words Here ↓

Pattern on center fold

fold

cut

cut

fold

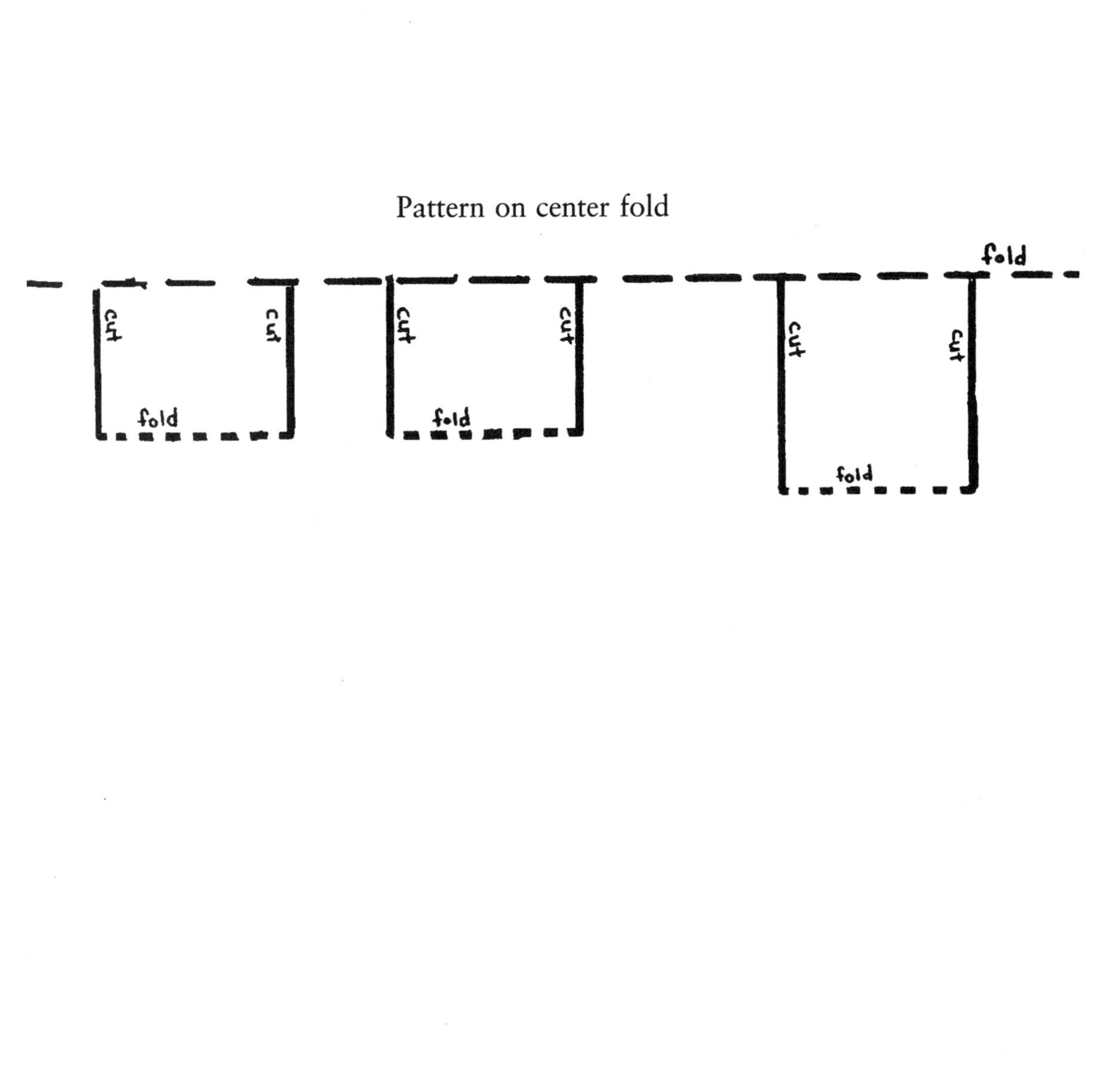
Pattern on center fold
fold
cut
cut
fold
cut
cut
fold
cut
cut
fold

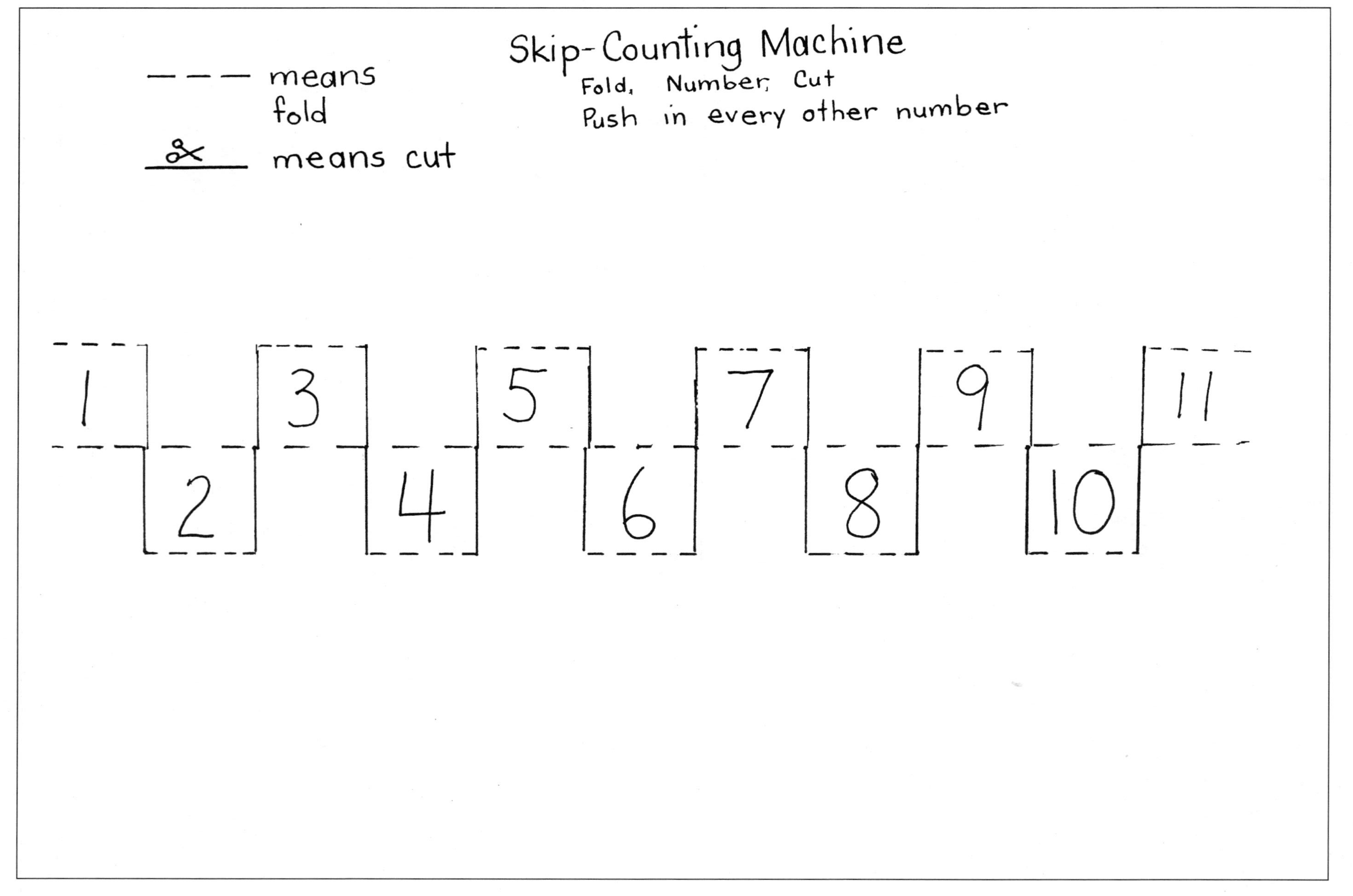

Skip-Counting Machine
Fold, Number, Cut
Push in every other number
— — — means fold
✂ ___ means cut
1
3
5
7
9
11
2
4
6
8
10

Make Your Own Alphabet-Key Word Chart		Aa	Bb
Cc	Dd	Ee	Ff
Gg	Hh	Ii	Jj
Kk	Ll	Mm	Nn
Oo	Pp	Qq	Rr
Ss	Tt	Uu	Vv
Ww	Xx	Yy	Zz

RESOURCES

Professional Organizations

International Reading Association (IRA)
800 Barksdale Road, PO Box 8139, Newark, DE 19714-8139
Online: *www.reading.org*

National Council of Teachers of English (NCTE)
1111 West Kenyon Road, Urbana, IL 61801-1096
Phone: 877-369-6283 Online: *www.ncte.org*

Professional Magazines and Other Resources:

The Horn Book Guide to Children's and Young Adult Books. Published twice a year by The Horn Book Inc.
56 Roland Street, Suite 200, Boston, MA 02129

The Horn Book Magazine. Published six times a year by The Horn Book, Inc.

The Horn Book Guide Online, *www.hornbookguide.com.*

Book Links. Published six times a year
PO Box 615, IL 61054-7566
Phone: 888-350-0950 Fax: 815-734-5858 Online, new orders: *blnk@kable.com*

School Library Journal
245 West Seventeenth Street, New York, NY 10011
Phone: 800-959-1066

Instructor Magazine. Published eight times a year.
Phone: 800-544-2917 or 800-959-1676 (Magazineline) Online: *www.scholastic.com /Instructor* or *www.magazineline.com*

Arts and Activities. Published ten times a year.
Phone: 619-819-4520 Online: *www.artsandactivities.com*

School Arts and Activities. Published nine times a year.
Phone: 800-533-2847

Classroom Book Club

Scholastic Book Club.
Phone: 800-SCHOLASTIC (800-724-6527)

Magazines for Children

Highlights for Children
Online: *www.highlights.com*
National Geographic World
National Geographic Society, Washington, DC 20036
Ranger Rick
National Wildlife Association, 8925 Leesburg Pike, Vienna, VA 22184
Online: *www.nwf.org/kidzone*
Zoobooks
Wildlife Education Ltd., 12233 Thatcher Court, Poway, CA 92064-6880
Online: *www.zoobooks.com*

Commercial Products Mentioned in the Text

- *Cardboard book displays, post office boxes*: Calloway House has a large variety of fiberboard organizers, such as the large book displays and post office boxes I use in my classroom.

Calloway House Inc., 451 Richardson Drive, Lancaster, PA 17603-4098
Phone: 800-233-0290 Fax: 717-299-6754

- *Adhesive material*: I use Fun-Tak reusable adhesive to hang artwork and put artwork together (affixing parts of a mural on background paper, affixing illustrations to charts, and so forth). Several companies have similar products, available at teacher supply stores and hardware stores.

DAP Inc., 2400 Boston Street, Suite 200, Baltimore, MD 21224-4775
Phone: 800-543-3840, ext. 2804, or 888-327-8477 Online: *www.DAP.com*

- *Book covers*: Gaylord Brothers sells a wide variety of materials for covering and protecting books, including plastic covers and rolls of plastic in assorted sizes. I find the easiest material for classroom use to be the 12-inch-by-100-yard roll of book jacket plastic. It is helpful to share a roll and the cost with another teacher. If possible, ask your school to purchase a roll for all teachers to use.

Gaylord Bros., PO Box 4901, Syracuse, NY 13221
Phone: 800-448-6160 Online: *www.gaylord.com*

- *A reference for other classroom supplies*:

Lakeshore Learning Materials, 2695 East Dominguez Street, Carson, CA 90810
Phone: 800-421-5354 Online: *www.lakeshorelearning.com*

- *Little bear puppet (Shown in Chapter 3) and other puppets*:

Folkmanis Inc.: Furry Folk and Folktales, 1219 Park Avenue, Emeryville, CA 94608
Phone: 510-658-7678 Online: *www.folkmanis.com*

- *Electric pencil sharpener (sharpens multiple sizes of pencils)*: Two models: Boston Brown; Panasonic.

Office Depot, 910 El Monte Avenue, Mountain View, CA
Phone: 650-964-9249

- *Little tooth-shaped boxes, plastic tooth saver necklaces, and items for treasure box (Chapter 6)*:

Oriental Trading Company Inc.
Phone: 800-228-2269 Online: *www.orientaltrading.com*

- *Butterflies, caterpillars, butterfly garden*:

Insect Lore.
Phone: 800-LIVE BUG (800-548-3284)

- *Phonics Phones*: ($48 per case; 24 phonics phones per case)

CANDL Foundation, PO Box 18623, Huntsville, AL 35804
Phone: 800-633-7212 Online: *www.phonicsphone.org*

Chapter 1: Getting Ready to Teach

Professional Books

Perlmutter, J., and L. Burrell. 2001. *The First Weeks of School—Laying a Quality Foundation*. Portsmouth, NH: Heinemann.

Chapter 2: Designing and Setting Up Your First-Grade Classroom

Professional Books

Fisher, B. 1996. *Inside the Classroom: Teaching Kindergarten and First Grade*. Portsmouth, NH: Heinemann.

Morgenstern, J. 1998. *Organizing from the Inside Out*. New York: Holt.

Naisbitt, J. 1986. *Megatrends: Ten New Directions Transforming Our Lives*. 6th ed. New York: Warner.
Routman, R. 2000. *Conversations*. Portsmouth, NH: Heinemann.

Children's Books

Milne, A. A., illus. by E. Shepard. 1989. *Pooh's Library: Winnie-the-Pooh, The House at Pooh Corner, When We Were Very Young, and Now We Are Six*. Reissue ed. New York: Dutton.
Slate, J., illus. by A. Wolff. 2001. *Miss Bindergarten Gets Ready for Kindergarten*. Reprint ed. New York: Puffin.
Wells, R. 2003. *Voyage to the Bunny Planet*. Boxed ed. New York: Viking.

Chapter 3: Celebrating the First Day of School

Professional Books

Avery, C. 2002. *And with a Light Touch: Learning About Reading, Writing, and Teaching with First Graders*. 2d ed. Portsmouth, NH: Heinemann.
Bittinger, J., ed. 1989. *The Farmer and the Beet, Goldilocks and the Three Bears, The Gingerbread Man, The Three Little Pigs*. Big Books, Level A. Reading, MA: Addison-Wesley.
Dragan, Pat Barrett. 2001. *Literacy from Day One*. Portsmouth, NH: Heinemann.
McCarrier, A., G. S. Pinnell, and I. C. Fountas. 2000. *Interactive Writing: How Language and Literacy Come Together, K–2*. Portsmouth, NH: Heinemann.
Ohanian, S. 2001. *Books Day by Day—Anniversaries, Anecdotes, and Activities*. Portsmouth, NH: Heinemann.
Pinnell, G. S., and I. Fountas. 2003. *Phonics Lessons: Letters, Words, and How They Work: Grade 1*. Package ed. Portsmouth, NH: Heinemann.
Peregoy, S., and Boyle, O. 2000. *Reading, Writing & Learning in ESL*. Reading, MA: Addison-Wesley.

Sign Language References

Flodin, M. 1991. *Signing for Kids*. Berkeley, CA: The Berkeley Publishing Group/ Perigee Books
Kramer, J., and T. Ovadia. 2001. *You Can Learn Sign Language*. New York: Troll Communications.

Children's Books: A Sampling of Alphabet Books

Alda, A. 1998. *Arlene Alda's 1 2 3*. Berkeley, CA: Tricycle.
Anno. 1988. *Anno's Alphabet*. New York: HarperTrophy.
Ehlert, L. 1993. *Eating the Alphabet*. New York: Voyager.
Fleming, D. 2002. *Alphabet Under Construction*. New York: Holt.

Grover, M. 1993. *Accidental Zucchini (An Unexpected Alphabet).* New York: Harcourt.
Lionni, L. 1990. *The Alphabet Tree.* New York: Dragonfly.
Martin, B. Jr., and J. Archambault, illus. by L. Ehlert. 2000. *Chicka Chicka Boom Boom.* New York: Aladdin.

Nursery Rhymes

Cousins, L. 1999. *The Lucy Cousins Book of Nursery Rhymes.* Reissue. New York: Dutton.
Long, S. 1999. *Silvia Long's Mother Goose.* San Francisco: Chronicle.
Opie, I. A., ed., illus. by R. Wells. 1996. *My Very First Mother Goose.* Cambridge, MA: Candlewick.
———. 1999. *Here Comes Mother Goose.* Cambridge, MA: Candlewick.

Picture Books: Beginning of School

Ada, A. F., illus. by K. Thompson. 1995. *My Name Is Maria Isabel.* Reprint ed. New York: Aladdin.
Brown, P. 1978. *Hickory.* New York: HarperCollins.
Cohen, M. 1989. *When Will I Read?* New York: Aladdin.
Deacon, A. 2002. *Slow Loris.* New York: Kane/Miller.
Duvoisin, R. 2000. *Petunia.* New York: Knopf.
Fox, M., illus. by J. Vivas. 1994. *Tough Boris.* New York: Harcourt Brace.
Henkes, K. 1991. *Chrysanthemum.* New York: Greenwillow.
Imai, M. 1996. *Little Lumpty.* New York: Candlewick.
Kantrowitz, M. 1989. *Willy Bear.* Reprint ed. New York: Aladdin.
Kraus, R., illus. by J. Aruego. 1994. *Leo the Late Bloomer.* Reissue ed. New York: HarperCollins.
Lionni, L. 2002. *Frederick and His Friends: Four Favorite Fables.* Book and CD ed. New York: Knopf.
London, J., illus. by F. Remkiewicz. 1998. *Froggie Goes to School.* Reprint ed. New York: Puffin.
Numeroff, L., illus. by F. Bond. 2002. *If You Take a Mouse to School.* New York: HarperTrophy/Laura Geringer.
Penn, A., illus. by R. E. Harper and N. M. Leak. 1993. *The Kissing Hand.* New York: Child Welfare League of America.
Wells, R. 2000. *Timothy Goes to School.* New York: Puffin.

Bullies and Buddies

Bottner, B., illus. by P. Rathmann. 1997. *Bootsie Barker Bites.* New York: Paper Star.
Elliott, L. M. 2002. *Hunter's Best Friend at School.* New York: HarperCollins.
Henkes, K. 1997. *Chester's Way.* New York: Mulberry.
Lester, H., illus. by L. Munsinger. 1999. *Hooway for Wodney Wat.* New York: Houghton/Walter Lorraine.
Marshall, J. 1997. *George and Martha: The Complete Stories of Two Best Friends.* New York: Houghton Mifflin.

Naylor, P. R. 1994. *King of the Playground.* New York: Aladdin.
O'Neill, A. 2002. *The Recess Queen.* New York: Scholastic.
Rathmann, P. R. 1997. *Ruby the Copycat.* New York: Scholastic.
Varley, S. 1992. *Badger's Parting Gifts.* Reprint ed. New York: Mulberry.
Waber, B. 2002. *Courage.* Boston: Houghton Mifflin/Walter Lorraine.
Wilson, S., illus. by C. Cameron. 2002. *Grade School Alien.* Berkeley, CA: Tricycle.

Chapter 4: Managing Your Classroom and Motivating Your Students

Professional Books

Armstrong, T. 2000. *In Their Own Way.* New York: Tarcher.
Feeney, S., D. Christensen, and E. Moravcik. 2000. *Who Am I in the Lives of Children? An Introduction to Teaching Young Children.* 6th ed. New York: Prentice Hall.

Children's Books

Henkes, K. 1996. *Lilly's Purple Plastic Purse.* New York: Greenwillow.
Slate, J., illus. by A. Wolff. 2001. *Miss Bindergarten Gets Ready for Kindergarten.* Reprint ed. New York: Puffin.

Chapter 5: Connecting with Families

Professional Books

Ada, A. 2002. *A Magical Encounter: Latino Children's Literature in the Classoom.* 2d ed. Needham Heights, MA: Allyn and Bacon.
Harwayne, S. 1999. *Going Public: Priorities and Practice at the Manhattan New School.* Portsmouth, NH: Heinemann.
Taylor, D. 1998. *Family Literacy—Young Children Learning to Read and Write.* Portsmouth, NH: Heinemann.

Children's Books

Aliki. 1998. *Marianthe's Story: Painted Words, Spoken Memories.* New York: Greenwillow.
Cooke, T., illus. by H. Oxenbury. 1997. *So Much.* Reprint ed. Cambridge, MA: Candlewick.
Dorros, A., illus. by E. Kleven. 1997. *Abuela.* Reprint ed. New York: Pearson.
Fox, M. 1994. *Koala Lou.* New York: Voyager.
Garza, C. L. 1993. *Family Pictures/Cuadros de Familia.* San Francisco: Children's Book Press.

Henkes, K. 1986. Reissued 2002. *Grandpa and Bo*. New York: Greenwillow.
Hest, A., illus. by Jill Barton. 1999. *In the Rain with Baby Duck*. Reprint ed. Cambridge, MA: Candlewick.
Hoban, R., illus. by L. Hoban. 1993. *A Baby Sister for Frances*. Reprint ed. New York: HarperTrophy.
Joose, B., illus. by B. Lavallee. 1993. *Mama, Do You Love Me?* San Francisco: Chronicle.
Kraus, R., illus. by J. Aruego. 1986. *Whose Mouse Are You?* New York: Aladdin.
Mitchell, M. K., illus. by J. Ransome. 1998. *Uncle Jed's Barbershop*. New York: Aladdin.
Mora, P., illus. by C. Lang. 1984. *Pablo's Tree*. New York: Simon and Schuster.
Penn, A., illus. by R. E. Harper and M. M. Leak. 1993. *The Kissing Hand*. New York: Child Welfare League of America.
Polacco, P. 2001. *The Keeping Quilt*. New York: Aladdin.
Ringgold, F. 1996. *Tar Beach*. New York: Dragonfly.
Root, P., illus. by M. Apple. 2003. *The Name Quilt*. New York: Farrar Straus and Giroux.
Rosenberg, L., illus. by S. Gammell. 1997. *Monster Mama*. New York: Putnam.
Rylant, C., illus. by S. Gammell. 2001. *The Relatives Came*. New York: Atheneum.
Rylant, C., illus. by D. Goode. 1993. *When I Was Young in the Mountains*. New York: E. P. Dutton.
Soto, G., illus. by E. Martinez. 1996. *Too Many Tamales*. New York: Pearson.
Spinelli, E., illus. by M. Cocca-Leffler. 1992. *Thanksgiving at the Tappletons'*. New York: HarperCollins.
Steig, W. 1988. *Sylvester and the Magic Pebble*. Reissue. New York: Aladdin.
Steptoe, J. 2001. *In Daddy's Arms I Am Tall*. New York: Lee and Low.
Viorst, J., illus. by A. Lobel. 1988. *I'll Fix Anthony*. New York: Aladdin.
Waddell, M., illus. by P. Benson. 2002. *Owl Babies*. Reprint ed. Cambridge, MA: Candlewick.
Waddell, M., illus. by B. Firth. 1994. *Can't You Sleep, Little Bear?* Cambridge, MA: Candlewick.
Wells, R. 1987. *Hazel's Amazing Mother*. New York: Dial.
Williams, V. 1984. *A Chair for My Mother*. New York: Scott Foresman.
Zolotow, C., illus. by B. Shector. 1987. *A Father Like That*. New York: HarperCollins.
Zolotow, C., illus. by M. Sendak. 1990. *Mr. Rabbit and the Lovely Present*. New York: HarperCollins.

Chapter 6: Helping Children Work on Discipline and Self-Control

Professional Books and References

Charles, C. M. 2002. *Building Classroom Discipline*. Needham Heights, MA: Allyn and Bacon.
Dennison, P., and G. E. Dennison 1992. *Brain Gym® Teacher's Edition: Simple Activities for Whole Brain Learning*. Ventura, CA: Edu-Kinesthetics.
Faber, A., and E. Mazlish. 1999. *How to Talk So Kids Will Listen and Listen So Kids Will Talk*. New York: Avon.

Flodin, M. 1991. *Signing for Kids.* Berkeley, CA: Berkeley/Perigee.
Gibbs, J. 2001. *Tribes®—A New Way of Learning and Being Together.* Windsor, CA: Center Source.
Hannaford, C. 1995. *Smart Moves: Why Learning Is Not All in Your Head.* Arlington, VA: Great Ocean.
Kramer, J., and T. Ovadia. 2001. *You Can Learn Sign Language.* New York: Troll Communications.
Nelsen, J., and H. S. Glenn. 1996. *Positive Discipline.* New York: Ballantine.
———. 1999. *Positive Discipline A–Z: From Toddlers to Teens, 1001 Solutions to Everyday Parenting Problems.* 2d ed. New York: Prima.
Nelsen, J., Lott, L., and H. S. Glenn. 2000. *Positive Discipline in the Classroom: Developing Mutual Respect, Cooperation, and Responsibility in Your Classroom.* 3d ed. New York: Prima.
Nelsen, J., Escobar, L., Ortolano, K., Duffy, R., Owen-Sohocki, M.S.N., and D. Owen-Sohocki 2001. *Positive Discipline: A Teacher's A–Z Guide.* New York: Prima.
Phelan, T. W. 1996. *1-2-3 Magic: Effective Discipline for Children 2–12.* 2d ed. New York: Child Management.

Children's Books

Allard, H. G., illus. by J. Marshall. 1985. *Miss Nelson Is Missing.* Reissue ed. Boston: Houghton Mifflin.
Bang, M. G. 1999. *When Sophie Gets Angry—Really, Really Angry.* New York: Scholastic.
Everitt, B. 1995. *Mean Soup.* New York: Voyager.
Lester, H., illus. by L. Munsinger. 1990. *Pookins Gets Her Way.* Boston: Houghton Mifflin.
Polacco, P. 1995. *Babushka's Doll.* New York: Aladdin.
Sendak, M. 1991. *Pierre: A Cautionary Tale in Five Chapters and a Prologue.* New York: Harper.
Thayer, J. 1962. *Gus Was a Friendly Ghost.* New York: Morrow.
Udry, J. M. 1961. *Let's Be Enemies.* New York: HarperCollins.
Viorst, J. 1987. *Alexander and the Terrible, Horrible, No Good, Very Bad Day.* New York: Aladdin.
Wells, R. 1992. *Voyage to the Bunny Planet.* Boxed ed. New York: Viking.

Chapter 7: Our School Family: Creating Community, Managing Conflicts

Professional Books

Albert, L. 1989. *A Teacher's Guide to Cooperative Discipline: How to Manage Your Classroom and Promote Self-Esteem.* Circle Pines, MN: American Guidance Service.
Bridges, L. 1995. *Creating Your Classroom Community.* Portland, ME: Stenhouse.
Brunson, R., Z. Conte, and S. Mascar. 2000. *The Art in Peacemaking.* Washington,

DC: National Endowment for the Arts and the Office of Juvenile Justice and Delinquency Prevention.

Fisher, B. 1995. *Thinking and Learning Together—Curriculum and Community in a Primary Classroom.* Portsmouth, NH: Heinemann.

Kreidler, W. J. 1994. *Teaching Conflict Resolution Through Children's Literature—K–2.* New York: Scholastic.

Porro, B. 1996. *Talk It Out: Conflict Resolution for the Elementary Classroom.* Alexandria, VA: Association for Supervision and Curriculum Development.

Children's Books

Blaine, M. 1975. *The Terrible Thing That Happened at My House.* New York: Scholastic.

Juster, N. 1993. *The Phantom Tollbooth.* New York: Random House.

Lionni, L. 1985. *It's Mine!* New York: Knopf.

———. 1989. *Six Crows: A Fable.* New York: Random House.

McKee, D. 1986. *Two Monsters.* New York: Atheneum.

Polacco, P. 1992. *Chicken Sunday.* New York: Philomel.

Scieszka, J. 1989. *The True Story of the Three Pigs by A. Wolf.* New York: Viking.

Udry, J. 1988. *Let's Be Enemies.* New York: HarperTrophy.

Zolotow, C. 1963. *The Quarreling Book.* New York: HarperCollins.

———. 1969. *The Hating Book.* New York: HarperCollins.

Chapter 8: The Beginnings of Literacy: Children's Faces Looking Up

Professional Books

Blakemore, C. 2002. *Faraway Places—Your Source for Picture Books That Fly Children to 82 Countries.* Albany, WI: Adams-Pomeroy.

California Department of Education. 2002. *Recommended Literature: Kindergarten Through Grade Twelve.* Sacramento, CA: California Department of Education Press.

Fox, M. 2001. *Reading Magic: Why Reading Aloud to Our Children Will Change Their Lives Forever.* New York: Harvest.

Jennings, P. 2003. *The Reading Bug . . . and How You Can Help Your Child Catch It.* New York: Penguin Putnam.

Lewis, V., and W. M. Mayes. 1998. *Valerie and Walter's Best Books for Children: A Lively, Opinionated Guide.* New York: Avon.

Trelease, J. 2001. *The Read-Aloud Handbook.* 5th ed. New York: Penguin.

Children's Predictable Books: Cumulative Patterns, Rhythm, Rhyme, Repetition

Aardema, V., illus. by B. Vidal. 1992. *Bringing the Rain to Kapiti Plain: A Nandi Tale.* New York: Dial.

Ahlberg, J., and A. Ahlberg. 1999. *Each Peach, Pear, Plum.* New York: Penguin.
Alborough, J. 1997. *Where's My Teddy?* Cambridge, MA: Candlewick.
Blake, Q. 1995. *Mr. Magnolia.* London, UK: Randon House.
Brown, M. W., illus. by L. Weisgard. 1997. *The Important Book.* New York: HarperTrophy.
Burningham, J. 1990. *Mr. Gumpy's Outing.* Reissue ed. New York: Holt.
Carlstrom, N. W., illus. by B. Degan. 1996. *Jesse Bear, What Will You Wear?* New York: Aladdin.
Charlip, R. 1993. *Fortunately.* New York: Pearson.
Emberley, B., illus. by E. Emberley. 1987. *Drummer Hoff.* New York: Simon and Schuster.
Fox, M., illus. by P. Mullins. 1992. *Hattie and the Fox.* New York: Pearson.
Gag, W. 1996. *Millions of Cats.* Reissue ed. New York: Paper Star.
Hoberman, M. A. 1982. *A House Is a House for Me.* Reissue ed. New York: Puffin.
Krauss, R., illus. by C. Johnson. 1989. *The Carrot Seed.* New York: HarperCollins.
Mahy, M., illus. by P. MacCarthy. 1987. *17 Kings and 47 Elephants.* New York: Dial.
Martin, B. Jr. 1992. *Brown Bear, Brown Bear, What Do You See?* New York: Holt.
Merriam, E., illus. by D. Gottlieb. 1994. *Train Leaves the Station.* New York: Holt.
Numeroff, L., illus. by F. Bond. 1997. *If You Give a Mouse a Cookie.* New York: HarperTrophy.
Rosen, M., illus. by H. Oxenbury. 2003. *We're Going on a Bear Hunt.* New York: Aladdin.
Sendak, M. 1991. *Chicken Soup with Rice: A Book of Months.* New York: Pearson.
Tabak, S. 1999. *Joseph Had a Little Overcoat.* New York: Viking (Penguin Putnam).
Van Laan, N., illus. by M. Apple. *Sheep in a Jeep.* Boston: Houghton Mifflin.
Van Laan, N., illus. by G. Booth. 1992. *Possom Come A-Knockin.* New York: Knopf.
Van Laan, N., illus. by M. Russo. 1995. *The Big Fat Worm.* New York: Knopf.
Wood, A., illus. by D. Wood. 1991. *The Napping House.* New York: Harcourt.
Zolotow, C., illus. by J. Steptoe. 2000. *Do You Know What I'll Do?* Revised ed. New York: HarperCollins.

Other Great Read-Alouds

Asch, F. 1999. *Happy Birthday, Moon.* New York: Aladdin.
Bemelmans, L., and A. Quindlen, introduction. 2001. *Mad About Madeline: The Complete Tales.* Reissue ed. New York: Viking.
Brown, M. W., illus. by C. Hurd. 1977. *The Runaway Bunny.* New York: HarperTrophy.
———. 1991. *Goodnight Moon.* New York: HarperCollins.
Burningham, J. 1993. *Avocado Baby.* Reissue ed. New York: HarperCollins.
———. 1996. *The Shopping Basket.* 2d ed. Cambridge, MA: Candlewick.
Cannon, J. 1993. *Stellaluna.* New York: Harcourt.
DePaola, T. 1988. *Strega Nona.* New York: Aladdin.
Ehlert, L. 1991. *Red Leaf, Yellow Leaf.* New York: Harcourt.
———. 1999. *Snowballs.* New York: Voyager.

Gardiner, J. R., illus. by G. Hargreaves. 1988. *Stone Fox*. New York: HarperTrophy.
George, J. C. 2001. *Nutik, the Wolf Pup*. New York: HarperCollins.
Harper Collins Treasure of Picture Book Classics: A Child's First Collection. 2002. New York: HarperCollins.
Henkes, K. 1996. *Lilly's Purple Plastic Purse*. New York: Greenwillow.
Hurd, T. 1998. *Art Dog*. New York: HarperCollins.
Johnson, C. 1981. *Harold and the Purple Crayon*. New York: HarperCollins.
Lawson, R., illus. by M. Leaf. 1997. *The Story of Ferdinand*. New York: Puffin.
Lester, H., illus. by L. M. Munsinger. 1990. *Tacky the Penguin*. Reprint ed. Boston: Houghton Mifflin.
Macaulay, D. 2002. *Angelo*. Boston: Houghton Mifflin/Walter Lorraine.
Meddaugh, S. 1995. *Martha Speaks*. Reprint ed. Boston: Houghton Mifflin.
Parrish, P., illus. by F. Siebel. 1992. *Amelia Bedelia*. New York: HarperCollins.
Polacco, P. 1996. *Rechenka's Eggs*. New York: Paper Star.
Potter, B. 1902. *The Tale of Peter Rabbit*. London, UK: Warne.
Rathman, P. 1995. *Officer Buckle and Gloria*. New York: Putnam (Penguin Putnam).
Rey, H. A. 2001. *The Complete Adventures of Curious George*. Boston: Houghton Mifflin.
Salley, C., illus. by J. Stevens. 2002. *Epossumondas*. New York: Harcourt.
Sassa, R., illus. by M. Simont. 2001. *The Stray Dog*. New York: HarperCollins.
Schneider, H. 2000. *Chewy Louie*. Flagstaff, AZ: Rising Moon.
Sendak, M. 1988. *Where the Wild Things Are*. New York: HarperCollins.
Seuss, Dr. 1957. *How the Grinch Stole Christmas*. New York: Random House.
Shannon, D. 1998. *No, David!* New York: Scholastic.
———. 1999. *David Goes to School*. New York: Blue Sky.
———. 2002. *Duck on a Bike*. New York: Scholastic/Blue Sky.
Simmons, J. 2003. *Come Along, Daisy*. Boston: Little, Brown.
———. 2000. *Come On, Daisy/Eja, Dejzi!* English-Arabic ed. London, UK: Miller.
Steig, W. 1998. *Pete's a Pizza*. New York: HarperCollins.
Stevens, J. 1995. *Tops and Bottoms*. New York: Harcourt Brace.
Sturges, P., reteller, illus. by A. Walrod. 1999. *The Little Red Hen (Makes a Pizza)*. New York: Dutton.
Van Allsburg, C. 1985. *The Polar Express*. Boston: Houghton Mifflin.
White, E. B., illus. by G. Williams. 1999. *Charlotte's Web*. New York: HarperTrophy.

Easy Readers and Chapter Books

Hoff, S. 1993. *Danny and the Dinosaur*. Reprint ed. New York: HarperTrophy.
Lobel, A. 1972. *Frog and Toad Together*. New York: HarperCollins.
———. 1976. *Frog and Toad All Year*. New York: HarperCollins.
———. 1979a. *Days with Frog and Toad*. New York: HarperCollins.
———. 1979b. *Frog and Toad Are Friends*. New York: HarperCollins.
Park, B. 2001. *Junie B., First Grader at Last!* Junie B. Jones series, No. 18. New York: Random House.
Rylant, C., illus. by S. Stevenson. 1996. *Henry and Mudge: The First Book*. New York: Aladdin.

Seuss, Dr. 1957. *The Cat in the Hat.* New York: Random House.
———. 1960a. *Green Eggs and Ham.* New York: Random House.
———. 1960b. *One Fish Two Fish Red Fish Blue Fish.* New York: Random House.
———. 1963. *Hop on Pop.* New York: Random House.
Van Leeuwen, J., illus. by A. Schweninger. 1999. *Amanda Pig, Schoolgirl.* New York: Puffin.

Poetry

Carle, E., illus., and L. Whipple, comp. 1999. *Eric Carle's Animals, Animals.* New York: Puffin.
DeRegniers, B., ed., various Caldecott illus. 1988. *Sing a Song of Popcorn: Every Child's Book of Poems.* Reprint ed. New York: Scholastic.
Kennedy, X. J., and D. M. Kennedy, illus. by Jane Dyer. 1992. *Talking Like the Rain.* Boston: Little, Brown.
Kuskin, K., illus. by S. Ruzzier. 2003. *Moon, Have You Met My Mother? The Collected Poems of Karla Kuskin.* New York: HarperCollins/Laura Geringer.
Lobel, A. 1988. *Whiskers and Rhymes.* New York: Morrow.
Moore, L., illus. by J. Ormerod. 1992. *Sunflakes: Poems for Children.* New York: Clarion.
Prelutsky, J., ed., illus. by A. Lobel. 2000. *The Random House Book of Poetry for Children.* New York: Random House.
Prelutsky, J., illus. by G. Williams. 1986. *Ride a Purple Pelican.* New York: Morrow.
Watson, C., illus. by W. Watson. 1987. *Father Fox's Pennyrhymes.* Reprint ed. New York: HarperTrophy.
———. 1992. *Catch Me and Kiss Me and Say It Again.* New York: Puffin.

Folk and Fairy Tales

Aardema, V., illus. by P. Mathers. 1998. *Borreguita and the Coyote: A Tale from Ayutla, Mexico.* Reprint ed. New York: Random House.
DePaola, T. 1981. *Fin M'Coul: The Giant of Knockmany Hill.* New York: Holiday House.
———. 2002. *Adelita—A Mexican Cinderella Story.* New York: Putnam.
Galdone, P. 2001. *Nursery Classics: A Galdone Treasury.* New York: Clarion.
McDermott, G. 1988. *Anancy the Spider: A Tale from the Ashanti.* New York: Holt.
———. 1993. *Raven: A Trickster Tale from the Pacific Northwest.* New York: Harcourt.
———. 2001. *Jabuti the Tortoise: A Trickster Tale from the Amazon.* New York: Harcourt.
Sierra, J., illus. by S. Vitali. 1996. *Nursery Tales Around the World.* New York: Clarion.
Slobodkina, E. 1988. *Caps for Sale: A Tale of a Peddler, Some Monkeys and Their Monkey Business.* New York: HarperCollins.
Stevens, J. 1995. *The Three Billy Goats Gruff.* New York: Harcourt Brace.
Wattenberg, J. 2000. *Henny Penny.* New York: Scholastic.
Wiesner, D. 2001. *The Three Pigs.* New York: Clarion.
Zelinsky, P. 1986. *Rumplestiltskin.* New York: Puffin.

Chapter 9: Reading Isn't Just Curriculum, It's a Miracle!

Professional Books

Bear, D., et al. 1999. *Words Their Way: Word Study for Phonics, Vocabulary, and Spelling Instruction.* 2d ed. New York: Prentice Hall.

Condon, M., and M. McGuffee. 2001. *Real ePublishing, REALLY PUBLISHING!* Portsmouth, NH: Heinemann.

Cunningham, P., and D. Hall. 1994. *Making Words: Multilevel, Hands-on, Developmentally Appropriate Spelling and Phonics Activities.* Carthage, IL: Good Apple.

———. 2000. *Making More Words: Multilevel, Hands-On Phonics and Spelling Activities.* Cathage, IL: Good Apple.

Cunningham, P., D. Hall, and R. Allington. 1999. *Classrooms That Work: They Can All Read and Write.* Reading, MA: Addison-Wesley.

Cunnhingham, P., D. Hall, and C. M. Simon. 2001. *The Teachers Guide to the Four Blocks.* Greensboro, NC: Carson-Dellosa.

Fisher, B., and E. F. Medvic. 2000. *Perspectives on Shared Reading—Planning and Practice.* Portsmouth, NH: Heinemann.

Fountas, I. C., and G. S. Pinnell. 1996. *Guided Reading: Good First Teaching for All Children.* Portsmouth, NH: Heinemann.

———. 1999. *Matching Books to Readers: Using Leveled Books in Guided Readings, K–3.* Portsmouth, NH: Heinemann.

Hall, D. P., and P. M. Cunningham. 2002. *Month-by-Month Phonics for First Grade: Systematic, Multilevel Instruction.* Greensboro, NC: Carson-Dellosa.

Holdaway, D. 1984. *The Foundations of Literacy.* Portsmouth, NH: Heinemann.

Miller, D. 2002. *Reading with Meaning: Teaching Comprehension in the Primary Grades.* Portland, ME: Stenhouse.

Routman, R. 1995. *Invitations: Changing as Teachers and Learners K–12.* Portsmouth, NH: Heinemann.

———. 1999. *Conversations: Strategies for Teaching, Learning, and Evaluating.* Portsmouth, NH: Heinemann.

———. 2002. *Reading Essentials: The Specifics You Need to Teach Reading Well.* Portsmouth, NH: Heinemann.

Spann, M. B. 2001. *The Scholastic Big Book of Word Walls: 100 Fresh and Fun Word Walls, Easy Games, Activities, and Teaching Tips to Help Kids Build Key Reading, Writing, Spelling Skills and More!* New York: Scholastic.

Taberski, S. 2000. *On Solid Ground: Strategies for Teaching Reading K–3.* Portsmouth, NH: Heinemann.

Weaver, C. 2002. *Reading Process and Practice.* 3d ed. Portsmouth, NH: Heinemann.

Children's Books

Bradby, M., illus. by C. K. Soentpiet. 1995. *More Than Anything Else.* New York: Orchard/Jackson (Scholastic).

Carrick, D., illus. by E. Bunting. 1990. *The Wednesday Surprise.* New York: Scott Foresman.

Cowley, J. 1990. *Mrs. Wishy Washy.* Big Book. New York: Wright Group/McGraw-Hill.

Fox, M. 1992. *Hattie and the Fox.* New York: Scott Foresman.

Hoberman, M., illus. by M. Emberley. 2002. *You Read to Me, I'll Read to You: Very Short Stories to Read Together*. Boston: Megan Tingley and Little, Brown.
Juster, N. 1993. *The Phantom Tollbooth*. New York: Randon House.
Langstaff, J., illus. by N. W. Parker. 1991. *Oh, A-Hunting We Will Go!* New York: Aladdin.
McPhail, D. 1997a. *Edward and the Pirates*. Boston: Little, Brown.
———. 1997b. *Santa's Book of Names*. Boston: Little, Brown.
Mora, P., illus. by R. Colon. 2000. *Tomas and the Library Lady*. New York: Dragonfly.
Preiss, B., illus. by J. Mathieu. 1973. *The Silent E's from Outer Space*. New York: Western.
Sendak, M. 1991. *Pierre: A Cautionary Tale in Five Chapters and A Prologue*. New York: Harper.
Shaw, N. 1997. *Sheep in a Jeep*. Big Book. Boston, MA: Houghton Mifflin.
Stanley, D., illus. by G. B. Karas. 2001. *Saving Sweetness*. Reprint ed. New York: Puffin.
Turner, P., illus. by W. Turner. 1999. *The War Between the Vowels and the Consonants*. New York: Farrar Straus and Giroux.
Walsh, H. S. 1995. *Mouse Count*. Big Book. New York: Voyager.

Chapter 10: Creating and Maintaining Literacy Centers

Professional Books

Marriott, D., and J. Kupperstein, ed. 2001.*What Are the Other Kids Doing While You Teach Small Groups?* Huntington Beach, CA: Creative Teaching.
Optiz, M. 1999. *Learning Centers (Grades K–4)*. New York: Scholastic.
Owocki, G. 1999. *Literacy Through Play*. Portsmouth, NH: Heinemann.
Johnson, P. 1992. *A Book of One's Own: Developing Literacy Through Making Books*. Portsmouth, NH: Heinemann.
———. 1993. *Literacy Through the Book Arts*. Portsmouth, NH: Heinemann.
———. 1997. *Pictures & Words Together*. Portsmouth, NH: Heinemann.
———. 2000. *Making Books*. Ontario, Canada: Pembroke.
Trelease, J. 2001. *The Read-Aloud Handbook*, 5th ed. New York: Penguin.

Chapter 11: Teaching Writing: From Scribbles to Authorship

Professional Books

Bissix, G. 1980. *Gnys at Wrk—A Child Learns to Write and Read*. Cambridge, MA: Harvard University Press.

Bridges, L. 1997. *Writing as a Way of Knowing*. Portland, ME: Stenhouse.
Calkins, L. M. 1994. *The Art of Teaching Writing*. Portsmouth, NH: Heinemann.
———. 2003. *Primary Units of Study*. Portsmouth, NH: Heinemann.
Cary, S. 2000. *Working with Second Language Learners*. Portsmouth, NH: Heinemann.
Gallagher, P., and G. Norton. 2000. *A Jumpstart to Literacy—Using Written Conversation to Help Developing Readers and Writers*. Portsmouth, NH: Heinemann.
Graves, D. 1994. *A Fresh Look at Writing*. Portsmouth, NH: Heinemann.
———. 2003. *Writing: Teachers and Children at Work*. 20th anniversary ed. Portsmouth, NH: Heinemann.
Hall, D., and P. Cunningham. 2002. *Month by Month Phonics for First Grade: Systematic, Multilevel Instruction*. Greensboro, NC: Carson-Dellosa.
Johnson, P. 1993. *Literacy Through the Book Arts*. Portsmouth, NH: Heinemann.
———. 1997. *Pictures and Words Together: Children Illustrating and Writing Their Own Books*. Portsmouth, NH: Heinemann.
———. 1998. *A Book of One's Own: Developing Literacy Through Making Books*. Portsmouth, NH: Heinemann.
McCarrier, A., Pinnell, G. S., and I. Fountas. 1999. *Interactive Writing: How Language and Literacy Come Together, K–2*. Portsmouth, NH: Heinemann.
Routman, R. 2003. *Reading Essentials*. Portsmouth, NH: Heinemann.
Smith, F. 1988. *Joining the Literacy Club*. Portsmouth, NH: Heinemann.

Children's Books

Ada, A. F., illus. by L. Tryon. 2001. *With Love, Little Red Hen*. New York: Atheneum/Simon and Schuster.
Ahlberg, A., and J. Ahlberg. 1986. *The Jolly Postman or Other People's Letters*. Boston: Little, Brown.
Cronin, D., illus. by B. Lewin. 2000. *Click, Clack, Moo: Cows That Type*. New York: Simon and Schuster.
———. 2002. *Giggle, Giggle, Quack*. New York: Simon and Schuster.
Heide, F. P., and J. H. Gilliland, illus. by T. Lewin. 1990. *The Day of Ahmed's Secret*. New York: Lothrop.
Teague, M. 2002. *Dear Mrs. La Rue: Letters from Obedience School*. New York: Scholastic.
Williams, V. B. 1999. *Stringbean's Trip to the Shining Sea*. New York: Mulberry.

Chapter 12: Math Matters

Professional Books

Abrohms, A. 1999. *1001 Instant Manipulatives for Math, Grades K–2*. New York: Scholastic.
Addison-Wesley. 1997. *Mathematics Their Way—Beyond the Book—Activities and Projects from Classrooms Like Yours*. Menlo Park, CA: Addison-Wesley Longman.
Baratta-Lorton, M. 1995. *Math Their Way*. Menlo Park, CA: Addison-Wesley.

Burns, M. 1993. *Math and Literature: Book One (K–3)*. Sausalito, CA: Math Solutions.

———. 2000. *About Teaching Mathematics: A K–8 Resource*. New York: Pearson.

Celebrate 100 Kit (Grades K–2), The. 1999. New York: Scholastic.

Clarke, J. 2002. *Shoe Box Math Learning Centers: 40 Easy-to-Make, Fun-to-Use Centers with Instant Reproducibles and Activities That Help Kids Practice Important Math Skills—Independently*. New York: Scholastic.

Copley, J., ed. 1999. *Mathematics in the Early Years*. Reston, VA: National Council of Teachers of Mathematics.

———. 2000. *The Young Child and Mathematics*. Washington, DC: National Association for the Education of Young Children.

Evans, C., A. Leija, and T. Falkner. 2001. *Math Links—Teaching the NCTM 2000 Standards Through Children's Literature*. Englewood, CO: Teacher Ideas.

Hechtman, J., D. Ellermeyer, and S. Grove. 1999. *Teaching Math with Favorite Picture Books*. New York: Scholastic.

Ritter, D. 1995. *Math Art—Featuring 33 Innovative Art Projects*. Cypress, CA: Creative Teaching.

Children's Counting Books

Anno. 1986. *Anno's Counting Book*. New York: HarperTrophy.

Bang, M. 2003. *Ten, Nine, Eight*. Reprint ed. New York: Scott Foresman.

Carter, D. 1988. *How Many Bugs in a Box?* New York: Little Simon.

Christelow, E. 1990. *Five Little Monkeys Jumping on the Bed*. New York: Pearson.

Crews, D. 1995. *Ten Black Dots*. New York: Mulberry.

Dee, R., illus. by S. Meddaugh. 1990. *Two Ways to Count to Ten*. New York: Holt.

Demi. 1986. *Demi's Count the Animals 1 2 3*. New York: Grosset and Dunlap.

Duvoisin, R. 2000. *Petunia*. New York: Knopf.

Ehlert, L. 1992. *Fish Eyes: A Book You Can Count On*. San Diego: Harcourt Brace.

Falwell, C. 2002. *Turtle Splash! Countdown at the Pond*. New York: Greenwillow/HarperCollins.

Hoban, T. 1995. *26 Letters and 99 Cents*. New York: Mulberry.

McGrath, B. B. 1994. *The M&M's Chocolate Candies Counting Book*. Watertown, MA: Charlesbridge.

———. 1998. *The Cheerios Counnting Book*. New York: Scholastic.

Mickelthwait, L. 1998. *I Spy Two Eyes, Numbers in Art*. New York: Mulberry.

Morozumi, A. 1990. *One Gorilla*. New York: Farrar, Straus and Giroux.

Muñoz, P. R. 1996. *The Crayon Counting Book*. Watertown, MA: Charlesbridge.

Pallotta, J. 2001. *Underwater Counting: Even Numbers*. Watertown, MA: Charlesbridge.

Ryan, P. M. 1996. *The Crayon Counting Book*. Watertown, MA: Charlesbridge.

Sabuda, R. 1997. *Cookie Count: A Tasty Pop-Up*. New York: Little Simon.

Sierra, J., illus. by W. Hillenbrand. 2001. *Counting Crocodiles*. New York: Voyager.

Walsh, E. S. 1995. *Mouse Count*. New York: Voyager.

Shapes, Geometry, Patterns, Attributes

Burns, M., illus. by G. Silveria. 1995. *The Greedy Triangle*. New York: Pearson.

Friedman, A., illus. by K. Howard. 1995. *A Cloak for the Dreamer.* New York: Pearson.
Giganti, P. Jr. 1999. *Each Orange Had 8 Slices.* New York: Mulberry.

Computations

Birch, D., illus. by D. Grebu. 1993. *The King's Chessboard.* New York: Pearson.
Hutchins, P. 1986. *The Doorbell Rang.* New York: Greenwillow.
Leedy, L. 1997. *Mission Addition.* New York: Holiday House.
———. 2000. *Subtraction Action.* New York: Holiday House.

Place Value and Structure of the Number System

Leedy, L. 1995. *The King's Commissioners.* New York: Pearson.
Schwartz, D., illus. by S. Gammell. 1993. *How Much Is a Million?* New York: Mulberry.
———. 1994. *If You Made a Million.* New York: Pearson.

General Problem Solving

Grossman, B. 1996. *My Little Sister Ate One Hare.* New York: Crown.
Scieszka, J., illus. by L. Smith. 1995. *Math Curse.* New York: Viking.
Tang, G., illus. by H. Briggs. 2002. *Math for All Seasons.* New York: Scholastic.
———. 2003. *Math Appeal, Mind Stretching Math Riddles.* New York: Scholastic.

Hundreds Day

Cuyler, M., illus. by A. Howard. 2000. *100th Day Worries.* New York: Simon and Schuster.
Harris, T., illus. by B. G. Johnson. 2000. *100 Days of School.* Brookfield, CT: Millbrook.
Kasza, K. 1989. *The Wolf's Chicken Stew.* New York: Putnam.
Pinczes, E., illus. by B. Mackain. 1999. *One Hundred Hungry Ants.* Boston: Houghton Mifflin.
Ryan, P. M., illus. by B. Huang. 1996. *One Hundred Is a Family.* New York: Hyperion.
Slate, J., illus. by A. Wolff. 1998. *Miss Bindergarten Celebrates the 100th Day of Kindergarten.* New York: Dutton.
Sloat, T. 1995. *From One to One Hundred.* New York: Puffin.
Wells, R. 2000. *Emily's First 100 Days of School.* New York: Hyperion.

Calendar

Barner, B. 2003. *Parade Day: Marching Through the Calendar Year.* New York: Holiday House.

Shields, C. D., illus. by T. Kelley. 1998a. *Day by Day the Week Goes Round.* New York: Dutton.
———. 1998b. *Month by Month the Year Goes Round.* New York: Dutton.

Time

Carle, E. 1999. *The Grouchy Ladybug.* New York: HarperFestival.
Hutchins, P. 1994. *Clocks and More Clocks.* New York: Simon and Schuster.
Rathmann, P. 1998. *Ten Minutes Till Bedtime.* New York: Putnam.

Money

Brisson, P., illus. by B. Barner. 1993. *Benny's Pennies.* New York: Doubleday.
Hoban, L. 1999. *Arthur's Funny Money.* New York: HarperCollins.
McMillan, B. 1996. *Jelly Beans for Sale.* New York: Scholastic.
Viorst, J., illus. by R. Cruz. 1980. *Alexander, Who Used to Be Rich Last Monday.* New York: Pearson.
Wells, R. 2000. *Bunny Money.* New York: Puffin.

Measurement

Adler, D. 2000. *How Tall, How Short, How Faraway.* New York: Holiday House.
Lionni, L. 1995. *Inch by Inch.* New York: Pearson.
Myller, R., illus. by S. McCrath. 1991. *How Big Is a Foot?* Reissue ed. New York: Random House.

Chapter 13: Ya Gotta Have Art!

Professional Books

Baer, G. 1972. *Paste, Pencils, Scissors, and Crayons.* New York: Parker.
Carson, J. 1984. *Tell Me About Your Picture—Art Activities to Help Children Communicate.* Palo Alto, CA: Dale Seymour.
Hart, K. 1988. *I Can Draw! Ideas for Teachers.* Portsmouth, NH: Heinemann.
Marantz, S. S. 1992. *Picture Books for Looking and Learning—Awakening Visual Perceptions Through the Art of Children's Books.* Phoenix, AZ: Oryx.
Romberg, J., and M. Rutz. 1972. *Art Today and Every Day: Classroom Activities for the Elementary School Year.* New York: Prentice Hall.
Schuman, J. M. 2002. *Art from Many Hands—Multicultural Art Projects.* Worcester, MA: Davis.
Thompson, K. B., and D. S. Loftus. 1994. *Art Connections—Integrating Art Throughout the Curriculum.* New York: Goodyear.

Art History/Appreciation

Blizzard, G. 2002. *Come Look with Me: Enjoying Art with Children.* VA: Thomasson-Grant, Inc.

Kohl, M. A., and K. Solga. 1996. *Discovering Great Artists—Hands-on Art for Children in the Styles of the Great Masters.* WA: Bright Ring.

Metropolitan Museum of Art. 2002. *Museum ABC.* Boston: Little, Brown.

Micklethwait, L. 1993. *A Child's Book of Art: Great Pictures First Words.* New York: DK.

Children's Art/Activity/How-to Books

Blake, Q., and J. Cassidy. 1999. *Drawing for the Artistically Undiscovered.* Palo Alto, CA: Klutz.

Drawbreakers: A Drawing Book That We Start and You Finish. 2001. Palo Alto, CA: Klutz.

Hurd, T., and J. Cassidy. 1992. *Watercolor for the Artistically Undiscovered.* Palo Alto, CA: Klutz.

Irvine, J., illus. by B. Reid. 1988. *How to Make Pop-Ups.* New York: Morrow.

———. 1992. *How to Make Super Pop-Ups.* New York: Morrow.

Kistler, M. 1988a. *Drawing in 3-D.* New York: Fireside.

———. 1988b. *Mark Kistler's Draw Squad.* New York: Fireside.

Petrich, P., and R. Dalton. 1995. *The Kid's Arts and Crafts Book.* Concord, CA: NittyGritty Productions.

Children's Books with Art Themes; Illustrations to Use for Teaching Art

Anderson, H. C., illus. by J. Pinkney. 1999. *The Ugly Duckling.* New York: Morrow.

Andrews-Goebel, N., illus. by D. Diaz. 2002. *The Pot That Juan Built.* New York: Lee and Low.

Anholt, L. 1994. *Camille and the Sunflowers: A Story About Vincent Van Gogh.* New York: Barrons.

———. 1996. *Degas and the Little Dancer: A Story About Edgar Degas.* New York: Barrons.

———. 1998. *Picasso and the Girl with a Ponytail: A Story About Pablo Picasso.* New York: Barrons.

———. 2000. *Leonardo and the Flying Boy: A Story About Leonardo da Vinci.* New York: Barrons.

Bang, M. 1987. *The Paper Crane.* New York: Morrow.

Bjork, C., illus. by L. Anderson. 1985. *Linnea in Monet's Garden.* New York: R and S.

Carle, E. 2002. *A House for Hermit Crab.* New York: Aladdin.

Cohn, D., illus. by A. Cordova. 2002. *Dream Carver*. San Francisco: Chronicle.
Greenberg, J., and S. Jordan, illus. by R. A. Parker. 2003. *Action Jackson*. Brookfield, CT: Millbrook.
Hurwitz, J., illus. by J. Pinkney. 1993. *New Shoes for Silvia*. New York: Morrow.
Keats, E. J. 1981. *The Snowy Day*. New York: Viking.
Lionni, L. 1995. *Matthew's Dream*. New York: Knopf.
———. 1997. *A Color of His Own*. New York: Dragonfly.
Winter, J. 1998. *My Name is Georgia*. New York: Silver Whistle.
Winter, J., illus. by A. Juan. 2003. *Frieda*. New York: Scholastic/Arthur A. Levine.
Winter, J., illustrator; text by Johah Winter. 1994. *Diego*. New York: Knopf.

Chapter 14: Making Social Studies, Health, and Science Come Alive Through Literacy and Play

Professional Books

California Department of Education. 1993. *Literature for History-Social Science K–8*. Sacramento, CA: California Department of Education Press.
———. 2001. *History-Social Science Framework: Updated Edition with Content Standards*. Sacramento, CA: California Department of Education Press.
Gardner, H. 1993. *Frames of Mind: The Theory of Multiple Intelligences*. New York: Basic.

Children's Books: Home, Community, and Country

Anno, M. illus. by various artists. 1999. *All in a Day*. New York: Paper Star.
Burton, V. L. 1978. *The Little House*. Boston: Houghton Mifflin.
Caseley, J. 2002. *On the Town: A Community Adventure*. New York: Greenwillow.
Fanelli, S. 2001. *My Map Book*. New York: HarperCollins.
Gibbons, G. 1986a. *Department Store*. New York: HarperTrophy.
———. 1986b. *Fill It Up*. New York: HarperCollins.
———. 1986c. *The Post Office Book: Mail and How It Moves*. New York: HarperTrophy.
———. 1987. *New Road!* New York: HarperCollins.
Knowlton, J. 1997. *Geography from A to Z: A Picture Glossary*. New York: HarperCollins.
Krementz, J. 1989. *A Visit to Washington D.C.* New York: Scholastic.
Lobe, M., illus. by W. Opgenoorth. 1984. *The Snowman Who Went for a Walk*. New York: Morrow.
Maestro, B., illus. by G. Maestro. 1984. *Big City Port*. New York: Scholastic.
Martin, B. Jr., and M. Sampson, illus. by C. Raschka. 2003. *I Pledge Allegiance: The Pledge of Allegiance with Commentary*. Cambridge, MA: Candlewick.
McLerran, A., illus. by B. Cooney. 1992. *Roxaboxen*. New York: Pearson.

Developing Responsibility

Banks, K., illus. by G. Hallensleben. 2001. *Night Worker.* Farrar Straus Giroux/Frances Foster.
Barasch, L. 2000. *Radio Rescue.* New York: Farrar Straus Giroux/Frances Foster.
Brown, R. 1991. *The World That Jack Built.* New York: Dutton.
Cooney, B. 1985. *Miss Rumphius.* New York: Scott Foresman.
Demarest, C. 2000. *Firefighters A to Z.* New York: Margaret McElderry.
Houston, G., illus. by S. C. Lamb. 1992. *My Great-Aunt Arizona.* New York: HarperCollins.
Kalman, M. 2002. *Fireboat—The Heroic Adventures of the John J. Harvey.* New York: G. P. Putman's Sons.
McMullan, K., illus. by J. McMullan. 2003. *I Stink!* HarperCollins/Joanna Cotler.
Osborne, M. P., illus. by S. Johnson and L. Fancher. 2002. *New York's Bravest.* New York: Knopf.

Geography and Economics

Ancona, G. 1990. *Bananas: From Manolo to Margie.* Boston: Houghton Mifflin.
Brown, J., illus. by S. Bjorkman. 1996. *Flat Stanley.* New York: Pearson.
Paulsen, G., illus. by R. W. Paulsen. 1998. *The Tortilla Factory.* New York: Voyager.
Priceman, M. 1996. *How to Make an Apple Pie and See the World.* New York: Random House.

Cultural Diversity, Now and Long Ago: Other Times, Other Places

Cohen, B., illus. by M. Deraney. 1998. *Molly's Pilgrim.* Beech Tree.
Dooley, N., illus. by P. Thornton. 1992. *Everybody Cooks Rice.* New York: Pearson Learning.
Fleischman, P., illus. by K. Henkes. 1999. *Westlandia.* Cambridge, MA: Candlewick.
Gray, N., illus. by P. Dupasquier. 1991. *A Country Far Away.* New York: Orchard.
Hendershot, J., illus. by T. B. Allen. 1987. *In Coal Country.* New York: Knopf.
Hoberman, M. A., illus. by fourteen illustrators. 1994. *My Song Is Beautiful: Poems and Pictures in Many Voices.* Boston: Little, Brown.
Hoffman, M., illus. by C. Binch. 1991. *Amazing Grace.* New York: Dial.
Kindersley, A., and B. Kindersley. 1997. *Children Just Like Me: Celebrations.* New York: DK.
Pinkwater, D. M. 1993. *The Big Orange Splot.* Reissue ed. New York: Scholastic.
Ross, D. 1972. *I Love My Love with an A.* London, UK: Faber and Faber.
Swope, S., illus. by B. Root. 2001. *Araboolies of Liberty Street.* New York: Sunburst.

Picture Book Biographies

Coles, R., and G. Ford. 2000. *The Story of Ruby Bridges.* New York: Scholastic.

Provensen, A. 1990. *The Buck Stops Here: The Presidents of the United States*. New York: HarperCollins.

Rappaport, D., illus. by B. Collier. 2001. *Martin's Big Words: The Life of Dr. Martin Luther King, Jr.* New York: Jump at the Sun.

Ryan, P. Muñoz, illus. by B. Selznick. 2002. *When Marian Sang: The True Recital of Marian Anderson*. New York: Scholastic.

Science

California Department of Education. 2002. *Literature for Science and Mathematics: Kindergarten Through Grade Twelve*. Sacramento, CA: California Department of Education Press.

Thomas, J. E., and D. Pagel. 1989. *The Ultimate Book of Kid Concoctions: More Than 65 Wacky, Wild and Crazy Concoctions*. Cleveland, OH: Kid Concoctions.

Dental Health and Tooth Lore and Legend

Bates, L. 1988. *Little Rabbit's Loose Tooth*. New York: Crown.

Beeler, S. B., illus. by G. B. Karas. 2001. *Throw Your Tooth on the Roof: Tooth Traditions from Around the World*. Boston: Houghton Mifflin.

Brill, M., illus. by K. Krenina. 1998. *Tooth Tales: From Around the World*. Watertown, MA: Charlesbridge.

Middleton, C. 2001. *Tabitha's Terrifically Tough Tooth*. New York: Phyllis Fogelman.

Munsch, R., illus. by M. Martchenko. 2002. *Andrew's Loose Tooth*. New York: Cartwheel.

Showers, P., illus. by T. Kelley. 1991. *How Many Teeth?* New York: HarperCollins.

Steig, W. 1986. *Dr. DeSoto*. New York: Scholastic.

Butterflies

Carle, E. 1994. *The Very Hungry Caterpillar*. New York: Scholastic.

Ehlert, L. 2001. *Waiting for Wings*. New York: Harcourt.

Ryder, J., illus. by L. Cherry. 1996. *Where Butterflies Grow*. New York: Pearson.

Sabuda, R., and M. Reinhart. 2001. *Young Naturalist Pop-Up Handbook: Butterflies*. New York: Hyperion.

Sandved, K. B. 1996. *The Butterfly Alphabet: Photographs*. New York: Scholastic.

Still, J., photographs by J. Young. 1991. *Amazing Butterflies and Moths*. Eyewitness Juniors, No. 9. New York: Knopf.

Professional Books: English/Second Language Teaching

Cary, S. 1997. *Second Language Learners*. Portland, ME: Stenhouse.

———. 2000. *Working with Second Language Learners: Answers to Teachers' Top Ten Questions*. Portsmouth, NH: Heinemann.

Krashen, S. 2003. *Explorations in Language Acquisition and Use*. Portsmouth, NH: Heinemann.
Peregoy, S. F., and O. F. Boyle. 2000. *Reading, Writing, & Learning in ESL: A Resource Book for K–12 Teachers*. 3d ed. Reading, MA: Addison-Wesley.

Children's Books: English/Second Language

Burningham, J. 2002. *Would You Rather?* New York: North-South/SeaStar.
Levine, E., illus. by S. Bjorkman. 1995. *I Hate English*. New York: Scholastic.
Wildsmith, B. 1997. *Brian Wildsmith's Amazing World of Words*. Brookfield, CT: Millbrook.

Chapter 15: Making Music

Music Appreciation

Aliki. 2003. *Ah, Music!* New York: HarperCollins.
Petty, K., and J. Maizels. 1999. *The Amazing Pop-Up Music Book*. New York: Dutton.

Collections of Songs to Sing

Delacre, L., ed., trans. by E. Paz, illus. by L. Delacre. 1989. *Arroz con Leche: Popular Songs and Rhymes from Latin America*. New York: Scholastic.
Diamond, C. 1998. *Charlotte Diamond's Musical Treasures—A Songbook with Activities for Teachers and Families*. Charlotte Diamond Music.
Newcome, Z. 2002. *Head, Shoulders, Knees and Toes: And Other Action Rhymes*. Cambridge, MA: Candlewick.
Raffi. 1993. *Children's Favorites*. New York: Amsco.
Raffi, illus. by E. Fernandes. 1996. *Rise and Shine*. New York: Crown.
Umansky, K. 1994. *Three Singing Pigs—Making Music with Traditional Stories*. London: A and C Black.
Warren, J., comp., illus. by M. Ekberg. 1983. *Piggyback Songs—New Songs Sung to the Tune of Childhood Favorites*. Boone, IA: Totline Publications.
———. 1984. *More Piggyback Songs*. Boone, IA: Totline Publications.

Children's Books with Musical Themes

Fitzgerald, E., and V. Alexander. 2003. *A-Tisket, A-Tasket*. Huntington Beach, CA: Philomel.
Gerstein, M. 2003. *What Charlie Heard*. New York: Farrar/Frances Foster.
Isadora, R., and C. Turner, Performer. 1991. *Ben's Trumpet*. New York: Mulberry.

Kuskin, K., illus. by M. Simont. 1986. *The Philharmonic Gets Dressed.* New York: HarperTrophy.

McPhail, D. 2001. *Mole Music.* New York: Henry Holt.

Moss, L., illus. by M. Priceman. 1996. *Zin! Zin! Zin! A Violin.* New York: Simon and Schuster.

Children's Sing-a-long Books

Bates, K. L., illus. by N. Waldman. 1993. *America the Beautiful.* New York: Macmillan.

Carle, E. 1992. *Today Is Monday.* New York: Putnam.

Guthrie, W., illus. by K. Jakobsen. 1998. *This Land Is Your Land.* Boston: Little, Brown.

Hoberman, M. A., illus. by N. Wescott. 2000. *The Eensy-Weensy Spider.* Boston: Little, Brown.

Hort, L. 2000. *The Seals on the Bus.* New York: Holt.

Kennedy, J., illus. by M. Hague. 1995. *The Teddy Bears' Picnic.* New York: Holt.

Langstaff, J., illus. by N. W. Parker. 1974. *Oh, A-Hunting We Will Go!* New York: Atheneum.

Langstaff, J., illus. by F. Rojankovsky. 1983. *Frog Went A-Courtin'.* New York: Gulliver.

Raffi, illus. by D. Allender. 1990. *Shake My Sillies Out.* New York: Crown.

Raffi, illus. by N. Wescott. 1999. *Down by the Bay.* New York: Crown.

Raffi, illus. by A. Wolff. 1997. *Baby Beluga.* Raffi Songs to Read. New York: Crown.

Tabak, S. 1997. *There Was an Old Lady Who Swallowed a Fly.* New York: Viking.

Weiss, G. D., and B. Thiele, illus. by A. Bryan. 1995. *What a Wonderful World.* New York: Simon and Schuster.

Zelinsky, P. 2000. *The Wheels on the Bus.* Pop-up ed. New York: Dutton.

———. 2003. *Knick-Knack Paddywhack!* (Interactive moving parts book). New York: Dutton.

Dance

Dillon, L., and D. Dillon. 2002. *Rap a Tap Tap: Here's Bojangles—Think of That!* New York: Scholastic/Blue Sky.

Gauch, P. L., illus. by S. Ichikawa. 2002. *The Tanya Treasury.* New York: Philomel.

Holabird, K., illus. by H. Craig. 1991. *Angelina, Ballerina.* New York: Crown.

Children's Records and CDs

Diamond, C. 1985. *10 Carrot Diamond.* Audio CD.

———. 2000. *Charlotte Diamond's World.* Audio CD.

Langstaff, J. 1996. *Songs for Singing Children.* Revels Records. Audio CD.

———. 2002. *John Langstaff Sings the Jackfish, and Other Songs for Singing Children.* Revels Records. Audio CD.
Palmer, H. 1969. *Learning Basic Skills Through Music.* CD.
———. 2000. *Easy Does It: Activity Songs for Basic Motor Skill Development.* Record Ar581. Educational Activities. Discount School Supply Catalog, 800-627-2829.
Raffi. 1996a. *Baby Beluga.* Audio CD. Rounder/Pgd.
———. 1996b. *The Singable Songs Collection.* Audio CD. Rounder/Pgd.
Smithsonian Folkways Children's Music Collection. 1998. Smithsonian/Folkways. Audio CD.

Chapter 16: Physical Education: Play Everything!

Professional Books

Blades, J. 2000. *Thinking on Your Feet: 100+ Activities That Make Learning a Moving Experience.* Richardson, TX: Action Based Learning.
Carnes, C., and M. Sutherland. 1992. *Awsome Primary Action Units—An Elementary School Primary Physical Education Book.* Carmichael, CA: The Education.
Dennison, P., and G. E. Dennison. 1992. *Brain Gym® Teacher's Edition: Simple Activities for Whole Brain Learning.* Ventura, CA: Edu-Kinesthetics.
Gardner, H. 1993. *Frames of Mind: The Theory of Multiple Intelligences.* New York: Basic Books.
Ortwerth, J., and M. J. Nicks. 1984. *P. E. Curriculum Guide.* Carthage, IL: Good Apple.
Steffens, C., and S. Gorin. 1997. *Learning to Play, Playing to Learn.* Los Angeles: RGA.
Tillman, K. G., and P. R. Toner. 1991. *You'll Never Guess What We Did in Gym Today! More New Physical Education, Games and Activities.* New York: Prentice Hall.
Wiertsema, H. 2002. *101 Movement Games for Children.* Berkeley, CA: Publishers Group West.

Children's Books

Day, A. 1990. *Frank and Ernest Play Ball.* New York: Scholastic.
Hest, A., illus. by J. Barton. 2002. *Make the Team, Baby Duck.* Cambridge, MA: Candlewick.
London, J. 2001. *Froggy Plays Soccer.* New York: Puffin.
McCully, E. A. 1992. *Mirette on the High Wire.* New York: Putnam (Penguin Putnam).
Welch, W., illus. by M. Simont. *Playing Right Field.* New York: Scholastic.

Music: Records, Audiocassettes, and CDs

Palmer, H. 1969. *Learning Basic Skills Through Music.* Vol 1. Record or CD.
———. 2000. *Easy Does It: Activity Songs for Basic Motor Skill Development.* Record AR581. Educational Activities. Discount School Supply Catalog, 800-627-2829.

Chapter 17: Assessing Your Children, Evaluating Yourself

Professional Books

Bridges, L. 1995. *Assessment: Continuous Learning.* Portland, ME: Stenhouse.
von Oech, R. 1998. *A Whack on the Side of the Head.* New York: Warner.

Chapter 18: Saying Good-Bye

Books for All Ages

Baycura, D., ed. 1999. *Patchwork Math 1 (Grades 1–3).* New York: Scholastic.
Blackburn, K., and J. Lammers. 1996. *Kids' Paper Airplane Book.* Boulder, CO: Workman.
Hensen, C., et al. 1994. *The Muppets Make Puppets! Book and Puppet Kit: How to Make Puppets Out of All Kinds of Stuff Around Your House.* Boulder, CO: Workman.
Nakano, D. 1994. *Easy Origami.* New York: Puffin.
Striker, S. 2001. *The Anti-Coloring Book: Creative Activities for Ages 6 and Up.* Owl.

INDEX